PLAYS FOR PLAIN PEOPLE

JAMES BRIDIE

PLAYS
FOR PLAIN PEOPLE

Lancelot

Holy Isle

Mr Bolfry

Jonah 3

The Sign of the Prophet Jonah

The Dragon and the Dove

CONSTABLE · LONDON

LONDON

PUBLISHED BY

Constable and Company Ltd.

10-12 *Orange Street*, W.C.2

INDIA *and* PAKISTAN

Orient Longmans Ltd.

BOMBAY CALCUTTA MADRAS

CANADA

Longmans, Green and Company

TORONTO

SOUTH AFRICA

Longmans, Green and Company Ltd.

CAPE TOWN

First published 1944
Reprinted 1945
Reprinted 1950

Printed in Great Britain by

RICHARD CLAY AND COMPANY, LTD.

BUNGAY

SUFFOLK

TO

ERIC LINKLATER

AUTHOR'S NOTE

Of the Plays in this volume *Holy Isle* was produced at the Arts Theatre in December 1942 by Mr Alastair Sim, with Miss Margaretta Scott, Miss Vivienne Bennett, Mr Herbert Lomas, Mr Bromley Davenport, Mr Norman Shelley and Mr Emrys Jones in the cast. Mr Michael Warre did the scenery.

Mr Bolfry was produced at the Westminster Theatre in August 1943 with Mr Alastair Sim as McCrimmon, Mr Raymond Lovell as Bolfry and Miss Sophie Stewart as Mrs McCrimmon. Mr Alastair Sim produced, and Mr Michael Warre and Miss Mary Purvis did the scenery.

Jonah 3 was done by the Unnamed Society of Manchester in November 1942, Mr F. Sladen-Smith producing it. It is a war-time version of my earlier play *Jonah and the Whale* The broadcasting version of the same play—*The Sign of the Prophet Jonah*—was done earlier in the year with Mr Ralph Richardson as Jonah. Miss Barbara Burnham produced.

The Dragon and the Dove was first shown at the Lyric Theatre Glasgow, under the title *The Niece of the Hermit Abraham,* in August 1942. It was produced by Mr E. Martin Browne, presented by the Pilgrims Players and decorated by Mr Ronald Long. Mr Denis Carey played Abraham, and Miss Sylvia Read Maria.

J. B

** These Plays may not be read or produced in public without reference to the author's agents, who are as follow:—

For *Lancelot* and *Mr Bolfry*: Christopher Mann Ltd. 45 Fountain House, Park Lane, London, W.1.

For *Holy Isle, Jonah 3, The Sign of the Prophet Jonah* and *The Dragon and The Dove*: Curtis Brown Ltd. 6 Henrietta Street, Covent Garden, London, W.C.2.

The Amateur performing rights of *Mr Bolfry* are controlled by Samuel French Ltd.

LANCELOT

A PLAY IN TWO ACTS

ACT I

SCENE I

Merlin's Retreat in the Welsh Mountains.

MERLIN *is half sitting, half reclining on a ledge of rock.* NIMUE *is on the ground with her head against his knees, idly turning over and throwing about a number of manuscripts.* MERLIN *is an old man, dressed mainly in goatskins.* NIMUE *is a small, dark creature with straight hair and cat's eyes.* MERLIN *is doting on her.*

The sun is shining. There are traces of some sort of picnic.

MERLIN. Nimue, there is one thing I should like to know.

NIMUE. So there *is* one thing the great Merlin doesn't know?

MERLIN. Who gave you your name?

NIMUE. The Lady of the Lake.

MERLIN. No. For she is a foolish and dull woman. A poet found your name. It is like a little waterfall trickling over green rocks.

NIMUE. Good of you to say so. . . . Merlin, are you going to do a trick?

MERLIN. A trick, my darling?

NIMUE. Yes. You brought me up here to teach me magic, and you have done nothing but tell me about yourself and myself, and anybody could do that.

MERLIN. There is magic in your name. Nimue!

NIMUE. That is nonsense. I want to see a trick.

MERLIN. What sort of trick would you like to see? Would you like me to change myself into a handsome young man?

NIMUE. No. I like old men best. I should like you to raise an evil spirit.

MERLIN. Why?

NIMUE. I want to see one.

MERLIN. It is wasting knowledge to raise evil spirits.

NIMUE. How is that? Can't you do it?

MERLIN. Yes, I can do it. Any enchanter can do it.

NIMUE. Then why not do it? You promised to teach me magic.

MERLIN. My dear, magic is only a very subordinate means

3   [3]

to an end.   We study magic, as we study astrology and Greek and the movements of the tides, to serve our purpose.

NIMUE.   And what is our purpose?

MERLIN.   To increase the sum of human happiness.

NIMUE.   You will increase the sum of human happiness if you make me happy.   And you will make me happy by raising an evil spirit.

MERLIN (*gently*).   I don't know, Nimue, if you follow my thought.   I am not a simple conjurer; or even a particularly wise man.   As I see it, I have been put into the world with certain faculties that I may use them for the benefit of the world.

NIMUE.   I think I shall go home now.

MERLIN.   No, my sweet friend, I shall do whatever you ask me.   Only listen to me.   In all my walking about in the world, I have never found a partner so apt, so compact of charm, intelligence and sympathy.   You and I will do great things.

NIMUE.   How can we do great things if you refuse to teach me magic?

MERLIN.   I have taught you a great deal of magic and I shall teach you more.   But I must make you understand my reasons.

NIMUE.   I thought your reason was that you loved me.

MERLIN.   That was only one of my reasons.   Another is that you are very intelligent.

NIMUE.   Very well.   Go on.

MERLIN.   You have heard of Abraham?

NIMUE.   The well-known Jew.   Yes.

MERLIN.   He was a breeder of camels and sheep.   By his magic he brought it about that he had the best camels and sheep in Asia.

NIMUE.   Shall we talk about something else?   I hate animals.

MERLIN.   Abraham talked of something else—to his wife Sarah, as I am talking to you.   He talked of breeding men.

NIMUE.   I'm not sure whether I understand you, but if I do, I may tell you I did not come here to be insulted.

MERLIN.   Pray forget for five minutes that you are a woman. I am telling you something of great interest.

NIMUE.   Very well.

MERLIN.   The great thought of Abraham was this: " I can, by using my wits and my knowledge, produce a stock of strong, beautiful camels who can survive the heat of the desert

[4]   4

and the terrors of the long march. These, my neighbours, are neither strong nor beautiful nor fit to survive. I have found out how to make the best kind of camel. I shall find out how to make the best kind of man." For man, my sweet friend, is plainly meant to be the noblest thing in creation.

NIMUE. He isn't.

MERLIN. That is true. But he will be. Abraham was only a farmer. He had not studied universal wisdom. He thought in terms of toughness and the capacity to survive. My own aim is to find the perfect man, living in the perfect state. I have made that the work of my life. I have found my solution.

NIMUE. You are the perfect man, I suppose?

MERLIN. No, no, no. I am only the instrument of the Almighty. I came to this savage land of Logris and there I found Uther Pendragon, the King of England. Him I mated with Ygraine of Tintagil, and they begat King Arthur. And with King Arthur was born order and discipline and honour in Logris.

NIMUE. Look.

MERLIN. What is it?

NIMUE. High up on that crag. A big golden eagle, spreading his wings to the sun. He has gone now. What were you saying?

MERLIN. I made the Age of Chivalry. That was only the first part of my work. I had created the time and the place in which the perfect man could be found and live and begin the new order of things. It is the bravest time since time began.

NIMUE. And you did it?

MERLIN. Humbly, I may answer that I did.

NIMUE. You must be very clever. And have you found your perfect man?

MERLIN. No. But when I have mated the best Knight in all the world to the daughter of King Pelleas of Corbin, I shall find him. They will have a son, and his name will be Galahad, and he will begin the New World.

NIMUE. But the champion Knight of the world is Sir Lancelot of the Lake.

MERLIN. Yes.

NIMUE. And Elaine of Corbin is the stupidest creature that ever was born.

MERLIN. Her father is a man deep in the mysteries. My perfect man must have the seeing eye.

NIMUE. But this is not practical. Lancelot loves the Queen. He will not look at Elaine.

MERLIN. It will not be necessary.

NIMUE. You have a plan? You will use magic?

MERLIN. Yes.

NIMUE. And may I help you?

MERLIN. I was counting upon that.

NIMUE (*embracing him*). Oh, darling Merlin! What shall we do?

MERLIN. We must first of all find where Sir Lancelot lies tonight. He is riding from the North. Bring me the ink bowl.

> [NIMUE *fetches a little gold bowl and pours some ink into it from a leather bottle.*]

His adventure is at an end. I saw him last riding into the forest of Lichfield by the Roman bridle-path. Tonight he will lie near Hereford. Look into the ink-pool.

NIMUE. I see nothing.

MERLIN. Wait. . . . *Homo, Sacarus, Museolameas, Cherubosca, Tetragammaton.* Amaymon, King of the East; Gorson, King of the South; Zimimar, King of the North; Goap, King and Prince of the West, I bind you with bonds from the third hour till dawn in the names of Ioth, Iglanabrath, El, Abiel, Anathiel, Athantos and Adonay. Show us the knight, Sir Lancelot of the Lake, where he lies in the full of the moon tonight. Fiat, fiat, fiat. Amen. . . . What do you see?

NIMUE. I see the bowling alley of an inn. It is lit by moonlight and all set about with apple trees in blossom. There is a knight fighting on foot with his back to a pillar of the inn archway. He is set upon by three knights. The moon casts a shadow, but I can see that the three are dealing heavy blows on the poor knight, and ever and again he strikes and drives them a pace or two back. He cannot live. . . . A light shows in the window above the arch. The window is opening. A tall man is standing at the window with the light making an aureole round him. He has vaulted over the sill and landed on the ground ten feet below. He has a sword in his hand. He goes fiercely at the three knights and drives them into the moonlight.

[6]   6

He has beaten a knight to his knees.   You look.   I do not like to see men killed.

[MERLIN, *muttering, looks into the pool.*]

The tall man was very strong.   His sword swung in the moonlight like a whip.

MERLIN.   It is Lancelot.   They are yielding to him as their master.   He is no master to dogs like that.   He will send them to Camelot to yield to the Queen.

NIMUE.   May I see him again?

MERLIN.   No.   You shall see him at Camelot when my plans are ripe.   And soon we shall lead him to Corbin to the Lady Elaine.

NIMUE (*shuddering slightly*).   I do not like the sound of that. . . . Whom did he rescue?

MERLIN.   Sir Kay the Seneschal.

NIMUE.   That boorish, brutal old man!   He should have let them kill him.

MERLIN.   He came early to the Round Table, before I could pick and choose.   Whoever he was, it was Sir Lancelot's duty to save him.

NIMUE.   Sir Lancelot is a fool.   He rescues stupid old men and spares his enemies to do him harm. . . . But a fool is happy.   Why don't you leave him in his happiness?

MERLIN.   He is not happy.   Happiness will come to mankind when I have made my man perfect in mind, body and spirit. . . .

NIMUE.   You will have made an intolerable prig. . . . Merlin, leave Lancelot alone.   You are horrible, moving men and women about on a chequered board, like the pieces in the Chinese game.

MERLIN.   My child, I myself am a man.

NIMUE.   I very much doubt it.   It is growing cold and dark.   Let us go in.

MERLIN.   You must not think I belittle the warm impulses of your generous heart when I say that you are wrong in supposing that my intentions towards Lancelot . . .

[*It grows dark.   They go in to* MERLIN's *hut.*]

SLOW BLACK OUT.

SCENE II

Part of the Bowling Alley of an Inn.

*It has a wall, overhung by a hawthorn in bloom. Against the wall is a
bench, and in front of the bench is a rough table. At one end of the
table is a stool. Moonlight is at odds with daybreak. A lamp is
on the table.*

SIR KAY, *an elderly man, dressed in armour like that of the knights in
the Bayeux Tapestry, is seated on the bench.* GWILYM, *Lancelot's
Page, is helping him out of his helmet.* LANCELOT, *with one foot on
the stool, is polishing his sword with a wisp of grass. He wears a
helmet and hauberk, but no other armour. His shield rests against
the table.*

LANCELOT.   How is it with you ?

SIR KAY.   I am better. I had been riding all night and
they were three to one.

LANCELOT.   Are you hurt ?

SIR KAY.   Bruised a little, but nowhere cut. I could have
dealt fairly by them if you had not come.   (*His helmet is off now.*)

LANCELOT (*holding the lamp to his face*).   I thought so. I
should have known you by your fair and courteous speech and
the urbanity of your manner.   Good morning, Sir Kay.

SIR KAY.   Good morning to you, Sir, whoever you are.

LANCELOT (*taking off his helmet and handing it to Gwilym*).
Take those helmets in and bring a jug of wine for Sir Kay.

[Exit GWILYM.]

SIR KAY.   I should have known you also. Sir Lancelot,
you are an admirable knight, but you cannot be persuaded to
mind your own affairs.

LANCELOT.   When you and your friends came into this alley,
my affair was sleep and pleasant dreams. If you wished me to
mind that, you shouldn't have roared like a bull for help.

SIR KAY.   I did not call for help. You must have been
dreaming.

LANCELOT.   I have said I was dreaming. And no doubt you
didn't call.   I am grateful to you for a very agreeable little fight.
Now stop growling and give me the news of the Court.

SIR KAY.   Where have you been ?

LANCELOT.   Wandering and fighting.

SIR KAY.   They miss you at Court.

[8]   8

LANCELOT. That is gentle of them.

SIR KAY. Every day the Queen asks for you.

LANCELOT. How is she?

SIR KAY. She wears well. . . . God's Body, my back aches. I wish I were twenty years younger.

LANCELOT. I wish you were.

SIR KAY. Do you? Why?

LANCELOT. Because I should kick you from here to Camelot for that speech.

SIR KAY. For what speech?

LANCELOT. You dared to speak irreverently of the Queen.

SIR KAY. Who? I? Nothing of the sort. I said . .

LANCELOT. Spare me what you said.

[GWILYM *brings in a jug of wine and two horn mugs.*]

LANCELOT (*ill-humouredly*).   Put them down there and go to bed.

GWILYM. I have bandages for Sir Kay upstairs. . . .

SIR KAY. I have told you I want no bandages.

GWILYM. It is nearly morning, Sir Lancelot. Need I go to bed?

LANCELOT. Yes. I think you have not slept much, and I cannot have you yawning on the journey. Whom were you serenading last night?

GWILYM. The landlady's daughter, my Lord.

LANCELOT. You hope to become a knight, some day?

GWILYM. Yes, my Lord.

LANCELOT. Remember that when you serenade landladies' daughters. Go to bed.

GWILYM. Good night . . . I mean, good morning, my Lords.

[*Exit* GWILYM.]

SIR KAY. The same old saint.

LANCELOT. I am no saint; but the boy is a good boy, and I am determined he will remain so.

SIR KAY. He seems a likely lad. When he puts on more beef he may make a formidable knight, poor devil.

LANCELOT. Why do you say " poor devil "?

SIR KAY. Because he is to be a knight. He must make vows; he must wear metal clothes; he must peacock and brag and be bumped and beaten and never call his soul his own. Do you call that a life?

SIR KAY.   It is the greatest life of all if a man has the grace and the courage to live it well.

SIR KAY.   I thought so once.   Not now.   I never had much grace, and my courage is an uneasy thing.

LANCELOT.   You are speaking at the back end of the night, after many hours of riding and fighting.   When you are planted on a good horse on a bright afternoon with your elbow gripping a lance and a good stretch of sward in front of you, I shall ask for your opinion.

SIR KAY.   It is easy for you to talk.   Horse or foot you have the better of any dozen of us.   We know it so well that the very sight of your shield loosens us in the saddle.

LANCELOT.   No!

SIR KAY.   But yes!   I'll wager on myself against any man who knows he is beaten before the fight begins.   If you dress me in Lancelot's crest and shield and surcoat, I'll cut through the mellay like corn.

LANCELOT.   Do you think so?

SIR KAY.   I don't think.   I know.

LANCELOT.   You shall have my armour.

SIR KAY.   Now?

LANCELOT.   Yes.   Now.   You shall ride in it to Caerleon upon Usk, and you shall fight in the Whitsun Tournament.

SIR KAY.   They expect you there?

LANCELOT.   All the better.   You will be Sir Lancelot and I shall be Sir Kay.   And if you have spoken the truth, you will carry off the prize and they will tumble me in the dust.

SIR KAY.   You are very kind.   I shall not fight at Caerleon. Your armour would bring Gawaine and the best of them against me like wasps round a honeypot.

LANCELOT.   Then you won't do it?

SIR KAY.   I'll take your armour.   It will be pleasant to get back to Caerleon in peace without knights errant challenging me at every ford.   As for you, you can play Sir Kay at Caerleon if you like.   You are a schoolboy and always will be.   And there are two or three scores I should like to see paid against some young birkies who rejoice to roll the old Seneschal on the ground.   I'll do it.

[10]

LANCELOT. Very well. But why do you call me a schoolboy? I am not so old as you are, but I have a hundred battles between me and the last of my youth.

SIR KAY. Because you are a schoolboy. Your mind is full of childish sports and masquerades. Your page is more of a man than you are.

LANCELOT. Has that speech any meaning, or are you simply growling over your bone?

SIR KAY. He seems to have the enterprise to make love to his landlady's daughter. You could have your pleasure with all the ladies in the land, and you creep about like a bald-headed monk.

LANCELOT. My good Sir . . .

SIR KAY. I know. I know. They say you would be the devil's own fellow if . . . you needn't get angry . . . if you weren't in love with the Queen. They say you never married because of that.

LANCELOT. I cannot tell people what they ought to say of me. They can say what they please. If a man is married, it is his duty to stay with his wife and give over arms and tournaments, battles and adventures. As for paramours, with them I have nothing to do. Partly for the fear of God and partly because I have seen that lechers and adulterers are never happy or fortunate in wars. Their minds stray and their bodies slacken and they are beaten by lesser men than themselves. Their happiness is more among the blankets than among the banners, and to fight without happiness is wickedness and folly. Knighthood is a hard vocation. You were right in that. A man must be taut and strong like a good bowstring. It is only so that he can hear the call and meet the shock and see through the forest of lances to the glory beyond.

[SIR KAY *has fallen asleep with his head on the table.*]

Sir Kay! . . . Poor old man! The May blossom is falling on his head. There was whiteness before it fell. God send that I die in battle, and never grow old and crabbed and feeble. . . . Wake up, Sir Kay. It is morning.

SIR KAY. Eh? What's that? I wasn't asleep. I heard every word you said. The boy's a good boy and he'll do very well. And I'll change armour with you and we'll meet at Caerleon.

[*A cock crows.*]

LANCELOT.   There's the good knight, Sir Chanticlair of the Barnyard, with his spurs and his golden corselet and his scarlet crest!

SIR KAY.   And his forty concubines.

LANCELOT (*laughing*).   Go to bed, you sinful old man! You must have more sleep before sun-up.   Come, I'll help you.

SIR KAY.   Let me alone.   I can walk by myself

[LANCELOT *takes the lantern with one hand and helps* SIR KAY *along with the other.*]

CURTAIN.

SCENE III

The ante-room of the Royal Pavilion at Caerleon upon Usk. A rostrum with two or three steps leads up to a window overlooking the tilting ground. Three Servitors called HOB, GIB *and* JOAN *are clearing up the disorder in which relays of aristocratic persons have left the place.* HOB *is forty,* JOAN *is twenty,* GIB *is seventeen.* GIB *finds difficulty in keeping away from the window. A tremendous clamour is coming from the tilt yard.*

HOB (*shouting above the tumult*).   Come away from that window and get on with your work.

GIB.   Oh, beautiful!   Oh, well hit, Sir Kay!   Well hit!

[*The tumult dies down and stops altogether as a single trumpet sounds.*

KING ARTHUR'S *voice is heard breaking the stillness.*]

ARTHUR (*without*).   Go and abide!

[*A subdued chattering is heard, and* GIB *comes reluctantly from the window.*]

GIB.   He lifted Sir Sagramore off his horse like a forkful of hay.

HOB.   It will be " Well hit, Sir Kay " all over again if he comes in and finds the place like this.

GIB.   I think there will be only one more mellay.   There are hardly enough knights in the saddle to make a good one. I never saw anything like it.   Sir Kay must have been feeding himself beef.

JOAN.   Silly lot of fools.

HOB.   You keep your tongue to yourself, my girl.   If the gentry like to bash each other about, it's none of our business. We must get on with our job.

JOAN.   Get on with what job?   Fetching and carrying for a lot of silly fools.

HOB.   Hold your tongue.

GIB.   It makes you think, doesn't it?   Everyone thought this would be the tamest Whitsun jousting we have ever had. Lancelot away, and Lamorake dead, and Palomides away, and Tristram in Cornwall.   And look at it.   I never saw better.

HOB.   You haven't seen much.

GIB.   Sir Gawaine will have to turn out, after all.   He won't let Sir Kay carry the tournament.   Sir Kay will give him a good fight, today.   I hope they have it out on the ground. I like Sir Gawaine best with his boots on the turf.

JOAN.   I don't like Sir Gawaine at all.

HOB.   What is the like of you doing with likes and dislikes? Who do you think you are?   The Queen of Orkney or something?

GIB.   I hope Sir Gawaine fights.

HOB.   I hope he does.   He'll keep Sir Kay quiet for some weeks.   He has an overhead swing that would split Snowdon.

GIB (*at the window*).   Oh, look!   His page is taking down his shield from in front of his tent.   He's mounting.   His three brothers are with him.   He's taking the opposite end from Sir Kay and Sir Bors and Sir Dinadan.   Now we'll see something. . . .   The King is going to drop his baton.

[*The* OTHER TWO *leave their work and come to the window.*
[*Four trumpets sound.*]

HERALDS (*without*).   Laissez les aller!

[*A terrific row breaks out—cheering, galloping and the clash of armour.*]

GIB.   Go it, Sir Kay!   Ride, man, ride.   Aim low.   Oh, well hit, Sir!   A beauty.   Over he goes.   Mind your back! Look out!   Oh, well ridden, Sir!   Hit him, Sir Bors!   Hard, man, hard!   By gum, what a crack!   That's got him.   Now, Sir Kay . . . give yourself room . . . that's right. . . . It's Sir Gawaine. . . . Oh, good!   Spur him.   As hard as you can pelt.   I bet a million crowns on Sir Kay.

JOAN.   Go on, Sir Kay!   Go on, Sir Kay!

HOB.   He's down.   Sir Gawaine's down.

GIB.   Oh, lads, what a buffet!   Swords out now. . . . No. He's had enough!

JOAN.   He's limping away.

HOB.   It's all over.

[*A trumpet sounds.*]

ARTHUR (*without*).   Go and abide.

HOB.   For the Lord's sake, hurry.   They'll be here in a moment.

GIB.   Did you see him knock the cantels off Gawaine's shield?

JOAN.   He was like a thunderbolt.

HOB.   Sir Kay never struck that stroke.

GIB.   But I saw him.   Joan saw it too.   Didn't you, Joan?

HOB.   That wasn't Sir Kay.

[*Enter* SIR GAWAINE *and* SIR AGRAVAINE. GAWAINE *is a large, ferocious-looking oaf in a foul temper.   His brother,* AGRAVAINE, *is a handsome young fellow with beautiful manners, but a sinister look in his eye.* GAWAINE *tears off his helmet and gauntlets and throws them into a corner of the room, where the* SERVITORS *pick them up and retire into the background.*]

GAWAINE.   Give me a drink.

[HOB *runs to him obsequiously with a horn of sack.* GAWAINE *drains it and throws the lees in* HOB's *face.* HOB *bows and joins his comrades.*]

GAWAINE.   That's better.   It went down.   I was afraid that dog had twisted my gullet.

AGRAVAINE.   When his lance hit you, my dear Gawaine, I thought it had torn gullet and windpipe apart.   It was a comely stroke.   Our friend Sir Kay has greatly improved since we saw him last.

GAWAINE.   If that was Sir Kay, I'm the Lady of the Lake.

AGRAVAINE.   Who was it?

GAWAINE.   He had Sir Kay's armour and Sir Kay's horse and he rode stiffly with a long stirrup, like Sir Kay.   But Sir Kay never dealt me that stroke.   I felt my gorget was a loadstone drawing his spearhead.   One of three knights could have struck that stroke, and one of them is dead.

[14]

AGRAVAINE.   He is bigger than Sir Kay.   You should have fought him on foot.

GAWAINE.   Not I.   When I fight a man on foot, I like to know who he is.   Besides, I thought my neck was broken. When I find his name, I shall cut his throat when and where he pleases.

AGRAVAINE.   Even if it were Lancelot?

GAWAINE.   Lancelot?   Lancelot is in Carlisle.

AGRAVAINE.   Nevertheless, our counterfeit Sir Kay had a manner of dropping his left shoulder I thought that I had seen before.

GAWAINE.   Lancelot or no Lancelot, I'll cut his throat.

AGRAVAINE.   According to the rules of chivalry and your oath of knighthood, I hope.

GAWAINE.   Of course.

AGRAVAINE.   And now we shall learn.   Here comes the King.

GAWAINE.   Mordieu!   Then I'll be going.   I can stand a hard knock or two, but I will not be the butt for bluff King Arthur's idea of a joke.

AGRAVAINE.   No.   Stop.

[*As* GAWAINE *hesitates*, ARTHUR, GUENEVERE, SIR LUCAN THE BUTLER, SIR DINADAN *and* SIR LIONEL *and two of the* QUEEN'S LADIES *enter.*]

ARTHUR.   Ha!   Gawaine!   Where are you going?

GAWAINE.   Sir, I was going to wash off some of this dust.

ARTHUR.   Nay, but why?   You rolled in it as if you loved it.

[*Some laughter.*]

GAWAINE.   Sir, it may please you to think so.   But if any of your gentlemen who are so much amused envy me this dust, by Our Lady, I will give them as much of it to eat as they please. And as soon as they please.

ARTHUR.   Come, come, Gawaine.   You must not take your beating badly.

GAWAINE.   I am not enough accustomed to beatings to take them well.

ARTHUR.   I think you forget yourself.   We shall ask another of our old gentlemen to give you another lesson.

GAWAINE.   No old gentleman struck me that stroke.

ARTHUR.   Indeed ?   We had thought that Sir Kay was past his first youth; he must have drunk from some well.   We must ask him where it is.   Must we not, my Lady ?

GUENEVERE.   What did you say ?   I wasn't listening.

ARTHUR.   Gawaine says that Kay has been rejuvenated. (*To* LUCAN.)   Where is he, Lucan ?

LUCAN.   They are searching for him, my Lord.

ARTHUR.   He must know that he has won the prize.

LUCAN.   Yes, my Lord.

ARTHUR.   When I sounded " Go and abide " he rode out of the ring.   Strange conduct.

DINADAN.   He is here, my Lord.

> [LANCELOT *enters and kneels before the* KING *and* QUEEN. *He wears his vizor down and is not recognised. He is battered and dusty, but bears himself proudly.*]

ARTHUR.   Ah, there you are.   Why did you not ride to the dais ?

GUENEVERE.   Were you hurt ?

LANCELOT (*gruffly*).   No, my Lady.

ARTHUR.   Never mind, never mind.   You have done very well.   Only one thing troubles me.   You are not Sir Kay.

LANCELOT.   No, my Lord.

ARTHUR.   You have his armour and shield and horse and some of his tricks in the saddle.   But you are not Sir Kay.   By the rules of Chivalry, you may remain Unknown.   But we know who you are not.   You have not his looks nor his voice nor, if he will forgive me, his skill in battle.

LANCELOT.   No, my Lord.

ARTHUR.   We should be interested to know who you are. We know only three knights who could have done what you have done today.   But one is in Carlisle, one is in Cornwall and the third is in Brittany.

GUENEVERE.   We need not question this knight further.   He is not in Carlisle.

ARTHUR.   Take off your helmet.

> [LANCELOT *takes off his helmet.*]

My dear fellow, I thought you had deserted us.   Get up. Sit down.   You must be tired.

[*He motions* LANCELOT *to a seat beside the* QUEEN. *There is an agreeable sensation in the Court as the* KNIGHTS *recognise* LANCELOT. GAWAINE *and* AGRAVAINE *draw together and look black.*]

ARTHUR.   Now you must tell us everything you have done since we saw you last.   We didn't expect to see you till the Autumn Ridings.   Where is Sir Kay?   Have you killed him?

[SIR KAY *appears from among the crowd.*]

SIR KAY.   I am here, my Lord.

ARTHUR.   Ah, so you are!   Now, Sir Lancelot!   The giant is dead, and I feel sure that the miles between here and Carlisle are full of recreant knights nursing their wounds and healing their broken bones; and heart-broken damsels who have had the misfortune to be rescued by this celibate knight.   Eh? Ha, ha!   Ho, ho!

LANCELOT.   Since you conquered your enemies, my Lord, you have made England very virtuous and dull.   I was hard put to it to find adventures.

GUENEVERE.   Then you've had a tedious journey?

LANCELOT.   Not entirely, Madam.   Indeed, when peace and the law shine on the land, then adventures are the rarest and sweetest.   We can pursue them in knightly fashion according to the rule.

GAWAINE.   Give me war any day.

GUENEVERE.   We can readily understand, Sir Gawaine, why you prefer war to tournaments.

GAWAINE.   You are very gracious, Madam.

ARTHUR.   Sir Lancelot is right . . . (*He says this line with a somewhat Blimpish air, for, in some respects, King Arthur is an etherealised Blimp*) . . . I have brought more than one war to a happy issue, but at the end of it I never felt that it had made me a better man.

LANCELOT.   In war the great and the simple, the high and the low, the knightly and the common, are seethed together in a pot.   The end is victory, not honour, and honour is lost in the chase.

GUENEVERE.   Chivalry cannot breathe in the dust of battle?

ARTHUR.   I should not go so far as to say that.   But what is the meaning of all this?   Here is the pattern of knighthood and

17   [17]

the prince of good companions home again breaking heads like a hero, and we sit philosophising like so many scabby old monks. Sir Lucan! I shall drink to the best man in Britain and the flower of all good knights.

> [SIR LUCAN *hands a loving-cup to the* KING, *and there is a noisy rush for the buffet as the* KNIGHTS *fill their bowls.*]

ARTHUR. Sir Lancelot of the Lake!

OMNES. Sir Lancelot!

LANCELOT (*drinking to the Queen*). Madam!

GUENEVERE. My very good knight!

> [*The* KNIGHTS *crowd round* LANCELOT, *and there is a noisy hum of conversation.* GAWAINE, AGRAVAINE *and* MORDRED *hold a little apart.*]

DINADAN. I knew you, you old shrew! You bull-headed old apostle of trouble!

LANCELOT. Dear old Dinadan, the cautious rider! How many falls did you get today, sweetheart?

DINADAN. None. My patron saint sent me a beautiful boil in exactly the right place.

BORS. But he was good last week, Lancelot. He put down four Irish knights with one spear.

LANCELOT. Rigid economy. . . . Hello, here's dear old Sir Kay. How are you, my friend? I'm afraid your armour is a little damaged. I think Gawaine spoiled your shield.

SIR KAY. You nearly spoiled Gawaine. He will love you no better for this day's work.

LANCELOT. Nonsense. Gawaine is a good knight. He can take hard knocks as well as he can give them. . . . Can't you, Gawaine?

GAWAINE. Yes.

LANCELOT. And he can give them! I felt my teeth rattle in my head.

ARTHUR. Now you are here you will abide. We shall hunt the boar tomorrow.

GUENEVERE. He hates us. He will not abide. He has told you he finds us dull.

ARTHUR. He didn't mean that. He was talking of the moors and deserts in the north.

GUENEVERE (*to* LANCELOT). Were you?

LANCELOT.   Madam, when you are cruel it is like a sudden thunder-cloud on an April day.   All the birds and beasts fall silent.   I have no words to say except that I am at your command.

ARTHUR.   Then tell him to stay.

GUENEVERE.   The King desires you to stay and hunt with him. . . . Will you stay?

LANCELOT.   Willingly, Madam.

ARTHUR.   And tonight we shall have such a feast as Camelot has never seen.

GAWAINE (*raising his drinking-vessel*).   The Queen and Sir Lancelot!

AGRAVAINE (*with rather more meaning in his voice than Gawaine*).   The Queen and Sir Lancelot!   Happy days and nights.

SIR BORS.   The Queen!

[*The faint shadow of embarrassment at* AGRAVAINE'S *tone blows over and the toast is drunk with great jollity.*]

ARTHUR.   Sir Agravaine, I thank you for your phrase. Happy days and nights.   We shall crown the happiest of days with a night of wine and song and tales of great deeds.   Never was there a day like this nor a land like the land of Logris nor a company like the company of the Round Table.   This is the bravest time since time began. . . .

[*While he is speaking* NIMUE *appears in the doorway.* GUENEVERE *draws his attention to her.*]

ARTHUR.   Eh?   What's that?   Oh!   Lady, you are welcome.   And if you bring an adventure you are doubly welcome. I had it in my mind that I should not sit down to dinner till I had seen an adventure.   Sir Lancelot says I have banished them from the land.

NIMUE.   Is Sir Lancelot here?

ARTHUR.   He is.

NIMUE.   Which is Sir Lancelot?

LANCELOT.   Here.

NIMUE.   My Lord, my Lady and Sir Lancelot, I have come to your Court for help.

ARTHUR.   For whom?   What is the adventure?

NIMUE.   I come from King Pelleas of Corbin.

19   [19]

ARTHUR. King Pelleas is a very noble knight. A little eccentric, but a very noble knight. What can I do for King Pelleas?

NIMUE. His city is troubled with a great serpent. With a great serpent that comes up from the tombs and goes silently through the streets at night and in by the little windows, stealing babies from their cots and putting the town in fear. In Corbin there is no knight found who can find and face the monster, and it has come to King Pelleas in a dream that it must be slain by the best knight in all the world. So I have come for Sir Lancelot.

ARTHUR. When Sir Lancelot is rested and refreshed no doubt he will accept your adventure. But not tonight.

NIMUE. It must be tonight. He must ride today and to-night, and tomorrow he will come to Corbin and kill the serpent.

GUENEVERE. But why? He has fought all day in the tournament. He is weary.

NIMUE. I have been deceived. I was told that when a Knight of King Arthur had been called to a quest he would leap from his death-bed to the saddle. I was deceived.

LANCELOT. Lady, there need be no more words. . . .

[*The* QUEEN *restrains him.*]

ARTHUR. You come from King Pelleas. Have you any sign that you come from King Pelleas?

NIMUE. I have his jasper ring that was cut from the breast-plate of the High Priest Caiaphas. . . . Look! Here it is. The little cup cut on it is the Holy Grail.

[*She crosses and shows the ring to* KING ARTHUR.]

ARTHUR. I have heard of this ring.

NIMUE. In the dream of the Fisherman King a leopard of king's blood attacked the serpent and killed him in the full of the moon. The moon is full tomorrow.

GUENEVERE (*furiously*). King Pelleas is a limping fool and a superstitious old madman. Everybody knows that. Everybody laughs at him. His castle is more like a church than a castle. He dreamed of the serpent too. There is no serpent. He lives in dreams. He is so dazed with the sound of church bells and besotted with incense that he doesn't know the truth from lies. I say you shall not go.

[20]   20

ARTHUR. This is very extraordinary conduct, my dear. Sir Lancelot has been called to an adventure. He has been called in perfectly correct form. He must go or be shamed. I am surprised at you.

LANCELOT. Madam, if King Pelleas has dreamt this and there is no serpent I shall return the sooner.

GUENEVERE. It is a trap. It is an enchanter's trap. Look at that woman's eyes.

[NIMUE *casts down her eyes.*]

ARTHUR. You do the young lady an injustice. She is embarrassed.

LANCELOT. Madam, when I have killed this beast, trap or no trap, I shall return to the court. I give you my word. As to the adventure, I have no choice. Sir Bors, lend me a fresh suit of war-gear. If the lady will wait for me I shall make her a more sightly companion.

[*He kneels to the* QUEEN.]

LANCELOT. Madam, forgive me and wish me well.

GUENEVERE. I wish you well. But come back soon.

LANCELOT. As hard as I can gallop.

[*He kisses her hand, rises, bows to the* KING *and leaves the hall with* SIR BORS. NIMUE *curtsies and follows him.*]

GUENEVERE (*to* ARTHUR). Now what has become of your happy evening?

ARTHUR (*gently*). My love, I sometimes wonder if you do fully understand the principles of chivalry.

GUENEVERE. The principles of chivalry are . . . Arthur,
[*A trumpet sounds.*]
send Sir Bors and a dozen knights after him. It is a trap. We shall never see him again.

ARTHUR. You are tired. You do not mean what you say. You must not give way to these childish fancies.

GUENEVERE. Sir, my day of childish fancies has long since passed. I am an old woman. You will find it wise to listen to an old woman.

ARTHUR. Oh, tut, tut. Dear, dear. You must not speak like that. Old? Heaven's Grace, what a thing to say!

[*He leads her apart from the* KNIGHTS, *who withdraw respectfully upstage.*]

ARTHUR. What will the knights think of you?

GUENEVERE. How should I know? They think I am an old woman. I *am* an old woman.

ARTHUR. My dear, you are eternally young.

GUENEVERE. " My dear, you are eternally young! " Now you set your kingly seal on that truth. And yet forty-five years is not an eternity. Many queens can keep the devotion of their knights for more years than that.

ARTHUR. I don't understand you.

GUENEVERE. There was a day when I could have called Lancelot back with the half flicker of a frown.

ARTHUR. My Lady, you are making an exhibition of yourself. We shall go now to the Gate and see him ride out.

GUENEVERE. No. Go you. You were right. I am tired. I shall wait here till you come back.

ARTHUR. I think you ought to come.

GUENEVERE. No.

ARTHUR. Very well. Your ladies will be disappointed.

GUENEVERE. Take them too. Go now. I am tired. I am old and tired.

ARTHUR. You are not old.

GUENEVERE. Say that often to me in that voice and I shall be young again. Dear Lord Arthur.

ARTHUR. My dear Lady. (*He kisses her hand.*) Lords and Ladies, we shall go to the Gate to speed the quest. Follow me.

> [*Exeunt all but* GUENEVERE. *She sits by the table and plays idly with a wine-cup. To her,* LANCELOT. *He wears a new surcoat and carries his helmet under his arm.* GUENEVERE *looks up in delighted surprise.*]

LANCELOT. My Lady.

GUENEVERE. Well?

LANCELOT. You do not wish me to go on this quest?

GUENEVERE. No. It is no fair quest. It is a trap.

LANCELOT. I am too cunning an old beast to be caught in traps. But trap or no trap, I cannot ride while the Queen is angry with me.

GUENEVERE. These things are said to queens. But I am different from other queens in this, that I do not believe them.

LANCELOT. I did not say these things to a queen.

GUENEVERE. To whom, then?

LANCELOT. To the greatest and dearest Lady in all the world. It is not that I would die for you, Madam. I would do that readily for my Lord Arthur's wife. But for me there are only two ladies—the Mother of God and yourself.

GUENEVERE. Is that true? They say it is true.

LANCELOT. They may say what they will and it is true, Madam.

GUENEVERE. God bless you, then, and speed you, Sir Lancelot. And this not only from Lord Arthur's wife.

[*She binds a handkerchief round his arm and withdraws a pace from him. They look at each other in silence for a moment.*]

But also from my Lord Arthur's wife.

[LANCELOT *bows in silence and goes out. Trumpet sounds.*]

CURTAIN.

SCENE IV

A room in the Castle of Corbin. At a refectory table KING PELLEAS, *a handsome, middle-aged man with a limp in his left foot,* DAME BRISEN, *an obvious witch,* NIMUE, ELAINE, *a handsome, stupid-looking young woman of about twenty, and* SIR LANCELOT *have sat down to dinner. Two or three extremely solemn-looking servitors stand behind them.* KING PELLEAS *is saying grace, and has obviously been saying it for a long time. Steam is rising from the dishes, but before the grace has finished the food is cold.* SIR LANCELOT *is somewhat impatient, but is always the perfect gentleman.*

PELLEAS. Hinc horror ille et stupor, quo passim scriptura recitat perculsos atque afflictos fuisse sanctos, quoties Dei praesentiam sentiebant. Quum enim eos videamus qui absente ipse securi firmique consistebant, ipso gloriam suam manifestante, sic quatefieri ac consternari ut mortis horrore concidant, imo absorbeantur, et paene nulli sint: colligendum inde est, hominem humilitatis, suae agnitione numquam satis tangi et affici, nisi portquam sed ad Dei majestatem comparavit. Ejus autem consternationis exempla crebra habemus tum in judicibus, tum in prophetis . . . adeo ut vox vox illa in Dei populo usitata foret: moriemur, quia Dominus apparuit nobis. Ideo et

23   [23]

historia Job ad prosternendos suae stultitiae, impotentiae,
polutionis conscientiae homines, pitissimun semper argumentum
a divinae sapientiae, virtutis, puritatis descriptione ducit.   Neque
frustra: videmus enim ut Abrahammellius se terram et pulvarem
adnoscat, ex quo propius ad conspiciendam Domini gloriam
accessit . . . ut Elias retecta facie ejus accessum exspectare
non sustineat . . . tantum est in aspectu formidinis.   Et quid
faciat homo putredo ac vermis, quum ipsos quoque Cherubim
velare, ipso pavore, faciem suam oporteat . . . ?   Hoc scilicet
est quod dicit propheta Jesiias . . . erubescet sol et confundetur
luna quum Dominus exercituum regnaverit; hoc est, ubi
claritatemsuam extulerit ac propius admoverit, lucidissimum
quodque prae illa tenebris obscurabitur.   Utcunque tamen Dei
nostrique notitia mutuo inter se nexu sint colligatae, ordo recti
docendi postulat ut de illa priore disseramus loco, tum ad hanc
tractandam postea descendamus. . . . Fiat . . . Amen. . .
Et Amen. . . . . And now, Sir Lancelot, fall to!   I hope you
have a good appetite.

LANCELOT.   Some of it at least has survived.

PELLEAS.   My daughter Elaine has superintended the
preparation of these—these mercies, herself.

LANCELOT.   That is very kind of her.

PELLEAS.   She is an excellent cook.   Is she not, Dame
Brisen?

BRISEN.   Indeed, she is, King Pelleas.

PELLEAS.   If a girl is allowed to be idle I find that inevitably
her thoughts stray to the practice of sorcery and such abomina-
tions.   Satan, they say, finds some mischief still for idle hands
to do.

LANCELOT.   So I have been told. . . . King Pelleas, if you
will forgive me for being blunt, I came to your very delightful
castle with some idea that my own hands were to be occupied.
You wish me to kill a serpent?

PELLEAS.   A serpent?   Ah, yes!   There was a serpent.
We shall talk of that later.

LANCELOT.   Forgive me, but may we talk about it now?   I
understood that the matter was urgent.

PELLEAS.   Oh, yes, urgent.   Certainly.   Most urgent.

LANCELOT.   I am very grateful, Sir King, for the reception
you and your people have given me.   The hundreds of little

girls strewing primroses—by the way, they ought to have been in their beds—the very excellent orchestra of lutes, citherns and tabors; the excellent choir of monks and nuns who sang the Song of Jubilation so beautifully; the prominent citizens who presented me with such a charming address of welcome; the finely proportioned and splendidly disciplined body of knights it was my pleasure to inspect—all these things gratified me very much. But so far I have not heard a single word about the serpent I came to slay.

PELLEAS.   There are two methods of encountering a monster of this nature. One is after prayer and fasting; the other is after a good meal and a good sleep. I sought for guidance in this matter, and have taken on myself the prayer and fasting. . . . Norman, fill up the Lord Lancelot's wine-cup.

ELAINE.   I shall do that.

BRISEN.   No, my darling, sit down. (*She rises.*) Dame Nimue and I have prepared a posset that is a heavenly remedy against fatigue. Sir Lancelot has ridden far today. (*She takes a golden cup from the sideboard.*) Nimue has tried it. She has ridden as far as Sir Lancelot and she is as fresh as a daisy. Are you not, my dear?

NIMUE.   Yes.

LANCELOT.   You are very kind. My Lord Sir Pelleas, I drink to you and to your fair daughter, and to you, my ladies! (*He drinks, and immediately looks a little startled.*) What is this?

BRISEN.   It is perfectly harmless. It is a recipe of my mother's. Don't you like it?

LANCELOT.   Very much. But I have a sensation of having swallowed a bowl of summer lightning. The hall seems to have grown brighter.

PELLEAS.   You have noticed that? This hall is sometimes illuminated by sudden bursts of radiance. At times we see the appearance of doves, fluttering among the beams.

LANCELOT.   If I have any more of Dame Brisen's posset it would not surprise me to see dragons fluttering among the beams.

NIMUE.   You are wrong. It is not the posset. This is a Holy place. Drink and do not fear.

BRISEN.   Fear is a strange word to use to Sir Lancelot. Are you afraid of my posset?

LANCELOT.   No.

BRISEN.   Then why do you look at it as if it were poison? Either your courage or your courtesy is at fault.

ELAINE.   You must not speak to Sir Lancelot like that. What will he think of us?

PELLEAS.   Take away his cup and give him what he asks for.

LANCELOT.   No.   I am sorry.   Dame Brisen, I have never tasted anything more delicious in my life.   This time I shall drink to you alone.   You have compounded a miracle!

[*He drinks to* DAME BRISEN.]

BRISEN.   You honour me too much.

LANCELOT.   Not at all.   You honour me too much.   I have never experienced such magnificent hospitality in my life. King Pelleas, you are known all up and down the country and round about and everywhere as a most godly and religious man. I am not myself a religious man.   I live by a simple and rather rough-and-ready code.   But I can respect your way of living. Please understand that.   And please don't misunderstand me when I say what a pleasure it is to find you such a broad-minded and hospitable person.   May I have the honour of drinking your health?

PELLEAS.   Certainly, Sir Lancelot.   It is your way of invoking a blessing on my poor house.

[LANCELOT *empties the cup.*]

LANCELOT.   King Pelleas . . . Dame Brisen, this is the most excellent stuff I have ever tasted.   I will not only kill your serpent for you.   I will kill a hundred million serpents and eat them one by one.   If you have any enemies, produce them.   I will deal with them.   And if anybody has the impertinence to say that your beautiful daughter Dame Elaine is not the second most beautiful, virtuous lady in the world, I will push my lance two yards through his breastbone and rid the world of a lying rascal. . . . Lady, if I could I would be your knight.   But I am vowed to be the knight of one lady, and one lady only, and her name I cannot speak even in this presence. . . . Shall we drink to her?

[DAME BRISEN *refills his cup.*]

To the great Lady who shall be nameless!   And to knighthood, honour and brave battles generously and nobly fought.

[*All drink.*]

ELAINE.   But you have eaten nothing.

LANCELOT.   I am going to eat the serpent.   Where is it?

[*He gets up, knocking over his chair.   He is very drunk, but he has his muscles under iron control.*   NIMUE *and* BRISEN *exchange glances.*   KING PELLEAS *rises.*]

PELLEAS.   Before you fight the serpent you have another part of the preliminary rites to fulfil.

LANCELOT.   And what part is that?

PELLEAS.   You must sleep.   I shall wake you when the moon is at its zenith, and then you will do what is to be done.

LANCELOT.   I am at your service.

PELLEAS.   I will show you to your room.

LANCELOT.   How long shall I sleep?

PELLEAS.   For two hours.

LANCELOT.   Very well.   I shall sleep for two hours.

[PELLEAS *leads* SIR LANCELOT *out.   The servants follow, carrying candles.*]

BRISEN (*to* ELAINE).   Go to your room.   We shall send for you when we need you.

ELAINE.   But Sir Lancelot is drunk. . . .

BRISEN.   Sir Lancelot is as I intended him to be.   Don't argue.   Go to your room.   I wish to talk to the Lady of the Lake.

ELAINE.   I wish Sir Lancelot weren't drunk.   He looks rather silly when he's drunk.   I wish you hadn't made him drunk.

[ELAINE *goes out complaining under her breath.*]

NIMUE.   She is a fool.

BRISEN.   She is none the worse for that.   She represents the finest stock in Christendom.

NIMUE.   So Merlin says.

[MERLIN *appears at the back.   He is dressed in a sad-coloured gown and wears a wreath of mistletoe about his head.*]

NIMUE.   Oh, there you are!   How did you get in?

MERLIN.   Never mind about that.   Have you done as I told you?

NIMUE.   Yes.   Dame Brisen hocussed his drink.   Perhaps too well.   He looked as though he might pass into limbo at any moment.

BRISEN. No, he won't. I have experience in these matters.

MERLIN. How is King Pelleas taking it?

BRISEN. He believes he has had guidance. In that state he is capable of any mischief.

MERLIN. And Elaine?

NIMUE. She is so stupid she'll do anything we ask her.

MERLIN. Good. Now move the table over there.

BRISEN. I shall call the servants.

MERLIN. Do as I tell you. And you, Nimue, help her.

[BRISEN *and* NIMUE *lift the table into a corner of the room.*]

BRISEN. Your friend is very peremptory.

NIMUE. Yes.

BRISEN. Nobody has eaten anything.

NIMUE. I am not surprised.

BRISEN (*to* MERLIN). What are you going to do? Make a magic circle?

NIMUE. Hush! Don't interrupt him. He is thinking.

BRISEN. Oh, thinking!

MERLIN. Where is the King?

BRISEN. He has gone with Sir Lancelot. . . Oh, here he is.

[*Enter* KING PELLEAS.]

PELLEAS. Merlin?

MERLIN. I am Merlin. Where is Sir Lancelot?

PELLEAS. Three knights carrying candles are leading him round and round the dark corridors of the palace. It is as you told me. He will be back here presently

MERLIN. He can walk?

PELLEAS. A little unsteadily, but remarkably well.

MERLIN. Everything is ready?

PELLEAS. Yes. . . . Merlin, this is very distasteful to me.

MERLIN. Why?

PELLEAS. I have never before played a trick on a guest beneath my roof.

MERLIN. It is not a trick. All that is to be done is necessary, except one thing. And on that one thing you insisted.

PELLEAS. Naturally I insisted. I am a priest as well as a king, and what is more, a man of principle. And my daughter is to be considered.

[28]   28

MERLIN. It is all right. There will be a marriage. It will make it more difficult, but your principles will be respected.

PELLEAS. I should not have consented on any other terms.

MERLIN. No? You would have defied the clear instructions of revelation?

PELLEAS. No. But it is a peculiar kind of revelation that disregards the Holy Sacrament of Marriage.

MERLIN (*kindly*). I do not think you realise, King Pelleas, the importance of this thing. Knighthood is the perfect state of mankind; even if nothing more were done it would survive long after you and I were dead—for ever. On this evening it is ordained by the powers of the air that there will be begotten in this palace the perfection of this perfect state, the perfect knight, who will be called Galahad and achieve the Grail and redeem the world by his greatness.

PELLEAS. Are you sure?

MERLIN. My dear sir, it was I who told Uther Pendragon that he should beget a son who would rule the land of Logris and lead the order of knighthood to perfection. I need hardly say that I allude to King Arthur. Besides, in your own way you have also had a revelation.

PELLEAS. I wish for this thing so greatly that it must be a revelation.

MERLIN. In the dark of the night voices came to you and told you.

PELLEAS. Yes, there were the voices too.

MERLIN. I wish this thing because it is to be. It is for this that life was put into the world.

PELLEAS. I wish this thing because through it the beauty of holiness will become manifest.

BRISEN (*aside to* NIMUE). They are well away. This sort of thing could go on all night.

[PELLEAS *stands in an attitude of prayer,* MERLIN *in an attitude of exaltation.*]

NIMUE. Hush! Men can do nothing without arguing themselves into it. They are quite happy.

[SIR LANCELOT *appears in the doorway. He is dressed in a long purple gown and carries his sheathed sword under his arm.* PELLEAS *and* BRISEN *disappear into the shadows.*]

LANCELOT. Where am I? A great wind blew out the candles and I lost my guides.

MERLIN. Do you know me, Sir Lancelot?

LANCELOT. Yes, you are Merlin. What are you doing here?

MERLIN. Is there in your heart a longing that you dare not speak?

NIMUE. Is there in your mind one you dare not name?

LANCELOT. I do not understand this.

MERLIN. This is the night of the full moon and of your heart's desire.

LANCELOT. I do not know whether I am awake or asleep.

MERLIN. It is of no great moment whether you dream or wake. This is the night of your expectation.

NIMUE. This is the night of your heart's desire.

MERLIN. There is another who speaks to you with silent words in this night of your desire.

NIMUE. She speaks to you with silent words she has not dared to utter.

MERLIN. The answer to the words your soul is speaking now in the silence of your heart. . . .

NIMUE. The words you both have spoken many times in question and answer and have known but have not heard.

MERLIN. The questioning and answering of your heart's desire.

LANCELOT. This is a dream.

MERLIN. Why not?

NIMUE. It is no dream. If it were a dream the words could be spoken and the longing fulfilled. The words cannot be spoken, but the longing will be fulfilled.

LANCELOT. What do you mean?

NIMUE. The Queen is here.

LANCELOT. The Queen?

NIMUE. It was at her bidding I came for you at Camelot.

LANCELOT. But she did not wish me to go.

NIMUE. At Camelot she was afraid. Tonight she will not be afraid.

LANCELOT. You are lying to me. How can the Queen be here?

MERLIN. How long have you slept, Lancelot?

LANCELOT.   I do not know.   My mind is in a cloud.   I remember nothing.

MERLIN.   You have slept for three days, and tonight the Queen is here.

LANCELOT.   Where is she?

MERLIN.   You are a knight of King Arthur.   You will be called to swear on the Rood that you neither saw the Queen nor spoke with her.   Therefore we shall bind your eyes and you will not speak.

LANCELOT.   But King Pelleas? . . .

MERLIN.   King Pelleas will be deceived.

LANCELOT.   What have you told him?

MERLIN.   I have told him that tonight you will marry a lady in a veil, whose name he may not know, and whose face he may not see.   He is a priest as well as a king, and tonight he will marry you to the Queen.

LANCELOT.   But . . .

MERLIN.   What is to be done will be done.

LANCELOT.   My mouth is dry and great bells are ringing in my head.   How can I be married to the Queen?   The King is alive.

MERLIN.   You cannot be married to the Queen.   He will talk words that have no meaning, like a priest in a stage play.

LANCELOT.   I can't do that to my host in his own house.

NIMUE.   Some fool told me once that you were the daringest knight and greatest lover in Christendom.   And now I hear you chattering and haggling like an old Jewess at a rag fair.   Do you want more of the posset to make you bold?   Or is your love for the Queen only a silly song to make the world think you a man?

LANCELOT.   Who are you, you spitting cat?

NIMUE.   I love the Queen and wish her a better lover.

LANCELOT (to MERLIN).   What do you want me to do?

MERLIN.   Go into that room.   Presently King Pelleas will bring you the lady in the veil.   Only she must not speak to you or you to her.   Do you swear that?

LANCELOT.   I swear that.

MERLIN.   Very well, then.   Bind his eyes

[NIMUE binds LANCELOT's eyes, and MERLIN leads him to the curtained exit at the back. NIMUE begins to sillaugh ently. MERLIN returns.]

MERLIN.   You have done very well.   He keeps most of his senses.   What are you laughing at?

NIMUE.   At a thought that pleased me.

MERLIN.   There is nothing to laugh at.   Tonight is one of the greatest nights in all history.

NIMUE.   I know.   You are doing the work of the great blind forces of the nether air.   It pleases you to think that.   It pleases me to think that you are doing a mean little, shabby, scurvy trick.

MERLIN.   Be silent!

NIMUE.   And that drunk fool there, the great lover!   Did you hear him boggle at deceiving his host?   It was against all honour and the laws of knighthood.   And because I jeered at him he has gone in there without a thought to cuckold his King. Or so he thinks, the bull-headed oaf!

MERLIN.   Nimue, you must be mad.   It is not like you to say such things.   If you believed what you say you could not be a party to this deed.

NIMUE.   When I was born a girl I was born a match-maker. Men only become panders when they are old.

MERLIN.   I wish to God I were too old to be a slave to an ill-tongued harlot!

NIMUE.   That's what you think of me?   Wait.   We shall see.   And don't begin to blubber, for here comes your partner, the pious Pelleas, leading the sacred cow.

[*Sacred music is heard.*]

[PELLEAS *and* ELAINE *enter, followed by* DAME BRISEN. ELAINE *is muffled heavily in a veil.* BRISEN *is fussily arranging it, so that none of her face can be seen.*]

ELAINE.   Don't do that.   It's too tight.   I can't breathe. I've got a bit of it in my mouth.

BRISEN.   It's got to be fixed properly.   He mustn't see your face, d'you hear?

PELLEAS.   I told you not to speak.   You swore that you wouldn't speak.   Elaine if I hear another whisper from you I shall send you back to bed. . . . (*To* MERLIN.)   Where is he?

MERLIN.   He is in the inner room.   He is blindfolded and the room is as dark as the Pit.   You will make your ceremony in the dark and come away quickly; if she does not speak it is safe.

[32]

PELLEAS.   Come, my child.

> [PELLEAS, ELAINE *and* BRISEN *go through the curtains.*]

MERLIN.   She is of a height with Guenevere and she walks like a queen.   I think our work is finished.   Where shall we go now?

NIMUE.   We?

MERLIN.   I am bound to you by fate.

NIMUE.   Then you must follow me.

MERLIN.   I will follow you.

NIMUE.   I know where I shall take you.   Come!

> [*Exeunt* NIMUE *and* MERLIN.   MERLIN *blows out all the remaining candles but one before he goes.   After a pause,* PELLEAS *and* BRISEN *enter the dark stage on tip-toe.* PELLEAS *takes the remaining candle and they go out.*]

THE CURTAIN FALLS.

SCENE V

The same.   Daybreak.

SIR LANCELOT *bursts through the curtain, roaring with rage.   He pulls* ELAINE *after him by the wrist and flourishes his sword with the other hand.*

LANCELOT.   Ah, you foul witch!   You false, traitorous hag! Come out.   Let me see you.

ELAINE.   Don't kill me!

LANCELOT.   Kill you?   I shall kill you, you traitor, you harlot!   You'll do no more witchcraft. . . . I am lost!   I am ashamed!   I'll kill you and the smiling devil your father and the witches who poisoned my drink.   I shall set this den of warlocks on fire and fill the moat with blackened skulls. Where is your father?

ELAINE.   I don't know.   I was to steal away when you were sleeping.   But it is daylight.

LANCELOT.   Why did you do this?   You must be sunk in wickedness, but there is no wickedness in your face.   Why did you do this?

ELAINE.   It was my father.

LANCELOT.   But why did you not hit him on the mouth when he spoke to you of this?   Your shame is greater even than my shame.

ELAINE.   I am not ashamed.   I am your wife.   Kill me now.   I am glad to have been your wife.

LANCELOT.   At least you are no coward.

ELAINE.   The wife of Sir Lancelot cannot be afraid.

LANCELOT.   Get up and look me in the eyes.   Do you know that you have done me the greatest of all treacheries?

ELAINE.   Yes.

LANCELOT.   Do you know that you have made me hate you above every living thing?

ELAINE.   Yes.

LANCELOT.   Do you know that you have killed your father and all his knights; for I cannot rest till I have brought an army against him to wipe this blot from my soul.

ELAINE.   Yes.

LANCELOT.   Did you think of these things when you lent yourself to this plot?

ELAINE.   I thought of them.

LANCELOT.   Why should I not kill you?   You have killed me.

ELAINE.   No.

[*They sit down on a bench,* LANCELOT *staring at* ELAINE *fixedly, and she returning his regard.   After a short pause he speaks again.*]

LANCELOT.   When you kill a man's life you kill him.   My life was to be better than a beast.   It was to act nobly and do great deeds and to honour my fellows and myself.   You have killed that with your mean thief's trick.   You made me dishonour my King and my Queen and myself.   What is there left for me but to kill and to kill and to kill and to die in a ditch? And for you, what was it drove you to this?

ELAINE.   I loved you.

LANCELOT.   How could it be that?   I was a drunken man embracing a shadow, an image.   You were less than nothing. Could you be content with that?

ELAINE.   Yes.   Yes, we are to have a son.

LANCELOT.   No.   I am going to kill you.   You and I are dead already.

ELAINE.   You are not going to kill me, and if you are dead you will live again in your son.

[LANCELOT *gets up and paces the room.*]

LANCELOT. I thought you were a fool. I thought I might spare you because you were a fool. But you are not a fool. I cannot understand. I am lost. I cannot understand. What am I to do?

ELAINE. If you forgive me you can stay here. Or if you don't forgive me you can stay here and learn to forgive me in time.

LANCELOT. You *are* a fool. That at least gives me solid ground beneath my feet.

ELAINE. I know I am a fool, but I think that was a very sensible idea.

LANCELOT. That I should live with you? And your detestable father? Whose sanctimonious smile I am about to carve out of existence with my sword?

ELAINE. You mustn't do that! Father is mad. He had a terrible experience before I was born. He trusted Sir Gawaine with his sweetheart. He thought Sir Gawaine was only a boy. But Sir Gawaine was a bad boy even then. He should have killed Gawaine and the woman then, but he laid his sword between them when they slept and went away and married mother. But he never got over it. It drove him to religion at last and he is too young to be religious.

LANCELOT (*sitting down again*). I have never known anybody like you. You are in danger of your life and you sit there calmly gossiping about your family. You are a strange creature, Elaine.

ELAINE. No, I don't think so. I expect you are too high-minded and noble to talk much to women. You would rather worship them than talk to them.

LANCELOT. By God, I believe you're right!

ELAINE. It is very dull for women, that.

LANCELOT. Dull?

ELAINE. You haven't thought how dull it is for them in this age of chivalry. They are driven to sorcery and all sorts of horrible things.

LANCELOT. You must not miscall the Age of Chivalry.

ELAINE. You told me a moment ago that I had killed it.

LANCELOT. No. You killed only me. You cannot kill knighthood.

ELAINE. I don't think I've killed you. I've only troubled you.

35   [35]

LANCELOT. You have troubled me so much that I do not know whether I am alive or dead. But you have taught me something.

ELAINE. What have I taught you?

LANCELOT. Elaine, all my life I have loved a Queen. I have loved her as if she had been a painted image of the Virgin in a church—adoring and asking nothing. But I have asked the Virgin for help, and I shall ask it from my Lady. I shall go to her and drink from the fountain of her woman's wisdom, and she shall show me what path I am to take. . . .

ELAINE. Oh, d'you think that would be wise?

LANCELOT. You have taught me that it would be wise.

ELAINE. I did not intend to. . . . If she tells you to burn Corbin Castle and kill father and me?

LANCELOT. You do not know the Queen. . . . Good-bye.

ELAINE. Is it good-bye?

LANCELOT. Yes.

ELAINE. But you don't hate me?

LANCELOT. No.

[LANCELOT *kisses* ELAINE; *takes up his sword and goes out.*]
[ELAINE *goes over to the refectory table and begins meditatively to eat a pear.*]

CURTAIN.

SCENE VI

CAMELOT, *a week later. There is no reason why the scene should not be the ante-chamber of the earlier scene. The* QUEEN *is sitting at the window, gazing out and working spasmodically at a tapestry frame. Three of her girls are working in the lower part of the room.*

FIRST GIRL. He looked lovely. He wore a cramoisie surcoat picked out with gold marigolds. He had a little round helmet with a beaten copper inlay. His shield was yellow and blue, showing a lady in olive green standing by the seashore. Iseult of Brittany that would be. He's mad about her. But it went terribly well with his brown skin and his big black eyes.

GUENEVERE. Who is that?

FIRST GIRL. What, Madam?

GUENEVERE. The knight you were talking of.

FIRST GIRL. The Saracen knight, Madam. Sir Palomides. The one who beat Sir Gawaine last autumn. He's terribly in love with the Queen of Cornwall. He won't look at anyone else. It's funny, a Saracen being so faithful. Especially as she just naturally won't look at him.

SECOND GIRL. You wouldn't if you had Sir Tristram.

FIRST GIRL. I don't know. He's very big and strong, and he has hair like ripe barley. But he hasn't the sort of grace of Sir Palomides. He's more the Gawaine type, only better looking, of course. The other sort looks far better on a horse. Like a tiger or a panther.

SECOND GIRL. Or a leopard . . . (*She giggles*).

FIRST GIRL. Well, Sir Lancelot *is* more the type. He's as big as Sir Tristram. But when he's on horseback he and his horse move like a couple of dancers.

GUENEVERE. Can't you work without chattering?

FIRST GIRL. Yes, Madam. They say Sir Lancelot is coming back, Madam.

GUENEVERE. What! Is there any news?

FIRST GIRL. They say a courier passed through riding to Guildford who saw him on the edge of the Kennet Marsh. He said he was riding slowly and looking at some swans flying above the mist.

GUENEVERE. He was riding towards Camelot?

FIRST GIRL. Yes, Madam.

GUENEVERE. When was he seen?

GIRL. Yesterday.

GUENEVERE. There is no word of what happened at Corbin?

FIRST GIRL. Not yet, Madam.

[*Enter* KING ARTHUR.]

ARTHUR. I have bad news for you.

[*The* QUEEN *springs up and stares at him with her hand on her heart.*]

You remember we said we should ride over to Whitechurch to see the fresh shoots in the larches? Well, I am sorry to tell you that your jennet, Magdalen, was cast last night and pulled her off hind fetlock. Gawaine says you won't be able to ride her for weeks. Of course, you could ride another, but I know your love for the beast. I went down to the stables and saw her.

[GUENEVERE *sits down again.*]

GUENEVERE.   Another day will do.

ARTHUR.   It is a pity.   The larches are at their best. . . .
And I forgot—I have a bit of news for you.   Gawaine and I
nearly laughed ourselves ill when we heard it.   Some of the
stable-boys had got hold of the story.   I couldn't believe it, but
they swore it was true.

GUENEVERE.   What story?

ARTHUR.   Do you remember Lancelot's quest?   He was
going to Corbin to kill a serpent for King Pelleas. . . .

GUENEVERE.   Yes.

ARTHUR.   Do you remember the little black-eyed villain who
came to fetch him?   D'you know, I smelt mischief whenever
she came into the hall.   A good-looking girl, though.   But
she has nothing to do with the story . . . (He laughs) . . .
Dear old stick-in-the-mud Lancelot—the bachelor knight!
And I should never have thought it of Pelleas.

GUENEVERE.   What is your story?   Tell it me.

ARTHUR.   I am telling you.   Of course, it may be nothing
but gossip.   Tell these girls to go away.

GUENEVERE.   The King wishes you to leave us.

[The GIRLS retire.]

ARTHUR.   The odd thing is, the serpent doesn't come into
the story at all.   If it were only gossip one would expect them
to make something of the serpent, wouldn't one?

GUENEVERE.   What has happened?

ARTHUR.   I'm telling you.   He's married.

GUENEVERE.   Married?

ARTHUR.   Yes.   To the King's only daughter.   Big,
leggy girl with eyes like a heifer.   I shouldn't have said she was
his sort at all, but one never knows.   And he's on his way back
here.   I call that the bravest thing he's ever done.   Dinadan
and Kay will make his life a hell.   It's a good thing he never
loses his temper.   But seriously, I am sorry about that jennet.
. . . You're not taking it too much to heart, are you?   You
could easily turn out with your mare.

GUENEVERE.   No.

ARTHUR.   You're looking pale.   It's a thousand pities
about the jennet.   A good run in the fresh air would do you a
world of good.   Are you ill?

GUENEVERE. No, I am quite well.

ARTHUR. Well, I thought I should look in and cheer you up. And I knew you'd be amused to hear about Lancelot. I hope he comes tonight. We shall have a feast and give him a rousing welcome—though he may not like it much. . . . Lancelot, of all people! And I didn't know he knew the girl.

[*The* KING *goes out, chuckling to himself.*]

[GUENEVERE *gets herself under control and strikes a little gong in the shape of a shield bearing Lancelot's arms.* FIRST GIRL *comes in.*]

GUENEVERE. Bring me Sir Gawaine.

FIRST GIRL. I think he is at the stables, Madam.

GUENEVERE. Then bring Sir Agravaine. Or any of the brothers. . . . Quickly!

FIRST GIRL. Very good, Madam.

[*Exit* GIRL.]

GUENEVERE. No. No. No. I don't believe it. I can't believe it. Never, never, never! I'd kill myself. But it isn't true! It isn't true! They are liars. It is a plot.

[*Enter* AGRAVAINE.]

GUENEVERE. Ah, Sir Agravaine, I am glad to see you! Will you sit down?

AGRAVAINE. I thank you, Madam.

GUENEVERE. I am distressed about my jennet. I hear she has strained a fetlock.

AGRAVAINE. Alas, yes, Madam!

GUENEVERE. Have you been to the stables today?

AGRAVAINE. Yes, Madam.

GUENEVERE. Have they had news of Sir Lancelot? We should have heard before this.

AGRAVAINE. There was some talk.

GUENEVERE. His adventure sped well?

AGRAVAINE. Very well indeed, they say.

GUENEVERE. What do you mean?

AGRAVAINE. They say he has won a wife.

GUENEVERE. Do you believe this story?

AGRAVAINE. I cannot tell. We had talk among ourselves about him when he went on the quest.

GUENEVERE. What talk?

AGRAVAINE.   We thought he was very urgent to go.   It would have been easy for him to rest for the night and make a quicker journey.

GUENEVERE.   You think he knew?

AGRAVAINE.   It is not for me to see into the mind of Sir Lancelot—in this as in other matters.

GUENEVERE.   Other matters?

AGRAVAINE.   Forgive me, Lady.   I meant nothing.

GUENEVERE.   Sir Agravaine of Orkney, if you mean nothing you should say nothing.   And do not dare to come to me with idle stories you have learnt by eavesdropping on ostlers and grooms.   I cannot punish you for this, but when Sir Lancelot returns he will not look kindly on those who play idle tricks with his good name.

AGRAVAINE.   Madam, I meant no harm.   And as for Sir Lancelot, he has returned already.   As I came to you he dismounted at the sally port.

GUENEVERE.   Are you sure?

AGRAVAINE.   Yes, Madam.

GUENEVERE.   That is very strange.

AGRAVAINE.   It is his habit to ride in by the main gateway. You would have seen him, Madam, from this window.

GUENEVERE.   No doubt.   This is a pleasant room.   It takes the evening sun.   My own room is gloomy in the daytime.

AGRAVAINE.   Madam, you will not tell Sir Lancelot what I said?   You asked me to tell you what I have heard.   I told you without malice.

GUENEVERE.   I know you did, Agravaine.   I shall not tell Sir Lancelot.   Indeed, I may not see him.   I do not think I shall come to the feast tonight, and no doubt he will wish to return to his wife.

[GUENEVERE *gives her hand to* AGRAVAINE *to kiss and leaves the room.   As she goes, enter* GAWAINE.]

GAWAINE.   Was that the Queen who left just now?

AGRAVAINE.   Yes.

GAWAINE.   She sent for me.

AGRAVAINE.   Fortunately I got here first.   I think I bear bad news with a better grace.   I enjoyed myself.   Her Majesty is a little indisposed.

GAWAINE.   How did she take it?

AGRAVAINE.   Full in the face.   She wanted to kill me.   You, she would have killed.

GAWAINE.   The Virgin Knight has arrived.

AGRAVAINE.   I could find it in my heart to be sorry for him.

[*Enter* LANCELOT.   *He is pale and distraught.*]

Welcome home, Sir Lancelot.

LANCELOT.   They told me the Queen was here.

AGRAVAINE.   She was a moment ago.

LANCELOT.   Does she know?

AGRAVAINE.   Yes.   The King told her.

LANCELOT.   Does she know that I am here?

AGRAVAINE.   That, too, she knows.   May Gawaine and I be permitted to offer our felicitations on your marriage?

LANCELOT.   It is kind of you.   Will you tell the Queen that I await her pleasure?

AGRAVAINE.   Willingly. . . .

[*He goes out.*]

GAWAINE.   You are a strange fellow.   You have done many astonishing things, but this is the most astonishing of all. We thought you God's own bachelor.

LANCELOT.   Did you?

GAWAINE.   Had you this in your mind for months?   Or did it take you suddenly?

LANCELOT.   Gawaine, forgive me.   I cannot talk to you. You are very kind, but I am in some little distress.   Will you be so good as to leave me for a little?

GAWAINE.   You wish to speak to the Queen?

LANCELOT.   Yes.   No.   Go away, like a good fellow. Leave me alone.   My head is in a turmoil.

GAWAINE.   It is a state more common before a wedding than after it.   I will leave you.

[*Exit* GAWAINE.   *After a pause, enter the* QUEEN.   LANCELOT
    falls on his knees.]

GUENEVERE.   You have something to tell me?

LANCELOT.   Yes, my Lady.

GUENEVERE.   Stand up, then.   We are old friends.   This is not the attitude for old friends.

LANCELOT.   My Lady, I have worshipped you for many a
year and have never asked of you anything than that I should
be your servant and your knight.   I have come to you now in
mortal distress to ask you to tell me what to do.

GUENEVERE.   If what I have heard is true you have already
decided what to do and done it.   Is it true ?

LANCELOT.   Yes, Madam.   But. . . .

GUENEVERE.   What is there for me to say, but that I hope
you will be very happy ?

LANCELOT.   Madam, I cannot tell you how I came to be in
this plight, because to do so would be to speak ill of King
Pelleas and his daughter.   But you must believe me I did not
seek this thing; and it has thrown me into a state of confusion
and bitterness I did not believe possible.

GUENEVERE.   You come to me to be relieved of this bitterness ?

LANCELOT.   Yes, Madam, indeed and indeed.   I come to
you as I would come to the shrine of Our Lady to beg you to
bring healing to my soul.

GUENEVERE.   And how do you propose that I should do
that ?

LANCELOT.   How should I know ?   I only know that you
can.   In my pain I have learned that.

GUENEVERE.   Who taught you ?   This woman ?

LANCELOT.   Yes, Madam.

GUENEVERE.   Do you love her ?

LANCELOT.   No, Madam.

GUENEVERE.   How am I to believe that ?

LANCELOT.   Oh, Madam, you must believe it.   Almost all
I am, almost all I have lived for, is broken and scattered in dust.
But not all.   You know what I have in my heart.

GUENEVERE.   Sir Lancelot, it was the common word that
you lived only for your honour and your Queen.   In the minds
of mean men I suffered for that.   But I did not care, for I was
content to rest partners with your honour.   Now where is your
honour and where am I ?   You dare to come cringing to me
like a beaten dog, hot from the embraces of this wretch ?   You
dare ! . . . How long have you been laughing at me ?   You
rode to a fine adventure ten days gone by, when I was the fond
fool who begged you to stay.   Did you tell your doxy the Queen

hung on you and would not let you go ?   Did you tell her that ?
Did you ?

LANCELOT.   No, Madam.

GUENEVERE.   How cunningly you acted your lies!   You
used to look at me as if you thought me young and lovely, hiding
your hatred and contempt.   Is she young ?   Is she lovely ?
Can you not answer me, you lying, treacherous dog ?   You
can be frank and honest with an old woman—with an old,
raddled, hideous woman.   Can't you speak ? . . .

[*She strikes him on the face.*]

LANCELOT.   For that and for all your other mercies I thank
you, Madam.   It is now all broken and gone.   All broken and
gone.

[*He gives an agonized cry and leaps through the window. The*
QUEEN *collapses in a snivelling heap.* AGRAVAINE *and* GAWAINE
rush in. GAWAINE *goes to the* QUEEN, AGRAVAINE *to the window.*]

GAWAINE.   Madam, what has he done ?   Shall we cut his
throat ?

AGRAVAINE.   He has torn off his coat.   He is running
through the gate like a mad thing.   He is gone.   . . Sir
Lancelot is mad. . . .

CURTAIN.

END OF ACT I.

ACT II

SCENE I

A Clearing in a Wood, in which is a very miserable charcoal-burner's hovel.

TIB, *the charcoal-burner's wife, a fat ragged woman, comes out of the hut.*

TIB. Dickon! Hi, Dickon!

DICKON (*without*). Coming, mother!

TIB. Hurry, then. The pot's boiling.

[DICKON *the charcoal-burner comes in. He is black with the dust of his trade and carries a heavy sack of charcoal.*]

DICKON. Where is everybody?

TIB. That's what I want to know. If they aren't quick the daft fellow will eat all the dinner.

DICKON. There is no word of the girl?

TIB. Keep your dear heart at rest. She should be here before nightfall. But you must wash your face and spruce yourself up to receive your grand daughter from the Court.

DICKON. What possesses her that she wants to come here?

TIB. She loves her parents. She was always a good girl.

DICKON. I hope she may be still. The Court is a gallus place for a young girl.

[*His wife brings him a rough bark bucket from behind the doorway, and he begins to wash himself.*]

TIB. Get that black off you. She will think she is the child of a pig of Mahomet, and her such a lady as no doubt she is now. Where are the boys?

DICKON. They took the cart and the donkey to Whitechurch with a load. They'll be back soon.

TIB. And where is the daft fellow?

DICKON. I sent him to catch a couple of rabbits for Joan's supper. By St Peter's trousers! it is all he is fit for. He is as much use about the kiln as a carbuncle on the back of the neck.

TIB. I don't know why you keep him. He's bone lazy.

DICKON. It's not that he's lazy. He's a willing poor soul. But he's no head and no hands. It's my belief he's a gentleman.

TIB. You said that before. You're afraid of him.

DICKON. Oh, he's as gentle as a lamb if you don't cross him.

TIB. Oh, he's a dangerous brute.

DICKON. Cock's body, no—not if you don't cross him.

TIB. I'll cross him to rights! Eating us out of house and home and too stupid to do a hand's turn.

DICKON. He killed a wild pig yesterday with a sharp ash stick and his own hands.

TIB. Yes, and he ate most of it too. And what will the forester say when he hears we've been killing wild pigs? The daft fellow will get us all hanged.

DICKON. I wouldn't advise the forester to lay a hand on him.

[LANCELOT *comes in. He is in rags and carries two rabbits. His eye has a crazy look, but he is very quiet. He gives the rabbits to* TIB.]

LANCELOT. Here they are. I am sorry for them.

TIB. Sorry for them?

LANCELOT. They were weak and afraid. They were alive, and now they are dead.

TIB. Take them in and skin them, and don't stand there chattering. And don't let me catch you at the pot! My daughter is coming from a long journey. We must keep some of the pot for her, and boil the rabbits later.

LANCELOT. Where does she come from?

TIB. From the Court at Camelot. You must be on your best behaviour. She is a lady.

LANCELOT. Are we to have dinner now?

TIB. I told you to keep your hands off the pot. You'll have dinner all in good time when the boys come back. Do as I tell you.

[LANCELOT *goes into the hut. Enter the* FOREST RANGER *with two* MEN-AT-ARMS. DICKON *and his wife cringe before them.*]

RANGER. Are you the charcoal-burner?

DICKON. Yes, your worship.

RANGER. How long have you lived in this forest?

DICKON. I do not know, your worship. Perhaps twenty-five years.

RANGER. You know that the game in this forest belongs to the King?

DICKON.   Yes, your worship.

RANGER.   You or your sons, or the three of you, killed a wild boar yesterday.

DICKON.   No, your worship.   Surely not.

RANGER.   I hope not.   I have just hanged your two sons, and I doubt that I shall have to hang you.

DICKON.   Hanged them, your worship?

RANGER.   My men and I met them on the edge of the wood with a cart.   I taxed them with the boar, and they were foolish enough to reply with dumb insolence.   The cart came in handy. . . . (*To his men*).   Search the hut.

TIB.   My sons, my sons!

RANGER.   You should have brought them up better, and if you snivel you will go the same way.   I like happy faces in my forest.

DICKON.   My lord, you will find nothing in the hut.   No master, don't let them go into the hut.

TIB.   My lord, I swear you'll find nothing there.

RANGER.   Hit the old trot on the head.   Set about it, boys. . . . (*To* DICKON).   And I hope for your sake you have eaten it all, feet, bristles and tushes, or I promise you you will hang too.

[LANCELOT *appears at the door.*]

RANGER.   Who is this?   Another of your litter?

DICKON.   No, master.   He is a poor daft fellow.   He is not ours.   We found him starving in the forest and gave him food and shelter.

RANGER.   A very Christian act.   Tell him to get out of the way.

DICKON.   Stand aside, lad.   My lord here is the Forest Ranger, and these are his men.   They have done hard justice on my poor sons, and we must not give them any more trouble.

LANCELOT.   What have they done to your sons?

RANGER.   Oh, it can speak, can it?

[*He strides forward to* LANCELOT, *and gives him a cut with his whip.* LANCELOT *promptly and silently breaks his neck, steps over his body and approaches the* MEN-AT-ARMS. *They back in front of him and then turn and run.* TIB *and* DICKON *gaze at him open-mouthed.*]

LANCELOT. Take this dog away and throw him in the sand-pit.

[DICKON *drags the body of the* RANGER *off.*]

I do not know how to skin rabbits.   Will you show me?

TIB.   Who *are* you?

LANCELOT.   I do not know.   Will you show me how to skin rabbits?   It is horrible to touch them.   I killed them, and they had done no harm.

TIB.   But you have killed a man!

LANCELOT.   You have been good to me and he had killed your sons.   Besides, he struck me with his whip.   It was right that I should kill him.   The rabbits had done no harm.

TIB.   They ate our kail.

[LANCELOT *sits down on a log.   He is anxious to understand her point of view.*]

LANCELOT.   When you say our kail, what do you mean?

TIB.   We planted the kail.   If we let rabbits live they would eat us out of house and home.   Besides, we cannot live on kail.   We must eat rabbits too.

LANCELOT.   It is very difficult.   The Ranger killed your sons because he thought they killed his wild pig.   If he did not kill them they would eat the King out of house and home, or, at least, deprive him of his healthful exercise.

TIB.   But my sons were men, and not rabbits.

LANCELOT.   If they were men, why are you not howling and weeping and running to where they hang?   Is that not what women do when their men-children are killed?

TIB.   The Ranger does not think we are better than beasts, and perhaps we have come to believe him.   Five of my sons have been killed in the forest.   I have howled and cried for a little, and then buried them.   It is the way of the world.

LANCELOT.   I think you deserve to be a beast.   But you do not look like a beast, and you have been kind to me.   You think that the kail is yours and that you have a right to kill the sons of the doe.   The Ranger thought the boar was his and that he had the right to kill your sons.   As for me, I thought nothing of breaking the Ranger's neck because it did not seem to me good that he should remain above the grass.   I do not understand that.   What is this right of which we are speaking?

If the world is built like a tower with the greatest at the top having rights over the lesser, and the lesser with rights over those beneath them, in time we shall come to the least, who have no rights at all; and if the tower is built on a foundation that has no rights, the tower will fall.

TIB.   I know nothing about your towers and your rights. I only know that my sons are dead and it cannot be helped, and that my daughter is coming home and we must make ready for her.   Who are you, that you know nothing of poor folk ?   We make charcoal to heat the furnace to smelt the iron to go to the smith to make swords and armour for the knights.   We must be content with that.

LANCELOT.   Do you believe in God ?

TIB.   The priest tells me I must, but the priest is in the same case.   It is for him to christen and marry and shrive the knights and to tend them when they are hurt.

LANCELOT.   The poor carry the knights in their arms.

TIB.   What is all this talk ?   My sons are dead.   You've killed the Ranger.   What is to become of us ?   They will send soldiers and burn the hut and put us all to the torture.

LANCELOT.   You can go somewhere else.   It should be easy to find a better place than this.

TIB.   But this is my home, and my daughter is coming, and God knows whether my daughter or the soldiers will be here first.

LANCELOT.   If the soldiers come you may leave them to me, but I cannot see why you should not go somewhere else.

TIB.   That is because you are a madman.   You never spoke to us before, and we wondered at that and thought it strange, but now you have spoken I would rather have you silent.   You talk madness.

[DICKON *returns, leading in* JOAN, *who appeared in Act One, Scene Three.   She is dressed in a decent travelling dress and is snivelling slightly.   She goes to her mother and kisses her.*]

DICKON.   There's your mother.   It's not a happy home-coming, but she is glad to see you.   The boys would have been too.   That's the mad fellow who killed the Ranger.

[JOAN *looks up at* LANCELOT *and starts.*

JOAN.   Who is he ?

[48]

DICKON. I told you—the mad fellow who killed the Ranger.

JOAN. I know him.

LANCELOT. You do not know me, young girl. I do not know myself.

JOAN. I know you. I've seen you before.

TIB. Where have you seen him?

JOAN. Riding in the lists at Camelot.

LANCELOT. Where is Camelot?

JOAN. Everybody knows Camelot.

LANCELOT. Is there a Queen in Camelot? And a round table? And a green lawn where men fight on horseback?

JOAN. Of course there is.

LANCELOT. I cannot stay here.

DICKON. Why not?

LANCELOT. I cannot remember. Your girl has said something that made me afraid. I do not know from what place she has come, but the name of the place makes me afraid. I cannot stay here and be afraid.

TIB. But what are we to do? You can't leave us to be burned and broken on the wheel.

LANCELOT. Go with her to that place. Go to that Queen. I do not know how I know, but I know there is death for me there and safety for you. Say to the Queen that the Mad Knight sent you. The clouds are thickening on my mind.

[*He stares at them for a moment, turns abruptly and goes out into the forest.*]

TIB. We must do as he says.

DICKON. But he is mad.

JOAN. He is not so mad but that he can give good advice. We must go back. Quickly.

TIB. Wait. I'll fetch the rabbits. . . .

CURTAIN.

SCENE II

A rocky, precipitous place. A slate-blue thunder-cloud darkens the scene. Thunder rumbles.

LANCELOT, *more ragged and dishevelled than before, stumbles along the path and halts almost exhausted.*

LANCELOT. This fellow who is with me is tired. This tired, ragged fellow. His feet are torn, his hands are torn, and the wounds in his feet and hands hurt me. Who are you, tired, ragged fellow? And who is this you hurt? He can see. He can hear. He can feel the grating of the rocks on his knees. But he cannot remember. He must go on and up with the tired, ragged fellow and see and hear and feel and not remember and not understand.

MERLIN (*calling from within a rock*). Lancelot! Sir Lancelot!

LANCELOT. Be quiet, you voices! I want to talk to the tired, ragged fellow. The shouting and whispering voices trouble me and do no help. I came here to escape those terrible, stupid voices, whispering and shouting, with no kindness in them and no meaning.

MERLIN. Lancelot!

[*A growing light illumines the dim figure of* MERLIN, *motionless in the heart of a rock.*]

LANCELOT. Who is Lancelot?

MERLIN. Do you know me, Lancelot?

LANCELOT. I do not know myself. How should I know you?

MERLIN. I am Merlin Ambrosius.

LANCELOT. I can see you dimly. Where are you?

MERLIN. I am crushed like a toad in the heart of this rock for ever—till my bones turn to stone. In a thousand years I shall be an object of great interest.

LANCELOT. How did you come there?

MERLIN. Through my folly and the enchantments of a woman.

LANCELOT. What woman?

MERLIN. Nimue of the Lake.

LANCELOT. No, I do not know her name. That is not the woman.

MERLIN. I solemnly assure you that it is. I trusted her and she bound me here. It is a mistake to suppose that one is ever too old to be a fool.

LANCELOT. That was not the name of the woman who made us mad—who made me mad and the ragged fellow who talks to me. I do not know her name.

[50]   50

MERLIN. No woman made you mad. You made yourself mad. You were sure of yourself, Lancelot.

LANCELOT. When one has reached certainty, then is the danger. When the world we have seen and made and set our feet upon turns upside down, then we go mad. Why do you call me Lancelot? Is that my name?

MERLIN. Yes.

LANCELOT. What is that certainty of which I was sure? I have lost it. Where is it? Give it back to me.

MERLIN. A state of certainty, my dear sir, is not an ideal state. I am in a state of certainty. The Round Table will dissolve. The armour of the Knights will become a handful of red powder and be blown away with the dust that made palaces for the King and kings and kings after him; and I shall still be here, with my hands by my side and my dead eyes staring. Nothing can be more certain.

LANCELOT. Is that all you have to tell me?

MERLIN. What do you want to know? It is my unhappy position that the only thing I can use is wisdom.

LANCELOT. I want to hear why the ragged fellow and I go on stumbling and talking, and why there seems to be no sense in our going and in our talk. There is nothing behind us but shadows, and I cannot discern the shape of the shadows.

MERLIN. You are a knight in the Court of King Arthur. You were the best knight in all the Court. You thought it a fine thing to be that and a fine Court to be in. You dressed yourself in things called honour, strength, chivalry, loyalty and I don't know what, until you believed yourself something different from what God made you. You were drunk with this belief. You thought yourself a flaming archangel surrounded by a glittering choir of angels. Life was very simple and beautiful. The laws of your little world sustained you in your pride, and the natural laws that gave you a clear eye and strong arms gave proof to you that your laws were right. You spoke set speeches and did set actions and gloried in your foolery, forgetting that God made you and that you were a man. You floated above the earth as people do in dreams. Then I came floating to you in my dream, and the two dreams burst like painted balloons.

LANCELOT. Why did they do that?

MERLIN.   Your dream was a schoolboy's day-dream—mine was an old man's vision.   The two could not live in the same air.

LANCELOT.   The shadows behind me take the shape of strong towers and pleasant palaces, green forests and lawns, tall men and gentle ladies.   I hear in the distance the sound of trumpets and gallant war-cries, and I hear the voices of comrades, gracious, knightly and virtuous.   In the skies above them walk ladies as bright as the saints of God.   Is that the Court of which you speak?   The Court of a golden-hearted King and a Queen peerless among all women.

MERLIN.   That is the Court of King Arthur in Logris.   It is strange that I should recognise it; because I know it now for a parcel of bullies and strumpets ruled over by a dolt.

LANCELOT.   One thing I remember.   I stood foot to foot with a big soldier, and he struck five heavy blows before I could answer with a heavier.   As these blows fell on my helmet, so your words fall on my head, and I have no word to answer you and lay you grovelling at my feet.   Have you spoken the truth?

MERLIN.   The truth has as many faces as a nightmare. You must find your own truth for yourself.   The Court you built in your mind has fallen to pieces.   Before many days the bullies and strumpets will also break.   Here you see the old bawd the first of them lost and tied in a rock.   The time of the rest of them will come soon.   Why should you think of them? You are a good man and a strong man.   Go back into the world and rejoice in your strength.   Why should you bind your eyes with lies?

[*The light on* MERLIN *fades and* LANCELOT *is left alone.*]

LANCELOT.   I am Lancelot.   I will go back to the valley.

[*Exit* LANCELOT.   *The darkness deepens and the wind is heard howling.*]

CURTAIN.

SCENE III

ELAINE'S *garden on the city wall at Corbin.* ELAINE *and* BRISEN *are gossiping.* KING PELLEAS *is sleeping in the sun.* PELLEAS *and* BRISEN *have perceptibly grown older, but* ELAINE *not much.* *Nevertheless, her ten-year-old son,* GALAHAD, *is playing with a puppy near the ramparts.*]

[52]

ELAINE.   I have changed my mind again.   I'll paint the room blue.

BRISEN.   But blue is such a cold colour, especially in winter.

ELAINE.   Not necessarily, if you choose the right blue.   I'll make it sea-blue, like the boy's eyes, with a frieze of yellow fleurs-de-lis for his hair.   It should look nice. . . . Laddie!

GALAHAD.   Yes ?

ELAINE.   Come back from those battlements.   How many times am I to tell you that ?

GALAHAD.   I can see hundreds of people, all running like little ants in an ant-hill.

ELAINE.   Let them run.   Do as you are told.

GALAHAD.   Why are they running ?

ELAINE.   Never mind why they are running.   They are only common people.

GALAHAD.   But they must have some reason for running.

ELAINE.   Common people don't need a reason for anything they do, darling.   That is why they are common.

GALAHAD.   But I want to see them.

ELAINE.   And I want you to stay away from the battlements.

GALAHAD.   But I can't see them if I stay away from the battlements.

PELLEAS (*waking up*).   What's the matter ?

GALAHAD.   Grandfather, I want to see the people and I am to stay away from the battlements, and I can't see the people if I stay away from the battlements.

ELAINE.   He will fall over.

PELLEAS.   Nonsense.

ELAINE.   It's not nonsense.

GALAHAD.   It is nonsense.

ELAINE.   Darling, that is not like you.   Your father never spoke to me like that.

GALAHAD.   How did he speak to you ?

ELAINE.   Always very nicely.   He was a great knight and a great gentleman.   He was a very perfect, gentle knight.

GALAHAD.   Shall I be a knight, too ?

ELAINE.   Yes, darling.   But only if you keep away from the battlements and don't look at common people.

GALAHAD.   But I want to see why they are running.

BRISEN.   Old Auntie Brisen will hold you by the belt, and then you can look over and see what is happening.

GALAHAD.   Oh, thank you, Auntie Brisen.

ELAINE.   Just for a minute, then.

PELLEAS.   You are spoiling that boy between you.

GALAHAD.   Oh, look! They are running to the West Gateway.   Do you think someone is coming ?

BRISEN.   I don't know, darling.

GALAHAD.   My father came in by the West Gateway.   He was dressed in armour with bits of gold on it, and they made a carpet of lilies and primroses by throwing them on the ground. They were glad to see him, weren't they ?

BRISEN.   Yes, very glad.

GALAHAD.   They had never seen such a splendid knight before.

BRISEN.   Never.

GALAHAD.   When is he coming back ?

BRISEN.   I don't know.   Very soon.

GALAHAD.   When is very soon ?   Is it ten minutes or a million years ?

BRISEN.   I can't tell you that.

GALAHAD.   Will he be dressed in armour ?   Will the people be glad to see him ?

BRISEN.   Yes, very glad.

GALAHAD.   Do you think they are running to meet him now ?

BRISEN.   No.

GALAHAD.   Why not ?

BRISEN.   Because they are not dressed up in clean smocks and they are not carrying flowers and flags.

GALAHAD.   Oh, look, there's a man coming through the gate !   What a big man he is !   Is he a knight ?

BRISEN.   No, dear.   He is only a ragged fellow. . . . He is very dirty and he looks half mad.

GALAHAD.   What are the people doing ?

BRISEN.   They are laughing at him.

GALAHAD.   Why is he not laughing ?

BRISEN.   I don't know.

GALAHAD.   They aren't glad to see *him*.

BRISEN.   I should think not.   There are plenty of dirty, mad people in this town.

GALAHAD.   A little boy has thrown a clod of turf at him. Why does he do that? It has hit the mad fellow on the face, but he goes straight on. They are shouting and throwing stones now. Why doesn't he kill them? They shouldn't throw stones.

[PELLEAS *gets up and comes to the balcony.*]

PELLEAS.   Well, well, well, what's all this? A riot? Dear, dear me! I cannot have riots in the sanctified town of Corbin. . . . Brisen, go and tell my guard to disperse the crowd. I don't know what they can be thinking of.

BRISEN.   Yes, my lord.

[*Exit* BRISEN.]

GALAHAD.   Why do they throw stones at the ragged man?

PELLEAS.   Human nature, I suppose. It is a pity.

GALAHAD.   It is a great pity. I should like to go and help the ragged man and cut off the heads of these people who are throwing stones.

PELLEAS.   Would you, my child? . . . Ah! There goes the guard. And just in time, too! They would have killed the fellow and I should have had to speak to them severely.

[ELAINE *joins them at the battlements. When she sees what is happening she pulls* GALAHAD *away.*]

ELAINE.   Father, I'm surprised at you. You shouldn't let him see sights like that.

PELLEAS.   Why not? He's going to be a soldier. He is going to be Our Lord's soldier.

ELAINE.   He won't be any better soldier if he can't sleep tonight. Really, father, you are terrible!

GALAHAD.   But I want to see the guard beating the people, or the people beating the guard. I want to see what happens to the ragged man.

ELAINE.   If you aren't good the ragged man will get you.

GALAHAD.   Oh, look! That was a *very* big stone, and it hit him on the brow. He has fallen down. The guard is carrying him into the castle.

PELLEAS.   It is very strange. I feel as if I had seen the ragged man before.

ELAINE.   And so do I. It is *very* strange. To me one ragged man is very much the same as another. Have they killed him?

PELLEAS.   No.   He is on his feet again.   He has thrown off
the guards.   How foolish!   They are only trying to help him.

GALAHAD.   Ooooooo! Oh! Oh! Oh! He threw the big
sergeant over his back.   He has taken a halbert from another
guardsman and is hitting them over the head with it.

ELAINE.   Come back from that battlement at once!   Father,
help me!   He is so strong for his age.

PELLEAS.   You must not fight with your mother, my child.
You must not fight with ladies at all.

GALAHAD.   Tell her not to touch me.   Don't you touch me.
I hate people touching me.   I will do as she says.

[*The* THREE *come down from the battlements.* DAME BRISEN *comes
running in.*]

BRISEN.   Oh, my lord, the madman!   He has beaten the
guard.   He is in the house.   He may come here.   Hide yourself.

PELLEAS.   Get behind me.

[*He seizes a stool by the legs and puts himself in an attitude of
defence.* LANCELOT *appears in a doorway. He is covered
with mud and bleeding and carries a halbert. He stares at the
group for a moment and then falls forward on his face.*]

ELAINE.   I said he would come back.   I said he would come
back.

[*She runs to* LANCELOT *and takes his head on her knee.* PELLEAS
and BRISEN *look at each other in astonishment.*]

PELLEAS.   What is this?

BRISEN.   Child, he is filthy!   You will spoil your gown.

ELAINE.   My dear, look up at me.   You are safe now.   No
one shall hurt you. . . . (*Shaking off* BRISEN.)   Go away.

PELLEAS (*approaching her*).   My child, you are beside yourself.   It is only the ragged madman.   He cannot hurt you now.
Look at me.   I am your father.

ELAINE.   I know that quite well.   Go and get a basin of
clean warm water and some linen rags.   He has fainted.

[GALAHAD *has been standing stock-still till this moment, staring at
his mother and* LANCELOT.]

GALAHAD.   Who is that, mother?   Is that my father?

ELAINE.   Yes, sweetheart, of course it is.   Make your
stupid grandfather do as I tell him.

[56]

GALAHAD (*to* PELLEAS). It is your turn to do as you are told.

PELLEAS. The Lord has manifested himself to me in many wondrous ways. But today he has excelled himself. Do you think it is Lancelot?

BRISEN. It may well be. I shall get the basin and the lint.

[*Exeunt* BRISEN *and* PELLEAS.]

ELAINE. Come and look at him. Don't be afraid. He is not dead.

GALAHAD. He is very big and strong.

ELAINE. He is the best knight in all the world. His eyelids are moving. Soon he will see you . . . Lancelot!

[LANCELOT *pushes her aside and raises himself on one arm.*]

LANCELOT. By God's blue hood! More witchcraft! . . . (*As he sees* GALAHAD). If you are a child and I am you, who is this bruised brute lying on the ground?

ELAINE. He does not know what you mean. You are frightening him.

GALAHAD. No, he isn't.

LANCELOT. No one will ever make that beautiful, stupid little face look afraid. He will beat his enemies and honour women and believe lies and die as ignorant as he was born. . . . (*To* ELAINE.) Where am I? Who are you?

ELAINE. Don't you know me, Lancelot?

LANCELOT. The old warlock in the rock called me by that name. The only name I have is Ragged Fellow and sometimes the Daft One. Under those names they beat me and pelt me with stones when I am thinking of other things, and now I am too weak to fight or to resist. What will your people do to me?

ELAINE. They will wash you and bind up your wounds and put you in a soft bed, and you will sleep and forget your sorrow.

GALAHAD. Why did he say he was weak? He threw the big sergeant as they throw sheep at the sheep-shearing.

LANCELOT. Who is that boy?

ELAINE. He is your son.

LANCELOT. I have no son. But I am so tired that I am ready to believe lies if they please me. This lie pleases me.

ELAINE. Rest your head on me and sleep. It will do you good to sleep. You will sleep and wake and sleep again, and

57

your hurts will be healed and you will wake again and be happy.
You have come home.

LIGHTS FADE OUT

SCENE IV

The same, some weeks later on a bright sunny morning. DAME BRISEN
is looking over the battlements. She turns as ELAINE *comes in.*

ELAINE.   I ran up to see him on my way back from church.

BRISEN.   How is he?

ELAINE (*cheerfully*).   He is very well.   Galahad is with
him.   I told him to come down and enjoy the sunshine.
These three weeks have made an enormous difference.   He's
so quiet and sensible and kind.

BRISEN.   Sensible?

ELAINE.   Well, his memory isn't very good yet, and he's
terribly obstinate.   I wish he would go to church.   It would
please father.   Father is terribly distressed that he won't go to
church.   He thinks it's so bad for the boy.

BRISEN.   But the boy goes to church.

ELAINE.   Yes.   He loves it.   He loves it so much that it
troubles me a little.   I don't want him to be a priest or anything
like that.

BRISEN.   Is that the only thing that troubles you?

ELAINE.   Yes.   I am unspeakably happy.   Of course, he
will have it that I am not his wife.   He isn't quite himself
yet.   But I think he likes me.   He follows me with his eyes
when I am fussing about the room.   And he has taken to the
boy.   There is no doubt of that.

BRISEN.   I wish you would let me put a little something in
his drink.

ELAINE.   What sort of something?

BRISEN.   It is a love potion.   Morgan le Fay gave me the
recipe.   It never fails.

ELAINE.   We shall play no more tricks on Sir Lancelot.
Besides, he would find out.   He is not so stupid as all that.
And if there is one thing he hates it is witchcraft.

[*Enter* KING PELLEAS.   *He looks depressed.*]

Good morning, father dear. The service was lovely this morning. I thought they sang the Benedictus better than they have ever sung it before. Laddie loved it. He caught my hand and held it tight.

PELLEAS. The basses were much better together than they have been. How is Lancelot?

ELAINE. He is very well.

PELLEAS. Did you speak to him about that matter?

ELAINE. What matter?

PELLEAS. I wish him to see Father Innocence. The man is spiritually starved. That is what is the matter with him.

ELAINE. I will not allow him to be bothered by Father Innocence or anybody else. You can leave his spiritual welfare to me.

PELLEAS. May I ask what steps you are taking to ensure his spiritual welfare?

ELAINE. I am giving him a big underdone beef-steak and two pints of goat's milk a day.

[*Enter* LANCELOT *and* GALAHAD. *They are obviously on affectionate terms.*]

LANCELOT. Good morning.

PELLEAS. Good morning. How do you feel yourself this morning?

LANCELOT. I am very well. And you?

PELLEAS. I have some slight indigestion that prevented me from sleeping. But I am much refreshed after my devotional exercises. I hope that before long we shall see you at the chapel.

LANCELOT. Do you?

PELLEAS. Galahad, your tutor is waiting for you in the schoolroom.

GALAHAD. Oh, not yet, grandfather! The Daft One is telling me a story.

PELLEAS. The what?

GALAHAD. The Daft One.

PELLEAS. My dear boy, no doubt you mean no harm by it, and you are very young; but I must most emphatically forbid you to use any such expression, especially . . .

LANCELOT. That is my name. Why should he not call me by my name?

ELAINE.   Come, father.   We were to talk to the tutor.

PELLEAS.   About what?

ELAINE.   You remember?   We agreed that he wasn't to teach Laddie Hebrew till next year.

PELLEAS.   Did we?

ELAINE.   Yes, of course we did.   Come along.   You come too, Brisen.

PELLEAS.   You may be right.   But I do not think a boy can begin too early to have a thorough grounding in Hebrew. Father Innocence had read through the Old Testament when he was four.

ELAINE.   Yes, and look at him now.

[ELAINE *hustles* PELLEAS *and* BRISEN *out.*   LANCELOT *and* GALAHAD *are left alone.   They sit on the parapet looking down on the village.*]

GALAHAD.   Your stories are different from the stories my grandfather tells me.

LANCELOT.   What stories does he tell you?

GALAHAD.   One day he saw a white hart walking daintily behind four lions.

LANCELOT.   One night he saw a great serpent winding about the streets of Corbin, but when I came to Corbin to kill it there was no serpent, nor ever had been.

GALAHAD.   But grandfather saw the white hart, and he knew that the white hart was Our Lord and the four lions were the four Evangelists.

LANCELOT.   Perhaps he did.

GALAHAD.   Do you ever see white pigeons with rainbows round their heads?   Or a gold cup floating through the air with nobody carrying it?

LANCELOT.   No.

GALAHAD.   Not when you were a knight?

LANCELOT.   When I was a knight it was enough for me to fear God, to honour the King, to ride straight, to keep my body clean and to be courteous to my enemies.   I thought that was enough.

GALAHAD.   Wasn't it enough?

LANCELOT.   No.

GALAHAD.   What is it you do in the charge when you break from the canter into the gallop?

LANCELOT.   You play the point of your lance in a little spiral till it is sighted on the centre of your adversary's shield. You move your own shield into a slant so that his spear-head may slip up it and over your shoulder, and you tighten the big muscles round your shoulder-blades, leaning a little forward, but not too much.

GALAHAD.   And what does it feel like when you hit him?

LANCELOT.   There is a heavy shock, and then you feel his saddle-girths give if you have struck him properly.

GALAHAD.   Will you show me how to use the lance?

LANCELOT.   Yes, some day.

GALAHAD.   Do you think the muscles round my shoulder-blades are big enough?

LANCELOT.   They will be.   They are the bow-strings that shoot the bolt.

GALAHAD.   Are you sorry for your enemy when he rolls in the dust?

LANCELOT.   No.   We must not insult our enemies by pitying them.   It is part of the game.

GALAHAD.   It must be a fine game. . . . Look there! Coming out of the shadow of the archway.   It's a knight on horseback.   People are cheering.   By God's blue hood, he looks splendid!   Much better than our knights in Corbin. Who can he be, do you think?

LANCELOT (*turning away from the parapet*).   God knows.

GALAHAD.   He sits his horse well.

LANCELOT.   And he fears God, honours the Round Table, and rides straight.   I do not doubt.

GALAHAD.   Well, shouldn't he?

LANCELOT.   If he is made that way and has nothing better to do.

GALAHAD.   He has gone under the second archway.   He is out of sight now.

[GALAHAD *comes down from the parapet and joins* LANCELOT.]

LANCELOT.   Did you ever build houses with toy bricks?

GALAHAD.   Once, when I was very young.

LANCELOT.   Did you build a great castle with a drawbridge and towers and battlements and bastions?

GALAHAD.   Yes.

61   [61]

LANCELOT. One day Dame Brisen was bustling about dusting and setting the room to rights and the swing of her skirt knocked your palace down.

GALAHAD. How did you know that?

LANCELOT. What did you do then?

GALAHAD. I was very angry, I should have kicked Brisen if I had not been taught to honour all women. I cried—only a little, but I cried. I was very small then.

LANCELOT. And what did you do next?

GALAHAD After a day I began building again.

LANCELOT. After a day! I took thirteen years.

GALAHAD. But you would be old after thirteen years. You would care nothing for toy houses.

LANCELOT. Did you build the same house or another one?

GALAHAD. Another one, of course. My mother helped me.

LANCELOT. I shall build another one.

GALAHAD. I don't know what you mean. All that happened long ago.

LANCELOT. That is also true. You are a wise fellow, Galahad.

GALAHAD. Grandfather told me that I must not pay too much attention to what you say.

[ELAINE *enters while he is speaking.*]

ELAINE. Grandfather was quite right, but you must not be impertinent. Run now to your tutor. If he is kept waiting he will be very angry. Quick. Run.

GALAHAD. I am not afraid of him.

[*Exit* GALAHAD, *running.*]

ELAINE. What were you two talking about?

LANCELOT. He is a clever boy.

ELAINE. I know that, dearest. He takes after you, I am afraid. He frightens me sometimes. I am so glad you have come back. He needs a father's hand. You and he will have great times together.

LANCELOT. Yes.

ELAINE. Father has been doing his best to make a pious little prig of him; but that will be all right now.

LANCELOT. Yes.

ELAINE.   Dearest, a visitor has come to the castle.   He said
he must see you.   I said he mustn't.

LANCELOT.   The knight who rode in a moment ago?

ELAINE.   Yes.

LANCELOT.   I shall see him.

ELAINE.   But, dearest, are you well enough?

LANCELOT.   I am back in my five dull wits, if that is what
you mean.

ELAINE.   He has come from Camelot.

LANCELOT.   That is no more to me than if he had come
from Tartary.

ELAINE.   Then why do you say it is nothing to you?

LANCELOT.   You spoke the word as if a demon had come
from hell.

ELAINE.   You won't let him persuade you to go with him
to Camelot?

LANCELOT.   Does he want me to go?

ELAINE.   I don't know.   Father tried to find out why he
had come, but he said his message was for you only.

LANCELOT.   What is his name?

ELAINE.   Sir Agravaine of Orkney.

LANCELOT.   I remember it dimly.   In my mind there is a
great fog over Camelot.   But I remember that. . . . Agravaine
. . . He had a brother.

ELAINE.   He is the son of King Lot of Orkney.   Sir
Gawaine is his brother.

LANCELOT.   And that name I remember too.

ELAINE.   That is good.   Your memory is coming back
quickly, and soon you will be well.   But you will not go back
to Camelot, not for a long, long time?

LANCELOT.   I shall never go back to Camelot.   I must
build a new house.

ELAINE.   Oh, where, darling?   I thought you were quite
comfortable here.   And it is a great joy to father to have us.

LANCELOT.   I shall build it here where we are now.   If
your father gives me leave I shall rule Corbin as men have a
right to be ruled.   I shall learn wisdom from my son and
contentment from you.   I shall not sail again from this port.

ELAINE.   But you were a great man in Camelot, and there
may be other lode-stones drawing you there.

63   [63]

[LANCELOT *embraces her*.]

I would do nothing to prevent you going to Camelot once or twice when you are strong and well. But not yet.

LANCELOT. I have told you that I will never see Camelot again. All my life is here.

ELAINE. That is good. You will soon be well. But you must live with us in Corbin for a long, long time and teach little Galahad to be a knight. . . . And you must eat and sleep and sleep and eat and get quite well and strong and laugh at Camelot and the foolish things that happened there.

LANCELOT. Where is Sir Agravaine?

[AGRAVAINE, *in full armour with his helmet under his arm, enters briskly*.]

AGRAVAINE. Here I am, Sir Lancelot.

ELAINE. I told you to wait.

AGRAVAINE. Lady, if my errand had not been urgent I should scarcely have dared to risk your displeasure. I move at command. It was not I who disobeyed you.

ELAINE. Sir Lancelot can give you five minutes. He is very much better, but he is not well enough for affairs of state.

AGRAVAINE. I am your humble debtor. Five minutes will do.

[*He bows to* ELAINE.]

[ELAINE *curtsies to him and goes out.* LANCELOT *stands motionless, looking at* AGRAVAINE.]

AGRAVAINE. Do you know me, sir?

LANCELOT. Yes. You are Sir Agravaine, the brother of Gawaine and Gareth.

AGRAVAINE. It gives me pleasure to hear you say so. The rumour was that your hurts had sorely confused you in your mind.

LANCELOT. What is your will with me?

AGRAVAINE. Why, none. Except to look in your face again. But there is another who will take no denial.

LANCELOT. Who is that?

AGRAVAINE. The Queen must see you.

LANCELOT. Why has she not forgotten me? I have forgotten her.

AGRAVAINE. Is that true?

LANCELOT.   When I shut my eyes I see her face twisted like that of a fiend.   When I stop my ears I hear her voice screaming and harsh with hate.   I can remember nothing more of her.

AGRAVAINE.   For a year we thought she would die.   And then she rose and went out maying like a woman in a dream. In all these years she has walked and talked and smiled like an image without a soul.   On Sunday she sent for me, and her soul had returned.   Her face was a mask, but there was torture in her eyes.   She said to me . . . "Agravaine, you must find Lancelot and bring him to me."

[LANCELOT *turns his back and looks over the parapet for a moment. He turns again and comes back to* AGRAVAINE, *making a helpless, hopeless gesture.*]

LANCELOT.   I shall get a horse.

AGRAVAINE.   We must ride at night.   The King does not know of this.

LANCELOT.   The King?

AGRAVAINE.   When you went the King believed what he did not want to believe, and the Queen and he have hated each other for thirteen years.

LANCELOT.   He had no reason to hate her.

AGRAVAINE.   In these matters the King does not act on reason. . . . You will ride with me tonight?

LANCELOT.   Yes.

CURTAIN.

SCENE V

The Queen's bedroom at Camelot. GUENEVERE *alone, before a mirror. The room is lit by two candles, and the moon shines through the window.*

GUENEVERE.   There was a cliff in Cornwall when I was young.   It was death to look down from the cliff.   The rocks below kept calling: "Throw yourself down!"   But the cliff was not to be denied.   The people went to the cliff and looked and looked.   So I look in my mirror.   I see and knew that I should see creeping cold and withering and death.

65 D

[*She gets up and places the candles so that they will not shine on her face when she receives* LANCELOT. *She sits on a chair and stares at the door.*]

GUENEVERE (*below her breath*).   And yet he will come.   He will come.   He will come.   He will come.

[*Enter* LANCELOT. *The two look at each other in silence.* LANCELOT *is unarmed. After a few moments he drops on one knee and bows his head.*]

Are you afraid to look at me ?   I am old.

LANCELOT.   That is not why I am afraid to look at you. You will never be old.

GUENEVERE.   Do you know why I sent for you ?

LANCELOT.   No, my Lady.

GUENEVERE.   And yet you came.

LANCELOT.   I thought I had forgotten you, but if you were among the shadows of Hell and called to me I should come.

GUENEVERE.   I have lived in these shadows for thirteen years and called to you continually.   Why did you not come to me then ?

LANCELOT.   I could not find a way.   Hell is very large.

GUENEVERE.   It is hell when we see our lives from beginning to end and they have no meaning.   That is why I have sent for you.   My life is nearing its end, and I dared not go down to the grave without. . . . A moment blazes up, and all the way from the beginning is set alight.   It must not escape.   My light is only the sunset, but it must not escape.   Do you hate me ?

LANCELOT.   Yes, Madam.

GUENEVERE.   Do you love me too ?

LANCELOT (*getting up*).   By God's life, I love you !   I have loved you since the bells of your wedding at Camelot beat the words into my brain.   I shall always love you and do nothing but love you until I die and rot.   I was not in hell when you called me.   I was in heaven, and I broke the golden gates and tore down the jasper walls and came to you.

[*He throws himself at the* QUEEN's *feet and puts his head on her lap.*]

GUENEVERE.   Why not before ?   Why not before ?

LANCELOT.   You were the Queen.

[66]

GUENEVERE.   I was never the Queen.

LANCELOT.   There is nothing but this.

[*A knocking at the door is heard thunderously.* LANCELOT *springs to his feet. The* QUEEN *clutches at her heart.*]

LANCELOT (*very quietly*).   Am I betrayed again?

GUENEVERE.   My God, no!   No, no, no!

AGRAVAINE (*without*).   Open the door!

GUENEVERE.   It is Agravaine.   Open the door.

[LANCELOT *opens the door.* AGRAVAINE *in his armour, with his vizor down, stands in the doorway. Behind him the corridor is full of armed knights, some carrying torches.* AGRAVAINE *strides into the room.*]

GUENEVERE.   Sir Agravaine, have you gone mad?

AGRAVAINE.   No, Madam.   But when my King is away its my duty to guard his honour.

GUENEVERE.   You talk to me of honour?

AGRAVAINE.   Yes, Madam.   If the word is unknown to you, you are about to see a little lesson which may enlighten you as to its meaning.

GUENEVERE.   What do you mean?

AGRAVAINE.   If Sir Lancelot is the courteous knight we take him to be he will come with us and we shall hang him quietly from the great apple tree in the orchard.   If not, Madam, I fear you will see an unhappy sight.

GUENEVERE.   But you brought him to me.

AGRAVAINE.   God's body, Madam!   Do you think I am a pimp?   Do you think the Knights of the Round Table will sit and smile and see their King made a cuckold? . . . (*To* LANCELOT.)   Come, sir, we are at your service.

[*The* QUEEN *throws herself in front of* LANCELOT.]

GUENEVERE.   You traitor!   You murderer!   Will you kill me?

AGRAVAINE.   If necessary, Madam.

LANCELOT.   Madam, forgive me.

[*He puts her aside.*]

Sir Agravaine, give me a horse and a sword and I will fight you to the death, according to the laws of knighthood.

AGRAVAINE.   The laws of knighthood are very well when one is the champion knight of all the world.   But you have

broken them by dishonouring your King and Queen. You
cannot cower behind them now.

LANCELOT (*shouting*). Sir Bors! Sir Kay! Sir Dinadan!
A moi! Lancelot!

AGRAVAINE. They are with the King, forty miles away.
You must shout louder.

LANCELOT. Let us go, the Queen and I. I have sworn
that I would never fight again.

AGRAVAINE. You sing a different tune from that you sang
a moment ago. We shall not ask you to fight. Leave your
strumpet and come with us.

LANCELOT. Say your prayers, dead man!

[*He pulls the cover from the bed and wraps it round his fore-arm
as a shield. He throws a candle to the ground and stamps it
out, seizing the candlestick for a weapon. He attacks* SIR
AGRAVAINE *with great fury, driving him into the doorway to
hamper the knights behind. He beats down his sword with the
candlestick, catches his dagger from his belt and stabs him
three times in the neck. He hurls him against the astonished
knights, throws a table in front of the doorway and stands on
guard.*]

I see that in all these years I have been forgotten at the
joyous Court of Camelot. That false dog should have told
you. I am Sir Lancelot of the Lake. I have struck a blow
or two in my time, and by God's blue hood I think I have more
to strike! Come, puppies, are you afraid? The old wolf is
waiting for you.

[*There is a stir among the knights, and* KING ARTHUR *enters. He
is followed by* GAWAINE, KAY *and* BORS.]

LANCELOT. I shouted loud enough, Sir Agravaine.

[*He laughs and salutes the* KING *with his sword.*]

ARTHUR. Bring lights!

[*Two or three* KNIGHTS *file in with torches and light other torches
in their sconces.* GUENEVERE *is sitting on the bed, staring at
the* KING *like a frightened rabbit. There is a silence.*]

GUENEVERE (*partly to herself and partly to* LANCELOT). Our
long love has come to a mischievous end, for they will kill you
and I shall die by the fire.

[*Another short silence.*]

ARTHUR. Agravaine spoke the truth.

[68]   68

LANCELOT.   No.   Agravaine was a liar, and I forced his lie down his throat with these hands so that he died.   My Lord King Arthur, I have been your poor and true knight and the knight of my Lady the Queen since first you knighted me.   I have fought your battles and taken the blows of your enemies upon my mortal body.   And as for my Lady Queen Guenevere, there is no knight under heaven that dare make it good upon me that ever I was a traitor to my King.   It has pleased her grace to have me in charity and to cherish me kindly more than any other knight, and I have tried to deserve her love.   I have fought her battles in the times past, and this battle, too, I shall fight; for she is faithful and good and true to her Lord.

GAWAINE.   If you butchered the whole Round Table it would not prove it a lie that this is night and you are in her bedchamber.

LANCELOT.   Your brother—God rest him!—could tell you why I am here, if he could speak.   I was trapped by the Queen's enemies.

ARTHUR.   Sir Lancelot, this is a grievous day.   I did not think that you, the best and noblest of my knights, would play me false.

LANCELOT.   My Lord, I have never played you false.

ARTHUR.   By the rules of knighthood it is necessary that you should say so, even at this time and in this place.   But it is not necessary that I should disbelieve the evidence of my eyes. You must die and the Queen must die, and because of that my heart is broken; not for the Queen, for I can get another, but for you, because you are the best knight who ever lived, and there is nobody to fill your place.

LANCELOT.   My Lord, I demand ordeal by battle.

ARTHUR.   You cannot do that.   You have been caught red-handed in a foul treason, and all your rights are forfeit.

SIR BORS.   My Lord, my rights are not forfeit.   I demand the right to fight for the good name of my Lady the Queen and for Sir Lancelot against Sir Gawaine or any knight you name.

ARTHUR.   Sir Gawaine will kill you.

SIR KAY.   Then he must fight me.   I am an old fellow, but I can still bite.

ARTHUR.   No, by God's thunder, no!   I am a Christian prince, and if I take my shield from before the laws of Christian

69   [69]

chivalry, Christendom will fall and the heathen riot over its ruins. The knight and the Queen must die.

LANCELOT. If the knight must die he knows of but one honourable way of dying. He will die fighting with his friends at his shoulders. Who are my friends in this company?

[SIR BORS *and* SIR KAY *and* SIR DINADAN *draw their swords and align themselves at his side.*]

DINADAN. I have got little happiness in your company, Sir Lancelot, you old shrew! But I shall die with you gladly.

[*One by one* OTHER KNIGHTS *join the group in silence, until they are a formidable party*.]

LANCELOT. My Lord, it seems I shall not die tonight. If it is your wish to vindicate Christendom upon my body I shall meet you and your knights on horseback on any field you name. As for the Queen, take care that you do her no hurt; for she has done you no wrong.

[*He salutes the* KING *again, solemnly this time, and the* CURTAIN FALLS.]

SCENE VI

The Hall at Camelot. PELLEAS *at the great window.* ARTHUR *sitting on a step in some dejection. Confused noises from without.*

ARTHUR. Draw the curtain.

PELLEAS. The preparations are well forward. Indeed, I think everything is ready. They have put the last faggot on the pile. The torches are in their stands. The steps she will mount have a nice bit of carpet on them. The knights' chargers are there with their grooms. There is quite a crowd at the barricades, and there are girls selling apples. A nice, quiet, orderly crowd. I think it will all be most impressive.

ARTHUR. For God's sake draw the curtain. I can't stand that noise.

PELLEAS (*drawing the curtain and coming down from the window*). Very well. But you mustn't take it so heavily. I know it means the breaking up of old associations; and it is always a painful thing to do justice, especially if one is doing justice on an old friend. But there is no other way.

ARTHUR. I know that. It was kind of you to come, Pelleas.

[70]   70

PELLEAS. If I can be of any help in your dark hour, I look upon it as a privilege. And the consolations of religion . . .

ARTHUR. Yes, yes. All the same, I'd have hushed it up if I could. But why on earth, if she wanted to let herself go, she would choose practically the middle of the Round Table!

PELLEAS. The heart of man is a dark place . . . and as for the heart of woman!

ARTHUR. I'm told . . . incineration . . . is not a particularly painful death.

PELLEAS. It is difficult to be sure. It is certainly rather painful to the onlookers. When I was young and enthusiastic I burned a few heretics. But as I grew older I found myself less able to support the sight of the poor wretches writhing in the flames. It may have been weak of me, but I asked permission of St. Agnes to have it done privately by professionals. The Blessed Saint granted that permission. I knew she would. It might have been more honest to ask some other Saint. But there it was. There it was.

ARTHUR. I have sent for her. I don't know what I shall say to her. At the trial she was very proud and faraway. As if the thing had no meaning. You'd better stay by me.

PELLEAS. Certainly, if you wish it.

ARTHUR. Somehow, when you're there and I'm talking to you, I always feel a better man.

PELLEAS. I'm glad of that.

ARTHUR. Pelleas, under what necessity must I put my wife to death?

PELLEAS. My dear Arthur, surely you know the answer to that. You are an instrument of the Moral Law.

ARTHUR. The Moral Law, eh?

PELLEAS. Yes, and the Ordinances of Holy Church, which are the same thing.

ARTHUR. Are they the same thing? Pelleas, I'm a plain man of my hands. I hope I'm as good a Christian as my neighbours; but if the fate of Guenevere depended on a book of rules laid down by a parcel of priests, she could die in her bed, so far as I was concerned. And yet I must kill her. Why must I kill her?

PELLEAS. Because you are her King and her Judge, and she has been condemned after a fair trial by her peers.

ARTHUR. She has no peers. She is . . . Never mind what she is. She *was* my love and my friend. It seems she did evil with Lancelot, who was also my friend. But of her Judges, of whom I was the chief, there is not one who has not done that evil so often that he has forgotten the half of it. What impelled those Judges to kill her? They didn't hate the evil she did. I don't hate that evil. Even in the autumn of my life, I still have a taste for it.

PELLEAS. Well . . . apart from the very natural passion of jealousy, which was given us to preserve the sanctity of the marriage tie . . .

ARTHUR. God's body, if I thought I had been actuated by that filthy vice, I should mount the pile of faggots myself. . . . No . . . I think it was that my honour was touched.

PELLEAS. Ah, yes. Honour. A good word. It does not occur in the New Testament, and in the Old Testament it has strange meanings, but it is a word of great power.

ARTHUR. It is not only a word. It is a spirit that tells me why the Queen must die.

[*Enter* GAWAINE.]

ARTHUR. Well, Gawaine? What is it?

GAWAINE. My Lord, you wished to see the Queen.

ARTHUR. Yes, yes. Is she here?

GAWAINE. Yes. Come in, Madam.

[*Enter* GUENEVERE.]

GAWAINE. Sir King, I ask you to remember that the affair was fixed for noon. We are already half an hour late. I hope that your farewells will be short.

ARTHUR. Sir Gawaine of Orkney, you forget yourself. Remember that I am your King.

GAWAINE. And remember you that too, Sir.

[GAWAINE *bows shortly and goes.*]

ARTHUR (*to* PELLEAS). A rude fellow. A rough fellow. But of sterling stuff.

PELLEAS. So I hope.

ARTHUR. He is the last of my great knights.

GUENEVERE. Great!

ARTHUR. What did you say, Madam?

PELLEAS. Madam, King Arthur and I hoped to find you in a mood more consonant to your latest hour.

[72]   72

ARTHUR. Well, Madam?

GUENEVERE. Well, Sir?

ARTHUR. The Court has decided that you are to die.

GUENEVERE. Yes.

ARTHUR. It is plain to you why you are to die?

GUENEVERE. Is it plain to you?

ARTHUR. Why do you ask?

GUENEVERE. I have not known you, in the past, to take much delight in the society of good King Pelleas. I think that you have called him as a doctor to your aching conscience.

ARTHUR. Before Heaven, Madam . . .

PELLEAS. Pardon me. . . . Madam, it ill befits you to speak of the King's conscience. Your concern is your own conscience.

GUENEVERE. Do you mean that I should be sorry for what I have done?

PELLEAS. I hope you are. Without the consciousness of sin there can be no repentance, and without repentance there can be no salvation.

GUENEVERE (*very quietly*). Sin? What is sin? I know that my soul had a great need, and that it is wicked to starve the soul . . . to allow the immortal part of us to diminish and die. If you mean to destroy my body for some sin that I have done, be sure that you know which sin.

ARTHUR. God damn it, woman, you might at least repent.

GUENEVERE. Will it make you happier in the wickedness you are about to do if I say I have repented? I have always striven for your happiness, my most dear Lord.

ARTHUR. There is no question of happiness. I shall never be happy again.

PELLEAS. Madam, Madam, do you think it is a happy occasion for any of us when we commit our friend to the flames? You should have had—you should have now—a little more consideration.

GUENEVERE. If it will make you a little happier, I shall tell you this: It is that I am deeply grateful to you and to my husband for what you are about to do. You will take my life when my heart is light and my spirit is glowing with benediction. You will kill me in the days when it has come to my knowledge that the foremost knight of all the world is my friend and my lover. Your gift is eternal life for that love which cannot now

73 D 2   [73]

ever grow old. I cannot tell by what reasons you justify this murder to yourselves. They are nothing to me. But when you kill me you will make me a glorious gift.

ARTHUR. Your love is dead now. Your lover has deserted you.

GUENEVERE. No. He is round me like a garment, like a royal robe.

PELLEAS. Woman, if you will not listen to us, let God speak to you.

GUENEVERE. He has spoken to me. He tells me to face death gladly because of what He has done for me.

PELLEAS. God did not tell you to commit adultery.

GUENEVERE. God is not such a fool. He does not send His messages in foolish words that have no meaning.

PELLEAS. No meaning! My dear Madam, you swore solemnly before God to be true to your husband. Have you forgotten that? You have broken your oath to your husband and to your God.

GUENEVERE. If I have given God a promise, he has released me from it. He gave my lord Arthur a place in my soul and then took him away. My lord Arthur is dead.

ARTHUR. Dead? I'm not dead.

GUENEVERE. I know that you are dead by the only means I have of knowing—that I know you no more. If I am alive, I cannot find you in my life. How can I think but you are dead?

ARTHUR. You'll find out soon whether I am dead or not, whore.

PELLEAS. My Lord, my Lord. I must ask you to withdraw that expression.

ARTHUR. Why?

PELLEAS. It is not suitable to the occasion.

ARTHUR. It is suitable to this damned woman. I'm dead am I, harlot?

GUENEVERE. You are dead and dead and dead and damned. One lives and breathes and fills all the world with the majesty of his being. He is my King and my Lover.

ARTHUR. If you speak his name you're a dead woman now.

PELLEAS. No, no. It must be the other way.

[ARTHUR *has drawn his dagger.* PELLEAS *restrains him with the powerful grip lame men have.*]

GUENEVERE.   His name is Lancelot.

[*Enter* GAWAINE, *bleeding and exhausted.* ARTHUR *is too blind with rage to notice that.*]

GAWAINE.   My Lord Arthur . . .

ARTHUR.   Are the faggots ready for this strumpet?

GAWAINE.   Yes, my Lord, but . . .

ARTHUR.   Take her, then.   Burn her.   Burn her bones and all.   Burn her ashes again till they are a smoke scattered in the wind.   None of her, not a trace, must sully the land of Logris.   Burn her.   Burn her up.

GAWAINE.   My Lord, the field . . .

ARTHUR.   What field?

GAWAINE.   The field is full of Lancelot's knights.   He came on us unaware through every gate in the town.   He broke us at the first charge.   My brothers are dead and flung on the wood-pile.   I am sorely wounded.

ARTHUR.   Draw back the curtain.

PELLEAS (*drawing the curtain*).   Sancta Mater, Communitasque Angelorum!

[*A trumpet sounds.*]

GAWAINE.   That's his trumpet.   Our knights have laid down their arms.

[*Silence.* ARTHUR *goes to the window.*]

LANCELOT'S VOICE.   King Arthur!

ARTHUR.   I am here, traitor.

LANCELOT.   Your city is in my hand.   Send down the Queen to me, and I shall ride out and leave you the field.

ARTHUR.   In a moment I shall throw down to you her dead body.

LANCELOT.   By God's blue hood, if you dare!   Break down the great door, lads.

[GAWAINE *and* PELLEAS *seize* ARTHUR *and wrest his dagger from him.*]

GAWAINE.   No, my Lord.

PELLEAS.   You must do as he says.

GAWAINE.   If you touch her it is death for us all.

[GUENEVERE *walks slowly to the window.*]

CURTAIN.

SCENE VII

*The theatre remains in darkness after the fall of the Curtain in the last
scene. A baritone bell and a tenor bell play a little ecclesiastical
duet and male voices are heard intoning a Latin hymn. As these
sounds die out the corners of the stage are gradually lit.* LANCELOT
and GUENEVERE *in the costumes of a monk and a nun appear before
the curtain at opposite corners. In the Colloque Sentimentale which
follows I should like their manner to be much less that of moaning
actors speaking verse or near-verse than the more matter-of-fact
tone used by cultivated people in describing their surgical operations.*

LANCELOT.   Are you awake?

GUENEVERE.   It may be. I feel neither heat nor cold, and
the sun has gone down.

LANCELOT.   Where are you?

GUENEVERE.   In a cell at the Abbey of Almesbury. Where
are you?

LANCELOT.   In Glastonbury with my four knights.

GUENEVERE.   How did you come there?

LANCELOT.   After our good-bye I rode with my four knights
all day and all that night in a forest, with my heart like to burst
with sorrow. In the morning I saw a hermitage and a chapel
that stood between two cliffs and heard a little bell ring to Mass.
When we had heard Mass, the hermit, who was a bishop, took
us in and gave us food and drink, and here I live and fast and
pray and sleep hard and wait for the ground to cover me.

GUENEVERE.   You and I came to Glastonbury in the hard,
bright daylight, and we dismounted from our horses and looked
each other in the eyes and knew that our lives were finished.
I said again what I said in my room when the King and the
torches came, our long love has come to an end.

LANCELOT.   And I said that might never be.

GUENEVERE.   It was a cold love, and the sun set coldly in
the rain.

LANCELOT.   It was all the love I had.

GUENEVERE.   I told you to go to your own country and to
your wife and to your son, and to rule there wisely and in peace.

LANCELOT.   And I said again, that might never be, for I am
Lancelot and you are the Queen, and we cannot be other than
we are.

[76]   76

GUENEVERE.   I said you were false to your wife and false to your son, Galahad, and false to yourself.

LANCELOT.   I said that there was one thing to which I could never be false.

GUENEVERE.   I told you that it was too late, that hope was gone.   I told you my purpose to give myself as a bride to the Lord Jesu Christ and to rest on His pity, till He should take me from my mortal body.

LANCELOT.   And I said, "My Sovereign Lady, your commands are the law of my life and I will faithfully endure.   I will betake me to penance and pray while my life lasts if I can find any good hermit, either grey or white, that will receive me."

GUENEVERE.   You took me by the hand.

LANCELOT.   I said to you, " And now, Madam, I pray you kiss me once and never more."

GUENEVERE.   I turned away from you and went through the high arched door.   We have never kissed and never shall.

LANCELOT.   I mounted and rode heavily through the morning mist, looking for those who should lead me gently to my grave, for I knew that my story was ended.   When I was a boy I took delight in the comradeship of fierce and noble knights, and felt myself from head to foot strong and terrible and magnanimous.   As I grew older, neither my strength nor my folly failed, and my head was warmed by the beauty and the bounty and the nobleness of my Queen.   I knew no other way of living.   I can find no other now.   A very little thing flawed my dream and cast me in the dust.   But for that dream I thank God who made me of this shape and of this cast of mind.   I cannot again ride or fight or love or build up what has fallen.   But the story of the man I am no more remains with me, and will remain.

GUENEVERE.   In all these years your spirit could not speak to mine in words.   How is it that you can speak to me now ?

LANCELOT.   I do not know.

GUENEVERE.   The fingers of the hands of our bodies clutch very weakly at the hem of our gowns.   Soon the hands will fall open and hold no more.

LANCELOT.   And then ?

[*The lights dim and go out.   The bells sound again.*]

[*The curtains part and show the dark interior of the Hermitage at Glastonbury. Vaguely outlined at the back is a pallet, on which* SIR LANCELOT *lies. Three* KNIGHTS *are sleeping on rough palliasses on the floor. The only light is a dim rushlight at a table. The* HERMIT BISHOP *is reading by that light, and* SIR BORS, *partly armed, is seated beside him on the floor.*]

SIR BORS.   He is sleeping now.   It is many days since he slept so peacefully.   He was the head of all Christian knights. There was no one to match him.   He was the courtliest knight that ever bore shield.   He was the truest friend to his lover that ever bestrode a horse.   He was the kindest man that ever struck with a sword.   He was the finest fellow that ever came among a press of knights.   He was the gentlest man that ever ate in hall among ladies.   He was the sternest knight to his mortal foe that ever put spear in rest.   I cannot believe that he will not ride again.

[*A silence, broken by a peal of laughter from* SIR KAY.]

(*Springing up*).   God's heart!   You will wake him.   Wake up, Sir Kay!   What ails you?

SIR KAY.   By the King of Heaven, why did you wake me? I was never in my life so glad and so well at ease.

SIR BORS.   Why?   Were you dreaming?

SIR KAY.   Sir Lancelot was with me, with more angels than I ever saw men on a single day.   And I saw the angels heave up Sir Lancelot towards Heaven, and the gates of Heaven open against him.

[*The* HERMIT BISHOP *gets up shakily and carries his rushlight over to* SIR LANCELOT'S *bed and stands peering into his face.*]

SIR BORS.   It is the troubling of dreams.   Be quiet.   Lie down and go to sleep.   You will wake him.

[*The* BISHOP *draws a blanket across* LANCELOT'S *face. The gesture attracts the attention of the* KNIGHTS, *and they turn towards him.*]

CURTAIN.

END OF THE PLAY

HOLY ISLE

A PLAY IN THREE ACTS

ACT I

SCENE I

Scene : The Palace of KING LOT *of Orkney at Kirkwall. The Throne Room is not an elaborate place. The furniture consists of a dais with a lounge throne covered with furs. On this* KING LOT, *a large, ginger-headed man in saffron clothes, with his hair long and plaited in the viking fashion and a small fuzzy beard, is stretched more or less at full length, playing ineffectively with a cup and ball. One knows he is a King by his gold circlet perched rakishly on his head. After two or three attempts he catches the ball and a* JARL-IN-WAITING *enters.*

LOT.   What is it ?   Why must you interrupt me ?   What is it ?

JARL.   Lord King, they have been waiting for two hours.

LOT.   Who have ?

JARL.   The Lord Bishop; Grettir Flatface, the gombeen man; and the young sailor they have brought with them. Also a monk.

LOT.   I'd better see them, do you think ?

JARL.   Yes, Sir, I think so.

LOT.   What do they want ?   I forget.

JARL.   The Lord Bishop would not tell me.   He said he had written to you.

LOT.   Because he knows I can't read.   The Queen has the letter.   I forgot to ask her what was in it.   She had better be here when I see them.   Tell her, will you ?

JARL.   It is not necessary to tell her Majesty anything.

LOT.   My dear Sir, if you are trying to be funny at the Queen's expense, I need hardly tell you what a hazardous enterprise that is.

JARL.   God forbid, Sir, that I should try to be funny at all.

LOT.   God forbid that you should.   My consort has a poor sense of humour.   You may find yourself suddenly turned into a wall-eyed goat.   Not a very difficult feat for Margause of Orkney, the eminent enchantress, but highly unpleasant for you.   And what do you mean by standing there chattering and my Lord Bishop cooling his heels in the ante-room ? Admit him at once.

[*The* JARL *bows, admits the* BISHOP (*round and fat*), GRETTIR (*a tough and prosperous man of business*), TORQUIL, *a young sailor with a crazy eye in his head, and a lean, middle-aged Friar called* MESS INNOCENCE. *The* JARL *withdraws.*]

Come in, Bishop, come in. I'm sorry to keep you waiting. I've been very busy. What with one thing and another, I find I have a very full day. And now what can I do for you?

BISHOP. Sir King, I wrote to you last Tuesday.

LOT. And very kind of you indeed, and a beautifully written letter, if I may say so. And now just tell me shortly in your own words exactly what you would like me to do.

BISHOP. Sir, the young man has brought the map.

LOT. Ah, the map. Good. Yes. Let me see it.

[TORQUIL *unrolls a map.*]

Yes, yes. Put it down on the platform. Sit down, sit down. Don't be afraid. Explain it to me in your own words.

[*The* KING *descends from his throne and sits on the dais.* TORQUIL *sits down opposite him at the other side of the map. The* BISHOP *looks over the* KING's *shoulder,* GRETTIR *over* TORQUIL's; *but as he gets more interested he sits on the throne for a better view.*]

LOT. By the Man of Hoy, what a lot of Ocean! Well?

TORQUIL. There is the Island, so please you.

LOT. Ah, yes, I see. The Island. It isn't a very big island.

TORQUIL. It is ten miles long by five miles across. It has a population of five thousand souls.

LOT. What's its name? I haven't got my spectacles.

TORQUIL. It is called Ultima Thule by our cartographers. The savages on the Island call it Ru-rhush (roo-roosh). That means The Island of the Sea. Ru is the word for Island, and Rhush is the word for the Sea.

LOT. Rooroosh. Odd name. Go on.

TORQUIL. We made it in eight days' sailing from Scapa. As his Grace no doubt explained to you, we had ill weather and were blown off our course. That is how we found the Island. It has a big, land-locked bay with deep harbourage for any number of ships. We made the bar by flashes of lightning, but we were no sooner in the bay than it fell as calm as a row of cucumbers. A marvellous landfall. There's a steep mountain

[4]   82

on the Island that traps the prevailing wind. They call it Cash-a-Ru.

LOT. Why?

TORQUIL. That means the Mountain of the Island.

LOT. Marvellous ingenuity they must have, thinking of all these names. Cash-a-Ru. Go on.

[QUEEN MARGAUSE, *a tall and sinisterly beautiful woman, enters, very quietly. As soon as he notices her,* GRETTIR *vacates the Throne with some precipitancy. She takes his place. The others don't see her for a little.*]

TORQUIL. We beached on a little sandy cove surrounded by trees. One remarkable thing is that the Island is pretty well wooded, in spite of its latitude. Conifers and oaks, with quite a deal of birch and mountain ash. Very pretty indeed.

LOT. Hello, my dear! I didn't see you. This young fellow is telling me all about his Island.

MARGAUSE. I know.

LOT. Do you mind if we go on?

MARGAUSE. Go on.

TORQUIL (*with some embarrassment—they are all afraid of the* QUEEN). Well, Ma'am . . . most of it's in the letter. . . . Is there any particular point . . . I mean to say . . .

MARGAUSE. What is your name?

TORQUIL. Torquil, Ma'am.

MARGAUSE. You are a sailor?

TORQUIL. Well, no. I've done a bit of sailing, of course; but I've been interested in a lot of other things. My father is a knight.

MARGAUSE. Of my brother, King Arthur?

TORQUIL. No. King Mark of Cornwall.

MARGAUSE. You are not a knight?

TORQUIL. Not yet. I suppose I shall have to be, some day. But I never could get very enthusiastic about tournaments.

MARGAUSE. You cannot be a coward, or you would not be a sailor.

TORQUIL. I suppose not, Ma'am.

MARGAUSE. You said you were interested in many other things. In what things?

TORQUIL. Oh, I like seeing different places. And how houses are built. And different languages. And how people

make things, and how they are governed, and their laws, and
how they work their fields and animals.   I like towns and
churches.   I like watching the monks illuminating their books
and painting their altar-pictures.   I'm not very fond of the sea,
but I like finding out how ships are built and handled; and
besides, the sea takes me to new places.

MARGAUSE.   You will know a great many new things when
you go back to Cornwall?

TORQUIL.   I hope so, Ma'am.   When I go back to Cornwall.

MARGAUSE.   You may not go back?

TORQUIL.   Perhaps I may, perhaps not.   There isn't
much . . . outlet in Cornwall.

MARGAUSE.   Not for a man of your ability?

TORQUIL.   If you put it that way.

MARGAUSE (*suddenly to* GRETTIR).   Who are you?

GRETTIR.   Grettir of the Flat Face, may it please your
Majesty.

MARGAUSE.   It isn't very flat.

GRETTIR.   It's flatter than my brothers', so please your
Majesty.   That's why I'm called Flatface.

MARGAUSE.   With what do you fill up your life?

GRETTIR.   I'm a business man.

MARGAUSE.   What is that?

GRETTIR.   I buy and sell things.   I finance copper mines
and tin mines, and do a bit in real estate and the like of that.
His Majesty here got his armour and horses and his Danish
Bodyguard through me.   I arrange things like that.

MARGAUSE.   That is very clever of you.   Is your father a
knight?

GRETTIR.   No, Ma'am.   I'm a self-made man.

MARGAUSE.   Ah!   At least you are honest enough to admit
it.   And who is the Reverend gentleman?

BISHOP.   That is Mess Innocence, Ma'am.   A brother of
the Columban, or Missionary Order.

MARGAUSE.   How do you do?

[*The* FRIAR *bows his head.*]

And now I am interrupting your business.   Please go on.

BISHOP.   This young man, Madame, took passage in a ship
from Ireland bound for the country of the Lapps.   They were
blown onto an uncharted Island inhabited, I regret to say, by

[6]   84

a heathen people.   He has shown, to my satisfaction, that it is just within the boundaries of my diocese.

GRETTIR.   He's got his head screwed on properly, this young man.   He found pyrites lying about thick, and he had the sense to bring some of it back.

TORQUIL.   They've got the most interesting sort of semi-civilisation there.   They're very primitive, of course, but they don't correspond to any other sort of people I've ever seen.   It's well worth looking into.

LOT.   Are they armed?   Could they put up any sort of a fight?

TORQUIL.   I didn't see any armed men.   They received us in the friendliest way.   We were the first strangers they'd seen for years.   I'd have liked to stay, but the Captain wouldn't wait longer than it took to undergird his ship and revictual. They've some sort of tradition that they came from the Eastern Mediterranean.   They were very reticent about it.   If I had a month or two there I could find out.

GRETTIR.   It's obviously a place that wants opening up.

BISHOP.   We must take them the light of the Gospel without delay.   Brother Innocence is ready to start.

LOT.   It's to take twenty-five knights, a hundred axemen, a hundred archers and four hundred pikemen.   I can't afford it, with the Strathclyde campaign on my hands.

GRETTIR.   I know where I can lay my hands on a regiment of Saxons dirt cheap.

LOT.   Not cheap enough for me.   How are they off for cattle?

TORQUIL.   It's good pasturage for hill pasturage, and it seemed to be very well stocked.

GRETTIR.   I've got a hunch about it, and I seldom make a mistake.

LOT.   It's all very well for you to have hunches.   You've got no responsibility.

GRETTIR.   Nobody, your Majesty, ever accused me of failing to back my hunches.

LOT.   It has always been a very extraordinary thing to me that people who do nothing all their lives except make wagers come to imagine that they have felt the same toiling and scheming and anxiety as those who have done the real working and fighting.   Now, if you were a practical man . . .

85   [7]

GRETTIR.   I like that!!   By Glory, I like that!

MARGAUSE.   The King and I are very glad you like it.   You will now, if you please, nourish your satisfaction in silence while your betters are discussing matters of high policy.   Bishop, you have been comparatively silent.   Will you be good enough to address us ?

BISHOP.   As a Christian priest I must, of course, agree with the King that violence is most undesirable.   He has spoken, if I may say so, like a Christian Prince.   So long as they commit no flagrant acts of aggression against the lieges, the inhabitants of this Island have a right to live their own life and to preserve their own independence, however small and weak they may be.   It is my duty as a Churchman to lay down this principle very clearly and boldly.

LOT.   Perfectly right.   Besides, we simply can't afford another expedition.   The people won't stand it.

BISHOP.   On the other hand, there are other principles to be taken into account.   As an instance, there is the principle of legitimate trade. . . .

GRETTIR.   Hear, hear.

BISHOP.   An inalienable human right vested in those who have the God-given energy and public spirit to practise that activity.   A world full of idle hands is swept and garnished for the entry of the Devil.   Faith without works, says St James, is dead.   And the Church is fully conscious of the stream of life poured into the veins of its Faith by the beneficent labours of Commerce.

GRETTIR.   My Lord, I thank you.   I thank you from the bottom of my heart.   You have said most eloquently what I have always felt, but have always been unable to express.   We are the instruments of a Higher Providence.

MARGAUSE.   I was under the impression that I told you to be quiet.

GRETTIR.   Your Majesty, I am sorry.   You must have noticed that I am a man of few words.   But there are times when I simply have to open my head and speak in my own blunt, business-like way.   I can't help it.   It's how I'm made.

MARGAUSE.   It's how you made yourself, isn't it ?   Rather a pity.   Go on, Bishop.

BISHOP.   There is a third principle, Madame, and then I

shall have done.   The Church has more than a right, it has a
duty, to bring light to those who sit in darkness.   Whatever
may be your Majesty's decision, I propose to send a mission to
this Island.   Grettir Flatface has been moved by the spirit to
equip for us a small vessel for this purpose.   He shall have, I
doubt not, his reward.   But it is only right that I should point
out this: That the success of the Mission would be assured if it
were accompanied by some proportion of your Majesty's Fleet.

LOT.   No, no, no.   I know what you're after, and you
can't have it.   I have all the islands I want.

BISHOP.   So be it.   If Brother Innocence attains the crown-
ing glory of martyrdom, it is his and the Church's gain.

LOT.   If you think I'm going to send a single galley to get
Brother Whatsisname out of any trouble he gets into, you are
very much mistaken.

BISHOP.   I cannot disguise from you, Sir, my disappointment
at your decision.   But, if the march of civilisation had depended
upon the support of monarchs, civilisation would not have
marched very far.   We must do what we can.   Failing your
patronage, we must trust in the patronage of the Blessed Saints.

LOT.   Oh, you can have my patronage all right.   But you
can't have any troops.

TORQUIL.   May I speak ?

LOT.   Yes, yes.   Certainly.   But don't take too long about it.

TORQUIL.   With the utmost respect, I think you've got hold
of the wrong end of the stick.   I don't think there should be
any question of conquering or exploiting . . .

BISHOP.   Stop, stop, stop, stop, stop!   You mustn't speak
like that.   If you had done the King and myself the favour
of listening to what we said . . . let alone recognising that the
King is a magnanimous and enlightened Prince and I a humble
but, I hope, devoted Minister of Religion . . . where was I ?
. . . Ah, yes!   If you had not, in the fashion of the very young,
allowed your attention to stray, you would have realised that
the question of conquest and exploitation has never arisen and
never could arise.

TORQUIL.   If that's so, I'm sorry, but . . .

BISHOP.   *If* that is so, young man ?   Really, now.   Really.

TORQUIL.   Well, take civilisation.   You did say you wanted
to civilise this Island.

87   [9]

BISHOP. If you mean that we had a purely altruistic impulse to introduce certain blessings and benefits, both spiritual and, perhaps, temporal, to that benighted spot, you have read our minds correctly.

TORQUIL. But the place *is* civilised. It's civilised already. It doesn't need our civilisation.

INNOCENCE. If the Pagan Night of Heathendom is compatible with civilisation, it is news to me.

MARGAUSE. What a beautiful voice you have, Father. And I was wondering whether you could speak at all.

TORQUIL. No, but honestly . . . I do think this expedition ought to go to the Island with an open mind. They may be simple and primitive, but they're kindly and industrious, and they have a system of laws that seems to work very well. I think we ought to go there from what the Greeks used to call the scientific motive: I mean, to get to know about them and all that. I'm glad we're not taking any troops. They'd just get drunk and want to fight and make trouble. What we want to do is to . . . is to . . . add to the sum of human knowledge, if I may invent a phrase. When we know all about them, we might even learn something from their ways of doing things and their way of looking at life. And so on. If you see what I mean.

INNOCENCE. I think we should leave this young man behind.

TORQUIL. Oh, you couldn't do that!

BISHOP. I am inclined to agree. He is a babbler. And I am not sure that he isn't a profane babbler.

TORQUIL. All I said was that we should go to the Island in the . . . in some sort of spirit of humility.

BISHOP. Then you expressed yourself very badly. Of course an expedition under the ægis of the Church will be conceived and carried out with the utmost humility. I have little doubt that, if we permit you to sail, even you might pick up a few hints in that very valuable virtue.

TORQUIL. But there can't be any question of my not sailing. I know the way and I know the people and . . .

BISHOP. We shall ponder on the matter.

GRETTIR. I think we should take him.

BISHOP. As you are paying the piper, no doubt you are entitled to call the tune. But, at the same time . . .

[10]

GRETTIR. I'm going myself.   I'll see that he doesn't talk too much.

LOT. When do you sail?

GRETTIR. As there seems to be no question of an escort, on Tuesday at High Tide, so please your Majesty.

LOT. Are you having any sort of ceremony?

BISHOP. I shall, naturally, be there to bless the ship and its company.

LOT. I shall be there too.

GRETTIR. I call that extremely handsome of your Majesty. It will be a great encouragement to all of us.   It will make the expedition a really official and high-toned affair.   Will her Majesty honour us with her presence?

MARGAUSE. No.

LOT. No? Oh, why not? Don't you approve of the expedition?

MARGAUSE. Whether I approve or not is beside the point. I am only a woman.

LOT. Oh, my dear! You may be only a woman, but you are a very remarkable woman.

MARGAUSE. I don't understand such matters.   Besides, I am going on Tuesday to my castle in Forres.

LOT. You didn't tell me.

MARGAUSE. Didn't I?

LOT. The audience is at an end.

[*He joins* MARGAUSE *on the Throne.*]

BISHOP. Our grateful thanks and our humble duty to your Majesty.

[*The party withdraws backwards, bowing at intervals.*]

LOT. What is all this about? You never told me you were going to Forres.

MARGAUSE. To where?

LOT. To Forres. You said just now that you were going to Forres.

MARGAUSE. Did I? Then perhaps I shall.

LOT. Holy Saints, what are you after this time?

MARGAUSE. I am too tired to invent any convincing lies for you this morning.   Perhaps in the afternoon I shall think of something.

LOT. I shall never be able to understand you.

MARGAUSE. No?

LOT. What *do* you think of this expedition? You read the Bishop's letter. You must have thought a lot about it. You might have given me a hint what to say.

MARGAUSE. You did very well.

LOT. But do you think there's anything in it? There must be, or old Flatface wouldn't go himself, let alone fitting out a ship. He's a mean old rat. I wish you'd let me know what you think.

MARGAUSE. I think the Sailor is a very remarkable young man.

LOT. I thought him a damned bore myself. A bit crazy, too. I'm going down to the stables. Care to come?

MARGAUSE. No, I think not.

LOT. So long, then. I'll see you later.

MARGAUSE. Possibly.

[*Exit* LOT, MARGAUSE *is left sitting on the Throne registering inscrutable purpose till she is nearly black in the face.*]

SCENE II

Scene : The Guest House at Ru-Rhush in the early morning. It is a sort of pyramid or cone, built of long, thin, unmortared stones. It is lit mainly by an aperture at what would be the apex of the cone if more than half of it were on the stage. This skylight or chimney has immediately below it an unlit log fire, piled in a circular granite hearth.

The back wall is divided by four cubicle-alcoves, separated by stone pillars. They are screened from the Audience by coloured woollen cloths, but the second and the fourth screens have been partly drawn back, showing untidy low beds with bearskin coverlets.

A long oak beam stretches across the tops of the pillars. It is painted with curious crude designs, quite meaningless, with a vague hint of both Celtic and Greek art in their composition. A big rectangular doorway, situated towards the Prompt side shows a prospect of a sunny, calm bay and part of a two-headed mountain. Three rough steps lead from the doorway down into the House. A double screen of leather and coloured cloth has been drawn back.

A lark is singing outside, and a deep diapason of snoring accompanies it from the third screened cubicle. Soon these sounds are joined by a song sung by a RU-WOMAN, *who comes bustling in, carrying a heap of garments and a couple of logs for the fireplace. She is sturdy and middle-aged, and wears a single garment of three different shades of blue. She dumps the logs and lays out the garments on a stone ledge on the O.P. side.*

Her song is in the Ru-Rhush language, and the air is rather like that of LAND OF HEART'S DESIRE *in Mrs. Kennedy Fraser's Collection.*

WOMAN.   Wah na clash-nye luf.   (Fawaway   clouded-not
                                                             the sky
            Blue ash Ru   Blue over the Island
            Pul wansha grash   Above pale bright sand
            Dwawmish na glumert.   Is a dream of the sun's.)

[*Enter* TORQUIL.   *He is in good form.*]

TORQUIL.   Oh, good morning to you.

WOMAN.   Good morning to you.

TORQUIL.   What is your name?

WOMAN.   My name is Ku.   It means The Wood Pigeon.

TORQUIL.   My name is Torquil.   I don't know what it means.

WOMAN.   It is a very peculiar name.

TORQUIL.   I am sorry.

WOMAN.   You mustn't be sorry.   It is the fault of your parents.   If any.

TORQUIL.   What do you mean by " if any " ?

WOMAN.   When the young men found the four of you, you were lying on the sand in a row, all wet.   You looked as if you had been carefully arranged in that row, and the sea is very careless.   We thought you might have been created there.

TORQUIL.   No.   We came from a ship.   We struck a reef, I think, in the middle of the night.   We must have split in two.   There was nothing left forward of the after-cabin where the owner and the priest and I slept.   Very soon that went too, and we three took to the water clinging to a spar.

WOMAN.   Three?   There were four of you.

TORQUIL.   Oh, yes.   There was the cabin-boy.

WOMAN.   What kind of boy?

TORQUIL.   The boy who was supposed to look after the cabin.   I hardly saw him.

WOMAN.   He is a peculiar kind of boy.

TORQUIL.   Indeed he is.   He was sick from the moment we cast off.

KU.   Strange things happen to people who are sick.

91   [13]

TORQUIL.   Poor little devil!   Isn't he up yet?   He ought to be helping you.

KU.   My mother when she was sick got very fat and my father got very thin.

TORQUIL.   Yes?

KU.   And before they were sick my mother was thin and my father was fat.   But I never heard of that change.

TORQUIL.   What change?

KU.   I shall never be able to remember your name.   I think we'll call you Shlup while you are on the Island.

TORQUIL.   What does Shlup mean?

KU.   It means a diver.   We shall call the other gentleman Snor because of the noise he makes when he is asleep.   Then there's the solemn gentleman in the long frock he wouldn't let me dry.   He has been outside all morning talking to himself in a peculiar way.   We'll call him Kaa, because that is our name for a crow, and he looks like one.   I am not quite sure what we shall call your cabin boy.   You say one thing about him and I think another, so it is a little difficult.   What name had your cabin boy in the place you come from?

TORQUIL.   I don't know.   We called him Hi You.

KU.   Hiyu is our name for a moor bird with a long beak. But the name for his hen is Wheet.

TORQUIL.   We had better call the cabin boy Hiyu.

KU.   Do you think so?

[GRETTIR *appears from his cubicle, wrapped in a blanket.*]

GRETTIR.   Eyahyah!   What about breakfast?

KU.   Good morning, Snor.   Your breakfast is in the kitchen—out through the door and first to the left.

GRETTIR.   Snor?   What do you mean by Snor?

TORQUIL.   It is to be your Island name.   It means Great-Prince-with-the-Adenoidal-Countenance.   My name is Shlup. You'd better pick up the Parson and make him have his breakfast.   I've had mine.   His name is to be Kaa.

GRETTIR.   Where are my trousers?

[KU *picks up his nether garments from the ledge.*]

KU.   Are these trousers?   How funny!

GRETTIR.   Here!   Hand them over.

[*He retires to his cubicle.*]

TORQUIL.   And it's time that young lubber got under way.

[*Going into first cubicle.*]

Hi! You! You young Son of a Gun! Show a leg there. Tumble up and look smart about it. . . . Oh! . . . I beg your pardon!

[*His jovial cries have been interrupted by a smothered squeal. He comes out of the cubicle precipitately and covered with confusion.* GRETTIR, *completing his toilet, appears at the opening of his cubicle.* TORQUIL *stares from* KU *to* GRETTIR, *opening and shutting his mouth as if he had words, but they would not come.*]

GRETTIR.   What's the matter with you?

TORQUIL (*pointing*).   He . . . she . . .

KU.   I told you. Didn't I tell you?

TORQUIL.   The cabin boy . . . she's not a boy at all!

GRETTIR.   How do you know?

[MARGAUSE, *with a sleepy look about her and a bearskin rug wrapped round her, appears at the opening of her cubicle.*]

MARGAUSE.   Never mind how he knew. Get me some clothes.

KU.   I thought of that.

[*She takes women's clothes from the heap on the ledge and gives them to* MARGAUSE.]

There you are. They are nearly new. We've been wondering what name to call you. I suppose you have a stupid, meaningless name like the rest of them. Perhaps we had better leave it over till She comes to see you. Yes, I think that would be the best plan. She will think of something.

MARGAUSE.   That will be very clever of her, whoever She is.

KU.   Oh, she's clever all right.

MARGAUSE.   But who is she?

KU. That's her name—She. She is the daughter of He. But he is now At One With The Earth, as all of us must be.

MARGAUSE.   Do you mean he is dead?

KU. Oh, no. He's not dead. He's part of a field of wheat. Besides, She is He as well as being She, just as I'm my father Tittur and my mother Mua. We don't die in Ru-Rhush, whatever people do in other places.

MARGAUSE.   I can't stand here any longer listening to non-

sense and catching cold.   When She comes I should like to
speak to her.   Tell her that, will you ?

[MARGAUSE *retires into her alcove and pulls the screen.*]

KU.   What did she mean by nonsense ?   She must be a
very stupid woman, that cabin boy of yours.   We keep on
giving bits of life away, and then a time comes when we give it
all away.   But that isn't being dead.   Being dead is when life
stops.   If your cabin boy talks like that to She, I don't know
what'll happen.   She is the only person on this island who is
allowed to lose her temper.

TORQUIL.   I hope that the lady we thought was our cabin
boy doesn't lose her temper too.

KU.   She had better not.

GRETTIR.   She is a most important person, I think you ought
to know.

KU.   I can't help that.   If she loses her temper she will
have to be dipped.

TORQUIL.   What is that ?

GRETTIR.   Hush!   She's just behind the screen.   She'll
hear every word.

KU.   I wouldn't tell you anyhow.   We don't talk about
such things.

GRETTIR (*taking* KU *aside*).   That lady is none other than
Queen Margause.   She is the wife of King Lot, and Queen
of the Orkneys.   She's the sister of King Arthur of England.
She's said to be the richest woman in the world.   And she is a
notorious Enchantress.

KU.   I don't know what all that is about, but I'd better get
her breakfast ready.   I'll call her Queen till She finds a name
for her.   Queen is our name for a peacock's wife. . . .
Queen, you'll find your breakfast in the kitchen in two or
three minutes.   Look sharp and don't let it get cold.

[*Exit* KU.]

GRETTIR.   What is there for breakfast ?

TORQUIL.   A sort of porridge.   Not bad.   No doubt from
the wheat from the field fertilised by the Father of She.   I must
find out about that.   I'm probably partly She's father already.

GRETTIR.   Stop waffling and try to think for a moment.
What on earth are we to do ?

TORQUIL.   About the Queen ?

GRETTIR.   Yes.

TORQUIL.   I don't know.

GRETTIR.   I never got such a shock in my life.

TORQUIL.   Neither did I.

GRETTIR.   Things were difficult enough as it was.

[*Enter* BROTHER INNOCENCE.]

GRETTIR.   Oh, there you are, Father.   Come over here, and talk very quietly.   Do you know what's happened?

INNOCENCE.   No.   I have spent the morning at my orisons.

GRETTIR.   Do you remember the cabin boy?

INNOCENCE.   The child who was sea-sick for all the journey? I, too, was sea-sick.   I did not much regard him.

GRETTIR.   He is the Queen of Orkney.

INNOCENCE.   You are pleased to be facetious.

TORQUIL.   No.   Unfortunately it is true.

INNOCENCE.   You mean that this wretched woman has joined the expedition in disguise?

GRETTIR.   That's right.

INNOCENCE.   Sancta Maria cum Sancto Josepho Multi-tudineque Angelorum!

GRETTIR.   You never said a truer word.

INNOCENCE.   She must be as if she had not been.   We must ignore her.

GRETTIR.   Nobody has ever managed to ignore the Queen of Orkney.

TORQUIL.   I'm not a bloodthirsty man.   I've never killed anything but a few partridges and rabbits; but I think we should kill her.

INNOCENCE.   These are terrible words.

TORQUIL.   Yes.   Now.   I can't explain why, but I know I'm right.

GRETTIR.   You can't do that.

INNOCENCE.   It is evil to take human life without long and prayerful meditation.

TORQUIL.   If I meditate I won't be able to do it.

[*He seizes a big billet from the fireplace.*]

GRETTIR.   Stop, you damned fool.   If there's any natural religion in this place they'll soon find out she's a witch.

95   [17]

INNOCENCE.   When I have Christianised the Island, I shall denounce her myself.

GRETTIR.   They'll do all the killing that's wanted.

INNOCENCE.   " Ye shall not suffer a witch to live."

GRETTIR.   Then the King will *have* to send a punitive expedition.   Sir Gawaine or King Arthur will, if he doesn't. Don't be a fool.

TORQUIL.   That's filthy treachery.   No, no, no.   I'll kill her in hot blood like a gentleman.

> [*He breaks from them and makes for the* QUEEN'S *alcove.* MAR-
> GAUSE, *dressed like a woman of the Island, appears before the
> screen, and he checks himself.*]

MARGAUSE (*after looking at him intently*).   So you are going to kill me, Torquil ?

TORQUIL.   Madame, I . . . (speech fails him).

MARGAUSE.   Put down that horrid log.   You must not kill me in that disgusting fashion.   Come nearer to me.

> [TORQUIL *approaches her with the gay insouciance of a rabbit
> approaching a stoat.*]

You must not batter and spoil my beautiful head, Torquil. You must take me by the throat with your strong young hands and hold tight till my breathing stops.   Lay down the log.

> [TORQUIL *drops the log with a clatter.*]

Let me see the strong hands that are so soon to choke me. You have spoiled them a little by heaving on ropes, but they are still the hands of an artist.   The long thumb and the little finger swing out from the rest.   They are a visionary's hands. You must let me, some day, tell your fortune.   But I forgot. There was something you had to do.

> [*She lifts his hands to her neck.*]

Now, strangle me.

> [TORQUIL *drags his hands away, but* MARGAUSE *keeps a grip on his
> wrists.*]

MARGAUSE.   You have changed your mind ?

TORQUIL.   Let me go.

MARGAUSE.   You don't want to kill me ?

TORQUIL.   With my whole heart I want to kill you; but I can't.

MARGAUSE.   Very well, then.

[*She lets him go.*]

Go over to your friends.   You may sit down, all of you.

[MARGAUSE *sits on the ledge.   The others squat on the floor.*]

Why did you want to kill me ?

GRETTIR.   Your Majesty, we tried to restrain this young man, but he was too strong for us.   I shall go now and fetch the guard, or whatever they've got on this Island, and have him arrested.

MARGAUSE.   But you and the priest were plotting against me too.

GRETTIR.   Oh, no, Madame!   We couldn't think of such a thing.   We are your Majesty's most humble, loyal and devoted subjects.   I got this bruise on my arm trying to stop him.

MARGAUSE.   Nevertheless, you were plotting against me. Why did you do that ?

GRETTIR.   On my soul and conscience . . .

MARGAUSE.   My dear Sir, you must find something far more formidable to swear by . . . if you must swear in a lady's presence.   Why do you wish me to be killed, Priest ?

INNOCENCE.   I do not wish you to be killed.

MARGAUSE.   Do you find me inconvenient ?

INNOCENCE.   Most inconvenient.

MARGAUSE.   In what respect ?

INNOCENCE.   Madame, I will be plain with you.   I am an Ambassador of the Church of Christ, sent to bring this Island to a sense of the beauty of holiness.   I find in you some beauty, but no holiness.   Your very presence menaces my mission, not to mention whatever mischief you may be contemplating.

MARGAUSE.   You think I am a wicked woman ?

INNOCENCE.   I think you bear a grievous burden of variegated sins.

MARGAUSE.   I lower the tone of your mission ?

INNOCENCE.   If you put it in that way, yes.

MARGAUSE.   You sit there between a sneak thief and a would-be murderer and say that to me !

INNOCENCE.   My companions are sinners, and for sinners there is the hope of redemption.   They are not the chosen instruments of the Devil.

[GRETTIR *is about to speak, but a look from* MARGAUSE *restrains him.*]

97 E   [19]

MARGAUSE. Does it occur to you, Priest, that I may not be the sort of woman you so generously describe? If I had been, would you be sitting there slandering your Queen when one word from her would silence you for ever? I am still Queen of Orkney. Grettir is my subject and Torquil is the son of a knight. Either of them could let the life out of that bag of bones if your lawful sovereign gave the order.

INNOCENCE. I am not afraid of you, Madame. Nor of them.

MARGAUSE. I know you are not afraid. I think you are the bravest man I ever saw. But you are a mistaken man. Why do you think I dressed myself in mean rags and dared the ocean to come with you?

INNOCENCE. I cannot tell.

MARGAUSE. Neither can I tell you. But I beseech you to think and to pray, and it may be that you will find in my act the elements of redemption even for a soul in such jeopardy as the soul of your Queen.

INNOCENCE. I pray that it may be so, Madame.

GRETTIR. May I be allowed to humbly express my satisfaction and, if I may say so, my deep admiration for the magnanimous way in which your Majesty has taken this most unpleasant incident. If there have been hasty words and actions—actions and words, if I may say so, that we all regret and would like to forget—you must remember that we have just been through a very trying time. With the notable exception of your Majesty, we are none of us quite ourselves yet. But I feel confident that the outcome of this very frank little discussion holds the best of omens for the future. One word more. I am not a man who makes a parade of his religion, but I think the worthy Father here will agree with me that the Hand of Providence has been very evident in the recent alarming series of events. The four of us were saved, almost by a miracle, from the wreck. Surely it is not presumptuous to suggest that Providence has also, almost miraculously, given us a leader and a guide in her Majesty, the gracious Consort of the anointed ruler of our State. Nay, more . . .

MARGAUSE. Have you had your breakfast?

GRETTIR. No, your Majesty.

MARGAUSE. Then go and have your breakfast. And take Father Innocence with you. I want to talk to Torquil.

GRETTIR.   Is it safe . . . to leave you alone with him?

MARGAUSE.   Quite safe.   Father, when you have leisure, we shall try to understand each other better, shall we not?

[INNOCENCE *bows*.]

GRETTIR.   We may go?

MARGAUSE.   You may go.

[*Exeunt* INNOCENCE *and* GRETTIR, GRETTIR *very elaborately*.]

Well? . . .

[TORQUIL *is silent*.]

Come and sit by me.

[TORQUIL *joins her on the ledge*.]

What impelled you to attack me in that extraordinary fashion?

TORQUIL.   It was Fear, Madame.

MARGAUSE.   Fear?

TORQUIL.   It is always Fear that makes us do extravagant and cruel things.

MARGAUSE.   Always Fear?   I don't think so.   Have you ever seen extravagance and cruelty springing from some other motive?

TORQUIL.   What other motive?

MARGAUSE.   Greed?   Or the lust for Power?   Or . . . Love?

TORQUIL.   It may be so.

MARGAUSE.   Love expresses itself in strange ways, Torquil.

TORQUIL.   Yes . . . I know . . . But. . . . No. Madame, I tried to kill you because I was afraid.

MARGAUSE.   Afraid of what?   Of me?

TORQUIL.   Yes. . . . No. . . . Madame, I have a curious feeling about this Island.

MARGAUSE.   Tell me.

TORQUIL.   Going up and down . . . and about . . . in England and in Ireland, in Alban and in Spain . . . everywhere . . . I've seen a great many people, living in their own way.   All kinds of people, rich and poor, but mostly poor people.   And nine out of ten of them—more than that—they were . . . don't laugh at me . . . they were Good.

MARGAUSE.   What do you mean by good?

TORQUIL.   They were kind and gentle and honest and friendly and patient and tolerant and brave and industrious, and even happy.   Everywhere they were like that.

MARGAUSE.   You must have been very fortunate in your acquaintances.

TORQUIL.   No.   Wait a moment.   They weren't all like that.

MARGAUSE.   You didn't, by any chance, find that some of them were stupid?

TORQUIL.   Oh, a great many of them were stupid.   Nearly all of them.   But that might not have mattered if only . . . The point is that there was always something that spoilt everything.

MARGAUSE.   What was that?

TORQUIL.   I'm not quite sure.   Sometimes it was a landowner who was so crazy with greed that the other landowners began to hate and fear him.   And then they became as crazy as he was.   Sometimes it was the land itself.   If the soil was too easy, the people became fat and idle and selfish.   If it was too difficult, they became hard and suspicious.   Sometimes they go so enthusiastic about governing themselves that everybody wanted to rule everybody else, and the stupid ones didn't know the difference between ruling and bullying.   And nearly everywhere there was some man not quite right in his head who couldn't fit in and always wanted to quarrel.   He made everybody round about fidgety, and that made them jealous and ready to take offence.   You know how it is when somebody can't help yawning or scratching himself.   The poor wretch goes on until everybody in the company is yawning or scratching too.   I saw a lot of that sort of thing in man-and-woman relationships too.   Men and women were all right until some itching individual came to live among them.

MARGAUSE.   I am afraid I cannot quite see whither this slightly indecent oration is leading us.   Never mind.   Go on.

TORQUIL.   No, but honestly. . . .   And there were all sorts of systems, too, that seemed to spoil everything.   I mean, there was one place where they roasted potatoes in their jackets, and very nice too.   Then a clever chap found that they were also very nice cut into bits and fried in boar's fat.   Then two asses came to the conclusion that they ought to be done either one way or the other.   Then they had a fight and everybody took sides.   When I was there they had just broken a man on the wheel for frying potatoes or baking them—I forget which.   The winning side had set some fool to making regulations for cooking potatoes, and fools of that sort never trust ordinary common sense. And there's any amount of common sense in the world, believe me, if they'd only let it alone. But some people must have their laws and rules and regulations and instructions . . .

MARGAUSE. But, Torquil, my dear, without rules and regulations we should have chaos.

TORQUIL. Perhaps. That may be. We ought to have rules to prevent the itching ones from robbing and killing each other and, may be, rules to restrain them from making rules.

MARGAUSE. I enjoy hearing you talk, but why did you try to kill me ?

TORQUIL. I was coming to that.

MARGAUSE. How nice ! Go on.

TORQUIL. This Island seemed to me to be the only place I had found where nothing had happened to spoil it all.

MARGAUSE. So you went at once to the Bishop and Grettir Flatface to see what they could do about it ?

TORQUIL. Well, yes, I . . . I thought . . .

MARGAUSE. You thought that the peace and beauty of the pigeon-loft would be enhanced by the introduction of two large, hungry Tomcats ?

TORQUIL. Oh, Madame, you don't understand. Besides, Grettir and the Monk aren't like that at all. They're simple souls. I could twist them round my little finger. . . . No. You were perfectly right in saying the Island was like a pigeon-loft. They're so helpless, you see. All their virtues are negative sort of virtues. They've no Tradition. They've no Art, or Religion, or Patriotism, or Philosophy, or Science to carry them through a danger period. Their Architecture's primitive. Their Agriculture's primitive. Now, Grettir's a marvellous executive. He has no ideas of his own, but if you give him ideas he gets them into practice at a tremendous rate. I'm no good at that sort of thing, but I'll feed him with ideas and keep a tight hand on him. Then I know you don't like Father Innocence, but he's a wonderful fellow. He's a musician, he's a scholar, he's a physician, he's an artist, he's an orator and he's a bit of a saint as well. Besides, my experience is that there's nothing so good for *steadying* a people as a good sound religious background.

101   [23]

MARGAUSE.   Grettir and the Bishop wanted to send soldiers;
I suppose they have a steadying influence too?

TORQUIL.   They have, in a curious kind of way.   I suppose
a little discipline is a good thing, too.   But that was only a makeshift idea, and I wasn't very keen on it.   Grettir thought we'd
be able to get down to what he called business more quickly if
we appeared to have some backing.

MARGAUSE.   And what is this " business " to which Grettir
wants to get down?

TORQUIL.   I've just told you.   I believe in this people.   I
think it will take very little to make them the most wonderful
people in the world.   Man doesn't live by goodness alone.   He
needs an intenser form of life, or he'll die.   I shan't touch the
groundwork of their common way of living.   That would be
to spoil everything.   But I'll make poets and artists and craftsmen and philosophers to teach them the meaning of their goodness . . . to key up their happiness to ecstasy.

MARGAUSE.   You think that I would not be helpful to this
project?

TORQUIL.   Oh, Madame, I have seen enough of you to be
sure that you will never be happy unless you are pulling the
Devil by the tail.   You love excitement and passion and
intrigue and danger.   I have come to save the Island from these
things.   So I had the impulse to kill.

MARGAUSE.   Perhaps it is true that you have seen enough of
me to come to an opinion.   You accidentally saw a good deal of
me this morning.   But do you know why I came on this voyage?

TORQUIL.   No, Madame.

MARGAUSE.   I am not sure that I know myself.   But I think
it must have been maternal instinct.

[KU *comes scurrying in.*]

KU.   Oh, there you are?   Where are the others?   She is
coming up the path.   She will want to see them all.

[*If the Actor who is playing* TORQUIL *feels that he can make his
long speeches better walking excitedly up and down, he may do
so.   If not, he rises at this point and goes up stage.* KU *runs to
the door and shouts:*]

Snor!   Kaa!   Come quickly!   Come in here!

[KU *fusses about, tidying beds, adjusting screens and talking all the
time——*]

[24]   102

There's no need to be afraid.   Unless something has happened to make her angry, there's nothing at all to worry about.   I think you'll like her.   I hope She likes you.

[*Enter* GRETTIR *and* INNOCENCE.]

GRETTIR.   What's the matter ?

KU.   Oh, there you are ?   I was telling Shlup and Queen not to get excited.   And don't you get excited either.   She may just have a look at you and go away.   It all depends what kind of a mood She finds herself in.   She's sometimes a little funny that way.   It's knowing so much, I suppose.   I should think her head sometimes almost splits with all the knowledge that is in it.   It saves the rest of us on the Island so much trouble to have somebody who knows everything.   Now, you don't need to say anything.   Just wait for her to speak. . . .   She can't be far off now.   I'll go out and have a look—see.   Just stay here.   And don't get worried.

[KU *goes out.   She is seen through the doorway, shading her eyes with her hand.*]

MARGAUSE (*to* TORQUIL).   Have you seen this woman ?

TORQUIL.   No, Madame.   On my last visit she was in retreat.   She was meditating, they said.

[*A short pause.* KU *re-enters.*]

KU.   She is coming.   Now, don't speak till She speaks to you.   Stand over there in a row.

[*As she is watching the doorway,* KU *does not see that* MARGAUSE *has not moved from her seat.* SHE *enters, followed by* WAWA, QUA *and* KWOO. SHE *is dressed as a Chinese, though there are only a few traces of Chinese ancestry in her features.* WAWA *is a very old man, in a long grey gown, with a chain of oyster shells round his neck.* QUA *and* KWOO *are middle-aged men in knee-length tunics with wide sleeves in different shades of grey.* KWOO *is completely bald.* QUA *has a bushy, grizzled beard. All three men carry long, peeled holly-sticks.* KU *addresses* SHE *respectfully, but without any obeisance.*]

KU.   She, these are the people who were found on the shore. Their names are Kaa, and Snor and Shlup and—and——   Oh, yes, and Queen.

[*She signals behind her back for* MARGAUSE *to get up.* MARGAUSE *ignores this.*]

103   [25]

MARGAUSE (*to* KU).   Bring a seat for the lady.

[TORQUIL *finds a little stool and moves it to face* MARGAUSE.]

MARGAUSE (*to* SHE).   You may be seated.

SHE (*after a very short pause*).   I thank you.

[SHE *sits down.*]

MARGAUSE.   Will you present these gentlemen to me?

SHE (*without looking round*).   The man with the white beard is Wawa.   He is our oldest Judge.   The man with the short beard is Qua, the Seagull.   He is a fisherman.   The bald man is Kwoo, the Owl.   He works with his head.   That is why he is bald.

MARGAUSE.   That is very interesting.   Do you have many baldheaded men on your delightful little Island?

SHE.   No.   Kwoo is the only one.

MARGAUSE.   He must be very proud of his beautiful shiny bald head.

SHE.   No.   He is not proud.   We do not encourage pride.

MARGAUSE.   How right you are!   But you must remember that there is such a thing as proper pride.   For example, you must take a pride in this perfect little community you govern so well.

SHE.   I do not govern this community.

MARGAUSE.   Oh?   I understood that you did.

SHE.   We have no government here.   I have heard of governments.   Their purpose is to keep the wicked in order. Here we try as far as possible to refrain from being wicked. Our reward is to have no government.

MARGAUSE.   Oh! . . . You must forgive my mistake. You and these gentlemen had the outward and visible appearance of being a chieftainess and her counsellors.

SHE.   No.   We are the Ponderers.   The people put questionings to us and, if we are able, we reply to their question-ings.   A whimsical, half-witted fellow on the Island has given us the by-name of Brains Trust.   We are often called that in jest.   But we are correctly called the Ponderers.

MARGAUSE.   Why?

SHE.   Because we ponder.

MARGAUSE.   I see.

SHE.   Is there anything else that you would like to know? While we ponder the answers to the questionings of our own people, it is our custom with strangers rather to ask questions than to answer them.

KU. I told them that, She.

MARGAUSE. But the old gentleman is a Judge. You said he was a Judge. What is the good of a Judge if you have no criminals?

SHE. We have wrong-doers, if that is what you mean. The Judge advises the people what to do with wrong-doers, if they ask his advice.

MARGAUSE. And the people punish the wrong-doers themselves?

SHE. They do not punish them. They deal with them.

MARGAUSE. How?

SHE. It depends upon what wrong has been done. If the wrong is Anger or the result of Anger, we first take the person who has been the cause of Anger in another. We send him to the top of the mountain for a certain time to consider in what respects he can make himself less offensive to his fellow-being. We then take the angry person and dip him.

MARGAUSE. Dip him?

SHE. We put him in the sea and hold his head under water for a certain time. This cools his blood and cleanses him of his passion. We find this method useful for all passions of any sort whatever. If there is doubt as to which person has offended, we dip both, and then send them up the mountain. Very conveniently, the mountain has two summits more than a mile apart. And now, if you please . . .

MARGAUSE. One moment. You said that the purpose of government was to restrain the wicked. Surely a government has other purposes.

SHE. What purposes?

MARGAUSE. Well . . . to put it at its simplest, to protect the country from War, Famine and Pestilence.

SHE. Do governments do that?

MARGAUSE. We were talking of their purpose. Many of them, no doubt, are disappointing in practice.

SHE. If a people cannot protect itself against Pestilence, Famine and War, I doubt if a government will protect it. We have no pestilence because we live principally in the open air and because we discourage visitors. We have no famines because we know if we do not sow and reap and bind and thresh and stow away, we shall starve. We have no wars, because we do not allow either gods or devils on this Island. The pebbles on our beaches are clean. Our cliffs are clean. And we give gods and devils to the mighty, cleansing sea.

MARGAUSE. If the King of Orkney had not been a wobat wallidrag and an idle rascal, your way with gods and devils would not have saved you from War.

SHE. I do not know who is the King of Orkney, but if he comes we shall ponder him. And if he is a god, we shall put him in the sea, and if he is a devil, we shall put him in the sea. The sea is grateful for these small sacrifices.

MARGAUSE. You would have no time to ponder him.

SHE. Then we should put him in the sea without pondering.

MARGAUSE. I see that it is high time we had to come to your Island.

SHE. Why have you come to our Island? Who are you?

MARGAUSE. We are the Teachers.

SHE. You have come to teach us?

MARGAUSE. Yes.

SHE. We are always willing to learn. And the sea gave you to us. The sea has no purpose, that we should look upon its gifts with suspicion. For a little you may teach us. But if you bring us gods or devils we shall give back its gift to the sea.

[SHE *rises and, without further ceremony, leaves the Guest House, followed by* WAWA, QUA *and* KWOO. KU *looks from face to face of the Strangers in a puzzled fashion and follows them.* MAR-GAUSE *rises.*]

MARGAUSE. And now, what shall we teach them?

TORQUIL. ⎫
INNOCENCE ⎬ The first thing . . . I beg your pardon . . .
GRETTIR. ⎭ No, please . . .

GRETTIR. The first thing is to overhaul all possible resources —to explore every avenue—to leave no stone unturned . . .

TORQUIL. The first thing is to get a clear idea as to the real object of our planning . . .

INNOCENCE. The first thing is to testify to Eternal Truth.

CURTAIN.

END OF ACT ONE.

[28]

ACT II

The same as in Act I, *Scene* 2, *except that the log pile has been removed.*
INNOCENCE, *from a rough pulpit, is preaching to the* PONDERERS, *who are sitting on a semi-circle of stools quite near him.* GRETTIR *is sitting on the floor against a pillar. He is sound asleep. On three more stools near the door are seated* BA, *the Goat, and his wife* TRIKA, *the Lark. They are a bucolic young couple, and are very much interested in what* INNOCENCE *is saying, though they can't make head or tail of it.* KU *is on the third stool. She is difficult to recognise, as* MARGAUSE *has smartened her up considerably. Her garments are much the same, but they are more jauntily worn, and she has earrings, a necklace and bracelets made of shells. Her hair is braided and curled and she wears a very violent make-up. Her finger-nails are crimson, and she cannot keep her eyes off them.* TORQUIL *is leaning restlessly against the doorpost at the beginning of the Scene, but disappears half-way through* INNOCENCE'S *first speech.*

INNOCENCE. " And they heard the voice of the Lord God walking in the garden in the cool of the day; and Adam and his wife hid themselves from the presence of the Lord God amongst the trees of the garden. And the Lord God called to Adam and said: 'Where are you?' And he said, 'I heard your voice in the garden and I was afraid, because I was naked; and I hid myself.' And the Lord God said: 'Who told you that you were naked? Have you eaten from the tree I commanded you that you should not eat?' And Adam said: 'The woman you gave to be with me gave me from the tree and I ate.'

" And the Lord God said to the woman: 'What is this that you have done?' And the woman said: 'The snake beguiled me and I ate.'

" And the Lord God said to the snake: 'Because you have done this you are accursed above all cattle and above every beast of the field. On your belly you shall go and eat dust all the days of your life. And I will put enmity between you and the woman and between your seed and her seed; and they will bruise your head and you will bite their heels.'

" To the woman he said: 'I will greatly multiply your sorrow and your conception. In sorrow you will bring forth children; and your desire will be to your husband so that he will rule over you.'

"And to Adam he said: 'Because you listened to your wife and ate of the tree of which I commanded you, saying, "You shall not eat it," I have cursed the ground for your sake. In sorrow will you eat of it all the days of your life. Thorns and thistles it will bring forth for you, and you shall eat the grass of the field. In the sweat of your face will you eat till you go back again into the ground—for of it you were taken. Dust you are and to dust you will return.'

"And the Lord God said: 'The man has become one of us, to know good and evil. And now, lest he put out his hand and take also from the tree of life and eat, and live for ever . . .' For that, the Lord God sent him out of the garden of Eden to till the ground from whence he was taken. So he drove out the man; and he placed at the east of the garden of Eden Cherubim and a flaming sword which turned every way, to keep the way of the tree of life."

SHE. Thank you very much. It is a most interesting story and very well told; and it confirms us in our wish not to have gods on our Island.

INNOCENCE (*with mild severity*). You must not interrupt the service.

SHE. Why not?

INNOCENCE. Because it is a sacred rite.

SHE. If you mean what I think you mean, I must ask you not to hold sacred rites on this Island.

INNOCENCE. You forbid it?

SHE. I don't forbid anything. I ask you not to do it.

[*She gets up and goes to the pulpit.*]

Forgive me, please, for a moment. That box of yours seems to be a very good device for a story-teller to use, and I should like to tell you a story.

INNOCENCE. But this place is reserved for the Priest.

SHE. I know. But please lend me your box. If you don't, Qua will pull you out of it—without hurting you, of course. Qua is very strong. He picks up people without hurting them as a dog picks up its puppies. Please let me have the box. It is only for a minute.

[INNOCENCE, *very doubtfully, steps down from the pulpit and* SHE *takes his place.*]

My great grandfather told me this story. Once upon a time

there was an Island, like this, where they did not want to have either gods or devils. When a god-man came to them once, they tore up his magic book and threw him into the sea. But a child kept a torn piece of a torn page of the magic book and grew up to be a man and learned to read; and on the torn piece he read, " Blessed are the meek, for they shall inherit the Earth." He thought, " This is a very wonderful thing," and called his relations together, and they all began to ponder what the magic torn piece said, though they had had little practice in pondering. They builded a heap of stones and put the magic paper in the heap of stones and pondered in front of the heap every day at sun-up and sun-down. Then someone said, " We have been pondering for some time and we have not yet inherited the Earth." The man said to him, " That is probably because we are not meek enough." So it was decided that they should roll down a bank till they were giddy and then crawl on their stomachs up to the pile of stones and lie there with their noses in the dust.

The other people laughed at them first, and then they thought " This is very interesting." And soon they began to be meek too. Soon there were so many that the man had to make a small charge for admission. The people brought eggs and milk and bushels of wheat to be allowed to roll and crawl with the others. The man and his relations began to inherit the Earth.

A time came when there were so many people who wanted to be meek that several other piles of stones had to be built. Then people found they felt meeker if they howled and yelled when they were rolling and crawling. And then they decided what words and sounds they ought to make when they were howling and yelling. Then someone said, " We should be meeker if we hit ourselves on the head with stones when we approach the heaps." So some of them did this, and grew so bruised and proud of their meekness that they would hardly speak to the ordinary meek people.

This led to great arguments, too, as to whether it was meeker to bang oneself on the head with a stone, what sort of words ought to be howled and yelled, what was the exact meaning of blessed, what should be the shape of the heaps of stone and hundreds of other things. These arguments led to fighting, because nobody would give way. The head-bangers lost because there were fewer of them, and then the winners chose

one who was called The Meekest of All.   He was given a huge
castle and a tenth of all the produce of the Island to help him
to be meek and to make others meek as well.   A number of
other officers called the Most Meek, the Very Meek and the
Pretty Average Meek were appointed to assist him, and paid
according to their meekness.   After that if anybody did not
pay his dues, or was found banging his head with a stone, or
spoke rudely of The Meekest of All, he was covered with tar
and set on fire.   But in spite of this there was no peace on the
Island.   The Ponderers and I are of the opinion that the whole
thing was a great pity, and thank you very much, Kaa, for allow-
ing me to use your little box.

[SHE *steps down from the Pulpit.   The Stage Audience, in their
degrees of intelligence, are mildly amused by* SHE's *story, though
they do not laugh aloud or applaud.*   INNOCENCE *is not amused.*]

INNOCENCE.   Woman, the blasphemy of your foolish tale is
due to ignorance, and is not your fault.   Your ignorance, God
help me, is my fault.

QUA.   You are not very polite.

WAWA.   The Ponderers think that it is a good thing—indeed,
one of the best things—to be polite.

KWOO.   This man is certainly not very polite.

WAWA.   He is a barbarian.   There are no two ways about
it, he is a barbarian.

KWOO.   I cannot entirely agree with you, Wawa.   He has
a smooth appearance and a cultivated way of talking that are
not characteristic of barbarians as I understand them.

QUA.   Perhaps he has lost his temper.   Do you think we
should advise the people to dip him?

INNOCENCE.   I never lose my temper.

SHE.   He has said what is quite true.   He has said we are
ignorant.   But surely, Kaa, the best remedy for ignorance is
to ponder all things carefully and continuously, and that is
exactly what we do.

INNOCENCE.   No.

SHE.   No?

INNOCENCE.   No.   The Truth alone destroys ignorance,
and the Truth comes in a blinding flash of revelation.   When
it came to St Paul it was so terrible that he fell down in a fit.

QUA.   When I used to follow the sea I saw that happen
once or twice in seaport towns.   A man was telling this Truth

[32]   110

of which you speak. He was shouting it in a loud, screaming voice, and several of his hearers fell down in fits. Several women tore their clothes off and foamed at the mouth. I did not think that they were any the better for it. One of these towns, I remember, was called by us sailors, The Town of Thieves and Murderers. Many months after the fits we returned, and found it still living up to its name

SHE. Your kind of truth, Kaa, seems to me to be both disagreeable and ineffective.

INNOCENCE. Birth is disagreeable and often ineffective. Death is disagreeable and often ineffective. But you cannot escape·them. No more can you escape the Truth, though it should grind you to powder.

SHE. There is this to be said for you, Kaa, that you do not bring your goods to the market disguised in a cloud of honeyed words.

INNOCENCE. God forbid that I should.

SHE. Not that your story you told us a little ago was not a very sweet story. But what did it mean?

INNOCENCE. I was about to expound it to you when you unleashed a pack of words at me.

SHE. I am so sorry. Perhaps I do talk too much.

INNOCENCE. As the Orcadian peasants say, you could talk the hind leg off a donkey.

SHE. It is a strange saying. I do not understand how simple talk could remove a donkey's hind leg or any of his other three legs. It is perhaps a humorous saying?

INNOCENCE. It is intended to be humorous.

SHE. I see. Now, tell me, if your god sets such store by truth, why did he take such elaborate precautions to prevent Adam from learning it?

INNOCENCE. Because Adam, in his pride, had disobeyed the Lord.

SHE. But the command that Adam disobeyed was, " You must not learn the truth."

INNOCENCE. Adam was not ready for the truth.

SHE. It would have been dangerous to him?

INNOCENCE. Yes.

SHE. I see. It was a peculiar bit of the Truth his bite at the apple taught him . . . that he ought to cover up part of his body.

111

INNOCENCE.   Bites at the Truth are often useless and ridiculous.   The Truth must be swallowed whole.   I see that I need not despair of you yet.

KWOO.   But . . . but . . . but. . . . You come here. . . . You seem to be a man more or less like the rest of us. . . . You speak to us as if you knew this Truth.   Have you broken into this Garden of Eden, overcome the Cherubim and swallowed the Tree of Knowledge, root, trunk, branches and leaves ? It seems to me that either you've got little respect for the wishes of your god, or else you're telling us a pack of nonsense.

INNOCENCE.   The Lord had compassion on mankind, and has revealed the Truth to his Church.   Not so many years ago a Virgin conceived and bore a son to the Most High.   To witness to Eternal Truth, that son suffered cruel death under Pontius Pilate to wipe out the sin of Adam; and arose again on the third day.   All Truth was known to him and he made the Truth known to St Peter, the rock on whom the Church was built.   He gave him the keys to loose and to bind on Earth and in Heaven.   From him and from the Apostles I derive what knowledge and authority I have.   And I bear the injunction to preach the Word of Truth to the Heathen with all my might till I die.

[*Pause.*]

SHE.   I see, at least, that you are under some necessity— whether it be good or bad I do not know.   My friends and I will ponder these matters.   Kwoo!

KWOO.   Yes ?

SHE.   When you addressed Kaa just now, I noticed some asperity in your voice.   I think it would be best if you went up the mountain to the Southern Spur and awaited tranquillity till tomorrow morning at sunrise.   Let us go now.   Good morning, Kaa, and thank you very much.

[*Exeunt* SHE *and the* PONDERERS.   BA *and* TRIKA *begin to follow them, but whisper for a moment in the doorway and come back to* INNOCENCE, *who is standing in gloomy reflection.* KU *goes out past them.*]

BA.   Kaa, please, may we speak to you a moment ?

INNOCENCE.   Yes, my children.   What have you to say to me ?

BA.   It's about Trika and me.

INNOCENCE.   Ah !

TRIKA.   We're friends, you see.   Great friends.   Ba and me.   This is Ba.

INNOCENCE.   Yes?

BA.   Ba means the Goat and Trika means the Skylark.

INNOCENCE.   I see.

BA.   And we're great friends.

INNOCENCE.   Yes, yes.   Go on.

BA.   She's very pretty, isn't she?

INNOCENCE.   No doubt.

TRIKA.   I think Ba is beautiful.

INNOCENCE.   Not very.   He will pass.

TRIKA.   Oh, I hope so.   We liked your story, Kaa.

INNOCENCE.   Did you?

TRIKA.   It was a very nice story and very interesting.

BA.   We thought the old Gardener was a bit unreasonable. But perhaps the apples weren't ripe yet.

TRIKA.   We liked it better than She's story.   We thought the people in She's story were very silly.   I mean, who want to roll on the ground and bang themselves with stones?   It's much more natural to want to eat an apple.

BA.   And it was natural, too, for the Gardener to be angry, if he was saving up the apples till they were ripe.

TRIKA.   Was the Gardener dipped for being angry?

INNOCENCE.   No.   Of course not.   Certainly not.

TRIKA.   He should have been.   But I suppose it happened very long ago.

INNOCENCE.   Very long ago.

TRIKA.   That explains it.   I understand the story perfectly now.   You make things very clear.   You are cleverer than She.

INNOCENCE.   It is not a matter of cleverness.

BA.   Oh, yes it is.   And after the stories you said much cleverer things than She did, and She is the cleverest one on the Island.

TRIKA.   By a long way.

BA.   Would you teach us to be clever?   That's what we wanted to ask you about.

TRIKA.   Would you make us as good as She and the Ponderers?

INNOCENCE.   I could teach you to be better than She and the Ponderers.

TRIKA.   I don't think I could be that.

113   [35]

BA.   Yes, you could.

TRIKA.   Very well, if you say so.   Kaa, it's funny, I always agree with Ba.

INNOCENCE.   Do you?

TRIKA.   Yes.   But only since lately.   We didn't before that.   We were so astonished when we began to agree with each other that we went quite giddy.

BA.   Yes.   Both of us.   I still go all giddy when I see Trika coming along the path or when I touch her.

TRIKA.   When he touches me I go all tingling, like nettles. I don't come out in little blisters, of course, but it's like that, only nicer.

BA.   When Trika isn't there, I feel as if I'd been chopped in two.   That's funny, isn't it?

INNOCENCE.   Extremely odd.

TRIKA.   We have great fun, Ba making me tingle and me making him giddy.

INNOCENCE.   My children . . .

BA.   We talk a lot, too, of course.

INNOCENCE.   What about?

BA.   Oh, about this and that.

TRIKA.   We thought we would like to make a baby.

BA.   We talked a lot about that.

TRIKA.   I wanted it done properly, and we weren't very sure how, so Ba went and asked the Ponderers about it.

INNOCENCE.   And did they tell you?

BA.   Oh, yes.   It was quite simple, really.

TRIKA.   But it was best to make sure.

INNOCENCE.   Terrible.   What a country!   Terrible.

BA.   Oh, no.   It wasn't a bit terrible.   I'll tell you about it if you like.   First of all . . .

INNOCENCE.   No.   You must not tell me.   You must tell nobody.   It is disgraceful to talk of such things.

BA.   Is it?

TRIKA.   Oh;   Ba, they can't have told us properly.

INNOCENCE.   Listen to me.   Do you wish me to teach you?

TRIKA.   Yes, yes.   If you know better than the Ponderers.

INNOCENCE.   I shall not teach you licentiousness.   I shall teach you the Way of Salvation.

BA.   What is that?   Do the Ponderers know it?

INNOCENCE.   No.

[36]   114

TRIKA.   Oh, good! Will you start right away?

INNOCENCE.   Yes, if . . .

BA.   Are you going to live all the time in that cave by the well?

INNOCENCE.   Yes.

BA.   Could Trika look after it for you and keep it tidy and cook your food?   She is a very good cook.

TRIKA.   Yes. Ba told me I was. I cooked a salmon for him yesterday. He could hardly eat it, it was so good.

BA.   I kept looking at you.

TRIKA.   May we come, Kaa?

BA.   But if she came to your cave, Kaa, if you don't mind, she wouldn't be your woman friend, but only mine.

INNOCENCE.   Yes, yes.

BA.   It's a funny thing, but I wouldn't like you to kiss her, or anything like that.   Not unless you want to very much.

TRIKA.   And not very much even then. Will that be all right, Kaa?   It's not because I don't like you. You understand that, don't you?

INNOCENCE.   Yes, yes, yes. I will teach you down at my cave; but on certain conditions.

BA.   What are conditions?

INNOCENCE.   You must be baptised and you must be married at once.

TRIKA.   Are these things very painful?

INNOCENCE.   No. Not at all painful.

TRIKA.   Very well, then. Are you willing to be what's-is named and married, Ba?

BA.   Yes, of course, if you are.

INNOCENCE.   Come with me to the cave.

TRIKA.   Both of us?

INNOCENCE.   Yes.

[*As they are going towards the doorway, enter* TORQUIL. *He carries a rod and three fish.*]

TORQUIL.   Oh, hello, Trika!   How are you?

TRIKA.   Very well thank you, Shlup.

TORQUIL.   Where are you going?

TRIKA.   Ba and I are going with Kaa to the cave. We are going to be married.   Both of us.

INNOCENCE (*at the door*). Come, Trika.

TRIKA.   All right, I'm coming.

[*Exeunt* INNOCENCE, TRIKA *and* BA. TORQUIL *frowns at the fishing-rod for a moment, lays it down, and goes to the doorway.*]

TORQUIL.   Ku!   Are you there?   Ku!

[*Enter* KU.]

KU.   Yes?   I was just seeing the Ponderers down the path. What is it?

TORQUIL.   Will you cook these three fish for Queen and me and Snor?   Kaa is going to live at the cave.   He'll have to catch his own fish after this.

KU.   They are beauties.

TORQUIL.   They wanted to be caught.   I pulled them out in a few minutes, one out 'tother come on. . . . Hello! What's the matter with you?

KU.   What do you mean by what's the matter with me? I'm all right.

TORQUIL.   What have you been doing to yourself?   You look quite different.

KU.   Do I?

TORQUIL.   Yes.   You looked a decent sort of poor woman yesterday, but today you look like a Camelot street-walker.

KU.   What is a street-walker?

TORQUIL.   A lady who walks in the streets.

KU.   What are streets?

TORQUIL.   Rows of houses with churches and shops and things.

KU.   It must be beautiful to be a lady who walks in streets.

TORQUIL.   Who taught you to make a—an image of yourself?

KU.   Queen taught me.

TORQUIL.   Good gracious Heavens almighty!

KU.   She said I wasn't making the best of myself.

TORQUIL.   She did, did she?

KU.   She said the men would look at me.

TORQUIL.   Oh, the men will look at you all right.   And the children will howl for their mothers, and horses will take fright and bolt.

KU.   You are talking very unkindly.   You will make me angry, and I shall have to be dipped.

TORQUIL.   A very good idea   It would wash all that filthy mess off your face.

[*Enter* MARGAUSE.]

KU.   Oh, Queen! He says I will frighten the horses!

MARGAUSE.   What does he mean by that?

TORQUIL.   Madame, you shouldn't have done this.

MARGAUSE.   I will not have my maid looking as if she had been pulled backwards through a thicket. Go away, Ku. I want to talk to this man. He is jealous of you because he is hideous.

KU.   Oh, is that it? I don't mind telling you now I'm beautiful, but I used to be jealous too, sometimes.

[*Exit* KU, *in good spirits.*]

MARGAUSE.   You are a very vulgar fellow, Torquil.

TORQUIL.   I know that, Madame, but . . .

MARGAUSE.   While we are on the Island, you may call me Queen. And you must not bandy pleasantries with the servants.

TORQUIL.   The servants?

MARGAUSE.   I said the servants.

TORQUIL.   There are no servants on this Island.

MARGAUSE.   There are servants everywhere. What extraordinary ideas you have in your head.

TORQUIL.   They have a byword on the Island that no man is good enough to be another man's master.

MARGAUSE.   That may be true of the Island. I think very little of the men I have seen. But it certainly does not apply to me.

TORQUIL.   Well, there may be natural-born slaves, and no doubt you will find them and make them fetch and carry for you. But that's no reason why you should corrupt them.

MARGAUSE.   The woman fetches and carries for you.

TORQUIL.   I know, but that's different. There's nothing degrading in doing services for other people. But that's not the point.

MARGAUSE.   What is the point, then, please?

TORQUIL.   The fact that she does us little services shouldn't debar her from ordinary human intercourse.

MARGAUSE.   Your idea of ordinary human intercourse is to tell her that she is ugly enough to frighten horses?

TORQUIL.   Well, so she is. She's painted like a jumping-Jack. Why? In the hope that worthless men will crowd

117   [39]

round her with their tongues hanging out.   You've corrupted
a decent woman with vanity and low ambition.

MARGAUSE.   My dear child, the lives of the people of this
Island are dull, drab and monotonous.   They might as well be
cattle.   I can hardly bear to look at them.

[TORQUIL *goes away from her, sits down and begins to carve a piece
of wood with his knife.*]

TORQUIL.   Can't you ?

MARGAUSE.   You said they needed an intenser form of life.
You said so yourself.   Why should I not bring a little colour
and gaiety into the Island ?

[*She goes over to him and begins to ruffle his hair.*]

TORQUIL.   Don't do that.

MARGAUSE.   You have nice hair.   I like ruffling it.   Why
should I not give them a little colour, Torquil ?

TORQUIL.   Does that include bathing in the creek with the
whole Island looking on ?

MARGAUSE.   I didn't see anybody.

TORQUIL.   They saw you all right.

MARGAUSE.   You're a strange fellow, Torquil.   You should
have been a monk.

TORQUIL.   No, I shouldn't.

MARGAUSE.   By the way, Qua is coming to lunch today.

TORQUIL.   Who is Qua ?   Oh, the big Ponderer with the
beard ?   We've only three fish.

MARGAUSE.   Then you can go and catch some more.

TORQUIL.   Why should I ?   I am not one of the servants.

MARGAUSE.   There is nothing degrading in doing services,
Torquil.

TORQUIL.   I know that.   But the sooner you learn that you
are not Queen here, the better it will be for you and for me and
for everybody.

[*He stands up and faces her.*]

MARGAUSE.   Why must you quarrel with me, Torquil ?

TORQUIL.   Because I am too much of a coward to kill you.

MARGAUSE (*turning away*).   I thought we had forgotten
that.

TORQUIL.   Why should I have forgotten ?   I haven't
changed my mind.   You're an idle, mischievous woman and
you're helping to ruin my Island.

[40]   118

MARGAUSE. Helping, am I? I am not the only evil influence, then?

TORQUIL. No. The other two are nearly as bad. I thought I could manage Grettir, but he's got the bit between his teeth. He told me he was a radical, but I'll never believe a business man again. He's out for himself, and he doesn't care what damage he does. And now the Padre's had a step up and got his own cure of souls, he's as narrow-minded as any persecuting Bishop. He's making nothing but trouble. And I thought he was an educated man.

MARGAUSE. And what have you been doing, besides finding fault with your comrades?

TORQUIL. How can I do anything? I can't get a word in edgeways—what with Grettir teaching them money-grubbing, and the Priest teaching them to genuflect and cross themselves, and you teaching them I don't know what.

MARGAUSE. You were going to make poets and artists and craftsmen. How many have you made?

TORQUIL. You can't do that without creating an atmosphere and building up a sound organisation.

MARGAUSE. Have you been creating and building, or whatever you call it? You seem to me to spend most of your time fishing.

TORQUIL. I've done what I could.

MARGAUSE. What was that?

TORQUIL. Well, I've set them asking themselves whether this stupid Brains Trust is as remarkable as it thinks it is.

MARGAUSE. Isn't it?

TORQUIL. No. I went to a session. It was simply childish. A more ignorant, dogmatic. . . . Half of them think the world is round!

MARGAUSE. Does She think the world is round?

TORQUIL. I don't know what She thinks. She isn't a bad sort if she didn't see herself as a cross between a Delphic Pythoness and a Nun running an infant school. She puts on that Chinese face and won't let herself be drawn. The others are contemptible. I tripped them up on more than a dozen points of detail and then came away. The people were all laughing and cheering.

MARGAUSE. That must have pleased the Ponderers.

TORQUIL. I don't suppose it did. But we'll make no pro-

dress till we've got rid of them. They're hopelessly out of
gate. And I can't begin to organise with all this piety and
penny-in-the-slot springing up everywhere. I no sooner
hammer an idea into a thick head than Innocence or Grettir
comes and steals the head from under my nose. It happened
only a few minutes ago again.

MARGAUSE. Oh? How?

TORQUIL. I thought it was important to get hold of the
youngsters, and I'd been talking to a very clever little girl—
really a brilliant child, and quite unspoilt. And then I meet
that damned fellow Innocence dragging her practically by the
hair of her head to his blasted baptismal font and just on the
point of marrying her to a reactionary lout of a sheep boy. It
makes me sick.

MARGAUSE. How very sad for you. But I expect you'll find
another brilliantly clever little girl quite soon. And the good
work can go on.

TORQUIL. If you *will* misunderstand me, I can't help it.

[GRETTIR *enters breezily ; with him* WAWA *and* KWOO.]

GRETTIR. Ah, Queen! I've brought these two boys to
lunch. Do you mind?

MARGAUSE. Not at all.

KWOO. I don't know whether I ought to wait. You see,
I have some rather important business at—at the top of the
mountain, in point of fact.

GRETTIR. Hooey! You'll meditate better on a full stomach.
I always do. Sit down, sit down. And I don't mind telling
you I've got a surprise for you. We'll get the table out first.
Come along, Shlup, old boy, bear a hand. . . . We're camping
out here for a bit in the meantime . . . but . . . I think I
can promise you . . . something you never imagined in your
lives before.

[TORQUIL *sulkily helps him to pull a table downstage.*]

Set the stools, old boy, and fetch some cups.

[TORQUIL *obeys.* GRETTIR *goes to his cubicle and returns with a
goatskin water-bag.*]

Wait till my new house is built. That will be an occasion.
We'll knock chips off the firmament that night, eh, Kwoo?
Not that this isn't an occasion too. Eh, Wawa? By the
way, is there anything to eat?

MARGAUSE. Torquil. Go and catch two more fish.

GRETTIR.   Yes.   And hurry, there's a good chap.   I could eat a whale.

[TORQUIL *hesitates for a moment.   Then takes his fishing-rod and goes.*]

[GRETTIR, *with a great air of mystery, pours a dark liquid into four of the cups.*]

Now, just see what you think of that. . . . Just a minute. Wait.   Queen, I have the honour to ask you to drink to the health of Messrs Snor, Wawa and Kwoo.

MARGAUSE.   It will be a pleasure.   To Messrs Snor, Wawa and Kwoo.

GRETTIR.   Incorporated.

MARGAUSE.   Incorporated.

[*They drink.*   WAWA *and* KWOO *cough a little and look astonished.* MARGAUSE *gazes on* GRETTIR *with a mild surmise.*]

GRETTIR.   Do you recognise it ?

MARGAUSE.   Yes.   It is Heather Ale.

GRETTIR.   Heather Ale it is.

MARGAUSE.   It's very rough and oily.   But there's no mistake about it.   Where did you get it ?

GRETTIR.   Aha !   Drink up and have another, gentlemen. That's none of your Ru-Rhush swipes.   Not a headache in a gallon, and every drop sets your toe-nails sparkling.

[*He refills the cups.*]

MARGAUSE (*as one who expects an answer*).   Where did you get it ?

GRETTIR.   I bought the recipe before we started.   Cost me a pretty penny, but it's worth it.   Then there's a little brewery at the other end of the Island.   I bought that too.

MARGAUSE.   How did you buy it ?   You have no money.

GRETTIR.   My good Queen, you don't need money to buy things !   All you need is a good honest tongue in your head. How do you like it, Kwoo ?

KWOO.   Very much indeed.

GRETTIR.   I thought you would.   That's the stuff to help your meditations.

KWOO (*giggles*).   Hehehe.

GRETTIR.   What about you, Wawa ?

WAWA.   It's very pleasant.   Very pleasant.   Very pleasant indeed.

GRETTIR. Good. Have some more. There's plenty where it came from.

KWOO. Pardon me. If we are to talk business . . .

GRETTIR. Plenty of time for that. There's no harm in oiling the wheels of commerce in the meantime.

WAWA. I think Kwoo is right. Yes. I agree with his opinion. I think we would be better to come to an agreement first and then, perhaps, celebrate our arrival at an agreement in a leetle more of this very salubrious beverage.

GRETTIR. Just as you like. Just as you like. . . . Oh, HELLO!

[QUA *appears rather nervously at the doorway.*]

WAWA. Who's that? What's that? Oh, Qua! There you are, my dear fellow! Did you wish to see anyone?

QUA. Well, as a matter of fact, Queen invited me to lunch.

GRETTIR. Oh, ah! Did you, Queen?

MARGAUSE. Yes. Come in, Qua, and sit down.

GRETTIR. Well, Madame, I mean to say, it's a little awkward.

KWOO. You see, Qua, this is, in a measure, a private meeting.

GRETTIR. Yes, Queen. I really think it would be better if you put him off till another day.

MARGAUSE. Am I deceived, or does some miserable person dare to insult my guest? (*rising in full majesty*). If it is so, let him remember with whom he has to deal. By God's Blue Hood, it will go ill with him if he forgets!

GRETTIR. No, no. Of course not, your Majesty. It was a little misunderstanding. Only a little misunderstanding. The gentleman is very welcome.

MARGAUSE (*more amiably*). Of course he is. Come, Qua, and sit by me.

GRETTIR. Will you try a little sup of the Heather Ale, Qua? It is my own particular brew.

[GRETTIR *fills* QUA's *cup and* MARGAUSE *drinks to him.*]

MARGAUSE. I hear that you attended Father Innocence's service this morning, Qua.

QUA. Yes. I did.

MARGAUSE. Did you enjoy it?

QUA. No.

[44]   122

MARGAUSE. Oh? I have never heard Father Innocence preach, but I am told that he is very eloquent.

QUA. That's as may be, but I am very suspicious of Kaa.

MARGAUSE. That's what you call Father Innocence? I beg your pardon. Why are you suspicious of him?

QUA. I think he is a god-man.

KWOO. We all suspected that, Madame.

MARGAUSE. Suppose he is what you call a god-man. What then?

KWOO. I don't know. She is of the opinion that we should throw them in the sea. But we have never had to do that in my time.

GRETTIR. Oh, nonsense! Throw him in the sea? I never heard of such a thing.

KWOO. Well, that's what She said.

QUA. I think She is right.

GRETTIR. Oh, my goodness! Have another drink.

[*He fills again.*]

MARGAUSE. Are you a violent man, Qua?

QUA. No, no. What made you think that?

MARGAUSE. You have such beautiful big muscles.

QUA. No. But we are happy on the Island, and we don't want the people to be made unhappy. Besides, we should only throw him in the sea. We shouldn't hurt him. And I'm told that whales are always standing by to swallow god-men and take them to places where they are of some use.

MARGAUSE. You must be the strongest man in Ru-Rhush.

QUA. I am pretty strong.

MARGAUSE. If I were a man, I shouldn't like to have to fight you.

QUA. Nobody fights here.

WAWA. Unheard of. Unheard of.

KWOO. Fighting? Dear, dear, dear.

MARGAUSE. Have you never fought?

QUA. Once or twice when I followed the sea. With savages and sailors and such like.

MARGAUSE. Tell me about it. Tell me about your fights.

QUA. I've forgotten them.

MARGAUSE. But you can't forget things like that. It's very bad to try to forget things. The memory eats at your heart like a maggot. Do you never feel a dark pain at your heart?

QUA. Yes. No. I don't want to talk about it. . . . I
once killed a man. . . . I don't want to talk about it.

[*He drinks to hide his confusion.*]

GRETTIR. Madame Queen and gentlemen, I think perhaps
that now Qua is here we ought to tell him what has brought
myself and his colleagues together. As you know, Madame, I
like to be open and above-board in everything.

MARGAUSE (*drinking*). That is very true, Snor.

[*She laughs a little and becomes suddenly solemn.*]

GRETTIR. I thank you, Madame, from the bottom of my
heart. My dear Qua, I was very pleased to hear how much
you valued the happiness of your beloved Island—perhaps I
may be allowed to call it *our* beloved Island. . . .

WAWA. Certainly. Certainly.

KWOO. Hear, hear.

GRETTIR. For, I may honestly say, although I have only
been here for a comparatively short time, I have been here long
enough to know that I have found my spiritual home. I feel,
may I say? that in the truest sense I am one of you.

KWOO. One of the best.

GRETTIR. I thank you.

KWOO. Don't mention it. Do you mind if I help myself?

GRETTIR. Do. Certainly. Yes. Do.

[KWOO *helps himself and the others.*]

Now, if there is one thing I hate, it is ingratitude.

KWOO. Bad thing that. I hate it too.

WAWA. Very bad. Shocking. So do I.

KWOO. So do you what, old boy?

WAWA. Hate it. I always have.

GRETTIR. I should feel myself ungrateful indeed if I did
nothing, in my small way, to repay the many acts of courtesy
and kindness I have received since I arrived somewhat precipitately on your shores (*to* QUA). I said as much to your
colleagues this very morning.

WAWA. Eh?

GRETTIR. I was saying that I said as much to you this
morning.

WAWA. As much as what?

GRETTIR. I said I would do as much as in me lay to repay
you.

[46]

WAWA.   That's right.   That's exactly what you said.

KWOO.   I like a man who says a thing straight out and sticks to it.   That's what he said.

GRETTIR.   We have only discussed the project in the vaguest and most tentative terms.   Neither party is bound by anything that was said.   It was all entirely without prejudice.   I hope you realise that, Qua?

MARGAUSE.   What mischief is this you have been hatching?

GRETTIR.   Oh, Madame, mischief?   I must take exception, very grave exception indeed, to the words that have fallen from your lips.   In the whole course of my career . . .

MARGAUSE.   Then why don't you get to the point?

GRETTIR.   I am coming to the point.

MARGAUSE.   Then what is it?   Have you found a gold mine?

GRETTIR.   Not yet, Madame, but I have found what I believe to be considerable deposits of copper.

QUA.   On the Island?

GRETTIR.   On the Island.   And, I believe, in such considerable quantity that to neglect their development would be flying in the face of Providence.   It would be impious.   Accordingly I have prepared a little provisional scheme.   Indeed, I have gathered together a few sturdy fellows and, between ourselves, we have opened up workings already.

QUA.   Have you spoken to She about this?

GRETTIR.   Not yet.   Not yet.   It's essential, of course, that we should take her with us.

WAWA.   Quite, quite, quite, quite, quite?

KWOO.   What did you say?

WAWA.   I said, " Quite."

KWO.   And I entirely agree with you.

WAWA.   Absolutely unanimous.

GRETTIR.   Good, good.   But there's quite a lot of spade-work still to be done before we can present She with a concrete proposal.

QUA.   She won't approve.   I know her.   She won't approve.

GRETTIR.   Now, I'm quite certain you're doing her an injustice.

KWOO.   Most unjust.   You are exceedingly unjust, Qua. Surprised at you.

WAWA.   Eh?   What did he say?

QUA.   He made quite an uncalled-for remark about She.

WAWA.   What's She got to do with it?

GRETTIR.   Exactly.   Our friend has put his finger on the point.

QUA.   You'll find out what She's got to do with it.

GRETTIR.   Well, well, all in good time, no doubt.   All in good time.   In the meantime, you probably remember what the proconsul of Iberia said to the proconsul of Gaul.

WAWA.   What did he say?   What did he say?

GRETTIR.   He said, " Tempus inter potiones longum est."

WAWA.   What does that mean.

GRETTIR.   It means, " Drink up and have another one."

QUA.   No.

GRETTIR.   Yes.

QUA.   No.

MARGAUSE.   Yes.

QUA.   All right, then.   Just a small one.

[MARGAUSE *and* QUA *drink to one another.   The others help themselves.   The atmosphere mellows.*]

GRETTIR.   That's better.   And when it comes to issuing stock, we shall not forget you.

WAWA.   We shall never forget you, Qua.   Gone but not forgotten.

GRETTIR.   Indeed, we should be very happy to welcome you on the Board of Directors.

KWOO.   And I shall be happy too, Qua.   Very, very happy.

WAWA.   We're all happy.   It is a very happy day.   It is delightful to see so many happy faces.

GRETTIR.   I hope they'll be happier still when the mine begins to pay dividends.

KWOO.   Hear, hear.

WAWA.   Hear, hear.

MARGAUSE.   Have your young men begun to dig?

GRETTIR.   At the mine, Madam?   Well, as a matter of fact they have.

MARGAUSE.   That is wonderful.   Qua, my Sailor, shall we go down to Grettir's lovely mine and watch the beautiful young men digging, with their rippling strong backs and great hairy chests?

GRETTIR.   You'll make us all jealous.   Besides, what about lunch?

[48]   126

MARGAUSE. Lunch? Are we having lunch?

GRETTIR. Yes. It's a luncheon party to celebrate the floating of the company.

MARGAUSE. The company is floating beautifully. How lucky we are, Grettir, to have lunch with such very charming and clever and powerfully built people. Snor, when I perform the State opening of the mine, you must promise me something.

GRETTIR. Only too pleased, Madame.

MARGAUSE. You must ask the little Chink woman. I think it would be a treat for her.

GRETTIR. I call that exceedingly handsome of your Ladyship.

MARGAUSE. Not at all. She's got few pleasures and she's a dear little thing. Why are you all so much afraid of her?

WAWA. What did she say?

KWOO. She said we were afraid of She. Ridiculous. Absurd. Haha!

QUA (standing up). I am not afraid of her nor of any man or woman on the living earth.

MARGAUSE. Then why do you look like a whipped dog when She is in the room?

QUA. When I followed the sea we were once attacked by a Lochlann galley out from Stavanger. They rammed us and they boarded us, and one big fellow in chain mail from head to foot came at me with his axe. I burst the straps and buckles of his helmet with my fist. I took him by the throat and bent him back over the rower's bank till his back broke. I took his axe and I said, " Come on, boys "; and at it we went like Billy be Damned till the last of them was drinking salt water . . . (he sits down rather suddenly) . . . them that could drink. With some of them the salt water didn't get very far down, because their throats were cut.

MARGAUSE. That's the sort of man you are?

QUA. That's the sort of man I am.

MARGAUSE. So you sit on this little Island and get fat and old and do exactly what the lady tells you. You don't do yourself justice, Sailor.

QUA. I'll do myself justice.

GRETTIR. I hope we all will. Roman Justice. And remember what the Proconsuls said in 85 B.C. Kwoo! Your mug is empty.

KWOO. By Jove, so it is!

MARGAUSE.   Sailor, darling, don't look so gloomy!   Look
at your friends there and think merry thoughts.   Think how
like a skull Kwoo is.   And how hundreds and hundreds of
years from now, when we have all changed, he will look exactly
the same.   Dear Kwoo!   Will you sing me a song ?

> [KWOO *at once stands up unsteadily and begins to sing.*]

KWOO.   O, I had an old wheelbarrow
And I had a pig in a sty.
And somebody wheeled me home in the one
And in the other laid me down to lie.
For I had had a night with the Barley Brew,
The Barley Brew, the Barley Brew.
And all jolly fellows love the Barley Brew,
As they come toddling home,
Toddling home,
As they come toddling home.

You join in the Chorus.   It's no good unless you join in the
Chorus.

So we'll all have a night with the Barley Brew
The Barley Brew, the Barley Brew . . . &c.

> [GRETTIR *and* WAWA *join in the Chorus, dancing solemnly with
> their arms round each other's necks.*]

MARGAUSE.   Don't you adore seeing the little ones enjoy
themselves ?

QUA.   You don't like seeing them enjoy themselves.   You
like to see them playing the fool.

MARGAUSE.   Isn't that the same thing ?

> [KWOO *has now joined in the dance.*]

Look!   The little death's head is holding himself up by
hanging onto the old trool's beard.

GRETTIR. ⎫ Toddling home.
WAWA.   ⎬ Toddling home.
KWOO.   ⎭ As we go toddling home!

> [*Enter* KU *with a platter of baked fish.   She stands still in astonish-
> ment.*]

WAWA.

With my fal and my fal and my tiddley ow de dow . . .
Oh, look, look, look, see, see.   A beautiful lady!

Come, come, come.   Dance with me.

[*He makes a rush at* KU, *who drops the platter and runs out of the door.*]

[WAWA *runs out after her.*]

KWOO.   Stop him.   Come back.   Stop him!

[*He runs out after* WAWA.   GRETTIR *strolls over to the table.*]

GRETTIR.   Going very well, isn't it ?

MARGAUSE.   Delightfully pastoral.

GRETTIR.   Pity about the lunch, but we'll get some more. What about you, Qua ?   Have a spot.

QUA.   Damned old fools.

GRETTIR.   Oh, I don't know.   They're pretty keen business men.   You need a little relaxation after swinging a deal.   But seriously, old boy, you'd better come in with us.   Her Majesty will tell you it's a pretty sound proposition.

MARGAUSE.   I know nothing about it.

GRETTIR.   Now, you're not being fair to yourself.   You showed a pretty keen grasp of the business side of it a minute or two ago.

MARGAUSE.   It is a part of my station to appear to have a grasp of matters in which I have not the slightest interest.

GRETTIR.   Oh, come now.   We're doing a public service.

MARGAUSE.   A very dignified act.

GRETTIR.   Oh, Qua and I aren't ashamed of serving the public.   The service of our fellow-creatures is one of the noblest of all services.   Nay more, I have no hesitation   . .

[*Enter* TORQUIL *supporting* KWOO *and* WAWA.]

TORQUIL.   What's all this ?

KWOO.   We fell down.   Atcha, atcha and we both fell down.

MARGAUSE.   I hope you didn't hurt yourself—in the public service.

KWOO.   No, no.   Just fell down.

WAWA.   Let's get on with the party.   These women spoil the ball.

KWOO.   I think I ought to let you know how I feel.   I feel fine.

[*He slips on one of the fish and falls to the ground.*   TORQUIL *helps him up, hindered by* WAWA.]

WAWA.   Be careful.   I beseech you to be careful.

KWOO. Why? What care I? Where was I?

[*SHE appears in the doorway with* KU *in the background.*]

Oh, She! There you are, there you are, there you are! We are all going to be very rich, She. In a very little time you won't know your Island. But it is a secret. It is a great secret. Hush! Not a word. . . . We have had a very pleasant little gathering. Very pleasant and agreeable indeed. I wish you had come earlier. I . . . We missed you very much. Naturally. And now, I think I shall go for a little walk in the fresh air. . . . I think, Snor, you said that there was no more competent business? A little walk in the fresh air.

[*He goes out fairly steadily, brushing against the door-post to pass* SHE.]

WAWA. I was seeing him on his way to the top of the Mountain and we dropped in. Yes. We dropped in. Snor, here, very kindly asked us if we would rest here for a moment. Se we just—dropped in. Qua, are you going my way?

QUA. No . . . Yes. Perhaps I had better. By the way, She, I shall not be at the meeting this evening. I have—an important appointment.

[*He takes* WAWA *by the arm and helps him round the immobile* SHE *and out at the door.* KU *takes* WAWA's *other arm and the three disappear,* KU *saying, " Poor old man, he's not very well. Hold up, grandfather,"* &c.]

GRETTIR. If you will excuse me, perhaps I had better see my guests on their way. Perhaps you will be here when I come back. Good morning. I think it's going to rain.

[*Exit* GRETTIR. *The sky has gradually become overcast.* SHE *stands facing* QUEEN MARGAUSE *in a gloomy light.* TORQUIL, *at back, between them, looking at* SHE.]

SHE. My advice to you is that you should go down to the creek. You will find there a curragh with water and provisions. I think that you and your friends should go there now; and that you should sail out of the lagoon and never come back here any more.

[*Distant thunder.*]

TORQUIL. It is gathering up for the father and mother of a storm. We should be lost.

MARGAUSE. It is your desire that we, your guests, should go out in a cockleshell into a mighty storm?

SHE.   I have no control over storms.   I have been told that the binding and loosening of hurricanes is one of the perquisites of a Witch.

MARGAUSE.   Suppose we do not accept your so generous and tender advice?   Suppose we do not go?

SHE.   Whatever you decide, we should give you back to the sea.

MARGAUSE.   Who is the one whose duty it is to commit us to the sea?

SHE.   Qua will arrange what is to be done.

MARGAUSE.   I do not think he will.

SHE.   Have you corrupted him too?   Your evil souls spread over my Island like the rust on the barley.

[SHE *goes wearily to the table and sits down.* MARGAUSE *and* TORQUIL *watch her intently.*]

We have a saying on the Island,

> " Shut the North window,
>   Shut quickly the South one,
>   Bar the one to the West,
>   But evil never came from the East."

It was on the East bay that the sea laid the four of you.

Long before my mother was born we killed the worshippers of the great Snake and tore down the altars where they had murdered our children.   We broke our spears and slings and arrows and threw our gold into the sea.   No rovers molested us for they feared the girdle of holiness that ringed our Island and the spirits of our dead watching over our fields.   For ten generations we have kept the Island clean.

MARGAUSE.   And empty.   It is an empty Island.

SHE.   No.   No.   No.   It is full of honour and friendship and the work of strong arms and hard hands.

MARGAUSE.   Your woman, Ku, told me a story.   Shall I tell it to you?

SHE.   I shall not hear it.   My ears are full of old voices crying shame on me.

MARGAUSE.   Nevertheless. . . .   Long before your mother was born there were three Giants in Ru-Rhush, and they lived in a cave.   And one day one of the Giants said, " I think I hear a cow mooing."   And a year and a day passed.   And then

the second Giant said, " What did you say ? "   And a year and
a day passed.   And then the third Giant said, " If you two
can't stop gabbling, you can have the cave to yourselves."

SHE.   It is the distant Island
Ringed by shining sea-horses,
Coursing against the white-swelling surge,
And it stands on feet of bronze.

Four feet of white bronze
Glittering through the lovely ages,
And on its ancient head
The coloured blossoms fall.

They fall from the Tree of Blossoms,
From whose boughs the birds call,
Naming the Hours as they pass,
Singing in sweet harmony.

Harmony never broken
By wailing of women
Or hiss of the traitor
Over the broad, kind fields.

Joy flew down to the land
That echoed with laughter and songs
Into Ru-Rhush, the calm place,
To nest and abide for ever,

To the kind land, the clear land,
To the sun-warmed cliffs
And the silver sea
And the long, long summer day.

MARGAUSE.   That is Tir nan Og.   That is the Island of
Youth and Dreams.   Perhaps we shall go there when we die.
But in the meantime there is life to be lived.

SHE.   What do you mean by life ?

MARGAUSE.   The time we spend between a very undignified
birth and a highly disagreeable death.   It is divided into small
spaces called minutes and hours.   We must tame those minutes,
or they will tick in our heads and drive us mad.   It is all very
well for your birds to sing to the Hours, but the Hours are
enemies and the birds are traitors.   Life is Time, and Time
is unbearable.   That is why man is a restless thing.   That is

[54]   132

why you must give your Islanders something to do, or they will rush down a steep place into the sea.

SHE. You must be a very idle person, Queen. The Islanders tame the earth till it gives them food, and sweep the sea till it gives them fish, and tend the herds till they give them clothing, and they build shelters for their families and barns for their grain. If you did those things, you would begin to love the hours and minutes instead of hating them.

MARGAUSE. And I should get dull-eyed and bow-backed like your Islanders.

SHE. They are not dull-eyed. They have thousands of things to see. They are not bow-backed. They have no masters and can look each other in the face. When they have done what they must do, they make songs to please their ears. They weave cloths to please their eyes. And they tell each other stories.

MARGAUSE. Stories! I have heard some of their stories.

SHE. The stories tell them that other people think and feel and act as they do. They bring to them the ever new surprise that they are not alone in the world.

MARGAUSE. Your songs are awful. Your clothes are hideous. And your stories are flat and wearisome.

SHE. Then bring us new songs and better stories and prettier clothes. But the things you have brought are not like that.

MARGAUSE. We have brought you nothing but ourselves. We are what we are. Do you wish to change us?

SHE. You are people who cannot leave your neighbours alone.

MARGAUSE. People who are indifferent to their neighbours might as well be toads in a rock.

SHE. This morning I came on a hundred young men digging for rubbish in the ground. A little later the fishermen came to me and asked me why they were not paid money for catching fish. They had never heard of money till you came.

MARGAUSE. What did you tell them?

SHE. I told them that money was rubbish and that it was only paid to idiots for finding rubbish.

MARGAUSE. What did they say to that?

SHE. They said they would like to dig for rubbish too.

MARGAUSE. And will they?

133   [55]

SHE.   How should I know ?   I don't know my people any
more.   That poor decent woman who cooks your food for you
is painted like an idol and postures like a cow dancing a hornpipe.
Half the men and women in the Island are talking through their
noses like your god-man.   They're all blown out with pride
and hatred.   They despise their brothers who are ignorant
and hate their brothers who are happy.   And they think they
can do what they like because another god-man took the responsibility five hundred years ago.   So they do wickedness
meanly and with no zest.   And the miners are tired and dirty
and fight among themselves for stupid bits of parchment.   And
where the mine is the Island is torn up and the air is filthy with
smoke.   I wish you had been indifferent, like toads.

TORQUIL.   If you would only come off your high horse and
listen to me . . .

SHE.   Why should I listen to you ?

TORQUIL.   Because I sympathise with nearly everything
you've said.   And I'm willing to help you.

SHE.   You brought these people here.

TORQUIL.   I can explain all that.

SHE.   What good will that do ?   They are cleverer than you
are.   And they've had practical experience and know what
they want.   You are only a chatterbox.

TORQUIL.   But if you would listen, you would see that I am
on your side.

SHE.   I have plenty of chatterboxes on my side.

MARGAUSE.   What is all this talk of taking sides ?   You and
your people have been very good to us.   We have nothing but
the kindest and most grateful feelings towards you.   But even
if we wanted your people to live in our way, how could we compel them to do it ?   We are only three foolish men and one
woman.   If your people are behaving strangely, it is because
they want to behave like that.   I don't see what we can do.
What do you want us to do ?

SHE.   I want you to go away.

MARGAUSE.   But, my good woman, we can't go away.   We
should be drowned.   I was very nearly drowned before and I
certainly don't want to repeat the experience.

SHE.   I shall give you a little ship and sailors.   Only, you
must go.

MARGAUSE.   I have been badly brought up.   The word

" must " has never been used to me.   You will forgive me if I
do not understand it.

TORQUIL.   What will you do if we stay ?

SHE.   I shall struggle and struggle and struggle against you
with all my heart and mind until you go away.

MARGAUSE.   Against four poor castaways ?   It would be a
very unequal struggle if it were possible.   But it is not against
us you will be fighting.

SHE.   What do you mean ?   I do not believe in Devils.

MARGAUSE.   You will be fighting against one of the natural
Forces.   Against human nature, my dear.

SHE.   I trust human nature if it is left alone.   But even if
you goad it into madness, I will fight it and you.

[SHE *gets up.*]

MARGAUSE.   You are determined to be our enemy ?

[*A clap of thunder,* SHE *flinches.*]

Ah !   There is the thunderstorm.   I thought it was coming.
You had better stay here till it passes over.   Or would you rather
go out and fight with Nature ?

SHE.   I hate thunderstorms.

MARGAUSE.   I love them.

[MARGAUSE *moves to the doorway and stretches out her arms to the
storm.* SHE *follows her.*]

SHE.   Let me pass, please.

MARGAUSE.   But you can't go out in this.   It's dangerous.

SHE.   I know.   Please let me pass.

[MARGAUSE *and* SHE *are facing each other from opposite sides of the
doorway.*]

I'm only an ignorant Island woman and you are a great
Queen, but I'll beat you.

[SHE *pulls her garments tightly round her and goes out.*]

MARGAUSE (*through roll of thunder*).   O sweet white lightning,
questing out of the sky, lay your long finger on that impudent,
obstinate, tiresome little creature and shrivel her to a cinder.

[*Coming back into the room.*]

I think that would be best.   Don't you ?

TORQUIL.   I don't know.

MARGAUSE.   Of course you don't know.   You know hardly
anything.   But, believe me, it would be best.   My God !

She almost persuaded me.   . . Why do you look so serious?
Has she persuaded you?

TORQUIL.   No.

MARGAUSE.   You are not going to desert us?

TORQUIL.   No, Madame.

MARGAUSE.   My little Shlup;

> [*She enfolds him suddenly in a passionate embrace to the accompaniment of a lively Towrowrow of thunder.*]

CURTAIN.

ACT III

*The same Scene as in Act II, except that some bright designs in primary
colours have been added to the hangings and a good deal of rough but
stylised furniture has been added. The log pile has been removed
and a basket fire has been erected in the corner of the dwelling. It
is smoking a little when the scene opens.* KWOO *is the only occupant
of the room. He is rocking two cradles. It is early morning—
two years after Act II.*

KWOO. Quiet then. Quiet then. There's nothing to
howl about. The daylight will soon be here. Your stupid
little Mammy will soon be here. All the nice ladies who
know how to manage little brutes like you will soon be here.
Don't cry. Old Kwoo is tired. Very tired. He needs a
little sleep at his time of life, does old Kwoo.

I know, I know. It's teething. It hurts a bit. I know.
Though what in the name of goodness you want teeth for, I
can't imagine. I was never really happy till I lost mine. But
people will insist on growing teeth. Nasty things, with their
gnashing and grinding and biting. You haven't been on the
Island very long, but you'll find that out. People who come
to the Island find things out sooner or later. Four people
came to the Island three long years ago. They all found out
things except one who knew too much before he came. If
he weren't a harmless idiot we should have to give him back
to the sea. The others have their faults, but they are all
right. The wicked old man has stopped doing harm and
wanders about in a dream smelling like an old wine cask.
The skinny sour man has stopped bullying us and goes about
smiling and pestering the Ponderer with his childish questions;
but his manners have greatly improved. The crazy-eyed
woman with the long black hair . . .

[WAWA *enters, drawing back the door-curtain and letting in a flood of
daylight. He is seen to be carrying a couple of babies' bottles
made of goatskin.*]

KWOO. Hello, Wawa! Is it you? Is it morning?

WAWA. It's long past morning. The sun has crossed the
summit of Cash a Ru.

KWOO. It is very active for its years. I must have dozed off.

WAWA (*giving babies their bottles*). Diddums then, the weeny, teeny, naughty ickle duckies. Did they want their nice bekky? What sort of a night did you have?

KWOO. A highly musical evening. Wooch! I am stiff.

WAWA. Have you had your breakfast?

KWOO. I had a bit of something an hour or two ago. I've got no appetite.

WAWA. Well, I hope you remembered we've got a Session this morning.

KWOO. What kind of a Session?

WAWA. A Ponderers' Session. We are the only two-ah-um-available. The Questioner may be here at any minute.

KWOO. Only one?

WAWA. Only one, so far as I know.

KWOO. The same one?

WAWA. Yes. The same one.

KWOO. He is becoming a perfect pest. I mean it.

WAWA. He has a great deal to learn.

KWOO. Had we better put these little beasts into the kitchen?

WAWA. No. Wait till Ku comes back. She may be any minute now. . . . They've been very lucky. They've had a fine night for it.

KWOO (*moving seats*). We'll sit over here and he can sit there. You'd better do most of the talking.

WAWA. Very well, very well. But you'll have to remind me of things.

KWOO. I'll prod you with this poker if you go to sleep.

WAWA. It isn't that I go to sleep. I can't remember things. How long is it since the Four Strangers came?

KWOO. Three years.

WAWA. It seems like yesterday.

KWOO. Everything seems like yesterday. And yesterday was an abominable day

WAWA. Everything seemed to go wrong.

KWOO. Everything did go wrong. . . . How the Four Strangers have changed! Except the young fellow and he is a born fool.

WAWA. Even he is a different kind of born fool since Queen deserted him.

KWOO. Hush!

[Enter INNOCENCE.*]*

INNOCENCE.   Good morning, gentlemen.

WAWA.   Good morning, Kaa, good morning.   A fine morning, a fine morning.   Won't you sit down?

INNOCENCE.   I thank you.

[He sits.]

KWOO.   Good morning, Kaa.

INNOCENCE.   Good morning, Ponderer.

WAWA.   Well, now, what's your difficulty today, hey? What can we do for you?

INNOCENCE.   Do you remember on Tuesday you told me that I had better, perhaps, do exactly what I liked?

WAWA.   Yes, yes.

INNOCENCE.   I tried my best all Wednesday.   But I couldn't be sure that I was doing *exactly* what I liked.

WAWA.   Hey?   Hey?   How was that, eh?

INNOCENCE.   I couldn't be sure what I liked.

WAWA.   A serious difficulty that, Kwoo.

KWOO *(dozing)*.   Eh?   Oh, no.   I shouldn't be surprised.

WAWA.   Give *me* the poker.

INNOCENCE.   And early on Thursday morning I had a most extraordinary dream.

WAWA.   Had you?   Had you?

INNOCENCE.   Yes.   It was all very vivid.   I dreamed I had a tame camelopard in my cell and I was feeding it chopped ptarmigan and cheese, when who should come in but my Bishop. I said, " Good morning, my Lord," and he said, " Good morning, my son."   And then he said, " I wouldn't give him that. He won't thrive on that."   And I said, " What shall I give him, my Lord? "   And he said, " I should feed him Father Abraham's boots."   And I said, " But I haven't got our Father Abraham's boots.   He died in them, and was buried in them." And he said, " Um!   That is certainly a difficulty.   But there is a Diocesan Conference going on just now.   We had better put the point to them."   So he took me to the Conference and there was I, sitting on a bench full of Bishops, with nothing on but a hair shirt and it was very short.   Then I awoke.   But before I awoke, I had an impression that it was the Day of Judgment.

KWOO.   What gave you that impression?

INNOCENCE.   I thought I heard a trumpet sounding.

(*Starting.*) What was that?   [*A trumpet sounds.*]

KWOO. Probably singing in your ears. What had you been eating the night before?

INNOCENCE. But I heard a trumpet now.

KWOO. Now?

INNOCENCE. While we were speaking.

KWOO. Wake up, Wawa. He says he heard a trumpet.

WAWA. A what?

KWOO. A trumpet. Just now.

WAWA. What had he been eating the night before?

INNOCENCE (*rising*). I am certain that I heard a trumpet.

KWOO (*kindly*). Sit down, Kaa. You are not very well. You have noises in your head. And the dream also shows that you are not very well.

INNOCENCE. Oh, do you think so? Is it serious?

KWOO. Oh, no. Wawa and I have pondered several cases like yours. What you must do is to take the weight off your stomach.

INNOCENCE. How shall I do that, Ponderer?

KWOO. Can you stand on your head?

INNOCENCE. I have never tried.

KWOO. A pity. It is also an excellent cure for bunions.

INNOCENCE. I could get Ba and Trika to hold me up by the feet.

KWOO. Excellent idea. Most excellent. Three times a day, after food. You have nothing further to suggest, Wawa?

WAWA. What? I? No. No. I don't think so. No.

[*All three rise.*]

INNOCENCE. Well, I am very much obliged to you, gentlemen. Very much obliged to you indeed. And if I think of anything else in the afternoon . . .

[*Fanfare, quite near now.*]

There it is again!

KWOO. Bless my soul, it *is* a trumpet!

WAWA. Shlup was practising yesterday on the ram's horn.

KWOO. That was played by a professional.

[*The* JARL *of the First Act suddenly appears at the door in full chain armour with his battle-axe at the ready.*]

JARL (*in a loud commanding tone*). Drop your swords and pikes and turn your faces to the wall.

[62]   140

KWOO.   But we haven't got any swords and pikes.

JARL.   Turn your faces to the wall, then, and don't answer back.

[*They obey. The* JARL *examines the room rapidly, pulling aside the alcove curtains and peering in. He stumbles on one of the cradles and a yell from it rises on the air.*]

JARL.   What's that?

KWOO.   A baby.

JARL.   Whose baby? Yours?

KWOO.   No, no. Not at all. Certainly not.

JARL.   Yours?

WAWA.   No. No. In point of fact, no.

JARL.   Yours?

INNOCENCE.   No, Sir Lachlan of the Cats, it isn't mine.

JARL.   What the . . . How do you know my name? Turn round.

[INNOCENCE *turns round.*]

One monk looks very much like another, but I should know that face. . . . Keep that infernal child quiet, somebody.

WAWA.   Did the little dumplekins get a f'ight from big soldjie man? Poor ickle pootlums and naughty soldier.

JARL.   Keep your personalities to yourself, will you?

WAWA.   Certainly. Certainly.

[*He gives the baby his beard to play with.*]

JARL.   Are you the Priest who sailed with Grettir Flatface from Kirkwall three years ago?

INNOCENCE.   I am, Sir Lachlan.

JARL.   Thank the Lord for that!   [*He goes to the doorway.*]
My Lord! My Lord! We're on the track at last! I've found the Monk!

LOT (*distant*).   Oh? Splendid! Hold on to him, then. I'm coming up!

[*The* JARL *takes off his helmet and wipes his brow.*]

JARL.   Don't you run away now. My Glory! What a piece of luck! We've combed every Island to the edges of the world, and we find it at last, by a cross wind.

[*Enter* KING LOT, *very splendid, with huge grey goose feathers on his helmet.*]

Here he is, Lord King. I didn't question him. I left that to you.

LOT. Quite right. Quite right. Let me see. What is your name, Father?

INNOCENCE. Innocence, my Lord.

LOT. Of course. I remember. Uncommon name. Well, what have you been doing here? Converting the Heathen?

[KWOO *and* WAWA *turn round gingerly and listen to the conversation.*]

INNOCENCE. Heathen? Oh, no, my Lord. Not Heathen.

[JARL *stands at the door watching.*]

LOT. These two gentlemen aren't Heathen, then? They look it.

INNOCENCE. My Lord, I have had occasion to revise many of my hasty judgments.

LOT. Indeed?

INNOCENCE. I have held too closely to the letter of the Law and thought too little of the spirit. What I have lost, perhaps, in confidence, I have gained in breadth of outlook.

JARL (*at door*). Hi! You! Come here, will you? . . . It's Torquil, my Lord. The young Sailor.

LOT. Oh? Good. I can't quite make out what this fellow is talking about.

[*Running footsteps and enter* TORQUIL. *He kneels on one knee to* LOT.]

TORQUIL. My Lord, thank God you've come. I saw your ships in the bay.

INNOCENCE. Just one word more. These Ponderers are very good teachers. And I find nothing whatever inconsistent between their teaching and that of those who . . .

LOT. Stop this rigmarole and tell me where the Queen is?

INNOCENCE. I cannot tell you that, Sir.

TORQUIL. My Lord . . .

LOT. One at a time. What do you mean, man?

INNOCENCE. I am not at liberty to tell you.

LOT (*seizing him by the throat*). By God's blue hood, I'll find means to make you! Out with it. Is she here . . . on the Island?

INNOCENCE. Yes.

LOT. Where is she, then?

INNOCENCE. If I told you, I should be breaking an unalterable rule which makes such things a matter of the strictest confidence.

[64]   142

LOT (*shaking him*).   Tell me the truth, man.   Tell me the truth !

TORQUIL.   My Lord, my Lord.   You'll kill him.   I'll tell you.

INNOCENCE.   Don't listen to him.   He has no right to tell you.

TORQUIL.   She is safe and well.   You will see her very soon.

LOT.   Why couldn't he say that at first ?

INNOCENCE.   You wouldn't let me.

TORQUIL.   My Lord, he isn't quite responsible.   You must be patient with him.

LOT.   Why ?

TORQUIL.   He has gone native.

LOT.   His Bishop will deal with that.

INNOCENCE.   Oh ?   Is my Lord here ?

LOT.   Yes.

INNOCENCE.   I am glad of that.   Very, very glad.

LOT.   Where's the Queen ?

TORQUIL.   My Lord, they have a barbarous custom here . . .

LOT.   By the Man of Hoy, if they've laid a finger on her I'll cut every gizzard in the Island.

KWOO.   I think I can explain, Sir.

LOT.   Explain ?   Explain ?   Explain ?   What do you mean by explain ?   Who are you, anyhow ?

KWOO.   My colleague and I have the honour to be humble members of the Court of Ponderers.   My name is Kwoo.   My colleague is Wawa.   The functions of this Court, to put the thing in a very few words . . .

LOT.   I have had enough of words.   Do you know who I am ?

KWOO.   I imagined that you might be Queen's husband, Sir.

LOT.   I am.   I've been hunting for my wife for three years, and you dish me out a pudding of words.   What—have—you—done with—my—WIFE ?

KWOO.   She has been dipped.

LOT.   What ?

KWOO.   And directed to the Mountain of Meditation.

WAWA.   With several others.

LOT.   Dipped ?   How ?   Where ?

KWOO.   In the sea.   You see, she lost her temper.

LOT.   She lost her temper ?

WAWA.   Yes.   She wasn't the only one.   It was a most discreditable business.

143   [65]

KWOO.   You see, Sir, it was about the babies.

LOT.   Babies ?   What babies ?

WAWA.   Here they are, Sir.   Nice little fellows.   Pulling away at their breakfast.   Chick, chick !   Cluck, cluck !

LOT (*after a short pause*).   Are these infants . . . are these my wife's children ?

KWOO.   Oh, no, Sir.   Not strictly speaking.

LOT.   What do you mean by strictly speaking ?

KWOO.   She adopted them.   Queen is very fond of children.

LOT.   Oh !

WAWA.   And Queen is a very strong-minded woman.

LOT.   You are presenting me with facts of which I was already fully aware.   But are you standing there and telling me that you dipped Her Serene Majesty, the Queen of Orkney, Strathclyde and the Lothians, in the sea ?   Or perhaps I did not hear you aright.

TORQUIL.   It's only fair to say that it was with her own consent.

LOT.   She consented to be immersed in the ocean by a pack of savages ?

TORQUIL.   I'm sorry to say, Sir, that her Majesty has gone a little native too.

WAWA.   She didn't entirely consent, Sir, when it came to the actual dipping.   She bit Qua.

LOT.   Bit what ?

WAWA.   Bit his hand.   Right to the bone.

LOT.   I have heard of Islands where the inhabitants had their heads turned round looking to the back instead of the front ; but I thought they were born that way.   I never imagined that it could be infectious.

KWOO.   You see, she had a row with She.   She was as much to blame as she was.   She lost her temper as badly as she did.   We dipped She too.

LOT.   What is all this charivari of She's ?

WAWA.   We are no respecters of persons on this Island.

TORQUIL.   The woman they call She is a sort of chieftainess on the Island.

WAWA (*proudly*).   She is a Ponderer.

KWOO.   You see, Queen adopted Trika's twins, because Trika was too silly to look after them.   And Queen wanted to put barley meal and a spoonful of Heather Ale in their goat's

milk, and She said that was all wrong.   And Queen said that
she had brought up six children and buried four, and that She
didn't know what she was talking about.   And then they had
words.

WAWA.   And everybody took sides.   And Queen slapped
She and Trika slapped Queen and Snor slapped Trika.   So they
all had to be dipped.

LOT.   I have never in my life heard of anything so squalid.
What has been happening on this Island?

TORQUIL.   Sir, you may well ask.   I hope that I am as free
from prejudice as my neighbours, but . . .

LOT.   You have changed too.

TORQUIL.   Sire?

LOT.   Let me think.   I remember you both quite well.
Both of you.   And the padre seems to have gone all to pieces
and you seem to have . . . tightened up, somehow.

TORQUIL.   I've recently had to exercise a good deal of
restraint.

LOT.   I remember you as an enthusiastic ass, but I don't
remember you as a prig.   What's happened to you?

TORQUIL.   Nothing has happened to *me*.

LOT.   You *are* a prig, you know.

TORQUIL.   As your Majesty pleases.

INNOCENCE.   We have all changed.   It has been a great,
an enlightening experience.   This is a Holy Island.

LOT.   You'll have to fill up some of the holes before I can
find my way about in it.   Stop sulking, you, and go on.

TORQUIL.   Sir, I have not changed in the least.   But I have
not forgotten that I come from the mainland.   The others
have.   That is all.

LOT.   That is not all.   Go on.

TORQUIL.   I found the Island.   I was prepared to give all
that I had, the last breath in my body, to help it to find its soul.
But of all the slack-minded, ignorant, obstinate, superstitious,
dyed-in-the wool barbarians . . .

KWOO.   Now, now, Shlup.   Be careful.   You will have
to be dipped.

TORQUIL.   I will not be dipped.   Just you try it!   And
don't call me Shlup.

LOT.   The Queen has gone to some Mountain.   Where
is it?

145   [67]

TORQUIL.   It is the only mountain in the Island.   They are inordinately proud of it.   It is the mountain behind this hovel. I shall show you the track.

LOT.   No, I'll find it myself.   Come with me, Lachlan. . . . Wait all of you here till I come back.   I haven't decided what to do.   No.   Padre, go down to the beach and tell them not to disembark the stores till I come back.   Take these two men with you.   The Quartermaster will want fresh water and some cattle.

KWOO.   But I was left in charge of the babies.

LOT.   Torquil will look after the babies.

TORQUIL.   My Lord, I don't know whether I could.   I've had no experience of . . .

LOT.   You'll get some now.   Be off, the rest of you.   Look sharp.   Come, Lachlan.

[*Exeunt, after some ceremony,* LOT, *the* JARL, INNOCENCE *and the* TWO PONDERERS.   *The* TWINS *begin to cry.*   TORQUIL *does his best to pacify them, but is soon at his wits' end.*]

TORQUIL.   Now, then.   Now, then.   It's all right. Mummy's coming.   You mustn't cry.   Here's a pretty thing for you.   And a pretty thing for you.   Damn!   The bottles are empty.   Now then.   Now then.   Oh, shut up, you little Devils.   You're driving me mad.

[*Enter* TRIKA *and* BA :   TRIKA *runs to the* TWINS, *who are instantly quiet.*]

TRIKA.   What were they doing to Mummy's precious pair ? Mustn't cry like that. . . . Hello, Shlup.   What are you doing here ?

TORQUIL.   Looking after your damned brats.

TRIKA.   I've just got down from the Mountain, I ran all the way.   I thought the Ponderers were here.   Ba and I want to see them.

TORQUIL.   Well, you can't see them.

TRIKA.   Oh, what a pity !   It's most important.   Isn't it, Ba ?

BA.   Yes.

TRIKA.   We were going to ask them about you, you see.

TORQUIL.   Me ?

TRIKA.   Yes.   You're always hanging about and bothering me when I don't want to be bothered, and Ba and I talked it over, and we decided that if it went on we would get angry and lose our tempers and be dipped, so we thought we'd ask the Ponderers, you see.

BA.   That's right.   [*He grins foolishly.*]

TORQUIL.   That's what you thought, was it?

BA.   Yes. We thought that. Trika and me.

TORQUIL.   Well, mind your own business . . . and take that grin off your face.

BA.   Eh?

TORQUIL.   Do you hear me? Take that grin off your face. . . . You won't, won't you? I'll show you whether I'm funny or not.

> [*He attacks* BA; *after a moment of astonishment,* BA *defends himself. The two roll together on the floor.*]

TRIKA.   Mind the cradles. Pull his hair, Ba. That'll make him stop. Wait a minute. Hold his head steady a minute and I'll pull it myself.

> [*Enter* QUA. *His arm is in a sling.*]

Oh, good morning, Qua. Shlup jumped at Ba, and I think they are fighting.

QUA.   What are they fighting about?

TRIKA.   About me, I think.

QUA.   They'd better stop. She is coming down the track.

> [*He lifts the combatants to their feet and sends* TORQUIL *staggering with a heavy push.*]

TORQUIL.   My God! Don't you hit me again!

QUA.   All right. But if you roll on the floor you will get hurt.

TORQUIL.   You shan't bully me. The day for bullying is finished, do you hear? We're going to have a little order on this Island at last. We'll see how you like it. I'm going down to the beach.

QUA.   All right. I'll come down presently and dip you.

TORQUIL.   See if you can dip the troops of the King of Orkney.

> [*Exit* TORQUIL, *in a passion.*]

TRIKA.   What a stupid fellow! He jumped at Ba without a word of warning. He is very rough.

BA.   That's right. I had the greatest job not hurting him.

QUA.   Well, don't discuss him now. The Ponderers will deal with him when they have time. I expect we shall be very busy for a day or two. Queen's man friend has arrived.

TRIKA.   But I thought she had lots of men friends.   I thought you were one.

QUA.   That's as may be, but I think this one is tied up like you and Ba.   He's looking for her.

TRIKA.   Oh, he's not going to take her away in all these ships, I hope.   Has he found her ?

QUA.   No.   He asked me the way to the top of the Mountain, and I put him on the wrong track.   I wanted time to ponder for a bit.

TRIKA.   It would be terrible if he took her away.   Who would look after the twins ?

QUA.   Can't you look after your own twins ?

TRIKA.   She's so much better at it than I am.   I keep forgetting all about them.   And she was lovely at the top of the Mountain. Singing.   And telling stories.   Even She was laughing.   The time passed like winking.

QUA.   You're not supposed to speak to one another at the top of the Mountain.

TRIKA.   Neither we did.   Queen did nearly all the speaking. And there's nothing about singing, is there ?

[*Voices heard singing* KU's *song of the First Act.*]

VOICES.   Wa na clash nye luf
               Blu ash Ru
               Pul wansha grash . . .

SHE (*without*).   No, no.   You said " grass."   You should say " grash."   It means sand.

[*Enter* MARGAUSE *and* SHE *with arms linked like two schoolgirls.*]

MARGAUSE.   Grash.   Like that.   Is that better ?

SHE.   Much better.   Grash.   It sounds like sand, doesn't it ?   Crunching beneath one's bare feet.

MARGAUSE.   Well, Trika, my dear.   How are the babies ?

TRIKA.   Oh!   I'd forgotten about them again.   I made them be quiet and then forgot about them.   I think they're all right.

MARGAUSE.   You didn't touch them ?

TRIKA.   No, Queen.

MARGAUSE.   You mustn't touch them.   Must she, dear ?

[*To* SHE.]

SHE.   I think she'd better not.   She's so careless.

MARGAUSE.   How right you are, darling. . . . What a

[70]   148

KU.   The bay is full of great ships.   They're roasting an ox on the beach.

GRETTIR.   Orkney?   Oh, yes.

QUA.   And fetch a skin of Heather Ale for the King.   He is probably as big a drunkard as you are.

GRETTIR.   Yes.   Certainly.   Heather Ale.   Surely.

TRIKA (*snivelling*).   My poor babies.   Who is to look after my poor babies?

KU.   We'll all look after them, dearie.   Take this duster. No wonder the poor god-man has gone off his head with you keeping house for him.   How many for breakfast, She?

SHE.   What did you say?

KU.   I asked how many were coming for breakfast?

SHE.   How can I tell?   I am not a prophet.   I cannot foresee anything.

QUA.   Hi!   Snor.   Get a move on, will you?   You're maundering about like a basking shark.

KU.   Don't speak unkindly to my little man friend.   He is doing his best   Aren't you, love?

GRETTIR.   I think so.   Where shall I put this?

[*He is hugging a skin of Heather Ale.*]

KU.   Down here.   Quick.   Here they come.

[KU *places a bowl of wind-flowers on a bracket near the door, and withdraws to the side of the doorway.*   Enter KING LOT *in a blazing rage.   He is followed by the* JARL *and by* TORQUIL, *who has got himself a little targe, a helmet and a sword.*   INNOCENCE, KWOO *and* WAWA *are seen in the doorway behind them.*]

LOT.   Where's that fellow with the gammy arm?   Oh, there you are.   Don't you know your own way about your own god-forsaken Island?

QUA.   Yes.

LOT.   Do you mean you do or you don't?

QUA.   I do.

LOT.   Then what do you mean by sending me along a track that led into the middle of a bog?

QUA.   It wasn't a bog; it was Snor's copper mine.

LOT (*with a sudden sinister calm*).   So you did it on purpose? You had the cold-drawn nerve to mislead me on purpose?   Do you know who I am?

QUA.   Yes.   You are Queen's man.

LOT (*exploding again*).   I am the man who is going to teach this Island manners.   And, by God's blue hood, you will take part in the first lesson.   I'm going to hang you!

TORQUIL.   If I might make a suggestion . . .

LOT.   Who the Hell are you? . . . Oh, you're here again, are you?

TORQUIL.   Yes, Sir.   I think perhaps you could give them a first lesson in discipline without going to such lengths.

LOT.   I'll go to the length of all the rope they've got; and there'll be an end of it for you, if you forget your place.   By the Eternal Thunder, I never heard of such a thing in my life! Body of me, I'll show them!

[*Enter* MARGAUSE *from the cubicle, dressed in all the splendour she has been able to collect in the Island during three years.*]

LOT.   My most dear Lady!   Are you safe?

MARGAUSE.   What is the meaning of this?

LOT.   The meaning of what, my dear?

MARGAUSE.   Why do you come into my apartment stamping and threatening and bawling like a bull?

LOT.   I was afraid of what might have happened to you.

MARGAUSE.   No matter of what you were afraid, it is no excuse for making an exhibition of yourself.

LOT.   Forgive me.   I was not myself.

MARGAUSE.   You were very much yourself.   It is time I took you in hand again.

LOT.   High time.   I have missed you, Margause.

[*He kisses her hand.   As she permits this, he proceeds to a respectful embrace.*]

MARGAUSE.   Your armour hurts.   Sit down by me at the table.   Snor, fill the King's cup.

[*The* KING *and* QUEEN *sit.*]

LOT.   Madame.

[LOT *drinks to* MARGAUSE.]

MARGAUSE.   Thank you.   Do you like our Heather Ale?

LOT.   It has a taste of damsons.   Madame, I am glad to have found you at last.

MARGAUSE.   I am glad too.   She!   Where are you?

[SHE *rises slowly from the fireside and comes to the table.*]
My Lord, I wish to present my kind hostess.

[LOT *holds out his hand to be kissed.   After a pause,* SHE *shakes it.*]

[74]   152

MARGAUSE. Sit down, She.   [SHE *obeys*.   LOT *stares at her*.]
She and her Islanders have made me happier than I have ever
been in my life. She is my very dear friend. I hope that she
will be yours.

LOT. I hope that she will.   [SHE *is staring at the* KING *now*.]

MARGAUSE. Oh, you do, do you ? (*Suddenly, to the* JARL.)
Ah, Sir Lachlan, it is pleasant to see you again. And how is
your wife ?

JARL. She is well, my Lady.

MARGAUSE. When do we sail ?

JARL. My Lord has not yet issued instructions.

MARGAUSE (*to* LOT). When do we sail ?

LOT. Eh ? Oh, yes. . . . I thought, perhaps. . . . It
may take some days to revictual and caulk the ships. And I
shall have to make some arrangements for governing the Island.

MARGAUSE. The existing arrangements are admirable.

LOT. I'm sure they are. Perhaps, when our Hostess has
leisure, she can tell me all about them.

MARGAUSE. I shall tell you all about them myself. We
shall sail today.

LOT. Today ?

MARGAUSE. At once. I am sick for home.

LOT. Well, if the tide . . .

MARGAUSE. Don't talk to me about the tide.   [*She rises*.]
Well, She, you have got your wish at last.

LOT. What is her wish ?

MARGAUSE. To be rid of us.

LOT. I don't know about that. We decided that the Island
must be explored and converted and developed. . . .

MARGAUSE. Yes, yes, I know.

LOT. And protected. I have taken a great fancy to the
Island. It reminds me of a song one of our harpers sang. . . .
How did it go ?

> . . . Ringed by shining sea-horses,
> Coursing against the something surge,
> And it stands on feet of bronze . . .

Oh, yes . . .

> Joy flew down to the land
> Into Ru-Rhush, the calm place,
> To nest and abide for ever.

> To the kind land, the clear land.

SHE (*rising in rapture*).

> The Inviolate land! . . .
> Inviolate now and for ever.

MARGAUSE.   Lot!   Come home at once.

[LOT *rises sheepishly,* SHE *as if waking from a dream. They join the* QUEEN *at the doorway. At the same moment* THE BISHOP *and* INNOCENCE *appear. They take positions on either side of the doorway to allow the party to go out.* LOT *bows out* SHE *first and follows leading the* QUEEN. *The rest follow them, leaving the* BISHOP *and* INNOCENCE *together staring at each other.*]

BISHOP.   I don't know what's the matter with you.   I think you must have gone daft.

INNOCENCE.   That is possible.   That may be.   I'm still a little muddled in the head.

BISHOP.   You have not performed the sacraments for at least six months?

INNOCENCE.   Yes.   That is true.   Yes.

BISHOP.   Then what on earth do you mean by it, man? Pull yourself together.

INNOCENCE.   I think it must be because I am learning the alphabet and find it rather difficult.

BISHOP.   The alphabet?   What do you mean by the alphabet?

INNOCENCE.   Our Lord taught us the alphabet very simply, and when His disciples had learned that, He went on to teach them the mysteries.   But we haven't learned the alphabet, have we, sir?   We don't know how to live at peace with our neighbours.   How can we understand the mysteries?

BISHOP.   What you need is a sea-voyage.

[*He leads* INNOCENCE *through the doorway as if he were a decrepit patient.*]

INNOCENCE.   I once thought I understood, but I'm not so sure now   I am not so sure.

[*Trumpet sounds, in distance.*]

CURTAIN.

END OF THE PLAY.

MR BOLFRY

A PLAY IN FOUR SCENES

*A parlour in the Free Kirk Manse at Larach, in the West Highlands of
Scotland. It is Sunday afternoon. The furnishing is austere. Two
walls are occupied by bookcases full of forbidding-looking books. On
the other wall are signed engravings of elderly clergymen. There is a
presentation black-marble clock on the mantelpiece. There are no
further concessions to decorative art. A lanky man in battle-dress is
lounging in the only comfortable chair, with his slippered feet on the
mantelpiece. His name is* CULLY. *When he speaks, it is with an
"educated" accent. He wears large horn-rimmed spectacles.
Through the window is seen an autumnal Highland landscape,
illuminated, for the moment, by a watery beam of sunshine. A
second soldier enters. He is small, sturdy, Hebraic and disconsolate.
His name is* COHEN.

COHEN (*singing, dirge fashion*). "Roll out the barrel; we'll
have a barrel of fun. . . ." Not half, we won't.

[*He finds a dishcloth in his hands and throws it back through the
open door.*]

CULLY (*in what he imagines to be Scots*). Hoots mon! Don't
ye no ken, you cannot sing on the Sabbath Day?

COHEN. Don't I know it!

CULLY. Where have you been, my dear Mr Gordon Monte-
fiore Cohen?

COHEN. Cleaning up the crimson dinner dishes. That's
where I've been.

CULLY. Don't you get enough polishing to do at the Camp?

COHEN. You've said it.

CULLY. Then what's the matter with you? Gone balmy?

COHEN. Not yet.

[*He sits down and absently takes out a cigarette.*]

CULLY. You can't smoke in here, cocky.

COHEN. Hell, no. (*He puts his fag away.*) Cor, stone the
crows, what a dump! What a billet! Cor darn my socks!

CULLY. You've only got your lousy ambition to thank for it.

COHEN. What do you mean ambition? Did I have any
ambition to get drafted up North to this perishing cold doorstep of
a country? Did I have any ambition to be billeted on an old holy,
sour-puss, praying bloody preacher? Tell me, I'm asking you.

157   [3]

CULLY.   You were ambitious to be the cleanest, best-behaved man in the battery, and that's why they picked you.

COHEN.   Oh, indeed.   And why did they pick you?

CULLY.   God knows.   They thought I needed a bit of religion, I expect.

COHEN.   What's the good?   Lord love me, what's the good?

CULLY.   They'll make you a bombardier all right.   This is only a small spot of purgatory, before they receive you into ever-lasting glory.

COHEN.   Bombardier?   Not me, they won't.   Not with a nose my shape and that old Nazi of a B.S.M. anti-semiting all over the ship.   Tin-eyed old beer-tank.   What you reading?

CULLY.   Meditations among the Tombs.

COHEN.   So help me, there isn't a decent cemetery to go to, let alone a cinema.

CULLY.   Why did you wash the dishes?

COHEN.   Something to do.   Just to pass the time.

CULLY.   Damned liar.

COHEN.   Well . . . I thought there might be a bit of fun in it.

CULLY.   Was there?

COHEN.   No fear!   They made her go to the matinee—the afternoon service, whatever you call it—the minute I offered. The nasty minds these holy blokes has.

CULLY.   Bad luck.

COHEN.   I'll be more careful next time.   A bit unsophistki-tated but quite a pretty little bit of stuff.   And a skirt's always a skirt.   And I ain't seen many round hereabouts.

CULLY.   I thought you were a respectable married man.

COHEN.   Hell, chum, I wouldn't be a married man if I didn't like a bit of skirt.   Be reasonable.   There ain't no harm in it. Read us a bit.   I'm right browned off, and that's a fact.

CULLY.   " Indulge, my soul, a serious pause.   Recollect all the gay things that were wont to dazzle thy eyes and inveigle thy affections.   Here, examine those baits of sense.   Here form an estimate of their real value.   Suppose thyself first among the favourites of fortune, who revel in the lap of pleasure; who shine in the robes of honour; and swim in tides of unexhausted riches; yet, how soon would the passing bell proclaim thy exit; and, when once the iron call has summoned thee to thy future reckoning, where would all these gratifications be?   At that period,

[4]

how will all the pageantry of the most affluent, splendid and luxurious circumstances vanish into empty air ? . . ."

COHEN.   I ain't got that.   Who's supposed to have murdered who ?

CULLY.   Nobody's murdered anybody.

COHEN.   Who's this bloke supposed to be talking to ?

CULLY.   To anybody.   To you.

COHEN.   He is, is he ?   Then he don't know me !   Swim in tides of unexhausted riches !   He don't say anything about skirts, does he ?

CULLY.   Oh, yes.   There's a lot about blokes dying and skirts howling over them.   Would you like me to read you a bit ?

COHEN.   No, I thank you.   I thank you kindly, I am much obliged, but I should not think of troubling you.   I don't like howling skirts, I like joyful skirts.   I'd give a week's pay to see one this moment.

CULLY.   You damp down your libido, cocky.   There aren't any skirts around here.

COHEN.   No.   And if there were, there ain't much to make them joyful.

[He goes to the window.]

What a country !

CULLY.   Well, the sun was shining last time I looked out.

COHEN.   Yes.   You can see across the loch.   They say hereabouts when you can see across the loch it's going to rain, and when you can't see across the loch it blooming well is raining.

[JEAN, *a tall, cheerful-looking young lady in a dressing-gown appears in the doorway.*]

JEAN.   Hello !

CULLY.   Oh, hello !

JEAN (to COHEN).   Hello ! you too,

COHEN.   Hello ! Miss.

CULLY.   Who are you ?

JEAN.   A joyful skirt.

COHEN.   You heard us talking ?

JEAN.   Yes.   I heard you.   I hesitated for years.   I was too shy to come in, till you said what you liked.   So then I came.

COHEN.   I'm sorry, Miss.   I'm not that sort of a chap at all. I'm not really.   But you know how it is, when two blokes gets chinning together.

JEAN.   Oh yes.   That's all right.   May I have a book ?

159   [5]

CULLY.   Oh, yes.   Please.

JEAN.   I didn't mean to interrupt you.

COHEN.   Not at all.   It's a pleasure.

JEAN.   I'm the Meenister's niece.

CULLY.   No.   Really?   Are you?

JEAN.   Yes.   My name's Jean Ogilvie.   What are your names?

CULLY.   Cully's mine.

COHEN.   Gunner Cohen, Miss.

JEAN.   What are your first names?

CULLY.   Tom.

COHEN.   Gordon.

JEAN.   Do sit down, Tom and Gordon.   I won't be a minute.   Are you from the gun position on the hill?

COHEN.   Yes.

JEAN.   I heard you were billeted here.   It must be pretty dull for you.

COHEN.   You have said it.

JEAN.   Where do you come from?   London?

COHEN.   Yes.   Little shop in the Borough Road.

JEAN.   You too?

CULLY.   More or less, yes.

JEAN.   So do I.   I'm a typist and teapot carrier at the Ministry of Interference.   I was blitzed about a bit, and they sent me for a week's holiday.   That's why I'm still in bed.

CULLY.   I see.

JEAN.   I only came yesterday.   The hills are nice, don't you think?

CULLY.   Very nice.

JEAN.   How do you like my uncle?

COHEN.   He seems a very nice gentleman.

JEAN.   And there's no doubt about my aunt being nice, so it's all very nice together—only dull.   I must try to see about getting you cheered up a bit.   But my uncle's so damned strict.

COHEN.   He is a bit, isn't he?

JEAN.   Yes.   It's funny.   He's very intelligent too.   I'm no match for him.   Are you intelligent?

CULLY.   I used to think I was.   Cohen certainly is.

JEAN.   Then we must tackle him tonight after evening service.

CULLY.   It will be a pleasure.

[6]   160

JEAN.   Will it be a pleasure to you too ? . . . I say, look here, I can't call you Gordon.   Haven't you another name ?

COHEN.   The boys sometimes calls me Conk.

JEAN.   May I ?

COHEN.   Yes, if you like.

JEAN.   Conk, will you help me with my uncle ?

COHEN.   Well, if it's not too much of a liberty in the gentleman's own house.

JEAN.   But it's for his good.   There's lots of things we could teach him.

COHEN.   I shouldn't be surprised.

JEAN.   Then that's settled.   I must run now. . . . What's this book ? . . . Oh, Greek, damn.   Never mind.   I feel much better.   I think I'll get up.

COHEN.   Won't you stay and talk to us ?

JEAN.   No, Conk.   My uncle doesn't think naked women are good for soldiers.   He'll be back any minute now.   Cheers. I'll see you later.

[*She goes out before the* SOLDIERS *have time to get to the door-handle. They make polite rushes and get to the door opposite one another.*]

COHEN.   After you, Claude.

CULLY.   Not funny.   How do you like her ?

COHEN.   What do *you* think of her ?

CULLY.   I don't know.   I haven't really seen her yet.

COHEN.   It seemed to me like you had a good look.

CULLY.   She was putting on an act.   She needn't have troubled.   I didn't come all the way up to the Heilans to be sparkled at.   I'm like old Wordsworth, Mr Conk.   I am one of them as likes a solitary Highland Lass to be a solitary Highland Lass.   I can get plenty " Come on, you chaps " stuff where I come from.

COHEN.   A bit hard to please.

CULLY (*resuming his chair and his book*).   Yes.

COHEN.   Looked a very high-toned bit of stuff to me.   You could see she was a lady.

CULLY.   There are no ladies nowadays.

COHEN.   In that case, I'll mizzle up to the canteen.   Coming ?

CULLY.   No.   Remember you've got to be back for supper at eight.

161   G   [7]

COHEN.   Hell, yes . . . (*at the window*) . . . and there's
the soft refreshing rain coming.   And there's the church
coming out.   And there's his holiness coming up the path.   I
can't make it.   No dodging the column this time, chum!

[*He sits down beside the table with a gesture of hopelessness.*]
A fatalist.   That's me.

[MCCRIMMON *enters.   He is a handsome, serious man of about fifty.*
He wears a turnover collar and a white bow tie.   He carries a silk
hat carefully in his hand.   Behind him come MRS MCCRIMMON, *a*
pretty little woman of forty, and MORAG, *the serving-maid, a girl*
of seventeen.]

MCCRIMMON.   Morag!   Put my hat in the box, girl.   And
take you great care of the nap this time.

[MORAG *takes the hat and goes out.*]
MRS MCCRIMMON.   Oh, Mr Cully!   The Minister's chair!
CULLY.   Sorry, Mrs McCrimmon.
MCCRIMMON.   Oh, it is all right.   It is all right, dear me.   A
man who defends my country is at liberty to sit in my chair, I'm
sure.   Sit ye down.
CULLY.   No thank you, Sir.   Cohen and I were thinking of
going out for a walk.
MCCRIMMON.   It is a nice thing, a walk.   You would be too
tired maybe to attend the afternoon diet of worship?   But I
forgot.   I am the stupid man.   You do not belong to our
communion.
MRS MCCRIMMON.   It's raining now, Mr Cully.   Maybe
you'd be better to stay in beside the fire.   I'll put some peats on
it, and the Minister will be in his study at his evening sermon,
and I'll be in the kitchen with Morag, so you needn't be bothering yourself.
MCCRIMMON.   Oh, there is no harm in the young men going
for a walk.   No harm at all.   You were reading?
CULLY (*showing him the book*).   Yes.
MCCRIMMON.   Well, well.   Hervey's " Meditations among
the Tombs."   An improving kind of a work in its way, but to
my mind he was a greeting bit body, that.   And not very sound
in his doctrine.   But he's dead longsyne, and no doubt he has
done you little harm with his greeting.

[MRS MCCRIMMON *is busy with the peats.*   COHEN *is helping her.*]
CULLY.   He makes very soothing Sunday-afternoon reading.

MCCRIMMON.   The Lord did not give his Day that you should
be soothed, young man.

CULLY.   Oh?   I was always told he did.

MCCRIMMON.   Those who told you so did you no service.
The Day was given for rest of the body, improvement of the
mind, and the ordinances of public and private worship.

CULLY.   Oh, but, Mr McCrimmon, surely . . .

MCCRIMMON.   Marget, will you bid Morag put my cup of gruel
in the study?   You will excuse me, Sir?   I have to make some
meditations of my own before my sermon.

CULLY.   At least I was trying to improve my mind.

MCCRIMMON.   Indeed, I hope so.   And now will you excuse
me?

[MRS MCCRIMMON *and* COHEN *leave the fireside*.]
[*Exit* MCCRIMMON.]

MRS MCCRIMMON.   Now, there's a clean fireside, and I think
there's nothing nicer in the whole wide world.   Don't you think
so, Mr Cohen, and you a family man?

COHEN.   You're right.   Not that I won't say them turf
fires take a bit of getting used to.

MRS MCCRIMMON.   If you handle them kindly you get a fine
steady glow.   And the smell of the burning peat is grand.

CULLY.   Like a burnt offering on the family altar.

MRS MCCRIMMON.   You're making fun of me, and that's fine;
but I wouldn't make jokes of things like that, Mr Cully.   Not
of sacred subjects.

CULLY.   I didn't think a good Presbyterian would think
altars particularly sacred.

MRS MCCRIMMON.   Maybe not, but they are no subject for
levity.

CULLY   I wasn't trying to be funny.

MRS MCCRIMMON.   That's all right, then.

CULLY.   I'll go up and get my boots on.   What about you,
Conk?

COHEN.   I've got my boots on.

MRS MCCRIMMON.   If you're going for a walk, I wouldn't go
anywhere you might be seen during the evening service.   There
might be talk, and you living with the Minister.

CULLY.   Right ho.

MRS MCCRIMMON.   And you'll be back for supper at half-past

eight, will you not ?   It's only pease brose, but there will be a
wee bit of cold ham for the pair of you.

CULLY.   Fine.   I'll remember.

[CULLY *goes out.*]

MRS MCCRIMMON.   He seems kind of vexed.   I hope I was not
too sharp with him.

COHEN.   Keep your mind easy.   He's been on the mat before
sharper-tongued people than you.

MRS MCCRIMMON.   Maybe he's not very used to the ways of
a Minister's house, only being here three days ; and none of them
the Sabbath.

COHEN.   That's it.   He's not used to it.

MRS MCCRIMMON.   He's a fine young fellow.   It's a pity
he's an episcopalian.

COHEN.   He's not that, Mum, whatever else he is.   He's
C. of E.

MRS MCCRIMMON.   Ah, dear me, now, he cannot help his
upbringing. . . . Look, the fire's glowing fine.   It's a homey
looking thing, a fire.

COHEN.   It is and all.

MRS MCCRIMMON.   And it growing so dark and gloomy out
bye.   I think we will have a storm.   It is not a nice walk you
will be having at all.

COHEN.   It helps to pass the time.

MRS MCCRIMMON.   Och, dear me, with me the time passes
without any help.   You would think there was scarcely enough
of it.

COHEN.   It hangs a bit heavy when you're used to city life.

MRS MCCRIMMON.   And what would you do, now, if you
were in the City at this very moment ?

COHEN.   Well, now you ast me, I shouldn't be surprised if I
sat down by the fireside and went to sleep.   I'd have read all the
Sunday papers by this time.

MRS MCCRIMMON.   Tuts, tuts !   Sunday papers !

COHEN.   But it'd be a comfort knowing there was places I
could go, if I wanted to.

[COHEN *heaves a deep sigh and suddenly takes a pocket-book out and
pushes a snap-shot at* MRS MCCRIMMON *as if it were a pistol.*]

MRS MCCRIMMON.   Oh !   What's that ?

COHEN.   Me and the trouble and strife.   Down at Southend.
That's the kid she's holding up to get took.

[10]   164

MRS. MCCRIMMON.   What a lovely boy!

COHEN.   He's a bit of all right; but he isn't a boy.   He's a girl.

MRS MCCRIMMON.   Amn't I the stupid one!   I should have known.

COHEN.   Don't see how you could, with all them clothes on.

MRS MCCRIMMON.   She's a bonny wee lass.   How old is she?

COHEN.   Eleven months there.   Had her third birthday last week.   There she is.   Sitting in the park with her blooming dawg.

MRS MCCRIMMON.   My, my, how they grow!   She'll be the great chatterbox now.

COHEN.   She's like her ma.   Got a lot to say and says it.

MRS MCCRIMMON.   She's got a look of you too.

COHEN.   Cor blimey!   I hope not.

MRS MCCRIMMON.   It's about the eyes.

COHEN.   She's a way of laughing with her eyes before the rest of her face gets going.

MRS MCCRIMMON.   What's her name?

COHEN.   Gladys.   Same as the old lady.

MRS MCCRIMMON.   You must miss them sorely.

COHEN.   Not half, I do.   Roll on the time.

MRS MCCRIMMON.   Roll on the time.

[*A pause.*]

COHEN.   No news yet from North Africa?

MRS MCCRIMMON.   Not yet.   He'll be twenty next month. Ninth of November.

COHEN.   You don't look like you'd a grown-up son.

MRS MCCRIMMON.   There's whiles I'm surprised myself.

[*They turn and look at a photograph of a Seaforth Highlander on the mantelpiece.*]

MRS MCCRIMMON.   That was taken the day he got his commission.

COHEN.   You'd be proper and proud of him that day.

MRS MCCRIMMON.   What's it you say?   Not half I wasn't!

[*She laughs.*]

You'll have us all speaking the fine, high English before you've finished with us.

COHEN.   You speak first-class English.   There's a bit of an accent, if you don't mind my saying so, but I can understand every word you say.

165   [11]

MRS MCCRIMMON.   Ah, well, now, am I not glad of that?
You will be finding us a wild uncivilised lot in the Highlands?

COHEN.   I wouldn't go as far as that.   You don't get the
same chanst as what we get up in London, but I wouldn't call
you uncivilised—except on Sundays.

MRS MCCRIMMON.   Well, well, we've all got our ways of
doing things, I suppose.   Is it a nice place, London?   It'll
not be all wickedness with eight million folk in it.

COHEN.   I wish you could see our little place in the Borough
Road.   Above the shop, it is.   Nice and handy.   And Gladys,
she keeps it a treat.   Pots and pans shining and a couple of
budgerigars in a gilt cage.   And always something tasty after
we puts up the shutters.

MRS MCCRIMMON.   She still keeps the shop open?

COHEN.   You bet she does.   Twicet she's had the window
blown in, but what does she care?   Out with the old broom and
bucket and on with the job.   Cor stone the crows, I shouldn't
have the nerve.   And I'm supposed to be a soldier.

MRS MCCRIMMON.   Och, now, you're a very brave soldier
too, I'm sure.

COHEN.   Not me.   I get the willies, sometimes, imagining
what's going to happen to me if the Gerries get busy on my gun.

MRS MCCRIMMON.   You'll be like us up here.   You've a
strong imagination.   There's whiles I can frighten myself more
than Hitler and Goering and that lad Rommel could do if they
were all in this room waving their pistols and making faces at
me.   I'll be lying awake at night with my head under the
blankets thinking there's devils and bogles and kelpies coming
down the chimney, though fine I know there's no such thing.
But when they dropped a big bomb on Aberdeen and me at a
shop door and knocked over with the blast with all my messages
flung mixty maxty, I wasn't afraid at all, at all.   I was just
angered.

COHEN.   That's right.   It's the same with Gladys.

MRS MCCRIMMON.   Not but what I put up a wee prayer, the
minute I could think about it.

COHEN.   The way you'd hear Gladys howling about the War,
you'd think old Hitler got it all up for her benefit.   But there's
no more howling when it comes to the bit.

MRS MCCRIMMON.   It's our imaginations.   They're an awful nuisance our imaginations.

[12]

[Enter JEAN—*now fully dressed.]*

My sorrow and my shame! What are you doing up and about, you bad girl?

JEAN.   I'm cured, Aunt Maggie.   It's the Highland air.

MRS MCCRIMMON.   You should think shame of yourself.   I told you to stay in bed till I said you could get up.

JEAN.   You know quite well that I never did what you told me.

MRS MCCRIMMON.   And that's a true word.   You've always been little better than a wayward wee rascal.

JEAN.   But I'm interrupting you.

MRS MCCRIMMON (*in some confusion*).   Oh, I was just having a wee talk with Mr Cohen.   You'll not have met Mr Cohen. He's one of the two gentlemen who are billeted with us.

JEAN.   I've met Mr Cohen and Mr Cully too.

MRS MCCRIMMON.   Dear me, when would that be, now?

JEAN.   Never mind.   And go on with your wee talk.   I'll go and speak to Morag and try to work up a bad cough for next time I come back.

MRS MCCRIMMON.   You are just terrible, and that's the only one word for you.   She has no respect for her elders, Mr Cohen. I'm real sorry for her poor mother.   And you'll just stay here and cheer Mr Cohen up, and I'll away be to the kitchen.

[Enter CULLY *in his boots.]*

Now, Mr Cully, you're surely not going out on an evening the like of this.

CULLY.   It does look pretty black.

MRS MCCRIMMON.   And there's the mists coming down from the ben.   I have seen me lost a hundred yards from the Manse door.

COHEN.   I'm not going out, you can bet your life on that.

CULLY.   I'll go myself, then.

JEAN.   I'll go with you if you aren't going far.   Mr Cohen can lend me his waterproof cape.

MRS MCCRIMMON.   Jean!

JEAN.   Well, Aunt Maggie?

MRS MCCRIMMON.   You're just out of your bed.

JEAN.   I told you I was all right now.

MRS MCCRIMMON.   And apart from all else, do you remember what day it is?

JEAN.   Yes.   Quite well.

MRS MCCRIMMON. What will people think? What will your Uncle say?

JEAN. I haven't the least idea what people will think, and Uncle Mac can say what he likes, and I'll be delighted. He has a beautiful, thrilling voice.

MRS MCCRIMMON. Oh, but, Jean . . .

JEAN. If you like, I'll promise you one thing. If Gunner Cully attacks my virtue, I shall defend it heartily. I am feeling very virtuous tonight.

MRS MCCRIMMON. Oh, Jean, that's awful talk! And it's not like you at all. I don't know what's come over you.

JEAN. Get your mackintosh cape, Conk, will you?

[COHEN goes out.]

MRS MCCRIMMON. I've half a mind to fetch your Uncle.

JEAN. Yes. Do. I haven't seen him today.

MRS MCCRIMMON. Oh, Jean! . . . It's all right in England, dearie, and there's no harm in it, I suppose; but surely you know what sort of place this is?

JEAN. Yes. It's got the best record for church attendance and the highest illegitimacy rate in the Kingdom. I don't respect it for either of these records, much. I'm not very keen on going to church, and I rather like behaving myself decently. So I propose to do exactly what I like. I hope you don't mind.

MRS MCCRIMMON. Well. . . . Don't go too far away, and see and be back in time for supper. I think I'll let Morag get the supper ready and go and lie down for a wee bit. I've a kind of a headache coming on, and it's still an hour and a half to the evening service.

JEAN. Oh, poor soul! Would you like an aspirin? I've got dozens.

MRS MCCRIMMON. No, no. It's only a wee headache. Don't be late.

JEAN. No. I won't be late. We won't go far.

MRS MCCRIMMON (going). I hope you have a nice walk.

JEAN. Please forgive me, Aunt Maggie. I'm an ill-tempered beast. I must be a bit nervy.

MRS MCCRIMMON. Yes. You would be after all those experiences.

JEAN. I wish I weren't going for that walk, but you see I've got to now, don't you?

CULLY.   I say, really, I'm not frightfully keen . . .

JEAN.   Shut up. . . . You see, Aunt Maggie, don't you ?

MRS MCCRIMMON.   Now don't be asking me if I see or if I don't see.   Away for your walk and don't bother me.

JEAN.   But we're friends, aren't we ?

MRS MCCRIMMON.   Och, I've no patience with you   Away with you and your havering.

[*She gives* JEAN *a tearful smile and goes out.*]

JEAN.   The fool I am, fighting about nothing.

CULLY.   I don't know.   I couldn't see what all the fuss was about.

JEAN.   This is a Wee Free Parish.   They think it's a mortal sin to be seen on the road with a strange young man—especially on the Sawbath.

CULLY.   I gathered that.

JEAN.   That's why they stick to hedges and ditches for their —social occasions.   Disgusting, superstitious pigs.   And they're not only immoral and hypocritical.   They're Devil-Worshippers.

CULLY.   I'd hardly put it that way.

JEAN.   They are.   I don't want particularly to go for a walk in the rain with you, but I'm not going to knuckle under to Devil-Worship.

CULLY.   What do you mean by Devil-Worship ?

JEAN.   Have you read any of these books ?

[*Indicating the bookcase.*]

CULLY.   Two or three.   They're very interesting.   I've just been cooling off a bit with Hervey on the Tombs.

JEAN.   Have you heard any of my Uncle's sermons ?

CULLY.   No.   I've denied myself that pleasure.

JEAN.   They don't worship God.   They worship the Devil. They call him God, but he's really the Devil.   All this holiness and censoriousness is to save their skins from boils and leprosy and their souls from damnation.   They think if they flatter this fiend and go through a few—rites of propitiation, he'll let them alone.   They're like savages tying red rags outside their caves to keep away demons.   I know them.   I've lived among them.   I'm one of them.

CULLY.   You may be right about the particular deity these people believe in, but I think you're wrong about the Devil.

JEAN.   How wrong?

CULLY.   Anybody who has thought a lot about the Devil has a great respect for him.

JEAN.   You mean they cringe to him.   That's what I'm saying.

CULLY.   No.   They don't cringe.   None of the fellows I'm thinking about knew how to cringe.

JEAN.   Who are they?

CULLY.   Milton, Goethe, William Blake, your own Bobbie Burns.

JEAN.   Robert Burns to you, please.   Well?

CULLY.   Even in the Old Testament all they could find against him was that he was rebellious and had a proper pride in himself and tried to educate people.

[*Enter* COHEN *with soldier's waterproof cape.*]

JEAN.   Oh, thank you, Conk.

CULLY.   Conk's ancestors made exactly the same charges against Christ himself.

COHEN.   Never mind about my ancestors.   What was your ancestors like in those far-off times?   Painted blue, they was.

CULLY.   They still are.   Come along, Jean, lets get some cold, damp, fresh air.

COHEN.   You don't want me to come with you, I don't suppose?

[*He helps* JEAN *on with the cape.*]

CULLY.   You can come if you like.

JEAN.   Yes, do.   I've got my own mackintosh upstairs.

COHEN.   No, thank you.   I'll settle down to a good book.

JEAN.   Oh, yes.   Good.   Do read the Institutes of Calvinism.   We want your opinion on them.

COHEN.   I've already got my opinion of most of these here books, lady.   I hope you have an enjoyable swim.

JEAN.   Gosh, yes.   It's raining cats and dogs.   Still, we must get out sometime.   Come on, Cully.   We'd better face it.   See you later, Conk.

COHEN.   Cheery bye.

[*Exeunt* JEAN *and* CULLY.   *When they are well away,* COHEN *opens the door carefully, leans against the jamb and whistles low and melodiously with his eyes on the passage ceiling.   After a few bars,* MORAG *comes in the door in some trepidation.*]

MORAG.   What is it you want?

COHEN.   Me ?   I was just whistling.

MORAG.   You cannae whistle on the Sabbath.   The Minister'll be hearing you.

COHEN.   Come in the office.

MORAG.   Oh, I couldna.

COHEN.   The Missus has gone to lie down.   The other two are out.   Come in a minute.

MORAG.   Well, just for a wee minute.

COHEN.   I got something for you.

MORAG.   Dear me, what can it be ?

COHEN.   Packet of chocolate.

[*He gives her packet of chocolate.*]

MORAG.   Now, are you not the kind man, man, no indeed yes.

COHEN.   Like chocolate ?

MORAG.   Och, I'm most terrible keen on the chocolates.   I could be sitting there eating the like for all eternity, whatever.

COHEN.   You're pretty easy on the eye.

MORAG.   Och, I don't know what you're saying, easy on the eye.

COHEN.   Got a boy friend ?

MORAG.   What would I be doing with boy friends, away up here in Larach ?   I've no patience with them at all, with their ignorance.

COHEN.   What's the matter with me, then ?

MORAG.   Nothing doing.

[*She pronounces this " Nuthun DOOOOun," with a dignified coyness unusual in most uses of the phrase.   After a brief attack and a token defence,* COHEN *succeeds in kissing her expertly. They disengage.*]

Dear me, aren't you the awful man, and a great danger to the neighbourhood.

COHEN.   Not me, and thank you very much.   Do you know what that was worth to me ?

MORAG.   It would not be much to a gallus rascal the like of you.

COHEN.   It was as good as a hundred Players, four pints of mild and bitter, and a gallon of Rosie Lee.   And now you better hop it.   I don't want you to be getting into no trouble.

MORAG.   Deed yes.   This is not the thing at all.

[*Exit* MORAG.]

[COHEN *registers mild satisfaction and then goes to the bookshelf. His spirits drop. He wearily chooses a book, without very much hope; takes it to the table and begins to turn over the leaves with a rather disgusted air. Noise of* CULLY *and* JEAN *in the passage.*]

JEAN.   No. Wait. I'll take them into the kitchen. You'd better take your boots off before you go into the parlour.

[COHEN *listens, is about to get up, but returns to his book. Presently* JEAN *comes in, a little bedraggled about the head and carrying her muddy shoes in her hand.*]

JEAN.   Hello, Conk.

[*She puts her shoes at the fireside.*]

Thank God there's somebody in the British Army with a little sense. What possessed that man to go out on a day like this, I do not know.

COHEN.   You didn't go far.

JEAN.   Quite far enough. What a day! It's getting dark, too. Another ten minutes and we'd have been hopelessly lost. We couldn't see a yard in front of us.

[*She takes off her stockings and hangs them on the fire-irons, while she is speaking.*]

I asked Morag to bring in a nice cup of tea. She was very doubtful. She rather thought she'd go to Hell if she did. I told her there was nothing in the Bible about having tea between one o'clock and half-past eight. I don't suppose there is, is there?

COHEN.   What of it if there is? All that stuff's a lot of hooey, if you ask me.

JEAN.   Are you an atheist?

COHEN.   I'm an agnostic.

JEAN.   Good. We'll make Uncle pull his socks up tonight. Talking of socks, I'd better go up and " put cla'es on my feet," or I'll be excommunicated.

[CULLY *enters, wearing his slippers.*]

JEAN.   Oh, hello! You've been very quick. I'm just going to tidy up. You'd better dry your shins at the fire.

CULLY.   Yes. Thanks.

[*Exit* JEAN. CULLY *dries his shins at the fire.*]

COHEN.   Any luck?

CULLY.   What do you mean by " Any luck "?

COHEN. Garn! Errcher!

CULLY. I've told you what I think of the young person.   I haven't had time to change my mind.   She's not my type.

COHEN. Any skirt's anybody's type in a place like this. You're a Cissy.   That's what you are.

CULLY. If you call me a Cissy, I'll fetch you a skelp on the jaw that'll make your teeth rattle.

COHEN. No offence.

CULLY. Take care that there isn't, you cock-eyed guttersnipe.

COHEN. All right, all right.

CULLY. And if you want to make offensive remarks, you'll kindly keep them strictly impersonal, if you understand what that means.

COHEN. Keep your hair on.   Who's making offensive remarks?

CULLY. You were winding yourself up into your most facetious vein.   You'd better unwind yourself.   I find your facetiae offensive.

COHEN. Ah, shut up and let me read.   It gives me a pain when you talk like a gory dictionary.

CULLY. What are you reading?

COHEN. Never mind.

CULLY. Why can't you keep your temper?

COHEN. I like that.   Who lost his temper?   You did.

CULLY. I asked you a perfectly civil question and you answered like a sulky kid.

COHEN. A bloke's got to be careful what he says to the great Goramity Mister Cully—him what writes to the Reviews. . . . What the Hell's biting you, chum?

CULLY. Nothing.   I'm sorry.   It's funny how chaps begin yapping like terrier pups when the weather changes.   Forget what I said.

COHEN. I accept your perishing apology. . . . It's five o'clock.   Five stricken hours till bedtime.

CULLY. Oh, as it's turned out, it may not be so bad.

COHEN. Not so bad as what?   A blinding Gerry Concentration camp at the blazing North Pole?

CULLY. I think we'll see some sparks flying.

COHEN. What sparks?

CULLY. Wait and see.   Our young lady seems to think she

has a mission to assault thrones, dominations, princedoms, virtues, powers, and crack their forced hallelujahs.

COHEN. She seems to think what's it?

CULLY. She's spoiling for a row with his Reverence.

COHEN. I don't see much good in that myself.

CULLY. No more do I.

COHEN. Live and let live, I always say.

CULLY. She says that too. Only she says his Reverence won't let live.

COHEN. Cor blind me, you got to make allowances. If you come to a place where there's niggers what likes bowing down to idols because it does them good, cor blimey, let them get on with it. They didn't ask you to come. They don't want your blooming interference.

CULLY. You're probably right, but she doesn't think so. I think we'll have quite a pretty fight.

COHEN. *He* won't fight. He's too blinking self-satisfied. He's got the Commanding Officer on his side.

CULLY. If he does, she won't have a chance.

COHEN. Yes, she will.

CULLY. You underrate his Reverence. I think you'll find he packs a pretty heavy punch.

COHEN. I never saw a skirt yet get the worst of an argument. All in, of course. No holds barred.

CULLY. We'll see. It might be quite a Pleasant Sunday Evening after all.

[MORAG *comes in with a teapot and three cups and a section of black bun. She is very nervous about it all.*]

MORAG. Oh, dear me, I wish to thank goodness Miss Jean would go away back to London. We'll all have our heids in our hands.

CULLY. What's the matter?

MORAG. Oh, where iss she? Drink your tea now quick, like good lads, before the Minister finds out. My sorrow, you cannae say, " No ", to her, she's that birsey.

[*Enter* JEAN. *She has changed her stockings, shoes and skirt and rearranged her hair.*]

JEAN. Oh, thank you, Morag. You are a Highland seraph.

MORAG. I may be a seraph or a geraffe or a camomile, but

haste ye now, Miss Jean, before the Mistress finds the dirty cups and teapot.

JEAN.   Awa wi' ye, you chittering oinseach!   There's nobody going to eat you.

MORAG.   I wouldna be over sure of that, Miss Jean.   Ochonorie!   It's a weary day for me.

[*Exit* MORAG, *lamenting.   The* OTHERS *sit round the table.*]

JEAN.   Gather round, chaps.   Do you both take sugar?

CULLY. } Yes, please.
COHEN. }

JEAN.   What a lot of sugar!   I suppose the Army's the generous donor.

COHEN.   They get our ration, you see, and neither of them takes it.

JEAN.   Thank the Lord for our gallant defenders.   Here's mud in your eye.

COHEN.   And in yours, Miss.

JEAN (*picking up the book* COHEN *has left on the table.*)   "The Discoverie of Witchcraft," by Reginald Scot.   You been reading this, Conk?

COHEN.   Glancing at it.   The spelling seems a bit cockeyed to me.

JEAN.   When I was a kid I used to stay here for the holidays. I sneaked in when nobody was about and read this book.   I didn't notice much wrong with the spelling then.   It frightened me out of my wits.   My Uncle found me reading it and gave me the telling off of my life.   I still feel beautifully frightened when I only look at the book.

COHEN.   Tells you how to raise the Devil and that.

JEAN.   Oh, does it?   I never got so far as that.   You draw cabalistic signs and repeat a spell, don't you?

COHEN.   I shouldn't be surprised.   Like the old boze in the opera.

JEAN.   It would be quite fun to try.

COHEN.   A waste of time, if you ask me.

JEAN.   I don't know.   He might tell us why the Wee Frees behave in that extraordinary fashion.

COHEN.   He might if there was any such things as devils.

CULLY.   What about the good old Battery Sergeant-Major?

COHEN.   Cor stifle me, don't you go calling him up now.

175   [21]

He's bad enough in the old monkey kit, but think what he'd be like in red tights! Old Mestify-toffles!

[*He laughs and chokes on his tea.* JEAN *thumps him on the back.*]

JEAN.   Take it easy, Conk.

COHEN.   I'm sorry. I had to laugh. Think of him blowing out flames instead of beer, with his fore and aft hanging to his near side horn. " Battery, tails up! "

[*He coughs again. Both* JEAN *and* CULLY *take a hand at thumping him on the back.*]

JEAN.   Oh dear, oh dear; the man'll choke himself.

CULLY.   Pull yourself together, Conk.

COHEN.   Easy on. Easy on. It's having a sense of humour. It'll be the death of me.

[*These lines are spoken simultaneously. As they are being spoken,* MCCRIMMON *enters without being noticed and watches the scene with an enigmatic expression on his face.* JEAN *sees him first; knocks the book off the table onto the floor; picks it up and hides it on a chair. Silence falls.*]

JEAN.   Oh, hello, Uncle Jock.

MCCRIMMON.   Good evening, Jean. Your aunt did not tell me that you were up and about.

JEAN.   I got up this afternoon. I'm ever so much better.

MCCRIMMON.   That is a blessing.

[*He sits down at the table.*]

JEAN.   Will you have a cup of tea?

MCCRIMMON.   No. I thank you.

JEAN.   It has turned into an awful night. Cully and I were out in it for a little.

MCCRIMMON.   Indeed?

JEAN.   Yes. It didn't seem to like us. It drove us in after a very few minutes. I suppose it was a lesson to us to do as the Romans do.

MCCRIMMON.   What Romans?

JEAN.   *You* know. When you are in Rome, you should do as the Romans do. I don't agree with that, do you? I mean, you couldn't do as the Romans do even if you wanted to. And they'd like you much better if you were just yourself. We used to laugh at the Japanese for wearing bowler hats and trying to talk slang. I think we were quite right. They were much nicer in those lovely silk dressing-gowns.

[22]   176

MCCRIMMON.   No doubt.

CULLY.   Of course, there's got to be some sort of compromise, hasn't there?   You can be yourself, I hope, without offending the local customs and prejudices.

JEAN.   Naturally.

MCCRIMMON.   We have a very peculiar local prejudice, Mr Cully, in this part of the country.   We have a prejudice against desecrating the Lord's Day.

JEAN.   Is that remark intended for our benefit?

MCCRIMMON.   Indeed, I hope that if you conseeder it seriously you may indeed benefit by it.

JEAN.   How have we desecrated the Lord's Day, as you call it.

MCCRIMMON.   Your consciences will tell you that.   And it is not I who have called it the Lord's Day.

JEAN.   Look here, Uncle, let's get this straight.   What are we supposed to have done?

MCCRIMMON.   You are my guests, and it is unbecoming that I should rebuke you; but, since you ask me, I have found you eating and drinking at unsuitable hours and indulging yourselves in unseemly levity and in that laughter that is like the crackling of thorns under a pot: and this on a day that we are enjoined to keep holy.

JEAN.   Uncle Jock, there are nearly seven hundred millions of Christians in this world, and nearly seven hundred millions of them wouldn't see an atom of harm in anything we've done today.

MCCRIMMON.   To be called a Christian is not to be a Christian.   You will find in the Gospel according to St Luke the words, "Why call ye me, Lord, Lord, and do not the things which I say?"

JEAN.   When and where did the Lord tell us not to have tea on Sunday afternoon?

MCCRIMMON.   In the Fourth Commandment.

JEAN.   The Fourth Commandment says nothing about tea.

MCCRIMMON.   Tea is included.

JEAN.   And buns.   Like a Sunday School Trip.

MCCRIMMON.   I have no inclination to listen to blasphemy.

JEAN.   It isn't blasphemy.

MCCRIMMON.   It is blasphemous to mock at the Ten Commandments.

JEAN.   The Ten Commandments are a set of rules for a wandering desert tribe.   And not very good rules either.   An American girl said they didn't tell you what to do.   They only put ideas into your head.

MCCRIMMON.   She would find elsewhere plenty of instructions what to do.   And the ideas were there already.

JEAN.   Anyhow, they tell us to keep Saturday holy, not Sunday.

MCCRIMMON.   If you were in a proper frame of mind, I would explain to you why.

JEAN.   What do you mean by a proper frame of mind?

MCCRIMMON.   A state of humility and reverence.

JEAN.   You mean I'm to swallow everything I'm told?

MCCRIMMON.   When you were a child you were not allowed to argue about your medicine.

JEAN.   I'm not a child now.

MCCRIMMON.   Ah, well, now, I'm not so sure of that.

JEAN.   I'm nearly thirty.

MCCRIMMON.   If you were Legion, you'd still be a bairn. You have all the signs and symptoms of infancy.

JEAN.   I'm glad to hear it, then.   But there's something about out of the mouths of babes and sucklings, isn't there?

MCCRIMMON.   Hath He perfected praise.   I did not observe that you were in the exercise of Praise, when I entered just now.   And since then I have not been aware of any high spirit of reverence.

JEAN.   I can't revere things I don't believe in.

MCCRIMMON.   You do not believe in the Word of God as it is revealed in His Holy Scriptures?

JEAN.   Oh, I believe lots of it, and I'd like to believe lots more: but when you put on that hangman's face and that awful voice and call it " The Word of God as it is revealed in His Holy Scriptures ", I go all shivery down to my stomach and I don't believe a word of it.

MCCRIMMON (*with a bland seriousness*).   Well, now, I have observed the same thing in my conversations with the atheists and infidels from England who come up for the fishing.   If I employ the sacred and beautiful words appropriate to the subject, they flinch and flee from my presence.   I must even abandon plain English and descend to their baby talk.   And yet I find that they have the presumption to set their opinions against the Gospel

[24]

with not even an educated schoolboy's vocabulary to support them.   It is very peculiar.   They are so ignorant that their own episcopalian meenisters, poor bodies, in ministering to them have wellnigh lost the power of human speech.   I have to wait till I see Father Mackintosh, the priest from Strathdearg, before I can converse in a civilised language forbye the Gaelic.

JEAN (*helplessly*). Do listen to that, Cully. If anybody dares to speak back to him, he makes a beautiful little speech showing that they're fools and ignoramuses—or ignorami or ignoramae—which is it, Uncle Jock ? You know I can only talk baby talk. What am I ? An ignorama ?

MCCRIMMON. The wee bit of Latin I once taught you has gone by the board. Mr Cully will tell you that ignoramus is not a noun.

CULLY. Oh, isn't it ?

MCCRIMMON. It is not. But I will talk to you in any language you please. What is it you want to know ?

JEAN. I don't want to know anything. At least, I don't want to know anything about religion. At least, I don't want to know anything about religion that you can tell me. Because I think you're all wrong. Absolutely and entirely wrong.

MCCRIMMON. That is your opinion, is it ?

JEAN. It isn't my opinion only. It's the opinion of all decent sensible people. You contradict your own book of words by making your holy day Sunday instead of Saturday; and by denying that it was made for man and not man for it; and by preaching original sin and election and predestination. . . .

COHEN. Stop the horses a minute. I like a good argument. It's like the Brains Trust. But I like to know what you're talking about.

JEAN. Original sin means that a baby is damned to Hell Fire even before it's born. Election means that only a little clique will ever get into the kingdom of Heaven and the rest haven't a chance. Predestination means that it doesn't matter two hoots what you do, because it was all fixed long ago. It's all a pack of nonsense.

COHEN. It sounds funny, all right.

MCCRIMMON. You do not believe in these doctrines ?

JEAN. I do not. I think your premises are wrong and your evidence is phoney. There's nothing in the whole thing that appeals to my reason. And if you don't appeal to my reason,

179   [25]

you need no more expect me to believe you than to believe a man who tells me he's a poached egg.   There might even be some sense in *that*.   Some men look like poached eggs.

COHEN.   That's the stuff to give him.   Reason all the time.

MCCRIMMON.   How far away is the sun?

JEAN.   I don't know.

CULLY.   About ninety million miles.

JEAN.   Yes.   That's it.   I'd forgotten.

MCCRIMMON.   Who told you?

JEAN.   I don't remember.   I read it in some book.

MCCRIMMON.   And you believed it?

JEAN.   Yes.   I suppose I did.

MCCRIMMON.   Did your reason tell you to believe it?

JEAN.   Yes.   Because it can be checked.   If it's a lie any expert could disprove it.

MCCRIMMON.   And when an expert had disproved it you would believe that it was a lie.   Very well, then.   I will tell you a wee story.

COHEN.   But if you don't believe experts, who are you to believe?

MCCRIMMON.   I will tell you, with your permission, a wee story: Once upon a time there was a wee wee fellow with the finest set of whiskers that ever you saw and his name was wee Stumpie Stowsie.

COHEN.   Cor blimey!

JEAN.   Shut up, Conk.

MCCRIMMON.   If there was one thing he was fond of it was a good swim.   He would be down in the pond every day and all day swimming with his whiskers.

One day he was swimming and thinking about nothing at all and up comes a snail as big as a whale.   " I'll swallow you as if you was Jonah," said the snail.   " Come on.   Do it," says the bold Stumpie Stowsie.   So the snail swallowed him, and it was peaceful and warm in the insides of the snail, and Stumpie was quite joco, like a tourist passenger on a steamboat sailing round the Western Isles.   But a time came when he thought and better thought, " Now am not I the silly one, dozing away in the insides of a great big snail when I might be settling down in a house of my own with a growing family to keep me cheery?" So he made a great todo in the insides of the snail till the snail was for no more of it, and he ups with Stumpie Stowsie and his whiskers into a forest that ran down to the seashore. So Stumpie he looks and he looks, and the verdure was that thick he could see nothing. So he climbs up a big palm tree to spy out the land.

COHEN. So along comes his Fairy Godmother on a magic carpet. Good night, children, everywhere.

MCCRIMMON. No. It was a kangaroo ass big ass a post office. But I am wearying you, with my havers.

JEAN. No. Honestly. We're enjoying it. It's like old times. Do you remember telling stories to Colin and me, on Saturday nights when we were wee tottums?

MCCRIMMON. I do, I do.

JEAN. You tell them so well! I believed every word.

MCCRIMMON. You don't believe this one?

JEAN. Of course I do, in a way.

MCCRIMMON. In what kind of a way? Would you put your experts on to prove it or to disprove it?

JEAN. No, of course not.

MCCRIMMON. But they would be very pleased, whatever, your experts. Indeed, now, a whole clacking of experts have been at that very story, proving it and disproving it till they were nearly black in the face.

CULLY. I see what you mean.

JEAN. I'm afraid I don't.

CULLY. He's been telling us the story of the Liver Fluke. It swims about in pools until it's swallowed by a water-snail. And then it's puked up onto a blade of grass. And a kangaroo eats the grass and the Fluke lays its eggs in the kangaroo's liver. Unless he does all these things the Fluke can't live. He seems to be very well named.

MCCRIMMON. So we are told.

JEAN. What a cad's trick!

MCCRIMMON. Are you referring to the Distoma Hepaticum or to your humble relative by marriage?

JEAN. To you. I call it cheating.

MCCRIMMON. But you believe my story now, I think.

JEAN. Yes, I suppose so.

MCCRIMMON. In both ways?

JEAN. How in both ways?

MCCRIMMON. When I took you into a world outside this world you readily suspended what you call your reason and believed in Stumpie Stowsie. When Mr Cully brought you back to earth and told you the story in another way, you believed it in another way without stopping to think. Your marvellous power of reasoning hadna much say in it either way, I'm thinking.

[He gets up, but stays at the table.]

It comes to this, that you wish to have the eternal world outside our wee temporal world explained to you in the language of the tuppeny-ha'penny general knowledge text-books. Such language is neither adequate nor exact. But I'll do my best. Use your eyes and look round you. Mr Cully and Mr Cohen, you'd be bonny-like soldiers if you had no discipline. For three hundred years Scotland disciplined itself in body, brain and soul on one day of the week at least. The result was a breed of men that has not died out even in this shauchly generation. You don't believe in Original Sin, Jean, you are telling me? Well, now, you could easily have had ten babies by this time if you had not preferred talking and sentimentalising about them. Then you would have found the truth that a baby has every sensual vice of which it is anatomically capable with no spirituality to temper it. You do not believe that mankind is divided into the sheep and the goats—the Elect and the Damned? Use your eyes and look around you. You may pity the Damned—and indeed it is your duty so to do. But you cannot deny that they exist.

You do not believe in Predestination? That is because you do not like it. If you only believe what is nice and comfortable, our doctrine is of no service to you. If I give you a crack on the head with a stick, you need not believe it; you need not believe in your dentist's drill or in the tax-gatherer's demand. Go on. Believe what is agreeable to you. I do assure you that you will be in such a continuous state of surprise that your eyebrows will jump off the top of your head. Even your heathen philosophers *knew* that Predestination was a fact, like Ben Nevis. You can go round it. You can go over it. But you are foolish to ignore it.

Do you believe that the body rises from the grave on the Great Day?

JEAN.   I believe that the spirit does.

MCCRIMMON.   In all my days I have never seen the interment of a spirit. You do not believe that the body can rise again,

[28]
                                                            182

though every spring and every day in a myriad forms you see that actual thing happening.   But it is folly to talk to you.   The Lord gave you a spiritual mind with which you might see the truth of these things.   But you are afraid of your spiritual sight. And 'deed I can hardly blame you.   Yet it is with that sight alone that you can apprehend spiritual truths.   Reason is a poor instrument for such a purpose.

CULLY.   The Fathers of the Church cultivated the spiritual mind ?

MCCRIMMON.   I believe some of them did.

CULLY.   They found in the world outside reason a lot of unreasonable phenomena.   They believed in transubstantiation and miraculous liquefaction and the remission of sins by priests and the efficacy of prayers for the dead.   They found warrant for all these things on the spiritual level.   Yet they are outside reason.   Do you believe in them ?

MCCRIMMON.   No.

CULLY.   Why ?   Because your reason rejects them ?

MCCRIMMON.   When I said that reason was a feeble instrument, I did not refer to my own reason.   But I must ask you to excuse me.   My evening diet of worship is in ten minutes.   It is in the Gaelic; and I must think for a little in the Gaelic before I am ready to speak it.   In the meantime I would feel very much obliged if you would respect my serious and conseedered opinion that today is a sacred day and should be observed, within these walls at least, with all due decorum.

CULLY.   Oh, yes, of course, but . . .

MCCRIMMON.   I thank you.   That is all I wished of you.   I shall see you at the evening meal.

[Exit MCCRIMMON.]

COHEN *(with the gestures of one drowned or dizzy).*   Help! Throw me a lifebelt, somebody.

JEAN.   I think you scored a hit, Cully.   His eyes flashed for a minute, but he broke off the engagement very quickly.

CULLY.   And very neatly.   He won handsomely on points.

JEAN.   Why didn't you chip in earlier ?

CULLY.   What's the good ?   He's a professional and we're only drivelling amateurs.   We're apt to forget that parsons are professionals.   Our English parsons are a bit like our professional soldiers.   They want us to forget that they know their job.

COHEN.   Why don't you shout him down, like you used to do in the barrack room?

CULLY.   He'd beat me at that too.   He's a chest on him like a bull.

JEAN.   He'd talk the hind leg off the Devil himself.

CULLY.   Would he?

JEAN.   I suppose so.   And he's so utterly wrong.   It kills everything that's gay and decent in life.   The other churches let you alone.   They sometimes go haywire and burn a few heretics, but most of the heretics are Calvinists, so it doesn't matter.

CULLY.   He made it look so damned logical for a bit.   It's his infernal totalitarianism I can't stand, though.

JEAN.   They seem to have a sadistic love for persecution for its own sake.

COHEN.   A lot of Nazis.

CULLY.   I don't know.

COHEN.   What do you mean, you don't know?

CULLY.   Do you know who invented modern democracy?

COHEN.   The thing we're fighting for?   No.   Lloyd George?

CULLY.   No.   Calvin.

JEAN.   I don't believe it.

CULLY.   You can look it up.   His system was a theocracy; but all its officials were elected by vote and responsible to God and to the electors.   And everybody in the community voted, so long as he behaved himself.

JEAN.   You're on his side?

CULLY.   I'm on nobody's side.   I'm a sort of Devil's Advocate.

JEAN.   I wish we could raise the Devil and get him to speak for himself.

COHEN.   You seemed to me to be doing your best.

JEAN.   Conk!   Your book!

[*She finds* REGINALD SCOT *on the floor.*]

We'll follow the printed instructions and have a shot.

CULLY.   That's an idea.   It will help to pass the time for Conk.

JEAN.   They are all in bed before ten.   We could sneak down quietly and try at, say, about midnight.

CULLY. I'm on.

COHEN. What's this? A séance?

JEAN. Yes. A sort of a séance.

COHEN. I went to a séance. Spoke to my grandfather. Cor blimey, the poor old perisher had gone off his head. Said he was happy.

JEAN. But what about your beauty sleep?

CULLY. That's all right. Four hours' sleep's enough for the likes of Conk and me.

JEAN. That's a date, then. We'll have to be very quiet.

[*At door.*]

CULLY. Where are you going to?

JEAN. I'm going to church.

COHEN. Cor blimey.

[*Exit* JEAN.]

END OF SCENE ONE.

THE CURTAIN IS LOWERED TO DENOTE THE PASSAGE OF SIX HOURS.

SCENE II

The Same. Darkness, except for the dull glow of the fire. Enter CULLY, *commando fashion, in gymn shoes. He lights the oil-lamp and turns it low. To him,* JEAN.

JEAN (*in a whisper*). Hello.

CULLY. Hello.

[*He suddenly embraces her with some violence.*]

JEAN. Damn you, what do you think you're doing?

[*She disengages forcibly and gets in a rousing slap to* CULLY'*s cheek.*]

CULLY. Sorry.

JEAN. I should damn well think so.

CULLY. I thought you wanted me to. I didn't know. I'm sorry. You see, I'm not much of an expert at amatory exercises. I never know whether they want to make love or not.

JEAN. What do you mean by " they "?

CULLY. Oh, anybody.

JEAN. Well, I'm not just anybody. I'm a friendly sort of creature; and when I pass a fellow-creature a cheery-oh I don't intend it as a mating call. Do you appreciate that?

CULLY. Yes. I think so.

JEAN.   And do you think you can manage to be friendly with me in a civilised fashion without getting into a continual state of excitement—or pretending to get into one ?

CULLY.   Yes, of course.

JEAN.   That's all right, then.   Sit down.

CULLY.   Thanks.

JEAN.   I'm not a puritan.   I suppose I've got the ordinary appetites.   But I think it's absolutely disgusting to go cuddling or guzzling one's way through life.   Do you agree, or are you just the ordinary pig-man ?

CULLY.   Yes.   You're perfectly right   I made a mistake. I've said I'm sorry.   I suppose it was a sort of compliment to your general attractiveness.

JEAN.   It's not a compliment at all.   It's a squalid insult.   It always has been, until the last few years.   Never mind.   You know now that " I'm not that sort of girl."   Forget about it. Where's your friend ?

CULLY.   I don't know.   I suppose he's making his own arrangements.

JEAN.   How beastly !   Go and fetch him.

CULLY.   I shouldn't think he'd like that.

JEAN.   Whether he likes it or not, do as I tell you.   If you mean what I think you mean, the sooner you two learn to behave yourselves the better.   You're my uncle's guests, and you must behave as if you were.   Where is he ?

CULLY.   I think he said something about the wash-house.

JEAN.   Wait.   I had better go.   I know my way in the dark; we musn't wake everybody up.   You wait here and keep cave.

CULLY.   You'll get wet.

JEAN.   There's a cape in the lobby and it's only a few yards.

[*She goes out.* CULLY *fetches the* DISCOVERIE OF WITCHCRAFT *and opens it on the table.   The clock strikes twelve.   Re-enter* JEAN *with* COHEN *and* MORAG.   *They are both fully dressed.* MORAG *is in some confusion of spirit, but is inclined to brave it out.*]

JEAN.   Come in and sit down here.

MORAG.   I'll away to my bed, Miss Jean.

JEAN.   You will not.   Do as I tell you.

[*All sit down at the table.*]

I'm surprised at you, Morag.

COHEN.   Aren't you surprised at me ?

JEAN.   Not a bit.

MORAG.   There was no harm in it.   No harm in it at all.
He was telling me about the wee talking birds he has got in a
cage down in London.

JEAN.   Well, he can go on telling you here.   Cully and I
don't mind.

MORAG.   This is not the thing.   This is not the thing at all.
Sitting in the parlour and the Minister upstairs in his bed.   It is
you that is the surprising one, Miss Jean, I am telling you.   Now
like a good lady, be letting me away to my bed.   I have my
washing to do, tomorrow's morning.

JEAN.   Sit still.   Maybe you'll hear something for the good
of your soul.

MORAG.   Oh, dear me, let you my soul alone.   It is two
minutes past twelve, and not the Sabbath day now at all, whatever.

JEAN.   That clock is ten minutes fast.   It's still the Sabbath
day.   Sit still and be quiet.

MORAG.   Oh, dear me.   My sorrow and my pain!

[*She mumbles a little in Gaelic and relapses into silence.*]

JEAN.   You were going to tell us about the birds, Conk.

COHEN (*grunts*).

JEAN.   Oh, very well, then.   We'll get on with the business
of the meeting.   Have you the book, Cully?

CULLY.   Yes.

JEAN.   Have you found the place?

CULLY.   Yes.

JEAN.   Let me see.   I've got a bit of chalk. . . .   Oh, but
this is terribly complicated!   We have to go out and bathe in a
spring; and we've got to have a lion-skin or a hart-skin girdle;
and we've got to have chest protectors with words on them;
and we've got to have a knife. . . .

CULLY.   That's all right.   We've all bathed quite recently,
and a tap's as good as a spring.   I've made myself a chest pro-
tector, and Conk and I have both got magic belts with brass
devices on them.   You can have them if you like.   Conk, give
the lady your belt.

COHEN.   I can't.   It's keeping up my respectability.

JEAN.   You're sure they will do?

CULLY.   Yes.   I know the drill pretty well.   I've written
Agla and the mystic signs on my jack-knife.   There it is.

187   [33]

[*He opens his jack-knife and throws it on the table.*]

JEAN.   Hush! Don't make a noise. You're wonderful, Cully.

CULLY.   You go ahead and make Solomon's Circle. That's it—on page 244. I'll read a sort of condensed version of the exorcism. It should do well enough. Get cracking, now. Give me a bit of chalk. I'll do the central diagram on the table.

[JEAN *draws a circle round the table and adds certain cabalistic signs.* CULLY *makes marks on the table itself.*]

JEAN.   Whom shall we call up, Cully?

CULLY.   It'll have to be a Duke of the Infernal Regions. They are free from midnight till four a.m. I should think Bealphares would be the best. He's the Golden Devil and a great talker.

COHEN.   I thought you sat in a circle with your hands on the table and played "Lead Kindly Light" on the gramophone.

CULLY.   We'll do that too, except the gramophone. Are you ready, Jean?

JEAN.   Nearly. What's this word? AGLA . . . EL. . . YA . . . PANTHON.

[*Standing up.*]

Righty-ho.

CULLY.   Give me the book and sit down. Turn down the light, Conk. Not too far, you fool.

[COHEN *lowers the light.*]

COHEN.   Do we sit with our hands touching?

CULLY.   Yes. Are you ready? Now keep very quiet.

[*He takes up the knife and points it at all in turn.*]

Fugiat omne malignum
Salvetur quodque benignum. . . .   Say Amen.

OMNES.   Amen.

CULLY.   *Homo. . . . sacarus. . . . musceolameas. . . che-rubozca*: I exorcise and conjure Bealphares, also called Berith, Beall and Bolfry, thou great and terrible divell, by the sacraments and by the unspeakable name TETRAGRAMMATON. I conjure and exorcise thee, Bealphares, by the virtue of all angels, archangels, thrones, dominations, principats, potestats, cherubim and seraphim that thou do come unto us, in fair form of man or womankind, here visible, before this circle and not terrible

[34]   188

by any manner of ways; and that thou do answer truly without craft or deceit unto all my demands and questions. Lemaac, solmaac, elmay, gezagra. Josamin, sabach, ha, aem, re, sepha, sephar, semoit, gergoin, letes. Amen. Fiat, fiat, fiat. Amen.

OMNES.   Amen.

[*The light turns blue.* MORAG *begins to whimper softly. There is a crash of thunder and the door swings suddenly open, revealing an elfish little gentleman in a glistening black mackintosh and a tall silk hat. His umbrella is open and dripping with water. He closes it.* MORAG *stands up to her full height and gives a piercing scream, which she checks by biting on the back of her hand.*]

MORAG.   It's unchancy to bring an umbrella into a hoose and it open.   It's unlucky.

COHEN.   For Gord's sake put up the light.

[*He turns up the lamp with a shaking hand. The* GENTLEMAN *takes off his mackintosh and hat and gives them to* MORAG, *with the umbrella.* MORAG *gingerly puts the umbrella upside down at the edge of the fireplace. He is dressed, to the astonishment of everybody, in exactly the same way as the* REV. MR MCCRIMMON. *His face is amiable and his hair is a silky black. He comes into the room with a light, springy step and takes his stance in front of the fireplace, beaming on the conjurors.*]

THE GENTLEMAN.   Well, ladies and gentleman, a most disagreeable evening.

[*He lights a big cigar by some sleight of hand and then looks at the clock.*]

Your clock is slow, I think.   It is just after twelve o'clock, as I happen to know.

[*He smiles benignantly, tucking his hands under his coat-tails. Enter* MCCRIMMON, *in nightshirt and dressing-gown.* MRS MCCRIMMON *behind.*]

Ah, Mr McCrimmon, I believe?   I am Dr Bolfry.   How do you do?

MCCRIMMON (*shaking hands uncertainly*).   How do you do?

BOLFRY.   I am very well, thank you.

[*He stands smiling on* MCCRIMMON.]

THE CURTAIN FALLS.

SCENE III

The Same, an hour later. The fire has been stoked up to a cheery glow, and illuminates BOLFRY *with just a suspicion of red light. He is reclining in the Minister's chair, with his feet on another chair. A bottle of " medicinal " whisky is on the mantelpiece, and he is obviously enjoying himself.* MCCRIMMON, *still in his dressing-gown, sits bolt upright at the far end of the table with a dazed expression on his face.* MRS MCCRIMMON, *with her back to the Audience, sits beside him.* JEAN *is on his other side. They both appear anxious about* MCCRIMMON, *who is certainly looking very strange.* CULLY *is next* MRS MCCRIMMON, COHEN *next* JEAN. MORAG, *completely pixilated, is just within reach of* BOLFRY, *and he is able to lean over and pat her hand or her knee affectionately from time to time.*

CULLY. I see. Yes. That's very interesting. But, you see, Mr Bolfry, we have got a little away from the conceptions of Good and Evil that were prevalent in . . . well, in your time. We have rather a different orientation, if you see what I mean.

BOLFRY. I see exactly what you mean. Your generation is not what you call orientated at all. Your scientific gentlemen have robbed you of Time and Space, and you are all little blind, semi-conscious creatures tossing about in a tempest of skim milk. If I may be allowed to say so, it all comes of thinking yourselves a little too good for your priests. You went prancing away from your churches and schoolrooms. And the first thing you did with your emancipated state was to hand yourselves over body and soul to a number of plain-clothes priests whose only qualification was that they were good at sums. That was very foolish of you. [*To* MORAG.] Wasn't it, my dear ?

MORAG. Yes, Sir.

BOLFRY. You can't organise and expound the sentient Universe simply by being good at sums, can you ?

MORAG. No, Sir.

BOLFRY. Just as I thought. And then you found that even sums were a bit too difficult. If you can't do a quadratic equation, all these pages of incomprehensible figures are too much of a strain on simple Faith. You went to a new sort of old gentleman who said to you, " Life, my dear brethren, is one long smutty story."

" Aha ! " you said, " This is a bit of all right. Why wasn't

I told this before ? "   But no amount of licentious conversation with serious-looking professors could cure the ache and restlessness in your souls.   Could it, my darling ?

MORAG.   Whatever you say yourself, Sir.

[*He helps himself to another drink.*]

BOLFRY.   That's an admirable whisky you keep, Mrs McCrimmon.

MRS MCCRIMMON.   We only keep it as a medicine.   Mr McCrimmon is a teetotaller.

BOLFRY.   Everything is a medicine, Mrs McCrimmon. Everybody in this world is sick.   Why is everybody in this world sick ?   A most profitable line of enquiry.   Why are we all sick, Morag ?

MORAG.   I think it is because we're all a bit feared of you, Mr Bolfry.

BOLFRY.   Feared of me ?   Feared of me ?   Dear, dear. Come, come.   You're not afraid of me, are you, McCrimmon ?

MCCRIMMON.   Get thee behind me, Satan !

BOLFRY.   What did you say ?

MCCRIMMON.   Avoid thee.   Get thee behind me, Satan !

BOLFRY.   Perhaps I should not have allowed you to get within that comfortable ring of chalk.   You must not speak to me like that.

MCCRIMMON (*throwing over his chair as he stands up*).   This is nonsensical.   It is an evil dream.   Presently I will be waking up.   What do they call you, you masquerading fiend ?

BOLFRY.   I have told you, Sir.   My name is Bolfry.   In the days of sanity and belief, it was a name not unknown to men of your cloth.

MCCRIMMON.   You are dressed like a minister.   Where is your Kirk ?

BOLFRY.   In Hell.

MCCRIMMON.   Are there Kirks in Hell ?

BOLFRY.   Why not ?   Would you deny us the consolations of religion ?

MCCRIMMON.   What I would deny you or grant you is nothing to the point.   You are a liar and the Father of lies. There cannot be a Kirk in Hell.

BOLFRY (*twisting suddenly round to look at the portrait of a clergyman hanging on the wall*).   Who is that ?

MCCRIMMON.   That is the worthy Doctor Scanderlands of Fetterclash.

BOLFRY.   How do you know?

MCCRIMMON.   It is an engraving of a portrait taken from the life.

BOLFRY.   The portrait was bitten into a plate with acid and printed in ink on paper.   The black ink and the white paper were arranged according as the light and shadow fell on the Doctor's face and bands and gown; so that the Doctor's friends cried in delight : " It is the very lineaments of the Doctor himself that we behold ! "   Would you recognise it as the Doctor if it were all black ink or white paper ?

MCCRIMMON.   If you came here, Sir, at the back-end of midnight to give us a lecture on the Art of Engraving, I can only observe . . .

BOLFRY.   Keep your herrings for the Loch, and do not drag them across my path.   Without this black and that white, there would be no form of Doctor Scanderlands that we could see ?

MCCRIMMON.   Maybe you are right.

BOLFRY.   The Artist could tell us nothing about the Doctor without them ?

MCCRIMMON.   He could not.

BOLFRY.   And neither you nor I nor anyone else can tell anything about Heaven or Hell, or this very imperfect makeshift of an Earth on which we stand, without our blacks and our whites and our greys, which are whites mixed with black.   To put it in simple words, we cannot conceive the Universe except as a pattern of reciprocating opposites—(to MORAG)—Can we, my love ?   No, of course we can't.   Therefore when I tell you that there are Kirks in Hell, I am telling you something that is at least credible.   And I give you my word of honour as a gentleman that it is true.

MCCRIMMON.   What do you preach in your Kirks ?

BOLFRY.   Lend me your pulpit and I will show you a specimen.

JEAN.   Oh, Uncle Jock, do !   You may never get such a chance again.

MCCRIMMON.   Sleeping or waking, dream or no dream, I'll have no blasphemy in this parish.

BOLFRY.   Blasphemy ?   I should never think of committing

blasphemy. I think I may say that I know my position better.
I am a Duke and a General of Legions. Only gutter devils are
impertinent to the Deity. . . . But won't you sit down ?

MCCRIMMON (*sitting*). I can make nothing of this.

BOLFRY. You disappoint me. You are a Master of Arts.
You are a Bachelor of Divinity. You are a theologian and a
metaphysician and a scholar of Greek and Hebrew. What is
your difficulty ? Don't you believe in the Devil ?

MCCRIMMON. He goeth about like a roaring lion.

BOLFRY. Not when I am sober. Answer my question.

MCCRIMMON. I believe in a personal Devil.

BOLFRY. And in Good and Evil ?

MCCRIMMON. Yes.

BOLFRY. And in Heaven and Hell ?

MCCRIMMON. Yes.

BOLFRY. And Body and Soul ?

MCCRIMMON. Yes.

BOLFRY. And Creation and Destruction ?

MCCRIMMON. Yes.

BOLFRY. And Life and Death ?

MCCRIMMON. Yes.

BOLFRY. Do you believe in the truth and inspiration of the
Bible ?

MCCRIMMON. Yes.

BOLFRY. Have you read the Book of Job ?

MCCRIMMON. Yes.

BOLFRY. " Now there was a day when the sons of God came
to present themselves before the Lord, and Satan came among
them."

MCCRIMMON. The Devil can quote Scripture for his own
purpose.

BOLFRY. An entirely suitable purpose in this case. . . . Mr
McCrimmon, I believe also in the things of which I have
spoken.

MCCRIMMON. And tremble.

BOLFRY. Not infrequently. But the point is this : Why, if
we hold all these beliefs in common, do you find anything odd
in my conversation or my appearance here ?

MCCRIMMON. I don't know.

BOLFRY. Tuts, tuts, man. Pull yourself together. If the
Creator Himself could sit down peacefully and amicably and

193 H   [39]

discuss experimental psychology with the Adversary, surely you can follow His example ?

MCCRIMMON.   Mr Bolfry, or whatever you call yourself, it is plain to me that you could talk the handle off a pump.   If you have a message for me, I hope I have enough Highland courtesy to listen to it patiently, but I must ask you to be brief.

BOLFRY.   Mr McCrimmon, I am not charged with any message for you.   Indeed, I think it will turn out that you and I are in agreement on most essential points.   But these young people have summoned me on a cold and dismal night from my extremely warm and comfortable quarters.   If you had instructed them properly, all this wouldn't have been necessary.   But we'll let that pass.   Do you mind if we go on from the point at which you rather rudely ordered me to get behind you ?

MCCRIMMON.   Go you on from any point you like.   You are whirling about like a Tee-to-tum.

BOLFRY.   Highland courtesy, Mr Cully.

MCCRIMMON.   And keep your tongue off the Highlands.

BOLFRY.   Mr McCrimmon, I may be only a Devil, but I am not accustomed to be addressed in that fashion.

JEAN.   Mr Bolfry . . .

BOLFRY.   One moment, please.   (*To* MCCRIMMON.)   Unless, Sir, you are prepared to exercise a little civility, I must decline to continue this discussion.

MCCRIMMON.   The discussion, Sir, is none of my seeking— no more than is your intrusion into my house and family circle. So far as I am concerned, you are completely at liberty to continue or to sneck up.

MRS MCCRIMMON.   Oh, John!   Tha's an awful like way to speak to a guest.

MCCRIMMON.   He is no guest of mine.

BOLFRY.   That is true.   I am Mr Cully's guest.   Why did you send for me, Mr Cully ?

CULLY.   I'm blessed if I know, now you come to ask.

BOLFRY.   The likeliest reason was that you were unhappy and afraid.   These are common complaints in these days. Were you crying for me from the dark ?

JEAN.   No.   We weren't.   My Uncle thinks he has got divine authority.   And he was using his confidence in that and his learning and his eloquence and his personality to bully us. We wanted a little authority on our side.

[40]

BOLFRY.   I see.   Thank you very much.

JEAN.   He's got the advantage of believing everything he says.

BOLFRY.   A great advantage.

JEAN.   You can't meet a man like that on his own ground if you think he's talking nonsense.

BOLFRY.   You can't discuss what brand of green cheese the moon is made of unless you accept the possibility that the moon is made of green cheese.   I see.   In what *do* you believe, Miss Jean ?

JEAN.   I believe that the Kingdom of Heaven is within me.

BOLFRY.   Is that all ?

JEAN.   That's practically all.

BOLFRY.   So far as it goes, you are quite right.   But you are also the receptacle of the Kingdom of Hell and of a number of other irrelevances left over in the process of Evolution.   Until you can reconcile those remarkable elements with one another, you will remain unhappy and have the impulse, from time to time, to raise the Devil.

JEAN.   Then we ought to study these what-do-you-call-'ems—these elements, and try to reconcile them ?

BOLFRY.   I didn't say you *ought* to.   I said you won't be happy till you do.

JEAN.   Then we ought to, oughtn't we ?

BOLFRY.   If you want equilibrium.   If you want happiness.

CULLY.   But surely the pursuit of happiness . . .

BOLFRY.   Yes, yes.   The pursuit.   A very different thing from catching your electric hare.   The happiest man is a general paralytic in Bedlam.   Yet you do not envy him.   He is in a state of death in life.   You naturally prefer life in death— probably because you are used to it. . . . You are not favouring me with much of your attention, Mr Cohen.

COHEN.   Sorry, Sir.

BOLFRY.   Why not ?

COHEN.   Well, Sir, if you want to know the honest truth, I'm bored bloody stiff.

BOLFRY.   You say that with an air of some superiority.   You must not be proud of being bored stiff.   Boredom is a sign of satisfied ignorance, blunted apprehension, crass sympathies, dull understanding, feeble powers of attention and irreclaimable weakness of character.   You belie your lively Semitic counten-

195   [41]

ance, Mr Cohen. If you are alive, Mr Cohen, you should be interested in everything—even in the phenomenon of a Devil incarnate explaining to you the grand Purpose in virtue of which you live, move and have your breakfast.

COHEN. It's all hooey, that. There's no such thing as a Purpose. It's a tele—teleo—teleological fallacy. That's what it is.

BOLFRY. Dear me! *Dear* me! Mr McCrimmon, you are an amateur of blasphemy. What do you say to that?

MCCRIMMON. The man is wrong.

BOLFRY. Another point on which we are agreed.

COHEN. I can't help it. I'm entitled to my opinion.

MCCRIMMON. In what sort of a world have you been living, man?

COHEN. In the Borough Road. Do you know it?

MCCRIMMON. Even in the Borough Road, do you find no evidence of Eternal Purpose?

COHEN. Not a bit.

BOLFRY. My dear goodness gracious me, I know the place very well, and it's simply bursting with Eternal Purpose.

MCCRIMMON. There's not one brick laid on another, there's not one foot moving past another on the dirty pavement that doesn't tap out " Purpose, purpose, purpose," to anybody with the ears to hear.

BOLFRY. Every one of your higher faculties is bent to some purpose or other. You can't make anything happen without a purpose. There are things happening all round you on the Borough Road. How in the world do you think they happen without a purpose behind them?

MCCRIMMON. Do you deny to your Maker the only respectable faculty you've got?

COHEN. All I can say is, if I've got a Maker and He's got a purpose, I can't congratulate Him on the way it works out.

BOLFRY and   ⎫ But my dear good chap, you can't possibly
MCCRIMMON, ⎬ sit there and . . .
   talking   ⎪ How can you have the presumption to sit
   together.   ⎭ there and . . .

BOLFRY. I beg your pardon.

MCCRIMMON. No, no. Excuse me. Please go on.

BOLFRY. Not at all. After you.

MCCRIMMON. It is not for you to congratulate or not to

congratulate.   Who is able to judge the Creator of Heaven and Earth ?

CULLY.   Well, who is ?

COHEN.   Yes, who is ?   Mind, I don't admit there's any such person.   But if there is and he give us a critical faculty, we got to use it, see ?

JEAN.   Conk's absolutely right.   You tell us to praise Him. What's the good of praise when you've no chance of blaming ? It doesn't mean a thing.

CULLY.   What happens to your reciprocating opposites, Mr Bolfry, if we can't be anything but a lot of sanctified Yes Men ?

COHEN.   Hallelujah all the time.   Not much encouragement to the Creator to stick to His job.

JEAN.   That's the stuff to give them, Conk !   And I thought you were too much the gentleman to open your head.

COHEN.   No offence meant, of course.

MCCRIMMON.   Young man, do you realise that your foolish words are jeopardising your immortal souls ?

COHEN.   That's all tinky-tonk with me.   We ain't got any immortal souls.

BOLFRY.   I begin to believe it.   Mr McCrimmon, it seems to me we cannot begin our battle for the souls of these persons until they realise that they have souls to battle for.

MCCRIMMON.   It is terrible indeed.   Our duty is plain.   We must wrestle with them.   We must admonish and exhort them.

BOLFRY.   It is my duty no less than yours.

MCCRIMMON.   But stop you a minute.   I know that this is only a dream, but there must be logic, even in dreams.   I understand you to say that you are a Devil.

BOLFRY.   But I am also, like yourself, a servant of One whom I need not name.

MCCRIMMON.   I am a very distressed man.   You must not quibble with me nor use words with double meanings.

BOLFRY.   I am bound by my contract with our young exorcist here to tell nothing but the plain truth.   My distinguished relative is in the same position as I.   I am the same Instrument of Providence as he who smote Job's body with boils for the good of his soul.

MCCRIMMON.   That is a way of looking at it.   Certainly it is a way of looking at it, whatever.

197   [43]

BOLFRY.   More than that, if it is of any interest to you, I am an ordained Minister of the Gospel.

MCCRIMMON.   Do you tell me that?   Where were you ordained.

BOLFRY.   In Geneva in 1570.

MCCRIMMON.   What did you say?

BOLFRY.   In Geneva, I said.

MCCRIMMON.   But in what year?

BOLFRY.   The year is immaterial.   I can't swear to it within two or three years.   But ordained I am.   And I have preached, among other places, in the High Kirk at North Berwick, to the no small edification of the lieges.

MCCRIMMON.   Will you swear to that?

BOLFRY.   Mr McCrimmon, my Yea is Yea and my Nay is Nay.

MCCRIMMON.   It is a most remarkable thing, but from what I have heard from your lips so far, your doctrine appears to be sound.

BOLFRY.   None sounder.   And now that you are satisfied, I have a proposal to make.

MCCRIMMON.   What is your proposal?

BOLFRY.   I propose that we adjourn to the adjoining sacred edifice and there admonish and exhort our brothers and sister in a place suitable for these exercises.

MCCRIMMON.   You mean in my Kirk?

BOLFRY.   Where else?   Is it not the place most suitable for a conversion?

MCCRIMMON.   It is suitable.   But all this is very strange.

BOLFRY.   All life is very strange.   Shall we go?

MCCRIMMON.   I cannot enter the Kirk in my nightshirt; though it is true that I have dreamed that same more times than once.

BOLFRY.   Go upstairs then and change.   I shall wait for you.

MCCRIMMON.   Well, well.   Come with me, Marget. . . . And in case I wake up before I come down again, Mr Bolfry, let me assure you that it has been, upon the whole, a pleasure to meet you.   I hope I have not passed the stage of learning . . . even from a—a Being of your—your Nature.

BOLFRY.   Sir, you are most polite.   I hope to be able to reciprocate the compliment.

[44]   198

[*Exeunt* MR *and* MRS MCCRIMMON, BOLFRY *holding the door open for them.*]

JEAN. I never heard the like of that!

BOLFRY (*mildly*). Of what, my dear?

JEAN. You're on his *side*!

BOLFRY. What did you expect?

JEAN. I don't know. I certainly didn't expect such a pious Devil!

BOLFRY. My dear young lady, you don't know everything, as you are very shortly to find out.

JEAN. If you want to know my opinion, I think you're drunk.

BOLFRY. Drunk? Dear me! Tut tut, tut tut!

[*He helps himself.*]

CULLY. Well, I don't know what you chaps feel, but I'd feel the better of a drink myself.

MORAG. No!

CULLY. What do you mean by No?

MORAG. Don't leave the circle. He'll get you if you leave the circle.

BOLFRY. She's quite right. Quite right. Quite right. You are a percipient little slut, my darling.

JEAN. But . . . I mean, it's all nonsense . . . but what happens on the way to church?

BOLFRY. Nothing. Nothing. The Holy Man will protect you. They have their uses, Holy Men. Not that I am really dangerous. But we are mischievous a little, and fond of experiments. Eve and the apple was the first great step in experimental science. But sit down, Mister Gunner Cully There is plenty of time. Let us continue our delightful conversation. Let me see. Where were we?

JEAN. Does it matter very much? You're the most inconsequent character I ever met.

BOLFRY. Oh, no, no. I follow the pattern. If there is one. Perhaps that's what's wrong with you young people. You don't seem to have any pattern. The woof, as it were, is flying loosely about in space. There is no drama about your associations. Now, I am very fond of the Drama. I have done a little bit in that way myself. To my mind the really interesting life is that which moves from situation to situation, with

character developing naturally in step with that orderly progress.
Now what is the matter with the four of you is that you haven't
a situation among you.   You are a quartette that has forgotten
its music.   We must do something about it.   Let me see.   Mr
Cully.

CULLY.   Well?

BOLFRY.   Here we have a common soldier who . . .

CULLY.   I'm not a common soldier.   I'm in the Royal
Artillery.

BOLFRY.   Here we have a young intellectual . . .

CULLY.   There's no need to use foul language.   Call me
what you like, but not that.

BOLFRY.   Very well, then.   Here we have a product of our
Universities and Public Schools.   I know I am correct there.

CULLY.   How do you know?

BOLFRY.   Because you can't listen patiently and because you
have no manners.   Here we have this delicately nurtured youth
cheerfully bearing the rigours of the barrack and the bivouac.
Why?   Has he a secret sorrow?

CULLY.   No, I haven't.   And I'm bearing the rigours
because I've blooming well got to.   I was stuck for a commission on my eyesight, but I'll be in the Pay Corps within a
month with any luck.   And then good-bye rigours of the
barrack and the bivouac.

BOLFRY.   None the less, an interesting character.   A philo-
sopher.   An observer of Life.   Obviously the juvenile lead for
want of a better.

CULLY.   Thank you.

BOLFRY.   Don't mention it.   There is about him a certain
air of mystery which we shall presently resolve.   The leading
woman, on the other hand, is cast along more stereotyped lines.
She is what happens in the third generation after one of the many
thousand Movements for the emancipation of Women.   So is
Mr Cully, by the way.

JEAN.   What in the world do you mean by that?

BOLFRY.   You are only faintly feminine and he is only
slightly masculine.   All these Women's Movements tend to have
a neutralising effect on the Human Race.   Never mind.   It
will make our little drama interesting to the psychologist, and
we are all psychologists nowadays.   We come now to what used
to be called Comic Relief.

COHEN. That wouldn't be me, I don't suppose?

BOLFRY. Yes. There is nothing dramatic about the Poor unless they are very funny or very tragic.

COHEN. Wotjer mean by the Poor? I ain't never had a bob I haven't worked for.

BOLFRY. That is what I mean by the Poor. As for the extremely charming little person on my right, I haven't decided whether she is funny or not. As she is an unsophisticated savage, she is probably significant of something which will no doubt emerge.

CULLY. What about the Minister?

BOLFRY. He will provide Personality. The drama will revolve about him and . . . ah, yes . . . his lady wife. As I had nearly forgotten all about her, she is probably the key to the whole business. There, my dear friends, are the Dramatis Personae. We have now . . .

COHEN. Where do you come in?

BOLFRY. I am the Devil from the Machine. Here we have our Persons in the Play. We know very little about them, because, so far, there is nothing much to know. We cannot imitate the old dramatists and describe them as Cully in love with Jean, Conk, in love with Morag, Jean, in love with Cully, Morag . . .

MORAG. Now, I am not, Mr Bolfry, no indeed at all. And you needn't be saying it.

JEAN. Nobody's in love with anybody else. Not here, anyhow. Why should they be?

BOLFRY. The animals went in two by two for a very particular reason. And when a drama has no other especial interest, it would be unkind to deny it a Love Interest. I think the least you can do is to fall in love as quickly as possible. You are wasting time.

JEAN. Except Conk and Morag.

MORAG. Now, Miss Jean! . . .

COHEN. We told you before we was only talking about budgerigars.

BOLFRY. Budgerigars! Love Birds! Brilliant images of tenderness and desire with every delicate feather-frond alive with passion! We taught them speech that they might teach us their mystery. And what did they say: " Cocky's clever. Cocky's clever. Chirrup, chirrup. Good morning, good evening."

That's all. And yet how much better do you express the primeval urgencies within you? "Cully's clever. Jean's clever. Chirrup. Good evening." I must teach you how to express yourselves better, young enemies of Death. Come, then. Why don't you tell Miss Jean what you think of her, Cully? She would be extremely flattered.

JEAN. No, I wouldn't. He's told me already what he thinks of me, and I've slapped his face. You're a silly old ass. If you've come here to talk about repressions and inhibited personalities, I wish you'd stayed in Hell. You know perfectly well that if it weren't for inhibitions every living thing on this earth would run down in a few minutes.

BOLFRY. Of course it would. And how shockingly you misunderstand me. I love repression. You repress your passion to intensify it; to have it more abundantly; to joy in its abundance. The prisoner cannot leap to lose his chains unless he has been chained.

JEAN. Then what *are* you talking about?

BOLFRY. About you. Come. I'll marry you.

JEAN. But I don't want to marry you.

BOLFRY. No, no. I mean, I'll marry Cully and you. I'll bind you by the strongest and most solemn contract ever forged in heaven. Think of the agonising fun and excitement you'll have in breaking it.

JEAN. No. Thank you very much.

BOLFRY. But why don't you do something? Why is the blood galloping through your not unsightly limbs? Why are the nerve cells snapping and flashing in your head if you are to wrap this gift of life in a napkin and bury it in a back garden.

JEAN. We are doing something.

BOLFRY. Indeed?

JEAN. We're fighting Hitler.

BOLFRY. And who is Hitler?

COHEN. Blind me, I'd 've thought if anybody knew the old basket, it'd be you.

CULLY. Do you mean to tell me that we've all gone to the trouble of fetching a damned medieval hypothesis out of Hell to tell us what life is all about, and now we have to tell *him*?

JEAN. Mr Bolfry, dearest, Hitler is the man who started the War.

[48]

BOLFRY. Is he? I thought I had done that. How is the War getting on? . . . No. Don't tell me. I'll try to guess.

[BOLFRY *helps himself to another drink.*]

I should think some lunatic has been able to persuade his country that it is possible to regiment mankind. I should think the people he has persuaded are my old friends the Germans. They are sufficiently orderly and sufficiently stupid so to be persuaded. I should conjecture that mankind has risen in an intense state of indignation at the bare possibility of being regimented. I should think that the regimenters will succeed in hammering their enemies into some sort of cohesion. Mankind will then roll them in the mud for a bit and then pull them out and forget all about them. They will have much more interesting things to attend to—such as making money and making love. . . . Ah, there you are, McCrimmon.

[*Re-enter* MR *and* MRS MCCRIMMON. MRS MCCRIMMON *is carrying a Minister's gown and white Geneva bands.*]

Well, my dear Sir, time is getting on. Shall we adjourn to the Kirk?

MCCRIMMON. No.

BOLFRY. No? But, my dear fellow, I thought it was all arranged.

MCCRIMMON. No. This is a dream, of course; but there must be decency even in dreams. Waking or sleeping, I will have no phantasmagorical equivocator preaching in my Kirk.

BOLFRY. A dream, eh? You think this is all a dream?

MCCRIMMON. What else can it be?

BOLFRY. What is the difference between a dream and a supernatural happening?

MCCRIMMON. The question does not arise. This is nothing but a highly circumstantial dream. I shall laugh at it the morning.

BOLFRY. The sign of a supernatural event is that it obeys all the laws of Nature except one. You will find that true of every supernatural event from the Burning Bush to the Resurrection.

MCCRIMMON. There is truth in that.

BOLFRY. Has your room changed? Have the people around you changed? Does the clock go on ticking? This is not a dream, Mr McCrimmon.

MCCRIMMON. I am troubled in my mind, but I can yet hold

fast to what there is to grasp.   I will have no spectre or Devil
preaching in my church.

BOLFRY (*in a low and sinister voice*).   By the Throne of
Thunder and the Canopy of Eternal Night . . .

MRS MCCRIMMON.   Now, now, then, Mr Bolfry, there's no
need to excite yourself.   You can preach here quite well.   See,
here's the wee reading-desk, and I've brought the Minister's
second-best gown and bands.   Put the desk on the table, Mr
Cohen.

[COHEN *puts a small reading-desk on the table.*]

There now, that's fine.   For Sabbath after Sabbath we had
the diet of worship in this wee room when the Kirk was being
done for the dry rot.   We'll pull the chairs round, and Mr Bolfry
will give us the grand sermon, I'm sure.

JEAN.   Yes, Mr Bolfry.   It would be better.   Give me the
gown, Auntie.

BOLFRY.   What is there in Creation or beyond it that cannot
be wheedled by women ?

[JEAN *and* MRS MCCRIMMON *close in on him and invest him in the
gown and bands.   He is a little tipsy.   The others arrange the
furniture for the Sermon.*]

MRS MCCRIMMON.   Well, well, that's no' very polite talk.
Put your arm through here and content yourself.

JEAN (*with the bands*).   How does this go, Auntie ?

MORAG.   There's a wee thingummy that catches behind the
collar.   Look you, I'll do it.

[MORAG *fastens the bands, while* JEAN *walks round for a front view.*
MRS MCCRIMMON *smooths the robe.*]

JEAN.   You look absolutely beautiful.

[BOLFRY *goes to the fireplace and surveys himself in the picture-glass.
The others sit down round the table in silence.   BOLFRY turns
and goes to the makeshift Pulpit.*]

BOLFRY.   You will find my text in the Gospel according to
William Blake, that Poet and Prophet who walked to the edge
of Hampstead Heath and put his finger through the sky.   " Now
is the dominion of Edom and the return of Adam to Paradise."

CULLY.   Ha !   Ha !

BOLFRY.   What are you laughing at ?

CULLY.   Paradise !   I can't help it.

BOLFRY.   You must not laugh at Paradise.

[50]   204

CULLY.   Have a look at your Paradise. . . . Hunger and filth and disease and murder.

BOLFRY.   Have a look at your Bible and don't interrupt my Sermon.   You sit there in your squalid, drab, killer's clothes, with your squalid, drab mind and see nothing but your little bodily rough-and-tumble in your little thieves' kitchen of a world.   Look up!   The real War is beyond and about it.   The War between Good and Evil.   The Holy War.   It is a War not to destroy, but to create.   It is like the war between man and woman.   If there were no war, God would go to sleep. The Kingdom of Heaven would wilt and wither.   Death would conquer both Good and Evil and there would be Nothing.   It is unbearable that there should be nothing.   The War must go on.

For what, you ask me, do these forces fight?   Their War Aims are plain.   My Führer fights for the New Disorder; for disorder is perpetual movement and movement is Life.   The Enemy has stated clearly his Ten Points, from Mount Sinai in a thunder storm.*   [We must not allow our reverence to stray from one single object.   We must not create works of Art, nor devote ourselves to them.   We must not conceive or propagate any idea about God that is not strictly true.   We must do no work on the seventh day of the week.   We must respect the Family.   We must not destroy life.   We must be faithful to our first love and desire no other woman.   We must not live on another man's efforts.   We must not lie about our neighbours. We must want nothing that another man has.]

To these are added two more powerful commands, spoken quietly on a hot and dusty day.   We must love the Holy Spirit with all our strength and we must love Tom, Dick and Harry as ourselves.

To effect these things is impossible.   It is admitted by the teachers that to do them is impossible to man; and man is the cleverest thing we know.   But to the Holy Spirit, they say, everything is possible.   By its Grace, they say, and by forcing the soul through Fire and Water up to Crucifixion itself man will at last achieve the impossible, which will be Victory.

I, the Devil, am Fire and Water.   I hoist the gallows and drive the pike between the ribs.   Without an enemy, there can be no Victory.   Honour me, then, for my part in your triumph.

* The lines within brackets may be omitted.

Honour me for the day when you spurn the clouds written with curses, when you stamp the stony laws to dust, " loosing the eternal horses from the dens of night ".

MCCRIMMON.   Rhetoric!   Rhetoric!   Rhetoric!   The Fathers have confuted you hundreds of years back.

BOLFRY.   So much the worse for them.

MCCRIMMON.   You are talking a parcel of old-fashioned Dualistic sophistications.   You are a Manichæan.

BOLFRY.   You are a liar.

COHEN.   Order, order!

MCCRIMMON.   I do not take issue with you for that word, because you are my own heart speaking in a dream.   But it is sorrowful I am that it should be so.

BOLFRY.   You are better than your neighbours, Mr McCrimmon.   They would say that because a truth was sorrowful or distasteful, or inconvenient, it was therefore not a truth.   That is why they will not believe what I have come to tell you; that Victory may go the other way.

MCCRIMMON.   What do you mean?

BOLFRY.   That the Gates of Hell may prevail against the armies of the Cherubim.   That Disorder may win the day.   If that were not possible, why do you wrestle and pray?

MCCRIMMON.   God forbid that it should be so.

BOLFRY.   God forbade Adam to eat an apple.

JEAN.   What will happen if you win this War?

BOLFRY.   Man's genius will burst its bonds and leap to meet the sun.   The living, glorious animal in you will riot in the fields, and the soul will laugh for joy, naked but not ashamed. Your Self will be triumphant.

When I win, Man will be an individual.   You may love your neighbour if you like, but all that is highest in you tells him to keep his distance.   You don't know him.   You will never know him.   You are no longer a thing in a herd, crouching against your neighbour's wool to keep you from the cold.   You are a man.   You are a woman.

Onward, Christian Soldiers, shuffling along shouldered with your heavy packs, and your blistered feet, and the fear of Hell in your eyes.   It's a rocky road to Zion, and what will you find when you get there?   Your officers lash you on with curses and punishment and flatter you with Hope.   There is no Hope in my country.   No man hopes for what he has.

[52]

What are the virtues that keep you going? Courage?
Honesty? Charity? I have them too. Courage is the
reaction to Fear. You are more afraid than I am. Honesty is
the reaction to lies. Charity is the reaction to hate and suspicion. My honesty spurns your superstitions. My charity
embraces both the sheep and the goats.

My flags are the Pride of the Eye and the Lust of the Flesh.
Their other names are Art and Poetry, and where they wave the
abomination of desolation can never be.

How long, O Lucifer, Son of the Morning, how long?
How long will these fools listen to the quaverings of impotent
old priests, haters of the Life they never know?

How long will they swaddle their strong limbs in dusty
parchments? How long will they shut out the sky from their
eyes with prisons of cold stone?

I tell you that all you have and all you know is your Self.
Honour your Self and set him free; for the Soul and the Body
are one, and their only home is the World, and their only life is
the Flesh and their only friend is the Devil.

Let the wild horses loose!

MCCRIMMON (*rising*). In nomine Patris Aeternis, Filii et
Spiritus Sancti, conjuro te, Sathanas. . . .

BOLFRY. Latin, eh? You've gone Papist, have you?
You don't know your own regiment, my man.

MCCRIMMON. Away with you! Away with you out of my
house!

BOLFRY. Take care, McCrimmon.

MCCRIMMON (*more quietly*). If you are, as I think you are, a
bad dream and the voice of my own heart speaking evil, I will
tear you from my breast if I die for it.

BOLFRY. Stay where you are. You said there was truth in
what I told you—" The sign of a supernatural event is that it
obeys all the laws of Nature except one." Think of that before
you act too rashly.

MCCRIMMON. You said you were here to free the Self from
its shackles. I am my Self, and myself is a Minister of the
Gospel. I will follow my inclination, look you. And what is
my inclination? It is to have the thrapple of you out by the
roots.

[MCCRIMMON *suddenly takes up* CULLY'S *knife. The* WOMEN
scream. BOLFRY *backs out of his pulpit and towards the door.*]

BOLFRY. You are not very wise, McCrimmon. You are not very wise.

MORAG. Stay in the circle. He will have you. He will have you.

JEAN. Uncle, don't be a fool.

MRS MCCRIMMON. Oh, no! Oh, no!

CULLY. Let him be. It's all right. Conk and I will look after him.

BOLFRY. You will have it, will you? Come along, then. Let's see you hunt the Devil over the moor.

[MCCRIMMON *breaks from* CULLY *and* COHEN *and makes for* BOLFRY. BOLFRY *throws the gown over* MCCRIMMON's *head and makes for the door. In a moment* MCCRIMMON *recovers himself and, flinging the gown over his shoulder like a cloak, follows* BOLFRY *through the doorway.*]

COHEN. Come on, Cully. There'll be murder done.

[*He runs through the doorway.*]

CULLY. Murder? Of what?

[*He follows* COHEN.]

MRS MCCRIMMON. Oh, such a like night to be out! And in his slippers, too. Well, well. We'll away to our beds.

JEAN. But, Auntie . . . But . . .

MRS MCCRIMMON. Och, we're dreaming all this. And I've a hard day's work before me tomorrow when I wake up. And moreover, when I do wake up, I'd like to it be decent-like in my bed. Away to your bed, Morag, girl.

MORAG. You're sure, now, we're only dreaming?

MRS MCCRIMMON. What else would we be doing, you silly creature? Away with you to your bed.

MORAG. Well, dear me, good night, then, Mem.

MRS MCCRIMMON. Good night, Morag.

JEAN. Good night, Morag.

MORAG. Good night, Miss Jean.

[*Exit* MORAG.]

JEAN. Do you think . . .? I mean to say . . .

MRS MCCRIMMON. Och, that girl's head is such a mixty-maxty of nonsensicalities, it'll be all the same to her in the morning, dream or no dream.

JEAN. What will be all the same in the morning? Do you think we *are* dreaming? Are you dreaming the same dream as I am, or are you just part of the dream? Is she dreaming too?

MRS MCCRIMMON.   I thought you knew enough about the Highlands to know that it is all one whether we are dreaming or not.

[*She begins to tidy up the room, moving the reading-desk to its proper place and shifting the chairs.*]

JEAN.   I don't think I'm dreaming.   I'm sure somebody has been here.   It was so absolutely real.   It's real now.

MRS MCCRIMMON.   Maybe Aye, maybe No.

[*She dusts off the chalk marks.*]

JEAN.   But there was a wee minister—you saw him too.

MRS MCCRIMMON.   Oh, aye, may be.

JEAN.   What are they doing out on the moor?   Uncle Jock went after him with a knife.

MRS MCCRIMMON.   As likely as not your uncle is up in his bed snoring.

JEAN.   Why don't you go upstairs and look?

MRS MCCRIMMON.   What difference would that make? Here or there, it's all one in a dream, if a dream it is.   And it's gey like one, I must say.   Forbye, I'm going up the stair this minute.   I'm blind with sleep.   We'll can tidy up in the morning, if there's anything to tidy.

JEAN.   I'll wait and see if they come back.

MRS MCCRIMMON.   Please yourself.

JEAN.   But, Aunt Marget . . . if it's a real man . . . if he's chasing a real man, with a real knife . . .

MRS MCCRIMMON.   Your uncle never did the like of that in his life.   That's why I know fine it's a dream.   Don't you fash yourself . . . and put out the lamp when you come up.

JEAN.   But if it's not a real lamp, what does it matter whether I put it out or not?

MRS MCCRIMMON.   It's unlucky to set the house on fire, even in a dream.   Good night.

JEAN.   Good night, Aunt Marget.

[*Exit* MRS MCCRIMMON.   JEAN *rubs her eyes, pinches herself, picks up the* DISCOVERIE OF WITCHCRAFT, *looks at it for a moment, slams it shut, and puts it back on the shelf.* JEAN *starts and turns round as* MCCRIMMON *enters followed by* CULLY *and* COHEN.   *All three look dazed.* MCCRIMMON *throws the knife on the table and the gown on the chair and stares into the dead fire.* COHEN *picks up the knife, rubs his thumb along the edge and shows it to* CULLY.]

COHEN.   No blood.   He can't have used it.

CULLY.   Yes, but . . . the Name I wrote on it.   Agla.
It isn't there.

COHEN.   Rubbed off, I expect.

CULLY.   It's damned funny.

COHEN.   It's all damned funny.   Do you think we're
crackers or what?

CULLY.   I don't know what to think.

JEAN.   Where's Bolfry?

COHEN.   He grabbed his hat and his coat and away he went
across the moor like an electric hare with his old Battle of the
Nile on his head.   His Reverence caught up with him on the
edge of the cliff.   Then he hit him.   With Cully's jack-knife,
I thought.   Anyways he . . . the . . . Bolfry, I mean . . .
he took a leap like a circus acrobat straight out and down into
the sea.   A 'undred blinking feet down.   Into deep water.
We couldn't do nothing about it.

CULLY.   And where he dived, the water boiled like a pot.
You saw it.   Why not say so?

COHEN.   I won't swear as how I didn't see it.   But it might
have been anything.   Atmospherics or a squall or something.

CULLY.   The sea was as calm as a millpond.   And the steam
rose to the cliff's edge.   Damnation, we've all gone mad.

[*He takes up the knife, rubs it vigorously on his sleeve, closes it, and
puts it in his pocket.* JEAN *has been staring at them and auto-
matically straightening the furniture.*]

JEAN.   Cully, what's happened?   What do you think has
happened?   What do you think, Cully?

CULLY.   I'm doing no thinking tonight.   Come along,
Conk.   Let's get down to it.   If I stay in this room any
longer . . .

COHEN.   Look at him.

[*He indicates* MCCRIMMON. *All three watch him as he slowly
picks up the bottle and pours the heel of it into* BOLFRY'S *glass.
He swallows the whisky neat at one gulp.*]

COHEN.   That's right, Guv'nor.   You need it.   Do you a
world of good, that, eh?

MCCRIMMON.   What did you say?

COHEN.   I said it'd do you good.

MCCRIMMON (*picking up the empty bottle and looking at it in a*

mournful, puzzled sort of way).   Do me good, do you think?
. . . Well, well.

[*He turns to* CULLY *and* COHEN.]

Gentlemen, I must ask your forgiveness.   It seems that I
. . . that I have forgotten myself.   When I was a Divinity
student there was a time when I was over-addicted to alcohol.
It is many years ago.   I thought that I had conquered the vice.
Indeed, I thought it.   But it seems I was over-confident.   I
have been too confident about too much.

JEAN.   Perhaps you should go to bed now, Uncle.

MCCRIMMON.   No doubt but you are right.   I cannot conceive how it happened.   My head is not yet clear, but my legs
seem to be doing their duty.   I will go to bed.   It is the black
disgrace of a fellow I am, and me a Minister. . . . Stop you,
though, am I right or am I wrong?   Was there another person
here?

JEAN.   How could there be?   There's only Cully and Conk
and me, Uncle Mac.

MCCRIMMON.   Dear me, that is so.   It is a terrible thing this
weakness of mine.   I thought for a moment . . . I will go
to bed.   You will put away this . . . evidence?

JEAN.   All right, Uncle Mac, I'll get rid of the dead man.

MCCRIMMON.   The dead man? . . . Ah, the bottle.   Do,
like a good girl.   I would not like to think . . .

COHEN.   That's all okey-doke.   We know how to keep our
traps shut.   We've forgotten all about it already.   That's right,
Cully?

CULLY.   That's right.

MCCRIMMON.   Tell me, was I violent at all?   I seem to
recall a lot of noise and rushing to and fro.

COHEN.   Nothing out of the ordinary.   You were a bit
excited, but always the gentleman.   My old grandfather used
to get a bit that way, but Lord bless you, he meant no harm by it,
and he was all right in the morning.

MCCRIMMON.   There was something I wanted to say.

JEAN.   It will do in the morning, Uncle Mac.

MCCRIMMON.   I will go to bed.

COHEN.   Need any help, Guv'nor?

MCCRIMMON.   No, I thank you.   You have been very kind
and very forbearing.   Good night.   Indeed, I am ashamed.

[*Exit* MCCRIMMON.]

JEAN.   Oh, dear?   I wonder.   Should we have explained?

CULLY.   Explained what?

JEAN.   I see.   There's that in it.

CULLY.   If you can explain, I wish you would.

COHEN.   If you ask me, I think we'd best forget about all this.   Unless it's a blooming murder and we're all in it.

CULLY.   If it's not a murder, I'm damned if I know what it is.   But it's not a murder.

JEAN.   Are you sure?

CULLY.   I'm not sure of anything in the whole Universe.

JEAN.   I'm a bit frightened.

CULLY.   By God, so am I.

[*He puts an arm round* JEAN.]

COHEN.   Oh, I don't know.   A cousin of the wife's went to one of them spiritualist meetings and seen a trumpet flying through the air.   But I says to her, " If you started worrying about things the like of that, you'd fetch up in the Silly House," I says.

CULLY.   You think there are . . . ?   Gosh, I nearly said it.

COHEN.   Said what?

JEAN.   That there are more things in Heaven and Earth than are dreamt of in our philosophy, Conk.

COHEN.   Oh, I don't know.   Depends on what your philosophy is.   Seems to me if there *was* SOMEONE up top-sides—and I'm not saying there is and I'm not saying there ain't —he wouldn't tell the likes of you and me what he was up to. Nor we wouldn't have much idea of what he was gabbing about if he did. . . .   Do you see the time?

CULLY.   Yes, by Jove!

COHEN.   Only three hours to good old Wakey-Wakey. Good night, Miss.   You waiting up a bit, Cully?

CULLY.   No.

COHEN.   Okey-doke.   Good night, Miss.

[COHEN *goes.* JEAN *and* CULLY *have separated and stand looking at each other.*]

CULLY.   Cully's clever, Jean's clever, chirrup-chirrup, good evening.   Only not so damned clever.

JEAN.   I'm still frightened.

CULLY.   May I kiss you now?   Would that help?

JEAN.   Oh, no, no, no, no!   It would make it worse.   But thank you all the same.

CULLY. Good night, then.

JEAN. Good night, my dear.

[*They shake hands and* CULLY *goes.* JEAN *puts out the lamp.*]

BLACK OUT.

SCENE IV

The Same. The following morning. Bright sunshine. JEAN, *in a spectacular dressing-gown, and* MRS MCCRIMMON *have just sat down to breakfast.* MORAG *has just brought in a cover and coffee.*

JEAN. Good morning, Morag.

MORAG. Good morning, Miss Jean. It's fresh herrings and bread-crumbs, Miss Jean.

JEAN. Isn't that splendid! There's nothing I'd like better. Did you sleep well last night, Morag?

MORAG. Yes, Miss Jean. I slept like a top all night, thank you very much. Coffee, Mrs McCrimmon.

MRS MCCRIMMON. Thank you, Morag.

[MORAG *goes.*]

For what we are about to receive, the Lord make us truly thankful.

JEAN. Uncle Mac isn't down yet?

MRS MCCRIMMON. No. He had a disturbed night, your uncle. I wanted him to have his breakfast in bed, but he's coming down. It's a beautiful day.

JEAN. How do you mean a disturbed night?

MRS MCCRIMMON. Oh, well. He has the indigestion whiles. And it's an awful thing for not letting you sleep very well. That's a beautiful dressing-gown you're wearing. Have I seen it before?

JEAN. No, Auntie. Didn't Uncle Mac sleep, then?

MRS MCCRIMMON. It is very nice. But, mind you, it is hardly what we are used to up in these outlandish parts. I don't say your Uncle will make a remark. He may and he may not. But he may not think it just quite the thing for breakfast. Mind, I'm not saying. But even on my honeymoon I always dressed for breakfast. It was just the way we had. Not that it's important.

JEAN. I'm sorry. I didn't sleep too well either.

MRS MCCRIMMON. Did you not, now? You shouldn't have got up. We'd have brought you your breakfast. Are you sure you're feeling all right?

JEAN. Oh, yes. Fine now. But it was a most peculiar night.

MRS MCCRIMMON. Was it so? You would be dreaming, maybe. I never pay any attention to such things. Will you be well enough to come down to the village with me today?

JEAN. No. Yes. I think so. Have the two soldiers gone?

MRS MCCRIMMON. Ah, yes. They have to be out for their runnings and their jumpings. They have breakfast up at the guns, poor souls. Nice lads, too. We are very lucky, whatever. Mrs McLean up by Offerance, she got some gey funny ones. But these are nice quiet lads.

JEAN. Aunt Marget . . . how did you sleep last night?

MRS MCCRIMMON. Oh, very well, I thank you. But nothing puts me up or down, from the moment I put my head on the pillow.

JEAN. I was wondering. I . . . You . . . I had an eerie dream last night, Aunt Marget.

MRS MCCRIMMON. Had you, dear? It was a wild night. It is a strange place up here in Larach, but, och, you get used to it. It might be something you ate.

JEAN. That's what I said to Morag. I mean . . .

MRS MCCRIMMON. I hope you won't be putting daft ideas into that lassie's head. It's full enough of daftness already.

JEAN. All right, Aunt Marget, I won't. Oh, good morning, Uncle Mac.

[MCCRIMMON enters. He is very solemn.]

MCCRIMMON. Good morning, Jean.

[He sits down.]

Heavenly Father, we thank thee for all these mercies. Sanctify them to our use. Amen. Well, that's a fine day.

MRS MCCRIMMON. Yes. Isn't it a beautiful day?

MCCRIMMON. It's not often you'll see Larach all over smiles the like of this, Jean. It's a great compliment to our visitor. It can be a wild place, Larach.

MRS MCCRIMMON. Indeed, that is so. I hope you don't object to the herring. There wasn't a single egg this morning. I don't know what came over the hens. It would be the storm, maybe.

MCCRIMMON. Aye, yes. The storm.

MRS MCCRIMMON. And now you two will have to excuse

me.   We're a wee thing late, and I have to check over the linen
for the washing before I go down for the messages.

MCCRIMMON.   Certainly, my dear.   Certainly.

[MRS MCCRIMMON *goes out.   She turns at the door and makes
mysterious signs to* JEAN *from behind her husband's back.   He
is not on any account to be worried.* JEAN *nods.*]

MCCRIMMON.   A man is a very curious thing.

JEAN.   Yes, isn't he?

MCCRIMMON.   Dear me, I did not think that I would behave
like that at this time of day.   It is a lesson to me.

JEAN.   Oh, it was nothing, Uncle Mac.   Nothing, really, at
all.

MCCRIMMON.   Nothing?   That one who should be an
example to the flock should give way to strong drink like a
beast?

JEAN.   Beasts don't give way to strong drink.   Besides, it
wasn't your fault.

MCCRIMMON.   A bottle of whisky!   Mind you, it is not
everybody who could drink a bottle of whisky and go up to bed
as straight as a die.   Pre-war whisky too.

JEAN.   But you didn't . . .

MCCRIMMON.   I must have.   It was full on the Lord's
morning, because I happened to notice.   Forbye it is not the
first time, the Lord forgive me.   But, Lord helping me, it will
be the last.   It comes on me about every five years.   But never
like this time.

JEAN.   How?   What happened?

MCCRIMMON.   That's the queer thing.   I don't know.   I
had a whirling vision that I was disputing with Beelzebub himself in this very room and racing over the moor with a knife in
my hand.   And then I found myself leaning against the
mantelpiece finishing off the bottle with the two lads tidying up
the room.   I aye throw the furniture about a wee.   Or I did
when I was that way.

JEAN.   It was a strange dream.

MCCRIMMON.   Never have I had a dream so real.   I could
see Beelzebub as plain as could be—in that chair and then
uttering blasphemies in my ears as if he were in the pulpit—in
my gown and bands.   I mind every word I thought he said.

JEAN (*breathlessly*).   What did he say?

MCCRIMMON.   I thought you and Marget and the lads were

215   [61]

here too.   He was telling you all to stamp the ancient Law into
dust and revolt against the Armies of the Lord.

[*He laughs.*]

Very plausible and persuasive he was, too.   I had an answer
for him, but he never heard it.   I was that angered I struck him
with my dirk and threw him into the Firth.   It wasn't a bad
answer, but I had a better.

JEAN.   What was your answer?   I mean, what would it
have been?

MCCRIMMON (*ignoring her question*).   It was my own mind
speaking.   We've got the queer, dark corners in our mind and
strange beasts in them that come out ranging in the night.   A
sophisticated black beast yon.   I never knew of him.   I
wonder, now, did I kill him?   If I did it was worth it all.
Mind you, there were points where he nearly had me.

[*He has been thinking aloud, but he becomes again aware of* JEAN
and turns to her.]

Of course, this was all a dream or a delirium, I canna right say
which.   But you learn things in these states.   It's a kind of a
twisted inspiration.   I learned one thing.

JEAN.   What was that?

MCCRIMMON.   That mankind turns to Almighty God as a
nettle turns to the sun.   And if the nettle had a fine, argufying
brain in it and a spacious command of words, it could do little
better and maybe a good deal worse.   We've a thing called
Faith in us, Jean, and we've no more command over it than we
have over our lungs.   Mind you, we can develop our lungs and
we can develop our Faith.   Maybe, I've neglected that a bit.
I was over proud of my head.   But in the middle of all the talk
it rose up within me and told me to strike the Devil dead . . .
in my delirium, mind you.   But it was awful like the real
thing.   A lesson to me.

[MRS MCCRIMMON *re-enters, ushering in* CULLY *and* COHEN.
CULLY *wears a brand-new Lance-Bombardier's stripe.* COHEN
carries a postbag.   He lays it down near the door.]

MRS MCCRIMMON.   Isn't this a nice surprise?   Come in,
boys, and have a cup of tea.

COHEN.   Look at him.   Lance-Bombardier Cully, Non-
Commissioned Officer in charge of his Majesty's Mails and the
same old Gunner Cohen, Lance Bombardier's stooge to same.

JEAN.   Oh, congratulations, Cully.

[62]   216

CULLY. Thanks very much.

COHEN. We thought we'd pop in. No good getting a dog's leg if you don't give the skirts a treat.

CULLY. How are you, Mr McCrimmon?

MCCRIMMON. I am well, I thank you. Indeed, remarkably well. And you?

CULLY. I couldn't sleep. Look here, Mr McCrimmon, it's no use pretending and telling lies. It's not fair to you. It's not fair to any of us. You weren't drunk last night.

MRS MCCRIMMON. Oh dear me, what a thing to say! As if the Minister would be!

MCCRIMMON (*rising*). What do you mean?

CULLY. Something happened last night that I don't understand, and we've got to thrash it out somehow.

MCCRIMMON. Do you mean that the—the—the—experience I had last night was shared by the whole of you?

[MCCRIMMON *sits down again in great perturbation of mind.* MRS MCCRIMMON *goes to him to soothe him.* JEAN *sits rigid.*]

MRS MCCRIMMON. Now, now, now, now. The best thing is to forget all about it.

COHEN. I told you that, Cully. You can't do any good.

CULLY. No, we've got to get it straight. There must be an explanation. We can't leave things that way. Look, Mr McCrimmon, do you know anything about Mass Hypnotism? I know they don't think there's much in it, but you know about the Indian Rope Trick, don't you? And the old necromancers who thought they were raising the Devil, they *did* induce a sort of suggestible state. I mean they sat down and deliberately hypnotised themselves with their spells and magic circles. I mean, what do you think? . . . Of course, you and Mrs McCrimmon weren't here at the beginning of the séance, but it's the only explanation that seems to me natural.

JEAN. You mean there was really nobody here?

CULLY. Yes. There must be a natural explanation. I know the other one's wrong.

JEAN. What other one?

MCCRIMMON. That I killed a man. I did not kill a man. How I know, I do not know, but I know it. I did not kill a man.

MRS MCCRIMMON. Of course you didn't, now.

CULLY. I'm sure you didn't. It's mass suggestion. Nothing happened. Look at the room. There are no signs of anything happening in this room.

MCCRIMMON. It is a peaceful room. Everything is natural. Everything obeys the Laws of Nature. It is the sign of a . . . let me see . . . it is the sign of a supernatural event that everything obeys the laws of Nature except one thing. No doubt you are right.

JEAN (*suddenly screaming*). The umbrella!! It's Bolfry's.

[*All look towards the umbrella on the hearth. There is a tense pause. Then the umbrella gets up and walks by itself out of the room.*]

MRS MCCRIMMON. Well, now, isn't that the queer like thing? And with all this havering, I was forgetting about your cups of tea. It isn't long infused, or have you time to wait for some fresh?

[*The* OTHERS *are too astonished to react to this.* MRS MCCRIMMON *pours hot water into the teapot and pours out cups. She talks all the time.* COHEN *and* CULLY, *in a trance-like state, take their cups.*]

Well, well, it seems you had a kind of a tuilzie with the De'il, after all. You're not the first good and godly man who did the like of that. Maybe you didn't kill him, but I'm sure you'd give him a sore dunt. And you're none the worse yourself.

It's a funny thing we should be surprised at seeing the Devil and him raging through the skies and blotting out the sun at this very hour. We're all such a nice kind of lot that we've forgotten there's any such person. Poor soul, him roaring away like a raging lion and nobody paying any attention to him with their fine plans to make us all the happy ones.

Will you be having another cup of tea, dear, now? You're looking quite white and peely-wally, and no wonder, dear me.

MCCRIMMON. I have nowhere seen such great Faith, no, not in Israel.

MRS MCCRIMMON. Drink you your tea.

Och, well, dear me, a walking umbrella's nothing to the queer things that happen in the Bible. Whirling fiery wheels and all these big beasts with the three heads and horns. It's very lucky we are that it was no worse. Drink up your tea.

[MCCRIMMON *smiles and takes her hand.*]

CURTAIN.

END OF THE PLAY.

JONAH 3

A NEW VERSION OF JONAH AND THE WHALE (1932)

Author's Note.—In my original stage version of " Jonah and the Whale " there are twenty-six speaking parts, to say nothing of supers. To perform such a play is difficult, if not impossible, in war-time conditions. I prepared a short play on the same theme for broadcasting, and, at the suggestion of Mr. F. Sladen Smith of the Unnamed Society of Manchester, I was tempted to combine the two plays in a way which will make stage performance more practicable. This new version requires little or no scenery and leaves scope for any eccentricities in production that may appeal to a modern Director.

The Curtain rises on a dark stage.   A NARRATOR *appears, lit by a Spot.*

NARRATOR.   In the deep sea-caves below the waters about the South Pole there lives a distressed and ancient Whale.   His great cruising days are over and he is so close to disintegration that Time and the sanctions of life and death have become for him misty and confused.   To such as he the waves of seas long evaporated, the forms of sea-creatures long washed to atoms, the voices of men long dead are as real as if the seas still beat, the fishes still swam and the men still spoke.   To that huge, dreaming beast came the voice of the Prophet Jonah.   It is nearly thirty centuries since the Whale last heard that voice, piping out in an agony of terror from its uneasy interior.   It is a calm and confident voice now.

[*The* NARRATOR *disappears.*]

[*The* GHOST OF JONAH *appears.   In the following dialogue the* WHALE *is indicated by its voice alone.*]

JONAH.   Ah, my dear Whale, I have found you at last!   Do you remember me?

WHALE (*as if reciting a lesson*).   I do not remember anything at all.   I am the Whale, that most deadly immortal monster.   I sail the oceans for ever and ever, lashing the sea in my wake, till you would have thought the deep to be hoary.   Or at least, so they say.   I do not remember anything at all.

JONAH.   And yet, Leviathan, you were once the instrument of Providence.

WHALE.   Was I?   In what respect?

JONAH.   Once upon a time you saved me.

WHALE.   And who are you?

JONAH.   I am a spirit hovering over the waters.   They are of interest to me, those great waters in which I nearly died frustrated and unfulfilled.   For even on them the doom that I foretold for Nineveh has fallen.   They are so polluted that even the sturdiest fish is hard put to it to live in them.   It is a pleasure to me to revisit them.   It is a pleasure to me to see you, dear majestic instrument of Providence, still held by a thread of life and brooding away time.

221

[3]

WHALE.   I am glad that a spirit can yet feel pleasure, but you have not yet told me who you are—or were, it does not matter which.   Not at this time of day.

JONAH.   I was Jonah the son of Amittai.   I lived in Zebulun in the little village of Gittah-Hepher.   It was a pleasant little town, full of fallible but worthy people.   I made it my business, in my not altogether humble way, to correct their fallibility and increase their worth.   I was not dissatisfied with the results of my efforts.   Indeed, I was more satisfied than any mortal man has a right to be.

One day in the cool of the evening some of my fellow townsmen and townswomen were sitting at the town gate.   I was a peculiar little man, though I say it who perhaps should not.   I was rather fat, and I had thick curly ginger hair and a small curly ginger beard.   When I looked at people straight in the eye they were afraid of me.   At that time the world was as it is now.   Men were hating each other and killing each other, and nobody knew what was going to happen next.   People were very anxious to know what was going to happen, whether it was good or bad, and soon it became known that I could tell them.

WHALE.   How did you know?

JONAH.   To tell you the truth, I don't think I really knew how I knew.

WHALE.   You didn't use the stars, did you?

JONAH.   My good gracious goodness, no!   Of course not.

WHALE.   Quite right, quite right.   I never used them myself, even for getting about from place to place; but I managed to get about all right.

JONAH.   I was fairly certain at the time that God told me what was going to happen; and the people were quite sure.   They came for miles to my little village, and I told them the truth in a very powerful baritone voice.   Some things I told them were easy, such as that if they were wicked they would be miserable.   Other things were more difficult.   I could tell them when the coppersmith's donkey would fall down a well, and when they might expect the soldiers to come ravening over their fields, and when it was going to thunder.   This sort of thing got me a greater reputation in the place than I could have got simply by telling them to be good.   It's very odd that.   However, one day some of them were sitting in the cool of the evening, blinking

at the yellow and olive haze on the dusty horizon, and recreating
themselves with idle conversation . . .

.   .   .   .   .   .

> [JONAH'S *presence and voice fade away. The lights go up on the
> gates of Gittah-Hepher. Three bearded men and two girls are
> sitting on the ground. A* SENTRY *with a big stick is indolently
> leaning against the gatepost watching them.*]

JOSIBIAH.   And the big bear said, " Who has been sleeping
in my big bed ? "

EUODIAS.   Yoi, yoi !

HASHMONAH.   Hush.

JOSIBIAH.   And the middle-sized bear said, " Who has been
sleeping in my middle-sized bed ? "   And the little bear said,
" Ach, ach, there is a girl sleeping in my little bed."   So the
noise of his cries awoke the fair Circassian, and she leaped through
the window and fled as far as her lower limbs could carry her.

HASHMONAH.   Praise Jahveh for her escape.

THE OTHERS.   Amen to that.

NAARAN.   How terrible to be eaten by a bear !

SHUAL.   Let alone three.

NAARAN.   Let alone three.

HASHMONAH.   It must have been a great lesson to her in
minding her own business.

SHUAL.   Indeed, indeed.

EUODIAS.   Yes, but . . .

HASHMONAH.   But what ?

> [*Enter* BILSHAN, *a handsome stranger with great brass ear-rings.*]

EUODIAS.   I feel . . . I mean . . . don't you think ?   I
mean if we all minded our own business, wouldn't we die of
being sick and tired of the horrible dullness of it ?

NAARAN.   That would be better than to die of being eaten
by bears.

SHUAL.   You are a wise woman, Naaran, and Euodias is a
silly chatterbox.   Ah, what, I ask you, is the good of Josibiah
telling a chittering jerboa like that all his wonderful and moral
stories ?

JOSIBIAH.   And true stories.   I knew the girl's father very
well.

SHUAL.   And true stories. . . . Eh ?

NAARAN.   No good at all.   I hope she is sorry she spoke.

223   [5]

HASHMONAH.   Indeed, I hope so.

JOSIBIAH.   And I hope so too.

SHUAL.   And, from the bottom of my heart, so do I.

BILSHAN.   She is quite right.

SHUAL.   Hey?

JOSIBIAH.   Ho!

BILSHAN.   The girl is quite right.

THE SENTRY.   Now, now, Sir.   None of that.

JOSIBIAH.   I have no specific recollection of asking you to interfere, you nasty sentry.   You are here to protect us and the rest of the village from thieves and lions.   The police should be seen and not heard. . . . I ask your pardon, Sir.   Your face seems familiar, but I don't know if I have the pleasure of your acquaintance.

BILSHAN.   No, you haven't.   I am Bilshan, a commercial traveller.   I dropped off the south-going caravan to see my cousin who lives, or used to, in your village.   He is dead, I find, poor devil.

SHUAL.   What a calamity!   Alas, alas!

BILSHAN.   Yes.   You probably knew him.   Old Thahash, the usurer.

JOSIBIAH.   Ah, yes.   Well, well, a fine old man, and a good usurer.   And you are his cousin?

SHUAL.   Yoi, yoi.   How sad to expect a welcome and to find instead a desolate hearth!

BILSHAN.   No, hog's bristles!   I didn't call on old Thahash expecting a welcome.   I had a proposition I thought might interest him.   However, it's nobody's business but his and mine, and I don't suppose it'd interest him now.   It'll be all the same two thousand years hence. . . . So you believe in curiosity, my darling!

EUODIAS.   Not if these gentlemen think it's improper.   I don't care what Naaran thinks.

NAARAN.   Oh, you don't, don't you?

EUODIAS.   No, I don't.   You've no experience of life.

SHUAL.   Experience of . . . Oh, tut, tut, hush, hush.

NAARAN.   I haven't, haven't I?   What experience have you, I should very much like to know?

HASHMONAH.   No doubt you would.   Hold your tongue. This gentleman would quite evidently like an argument.   Argument is an interesting and a beautiful exercise which is too readily

ruined by the shrill screaming of females. . . . You have come
to the right place, Sir, for a good argument. We have some
excellent debaters. Josibiah, there . . .

JOSIBIAH. No, no, Hashmonah. No, no. I can speak
well enough and eloquently enough if you give me time and a
subject I thoroughly understand, like the Creation, or the nature
of Dreams; but this gentleman has obviously seen a bit of the
world, and he has a cunning eye and a chest like a drum. No,
no. You must excuse me.

SHUAL. Oh, Josibiah, for the honour of our fair town of
Gittah-Hepher.

HASHMONAH. Please, Josibiah.

JOSIBIAH. No, no.

HASHMONAH. He may not be very eloquent, and you can
always contradict him and fly into a passion.

JOSIBIAH. No, I should be ashamed.

SHUAL. He looks to me rather the strong, silent type. I
don't believe he can talk at all.

JOSIBIAH. He is a commercial traveller.

BILSHAN (to EUODIAS). And you, you most utterly beautiful
one—and, by the way, I see you don't dye your toes as the wicked
ones of Phoenicia do. . . . This little goat went to market, this
little goat stayed at . . . Oh, don't do that! . . . Rather
funny, only a week or two ago I heard one of these fellows in a
quayside music-hall—Homers, they call them in the Levant—
singing a darned good song about that.

> "Rapidly crept, on the one hand,
>   Her feet, like small mice in a panic,
>   Under her petticoat's fringe."

What's your name ?

EUODIAS. Euodias.

BILSHAN. And yours ?

NAARAN. Naaran.

BILSHAN. Nice names. Now sit down here and I'll show
you what Uncle has brought all the way from Tyre for two nice
little girls.

JOSIBIAH. I don't think he really wants to argue at all.

HASHMONAH. That is just his tact. You don't suppose he'd
rather talk to those two silly little creatures. Take him on about
the Creation.

JOSIBIAH (*clears his throat, but thinks better of it*).   No, no.
He's busy.

THE SENTRY.   Beg pardon, gentlemen.

HASHMONAH.   Well ?

THE SENTRY.   May I speak ?

HASHMONAH.   You are speaking.   Go on.

THE SENTRY.   What I was thinking was, if you gentlemen
want to put up a good show for the good old town, what about
me running round and fetching the Prophet ?   It's not every
town that has a Prophet.

HASHMONAH.   Well . . .

SHUAL.   Ah, um . . .

JOSIBIAH.   Would he come, do you think ?

THE SENTRY.   He always comes along this way for a stroll
every evening, nearly.   He could just join in casual like.   I'll
go for him if you like, if you'll look after my stick.

HASHMONAH.   Very well, then, run.   Tell him that, if he's
not busy, it's rather important.

THE SENTRY.   My feet will be like the feet of a sandstorm.

[*He goes through the gate.*]

EUODIAS (*calling after him*).   Silly !   A sandstorm has no feet.

JOSIBIAH.   You are exposing your ignorance.   That was a
quotation.

HASHMONAH.   Don't let those silly girls worry you, Mr
Bilshan. . . . As a matter of fact, we were expecting the
Prophet at any moment, and we should so like you to meet him.

BILSHAN.   I should like to very much.   I didn't know you
boasted a Prophet in these parts.

HASHMONAH.   Oh, yes.   He was born here, as a matter of
fact.   He is very fond of the old place.   He lives most of the
year here.

JOSIBIAH.   You have probably heard of him.   It's Jonah, as
a matter of fact.

BILSHAN.   Jonah ?

SHUAL.   Yes.   Jonah, the son of Amittai, a very respected
fellow-townsman of ours in his day.

BILSHAN.   I seem to have heard the name Jonah.   I'm
afraid I'm not a very churchy man these days.   What with
meandering about among the heathen, I find it impossible to
keep track of the local religions, but I'll feel highly honoured by

[8]

an introduction.   I've always had a high regard for the prophets. They can do a man a lot of good in a district, if he gets on their soft side.

HASHMONAH.   Jonah, the son of Amittai, has no soft side.

SHUAL.   A fine soul.   An excellent soul.   We are very proud of him.

JOSIBIAH.   He has done some great work in this parish and in others.

HASHMONAH.   The taverns are empty.   The meeting-houses are full.   The old practise repentance, and even the young people have grown modest and thoughtful . . . with one or two exceptions.

> [*He puts* EUODIAS *and* NAARAN *in their places with a look.*]

JOSIBIAH.   It is quite a relief when he goes into the wilderness for a little.

SHUAL.   Hush.   He is coming.

> [*Enter* JONAH, *a simple, handsome, eloquent, consequential little fat man of about thirty years old.   He contrives to look rather dressy in his Prophet's rags.   He catches his garment on a wooden nail sticking out from the gateway, and turns to the* SENTRY, *who is following.*]

JONAH (*with a very formidable gentleness*).   I think I spoke about this before.   I am fallible, I may be in error.   But I think I spoke about this.

THE SENTRY.   Not to me, Master.   I haven't been long on duty.   I . . .

JONAH.   Didn't it occur to you that a horrid great nail sticking out like that might wound a citizen, or tear his garment ? Did the Lord give you eyes ?

THE SENTRY.   It's really the Sanitary Department's business, Master, and . . .

JONAH.   I am not interested in the Sanitary Department.   I asked you a question.   Did the Lord give you eyes ?

THE SENTRY.   Yes, Master, He did.   His name be magnified.

JONAH.   Use them, then.   And hands ?

THE SENTRY.   Yes, Master.

JONAH.   Hands capable of other acts than to brandish that stick to the terror of little boys ?

THE SENTRY.   Quite capable, Master.

JONAH (*in a terrible voice*).   Use them then—(*the* SENTRY

227   [9]

pulls out the nail)—. . . Ah, good evening, Josibiah. How are you, Hashmonah? I am glad to see you, Shual. And how are my sportive little she-camels, hey?

EUODIAS and NAARAN.   Quite well, thank you, Master.

JONAH.   You are good girls, I hope?

EUODIAS and NAARAN.   We try to be, Jonah.

JONAH.   Good, good. . . . Ah, I see we have a guest. Welcome, Sir, to Gittah-Hepher. You will find no more healthful spot in Palestine for a real restful holiday.

JOSIBIAH.   This is Bilshan, Jonah.

BILSHAN.   The son of Pethuel and Hodesh, his wife. I am a commercial traveller. I am very pleased to meet a gentleman so holy and celebrated as your good self.

JONAH.   It is always a pleasure to meet a wanderer; though what are we all but wanderers, if one looks below the surface of things?

SHUAL.   As you invariably do, Jonah.

BILSHAN.   What you say is perfectly true, Jonah. When people say to me, " How horrible not to have a home, a restingplace," I always reply, " Where is your home, your restingplace, your security of tenure, and for how long? "

JONAH.   A very proper observation.

BILSHAN.   A traveller may well be at rest, as a seagull is, hanging motionless between heaven and the waves that hurry ceaselessly beneath him. It's a matter of relativity, you see, Jonah. A man who runs through a crowd may well be the only stationary object in that crowd, and from one view-point— shall we say that of a flea in his ear?—he undoubtedly is.

JOSIBIAH.   Jahveh be praised I didn't join issue with this fellow.

JONAH.   All objective fact, then, depends on the view-point from which it is observed?

BILSHAN.   Surely.

JONAH.   Then it is in the power of any casual mountebank to turn the Universe upside down by the simple process of standing on his head?

THE ONLOOKERS.   Ho, ho, ho! Jonah had him that time. Hip, hip, hurrah!

ONAH.   My friends, I should appreciate your applause the more if I believed that you had the faintest idea what this gentleman and I are talking about. You remain if you will not

[10]

interrupt. On that condition alone. . . . Well, Sir, I am all attention.

BILSHAN. I hardly think you have quite followed my thought, Sir.

JONAH. Pardon me. One moment. I am only a simple prophet. I have not travelled to many places nor seen a great variety of people. These things possibly account for the fact that I am not accustomed to being spoken to in that manner.

BILSHAN. In what manner? I had no intention . . .

JONAH. You accused me of being unable to follow your thought. Your thought must be a good deal quicker on the wing before it is too rapid for me to overtake it, Sir, and pass it, Sir, and deliver it neatly tied up to the furnaces of reason, Sir. And good evening to you. I hope you will enjoy and profit by your sojourn in this neighbourhood.

BILSHAN. My dear Sir, don't be angry. I apologise humbly for my unfortunate figure of speech. We commercial travellers are notorious for our rough and haphazard locutions. And it is seldom one has the privilege of speaking to a prophet. Put down what I said just now to natural embarrassment and write it off my account. I am anxious to learn from you. Let us change the subject if you wish.

JONAH. The subject cannot be changed. I annihilated it two minutes ago. I am willing to overlook any little unpleasantness that has arisen. Is there any other subject upon which I can inform you?

BILSHAN. Why, yes, if you will be so courteous. To what do you attribute the obvious prosperity of this delightful town?

JONAH. Bilshan, this town was not always prosperous.

BILSHAN. No?

JONAH. No, indeed. At one time it was actually a nasty offence in the nostrils of Jahveh.

BILSHAN. Dear me.

JONAH. And if I did not continually wrestle with it and intercede with Jahveh for it, it would find itself in a very unpleasant position indeed.

BILSHAN. Yes?

JONAH. This parish, Bilshan, was only a few short years ago a pretty obvious target for thunderbolts. Every man, woman and child in it, every domestic fowl moved in continual jeopardy;

and their state was none the less shocking that they were unaware of the fact.   They were given up to every unseemly
hobby, from adultery to idolatry.   I can only assume that
Jahveh held His hand because He was stunned by their impu-
dence.   At that time I returned from my novitiate in the wilderness, and I solemnly assure you I was ashamed to tell Jahveh in
my prayers that I had been born in such a place.

BILSHAN.   Terrible.

JONAH.   My son, that is a true word.   Well, I wasted no
time.   There was none to waste.   I girt up my loins and got to
work.   And in three weeks the place was unrecognisable.

BILSHAN.   I feel sure of it, by Ishtar.

JONAH.   By whom?

BILSHAN.   I beg your pardon.   I was carried away.   I
mentioned Ishtar, a heathen goddess.   A piece of meaningless
foolery.   It isn't really swearing.   A mere reflex.

JONAH (*regarding him severely*).   Please be careful.   Please
be very careful.

BILSHAN.   Forgive me.   I shall try to be.   But tell me,
apart from girding your loins, how did you set about converting
these unfortunates into the worthy citizens and dear little persons I see before me this evening?

JONAH.   My friends are good enough to inform me that I
have an impressive personality and a considerable degree of what
is called magnetism.

BILSHAN.   Salesmanship, we call it.   Yes?

JONAH.   It is immaterial what you call it.   It is a gift.   I
know myself to have a fluent tongue and a good platform manner,
and I am humbly conscious of an intense enthusiasm for my
work.   I put all these gifts unreservedly at the disposal of my
fellow-townsmen.

HASHMONAH.   And we thank you heartily for it, Jonah.

SHUAL.   Indeed we do.

JOSIBIAH and THE GIRLS.   Yes, yes!

JONAH.   In three weeks, as I say, the ribald songs were silent;
the dancing feet trod warily and circumspectly.   The imbecile
grins were washed off the faces.   The gaudy, bawdy garments
were displaced by decent sackcloth.   The groves were cut down
and the images destroyed.   Gittah-Hepher was a different place.
The Lord delighted in it.

BILSHAN.   I see.   Jonah, what do you think of Nineveh?

JONAH.   I have never been there.   But I have heard of that inordinate and dreadful town.

BILSHAN.   If there is a magnificence in evil, you will find it in Nineveh.

JONAH.   There is magnificence in evil.   One who has fought with the Devil knows that.

BILSHAN.   Nineveh has fine streets and great temples.   It is seventy miles round.   The streets are full of people.   Sculptors and painters and architects and musicians and orators pay court to the Devil there.

JONAH.   They pay court to the Devil, do they ?   It doesn't need a Prophet of God to tell them the latter end of that.

BILSHAN.   Doesn't it ?

JONAH.   What do you mean, man ?

BILSHAN.   Nothing, nothing.

JONAH.   What do you know about God's Prophets ?   Do you know that to be possessed by God is the uttermost torment in the world ?

BILSHAN.   I can well believe it.   Only . . .

JONAH.   Only ?   Only ?

BILSHAN.   I know that in the sight of Jahveh Gittah-Hepher and Nineveh may well be of equal importance, and that a million well-dressed persons may well be weighed in His sight with three king-crabs on a desert island.   But I have been to Nineveh, and it is an impressive place.   Do you know, my darling (*to* EUODIAS), I have seen there such an ingenious little instrument—a chime of bells, worked by a miniature water-wheel and playing an immoral song ?

EUODIAS.   How interesting !

BILSHAN.   Isn't it, Sweetheart ?   I could interest you all night, telling you of the miraculous devices the people have employed, at one time and another, for their entertainment.

JONAH.   These things are vanity and wickedness.

BILSHAN.   That is exactly my point.   (*A silence.*)   Well, I have had a long and tiring journey today, and I rather feel like turning in.   I hope you ladies and gentlemen will excuse me.

JONAH.   Stop.

THE SENTRY.   Beg pardon, gentlemen, but it is closing time, gentlemen, please.

JONAH.   What ?

THE SENTRY.   The sun has dropped under the horizon. My orders are to shut the gate.

JONAH.   The sun!   If this were an occasion for a miracle I should pull that hot ball up again.   But it isn't.   Stop a minute. I have something to say.

THE SENTRY.   Very well, Sir.   But please remember my orders.

JONAH.   I will go to Nineveh.

BILSHAN.   Professionally, may I ask?

JONAH.   Nineveh is ripe for destruction like a rotten fig.   It is my duty to give warning.   I have great pity on Nineveh.

BILSHAN.   Nineveh will be highly gratified.

JONAH.   Jahveh will not send me to Nineveh for that city's gratification.

BILSHAN.   Well, I am a simple nobody, and I shouldn't dream of trying to influence one of Jahveh's prophets, but I happen to know Nineveh, and I warn you here and now, you will have to exercise tact, or you will quickly find yourself covered with bruises and floating down the Tigris.   Nineveh isn't Gittah-Hepher.   And good night to you, Prophet.   It has been a privilege to meet you.

[He goes through the gate.]

JOSIBIAH.   Oh, what an impudent dog!

HASHMONAH.   Pay no need to him, Master.   He is beneath your notice.

SHUAL.   Sentry, why didn't you strike him on the mouth?

THE SENTRY.   I was tooken aback, as the saying is.

HASHMONAH.   You will be reported for gross negligence.

THE SENTRY.   Negligence, how?   I ask you.   When gents are having a private conservation, what business is it of mine to shove in my nose like the stork in the story?   Eh?

HASHMONAH.   Don't you dare answer back.

SHUAL.   You are only making it worse.   Worse and worse.

THE SENTRY (*beginning to cry*).   This world is a dreadful place for poor dutiful men.   I have ten children and a wife, and how will they respect me when I am spoken to like that?

JONAH.   Go into the village, everybody.   Leave me!

THE SENTRY.   I must lock the gate, Master.

JONAH.   Never mind the gate.

THE SENTRY.   Oh, now, now, now, you will only get me into worse trouble.

JONAH.   I will lock the gate when I have finished what I have to do.   Light the lamp over the gate and go in.   Go in. Go in.

[*It is getting dark. The* SENTRY *lights the lamp and the rest follow him into the village, wishing* JONAH *good night as they pass him.* JONAH *does not reply. The actor will convey, without extravagance of gesture, that* JONAH *is a tormented man, seeking contact with his God.*]

[*After a short pause* EUODIAS *steals into the scene.*]

JONAH.   What do you want?

EUODIAS.   The stranger gave me a little lapis-lazuli frog.   I dropped it in all the excitement.

JONAH.   Let it lie.   There can be no blessing in a lapis-lazuli frog got from such a source.

EUODIAS.   It was very pretty.   It came from Nineveh.   I'm sorry.   Good night, Master.

JONAH.   Stop.   Don't go away.   What do you think of me, Euodias?

EUODIAS.   Oh, Master!

JONAH.   Do you think I'm a great Prophet?

EUODIAS.   Of course.

JONAH.   Why do you think so?

EUODIAS.   Oh, well, look at the way you speak, and the funny look about your eyes, and look at all the good you've done us, and look how frightened of you Hashmonah and Josibiah are.   I mean, it's obvious.

JONAH.   Do you think I'm inspired by Jahveh?

EUODIAS.   Yes.   Aren't you?   I mean, when Josibiah speaks we all know what he's talking about, but we never know what you're talking about . . . except, of course, when you're talking about sin . . . and even then you tell us a lot of sins we never even heard of.   I mean it's as if you opened your mouth and the words just happened.

JONAH.   Yes, yes . . . in a way they do.

EUODIAS.   You'll think me just a cheeky little thing, but it's marvellous to hear you speak, Jonah.   I think if you only recited the alphabet it would make us all cry.   I know it would me.

JONAH.   Then my words have no meaning to you?

EUODIAS.   No, no.   I don't mean that.   They're full of terrific meanings, only we feel them, you see, without properly understanding them. I mean, even when you said my name just now, it made me quite giddy. And, I mean, that shows you, doesn't it?

JONAH. No, it doesn't—unless you too are inspired. For when you said my name just now I too became a little faint. That's a curious thing, Euodias, isn't it?

EUODIAS. Oh, Jonah, do you think it's possible that I too may be inspired like Deborah and Jael?

JONAH (*looking at her gloomily*). It is unlikely, but it is possible.

EUODIAS. Oh! . . . . Then will you take me to Nineveh with you?

JONAH. Nineveh?

EUODIAS. Yes. Don't you remember? You said you were going to Nineveh.

JONAH. So I did. Or at least I suggested I might if my engagements permitted.

EUODIAS. Oh, Jonah, you said, " I will go to Nineveh ". Those were your very words.

JONAH. Hum. Ha. Well, we shall see.

EUODIAS. Well, that's all right. And you'll teach me on the way how to be a proper Prophetess, half woman, half snake; and won't it be splendid, the two of us standing hand in hand at the top of a lot of marvellous marble steps prophesying against all these well-dressed handsome rich people and terrifying the lives out of them? When shall we start, Jonah?

JONAH. I have not made up my mind; and in any event I shall certainly not take you.

EUODIAS. But you said you would. And I'd be such a help to you. And you said I was inspired. And I'm dying to see Nineveh.

JONAH. You will certainly not see Nineveh in my company. That is final.

EUODIAS. Why not?

JONAH. I decline to answer. It would be obvious to you why not if you were not a born fool. Quite apart from that, I should be perfectly justified at this moment in asking the Almighty to strike you suddenly dead. You have interrupted me and diverted my thoughts in an intolerable manner. Go away at once.

EUODIAS. But you let me talk to you and you were so kind

and gentle and I never dreamed . . . and now you talk about striking me dead and . . .

JONAH. Stop crying, Euodias. You mustn't cry. It isn't your fault. I'm not angry.

EUODIAS. I thought you liked me.

JONAH. I do like you, my dear, very much indeed. Jahveh sent you and other lovely things, like the oleander and the nightingale, to cheer and hearten men like me whom He has singled out to torture with His revelation. I don't think I shall go to Nineveh anyhow.

EUODIAS. You won't go to Nineveh ?

JONAH. No. I've had rather a trying time lately and a good many arrears of work to overtake, and Nineveh is really rather a big job, to tell you the truth, to be tackled by a provincial prophet. Perhaps later on in the year . . .

EUODIAS. I see.

JONAH. You see what, little one ?

EUODIAS. I thought you were a mighty Prophet. I worshipped you. All us girls did. And now I see that you are a cowardly little gas-bag. Very well. Tomorrow I shall paint my toes scarlet. I'll get Naaran to dig out her drum, and I know two boys who can play the trumpet, and I'll go dancing round the town at sunrise with nothing on and prophesy against *you*, Mr Jonah. And I bet I draw a bigger crowd than you can with your flames from Heaven that never arrive.

JONAH. Be silent, unregenerate and unmitigated harlot !

EUODIAS. Cowardy Custard !

JONAH. No one has dared to call me that before.

EUODIAS. They didn't know you. Good night, little Jonah.

[JONAH *catches her by the wrist.*]

JONAH. No. No. No.

EUODIAS. Go on. Beat me, now. I'll yell the place down, and you'd look a beautiful prophet fighting little girls after dark outside the village gate. Go on. Beat me.

JONAH. I wonder why I don't have you struck suddenly dead.

EUODIAS. Because you can't. That's why. You're no good at all.

JONAH. Yes. That's true. I can't. And I'm no good at all.

EUODIAS. Aren't you really a prophet ?

235   [17]

JONAH. Oh yes, I'm a prophet all right.   But I'm not much of a man.

EUODIAS. Yes, you are.   You're such a good man and so just to other people you can't be just to yourself.   You don't realise how good you are.   That's why you're hesitating about Nineveh.   You think you aren't good enough to tackle a big thing like that.   Well, you are good enough, and that's what makes me so angry.

JONAH. The barbarians have a saying, " Oh that some god would give us the inestimable gift of seeing ourselves as we appear to others."

EUODIAS. Exactly.   That's what I say.   And what's Nineveh anyhow ?   A noisy vulgar place, if what Bilshan says is true.   They want a good, honest, sturdy prophet from the country to make them sit up.   Do go, Jonah.   It will be a great experience.

JONAH. Very well.   I will go.   I have had a lesson to-night.

EUODIAS. And you'll take me ?

JONAH. No.   I have had another lesson tonight.   Come in.   It is growing cold.   I shall start tomorrow at sunrise.

[*Enter the* SENTRY.]

THE SENTRY. Now, Master, you haven't shut the gate, and that's not fair.   It will only get me into trouble and . . . Oh, good evening, Miss.   I didn't notice you.   I'm sure I beg your pardon, Sir.

[*He ostentatiously begins to busy himself about nothing in particular, whistling loudly as he does so.*]

JONAH. On your knees, you ugly son of perdition, and pray for forgiveness for the evil thoughts of your black heart.   Go in, young woman.

[EUODIAS *goes in through the gate.*   JONAH *sits in an attitude of deep thought while the* SENTRY *looks at him with an embarrassed air.*]

JONAH (*suddenly*).   Well, what are you waiting for ?

THE SENTRY. It's closing time, Rabbi.

JONAH. There is no such thing as closing time; we are living in eternity.

THE SENTRY. I don't know where you're living, Rabbi, but I am living in Gittah-Hepher, and my orders are to close the gate at sundown.

[*The light is fading rapidly.   It is nearly dark.*]

JONAH.   Well, carry out your orders, shut the gate.

THE SENTRY.   And leave you outside ?

JONAH.   Yes.

THE SENTRY.   Oh, but I couldn't do the like of that; the wolves would come and eat you.   Or the demons might come and carry you away.   And you know who would get the blame ? I would.   And I know you don't want to get me into trouble.

JONAH.   Do as I tell you, shut the gate.

[*The* SENTRY, *grumbling under his breath, shuts the gate with a great sound of creaking and clanking.*]

THE SENTRY (*sotto voce*).   A poor ill-used man, me.   A poor simple fellow, what never did anybody any harm.   Prophets ! It's my opinion we could do very well without prophets.

[SENTRY *disappears as the gate bangs shut.*   JONAH *shivers, draws his garment about him and sits down against the wall.*]

JONAH.   If I could only see clearly.   If I could only have a revelation.   Lord, in Thine infinite mercy . . . No, that won't do.   It's no good asking for a revelation.   I must wait for it.   The Word often comes when we are thinking of something else.   Now what shall I think about ? . . . No. . . . No, that won't do.   She is a very common little creature, and all compact a snare and deceit.   I must put her out of my mind. All compact a snare and deceit.   I must tell her so.   I shall rebuke her tomorrow.   It's my plain duty.   A good resounding rebuke.   That would be by far the most dignified course.   (*He yawns.*)   Where am I ?   There's something wrong.   Let me see.   I sat down outside the town wall.   And this is the town wall.   There's the crack in the dried mud, with the hole at the foot of it where the little green lizard came through.   And yet it has changed.   (*He rubs his eyes.*)   There is something wrong.

[*An amber light grows and comes until it reveals a tall young man dressed in white, leaning against the postern with a somewhat weary and casual air.*]

JONAH.   It's growing light.   And yet it isn't daylight.   It's after sunset.   It should be dark.   And yet the light grows and grows.   It will soon be so bright that I cannot look at it.   Someone is here.   Who is that ?   Who are you ?

ANGEL.   Are you Jonah ?

JONAH.   Yes, Lord.   But who are you ?

237   [19]

ANGEL. What are you doing here?

JONAH. I don't know. I just sat down to think for a bit. I was very worried.

ANGEL. What were you worried about?

JONAH. Oh, a lot of things. I have had a lot to worry me lately. I must have dropped off to sleep. I think I must be asleep now. I was very tired.

ANGEL. You are to get up and go to Nineveh.

JONAH. To Nineveh, Lord?

ANGEL. That is what I said.

JONAH. Well, to be quite frank, the idea had crossed my mind. Indeed, I went into the matter fairly fully. But Nineveh is a great, huge, rich city. I should be lost in Nineveh. I am only a simple village prophet. Besides, I am doing good work here. I don't know what they would do without me. And anyhow, it's a very long way to go. My feet have been giving me trouble. I think it's fallen arches or something. Besides, I'm not very clear about the way to Nineveh. Honestly, with the utmost humility and respect, I don't think I am the man to go to Nineveh. I think you must be making some mistake.

ANGEL. Have you finished?

JONAH. Yes, Lord.

ANGEL. Very well, then. You are to go to Nineveh, and cry against it. The wickedness of Nineveh has come up before the Lord.

JONAH. But, Lord, a man from Edom went to Nineveh last spring. They broke his bones and threw him into the river. It is useless to cry against Nineveh. They are deaf, and blind, and arrogant.

[*The light fades quickly. The* ANGEL *gradually disappears.*]

ANGEL'S VOICE (*through the darkness*). You may do precisely what you like about it. But you are like the Sentry. You have your orders. I advise you to obey them.

JONAH. He has gone. I am awake. Oh dear, oh dear, oh dear. What am I to do? . . . Stand up, Jonah. Take a deep breath. Keep steady, will you, my knees? What's the matter with you? . . . That's better. The Word of the Lord has come to you, Jonah, son of Amittai. And Nineveh is as nothing in the Lord's great eye. You are God's Prophet, Jonah, son of

[20]

Amittai. You are God's Prophet at last.   Sentry!   Open the gate.

[*He begins to beat on the gate. The* SENTRY *opens it, carrying a big torch. While he is opening the gate* JONAH *keeps hammering and calling, " Open the gate ".*]

JONAH.   Call the people.

THE SENTRY.   The people ?   What people ?

JONAH.   Call all the people of Gittah-Hepher.

THE SENTRY.   But they have gone to bed, Master.

JONAH.   Then get them out of bed.   Blow your alarm trumpet.

THE SENTRY.   But I can't blow the trumpet unless there are enemies, and I don't see any enemies.   And besides my mouth's full of biscuit.

JONAH.   Blow your trumpet, man.

[*The* SENTRY *unhooks a big ram's horn from the side of the gate and blows a loud blast.*]

THE SENTRY.   I hope you're going to take the responsibility for this.   I'm not supposed to blow the trumpet unless I see the enemy approaching.   And there isn't any enemy, not in these parts.   When I got up this morning I knew I should get into trouble.   I told my wife that.   " I'll get into trouble," I said. She said, " There's nothing new in that."   I said, " Never you mind about nothing new in that.   You mark my words, there's going to be trouble," I said.

[*A babel of voices is heard and the gateway becomes crowded with people all talking together and in various stages of undress.* JONAH *stands silent and rapt till a sufficient crowd has gathered.*]

JONAH.   People of Gittah-Hepher . . . (*A silence falls.*) People of Gittah-Hepher, I am a man as you are, a child of your streets; a man as you are, in nothing different but for this : that at His time and in His places the Lord seizes with His hands on the cords of my breast and opens my mouth to speak terrible and wonderful words.   I am a man as you are . . .

I am going on a long journey to walk strange paths, to hear strange tongues and to look into the hard strange eyes of those who do not know me, who are not my friends.   I am going because the tumult in my spirit drives me.   I am going alone, I am only a . . . People of Gittah-Hepher, for many months, it may be years, I shall stand no longer between you and the rage of Jahveh.   Walk in terror, then, with downcast heads and

239   [21]

lagging feet, for the rage of Jahveh, when it is awakened, will rend the mountains and split the firmament like a bursting wall. What account will it take of your miserable soft flesh and brittle bones, my pitiful little brothers? Take care, then, how you provoke the wrath of Jahveh. And these are my last words and my warning and my blessing till I come to you again. Shut the gate!

[*At this the attitude of the watchmen indicates that there is a wild rush. A hubbub of wails and screeches breaks out. The gate is closed, but before it finally shuts, EUODIAS breaks out and flings herself at the skirts of JONAH's rags.*]

EUODIAS. Take me with you, Jonah. Take me. I'll prophesy too. Take me with you.

JONAH. Euodias, let go. Go back at once. Do you hear?

EUODIAS. Lord, take me. I helped you last night. You know I did.

JONAH. Perhaps you did. When a man is in travail with a great idea, a woman may have a curiously calming effect on him. But when the idea is born, she is of no more use. So go away.

EUODIAS. That's not how it happened at all. What you said was . . .

JONAH. I have been very patient. Woman, won't you realise I am riding on a whirlwind of the spirit? You are nobody. You are nothing. Run away, like a good girl. I am possessed by what you can't possibly understand. (HASHMONAH, JOSIBIAH and SHUAL *run out of the gate.*) Don't you realise I can't even see you? I see the dawn full of splendid moving shapes; I hear tremendous and melodious voices. . . . Ah! . . . There you are! Take this poor girl back to her mother. I will pray for you, Euodias.

[*The townsmen lead EUODIAS weeping away. JONAH stands biting his thumb awhile in thought. Shrugs his shoulders. Makes a gesture of blessing towards the town, and marches resolutely away.*]

HASHMONAH. Well, Euodias, I hope you are thoroughly ashamed of yourself.

JOSIBIAH. What will Jonah think?

SHUAL. To think of the good man marching away to Nineveh all uplifted by his splendid send-off, and you go and spoil it all.

JOSIBIAH. A most embarrassing and regrettable incident altogether. Hi! Open the gate, there.

[22]

EUODIAS.   He won't go to Nineveh.

SHUAL.   Oh, what a thing to say!

EUODIAS.   He'd have gone if I'd gone with him to make him. But he's as frightened for Nineveh as a rabbit.   He won't go.

HASHMONAH.   Nonsense.   Be quiet.

JOSIBIAH.   Personally I don't care whether he goes to Nineveh or not, so long as he doesn't come back here for a little. Open that gate, will you?   (*The gate opens.*)   Keeping us all out in the cold morning.   What's that?

[*Music is heard.*]

EUODIAS.   Oh, hello!   They're dancing!   Wait for me, I'm coming!

[*She runs into the gateway, pulling off her outer garments. The three bearded men follow, uttering exclamations of concern, disapproval, and anticipation.*]

END OF SCENE I.

SCENE II

A blasted heath. The music that closed the first Scene grows wilder and wilder till it becomes blended with the far-away eerie howling of a jackal. Enter JONAH. *The music stops suddenly and only the long-drawn wail of the jackal is heard.*

JONAH.   What's that?   What's that?   It sounds sometimes like a crying child and sometimes like a lost soul. . . .   It's only a jackal.   You've heard jackals crying in the night before. But it's dark and lonely and I'm weary.

JACKAL.   Jo-o-owowow-onah!

JONAH.   It sounded like my name.

JACKAL (*clearly enough*).   Jonah.

JONAH.   It's still the jackal, but I'm sure I heard my name. What is it? . . .   Pull yourself together, Jonah.   It's the night and—and being so tired.   Three days and three nights.   I hardly stopped to rest.

JACKAL.   The sun set on your right, Jonah.

JONAH.   What if it did?

JACKAL.   If you had been going to the North-East it would have set on your left.   Nineveh is to the North-East.   Where are you going, Jonah?

JONAH. It's all imagination. Jackals can't talk. My imagination is playing me tricks.

JACKAL. You're going to Joppa, aren't you, Jonah? Here, boys, Jonah's going to Joppa. Jonah's running away!

JACKAL PACK. Away-ay-ay-ay.

JACKAL. O great bustard, flying up aloft! O starlings, chattering in your nests! O whistling kites! O bears, shambling among the rocks! Jonah is running away from God.

JACKAL PACK. Birds and Beasts: Away-ay-ay-ay. Jonah is running away!

JACKAL. O laughing hyena, who roams by himself, do you hear that? Jonah is running away from God.

HYENA. Ha! Ha! Ha! Hahahahahahahahahaha!

JONAH. O peace, rest! Will I never have peace? Will I never have rest? I cannot go to Nineveh. I dare not go.

JACKAL PACK. Away-ay-ay.

STARLINGS. Coward, coward, chattering, bragging coward!

JONAH. They are devils. I must make for the sea. I must put the blue water between me and the devils. I must go on. I must go on and on. The sea!

END OF SCENE II.

SCENE III

SAILORS *heard singing behind the curtain:*

"*Good-bye and Farewell to you, ladies of Joppa,*
Good-bye, fare you well; good-bye, fare you well.
Farewell and adieu to you, young Joppa Ladies.
Hurrah, my boys, we're Tarshish bound."

NARRATOR *appears before the curtain.*

NARRATOR. The sun is rising on the seaport town of Joppa, and the good galley, Sargon First, must cast off from the quay now if she is to catch the tide.

[*The curtain rises showing the deck of a ship. The* CAPTAIN *is talking to the* MATE. *A few passengers are settling down against the bulwarks.*]

CAPTAIN. A fair wind from the landward, Mr Mate.

MATE. Aye, aye, Sir. (*To passengers*). All you steerage passengers get forrard there. What do you think this is? A blistering hospital dormitory?

[The passengers move forward off the scene.]

CAPTAIN. Time we was casting off. I like running to schedule, and we ain't running to schedule. Besides, we'll miss the tide. What are we waiting for, Mr Mate?

MATE. There's a passenger running up the jetty.

CAPTAIN. Running, eh? So there is. Thundering Heliogabalus, he runs like a top-heavy dodo.

MATE. Hi! You, Sir. Hurry up there.

[Enter BILSHAN.]

CAPTAIN. Oh, good day to you, Mr Bilshan. I heard you were making the trip. It's a pleasure to see you, Sir.

BILSHAN. How are you, Captain? Good morning, Mr Mate. Well, we've got to keep on the move these days. The world won't wait for us.

MATE. No, by Ishtar, and no more we won't wait for that pot-bellied tunny fish if he don't get a hustle on himself. . . No hurry, Mister. Lord love you, we are only here to suit your crucified convenience.

JONAH *(without)*. I am being as quick as I can.

MATE. I believe it. By Baal, look at him, with legs on him like pack-threads and a belly like a kedge! yawning at the fareway, making faces with his starn.

BILSHAN. Looks like a good voyage, Captain.

CAPTAIN. Shouldn't be surprised; there's a fair wind from the southward and as pretty a horoscope as I ever paid for.

[JONAH comes aboard.]

MATE. All aboard, Sir.

JONAH. I'm sorry, I came as quickly as I could.

MATE. Stand by to cast off. Look alive there, you palsy-stricken dock rats. Cast off there, bosun. Look lively on the main sheet. Give way the starboard bank. Heave as she goes. Heave and break your hearts.

[The oarsmen begin to sing.]

CAPTAIN. See you later, Mr Bilshan. You'll have your old seat at my table.

BILSHAN. Thank you, Captain. *(To* MATE.*)* Well, we're off.

MATE. No thanks to our gentleman friend here. *[To* JONAH.*]*

CAPTAIN. Steady as you go, Mr Mate, the poor gentleman is tired.

MATE. This ship's full to the gunwale with tired gentlemen.

[*The* CAPTAIN *laughs and goes off.*]

MATE (*to* JONAH). Got your ticket?

JONAH. Yes. Yes. I have it somewhere.

MATE. Single or return.

JONAH. Single. To Tarshish.

MATE. Steerage. Stow your dunny-bag abaft the binnacle. I'll get you fixed later. You can cruise about here for a bit in the meantime, if this gentleman has no objection.

BILSHAN. None in the world.

JONAH. Thank you.

MATE. Much obliged. . . . Forrard there, easy as you go.

[*Exit* MATE.]

JONAH. Thank you.

BILSHAN. Don't mention it. That was a narrow squeak you had, Sir.

JONAH (*sitting on his baggage*). Yes.

BILSHAN. It's lucky for you the Skipper got a good horoscope this morning. He'd have left you behind as soon as look at you. . . . Hello!

JONAH. Yes?

BILSHAN. Haven't I see you before somewhere?

JONAH. No . . . no . . . I don't think so.

BILSHAN. Yes, I have. I never forget a face. Let me see. . . . You weren't so dressy, I think, and there was something about you . . . Oh, I know. What's the name of the place? Gittah. . . . Gittah-Hepher. That's it. Well, well, well.

JONAH. You must be making a mistake.

BILSHAN. No, Sir. That's not the sort of mistake I make. . . . Joshan . . . Boshan . . . Jonah. That's it. Jonah of Gittah-Hepher. You're the local Prophet, aren't you?

JONAH. I'm not Jonah. I—I think I know the man you mean. We are often mistaken for one another. But I assure you you are wrong.

BILSHAN. I should think you're a true prophet all right. You could never have made much of a reputation at lying. Let me see . . . let me see. . . . Oh, yes. . . . Aren't you in the wrong boat?

JONAH. No . . . no. I hope not.

BILSHAN. The usual route to Nineveh is to go up to Damas-

[26]

cus and to cross the desert by caravan. This is precisely in the
opposite direction.

JONAH. I know that. I have no intention of going to Nineveh. I—I never had. And I have no wish to prolong this
conversation. I think I shall go for a walk to the sharp end of
the boat.

BILSHAN. No, no. Plenty of time for that later. I'm
enormously interested. I threw a blue iris at you when you
had that very enthusiastic send-off from Gittah. Marvellous.
Didn't all that enthusiasm make you a little bit suspicious? It
did me. Never mind. What I really want to know is, what
are you doing on the Tarshish galley?

JONAH. Will you be so exceedingly kind as to mind your
own business?

BILSHAN. I wondered why you Gittah people made such a
point of minding one's own business. . . . What was the
trouble, Jonah? Oh, don't be so huffy. I won't give you
away. Embezzling the chapel funds?

JONAH. There were no funds and no chapel. Please leave
me alone.

BILSHAN. Ah. Too fond of the ladies, then. Charming
little creature that Euodias.

JONAH (assuming some dignity). If you knew me, Sir, as you
say you do, you would know that I am not entertained by foolish
talk. My name is Kish. I live in Gaza. I suffer from gall-
stones. My medical man has ordered me a sea-voyage. And
quiet, Sir, and quiet.

BILSHAN. I know Gaza well. What is the name of your
doctor?

JONAH. Did I say Gaza? I meant . . . No, I didn't.
You have no right to question me. You are a vulgar and
intolerable person.

BILSHAN. I am, am I?

JONAH. Yes. An inquisitive, gossip-mongering fellow.

BILSHAN. And what are you? A quack prophet.

JONAH. A what?

BILSHAN. A quack prophet.

JONAH. If you don't hold your tongue, man, I shall . . .

BILSHAN. What will you do?

JONAH. No, I can't do that now. God help me. I can't
do that now.

BILSHAN. Can't do what?

JONAH (*sadly and reasonably*). I thought for a moment of cursing you, Bilshan, but for the time being, and for reasons that are strictly private, I happen to know that my curse would be ineffective; and I am not like the uncircumcised who curse blind curses that for all they know may never be implemented. If it will satisfy you, I may tell you that I really intended to go to Nineveh.

BILSHAN. No, by Ishtar, it won't satisfy me. I am a student of human nature. Your mind must have been in an extraordinarily interesting state for several days. You left Gittah, heading north, forty-eight hours before me. I had a charming time in Gittah-Hepher, by the way, after you left. I thought I was fairly seasoned, but I couldn't stand more than a couple of days at it.

JONAH. At what?

BILSHAN. I never tell tales out of school. Go on, Jonah. I took it easy coming down to the coast, and I've been in Joppa for three days. You must have wandered backwards, north and south, doubling like a hare. Did you lose your way?

JONAH (*passionately*). No. But I must have some rest. Am I never to have any rest?

BILSHAN. Rest from what, Jonah?

JONAH. He called to me in a myriad voices when I went through the little villages going north. He shouted to me from the wilderness of Tob. I was deaf from His shouting and blind with His signs. I turned south, and His hands held me and tripped me and prevented me. . . . I am only a simple man. Who am I that I should go to Nineveh, that great city? . . . And one morning in the cold hour before sunrise I was sleeping in the lee of a big stone, and a fox barked and woke me, and I sat up and looked round at the grey foothills and the grey sky and He wasn't there; do you hear me? So I got up and took my pack and ran and ran.

BILSHAN. And you were still running this afternoon.

JONAH. Oh, no. I sat down sometimes. I even slept, in a sort of way—now and then.

BILSHAN (*yawning*). You must be tired. Well, we shall have a nice quiet chat about it all one of these days. I could have sworn that little Euodias had something to do with it.

JONAH. No, no. You don't understand. I'm not that sort of man at all. You are . . .

[28]

BILSHAN.   You'll excuse me, won't you?   I've got to see the steward about one or two things.   Are you a good sailor?

JONAH.   I don't know.   I've never been on the sea before.

BILSHAN.   Ah, you're having beginner's luck, then.   Sea like a sapphire mirror and a good following wind.   And although the accommodation is pretty lousy on this line, they're sturdy old tubs and they feed you well.   Darned well.   I should have a sleep if I were you.   Well, a ship isn't a big place.   We'll bump into one another some time.

[BILSHAN *strolls off, humming a stave of the shanty.*   JONAH *settles himself to sleep.*]

JONAH.   Ach!   I nearly started my prayers.   Be careful, Jonah.   Take no risks.   Don't draw attention to yourself. Take care.   Take care. . . .   No, Jonah.   It's all right. Pull yourself together.   It's all right.   It's the want of sleep. For seventy-two hours I have had no rest and no sleep.   I can sleep now.   I can sleep.   I can sleep.

SAILORS (*singing off*).

> A girl asleep with a blue dress on
> (Shake her, Johnny, shake her).
> An unsafe couch, she's resting on,
> (Shake her, lads, and wake her).
>
> Oh, shake her, and wake her;
> For we are bound away to Tarshish,
> Poor old man!

[*Sea music.*]

JONAH (*drowsily*).   Demons cannot cross the water.   There are no demons to mock me here.   There is only the creak of the cordage, and the rattle of the oars.   The sea is my friend. The sea is the only friend for a lost man.   I am lost now, and cannot be found.   There is nothing to do but sleep.

[*He goes to sleep.   Soft music grows gradually loud and sinister and the ship noises grow more intense.*]

WHALE.   Jonah!

JONAH (*in his sleep*).   Eh!   What's that?

WHALE.   Jonah!   Here I blow.

JONAH.   Ach!   Who is it?   Am I awake or asleep?   Is that Jahveh?

WHALE.   No, I am the Whale, that most deadly immortal monster.   Lie still, Jonah.   Lie very still.   You are asleep,

Jonah, you can't move, you are fast asleep. I am the Whale,
Jonah, the mightiest of living things.   There is nothing in the
deep waters or on the silly dry land to compare with me, Jonah,
to compare with the ferocity and majesty of my great driving
snout, to compare with the fury of my dreadful tail.   I beat
the sea before me into a foam, and lash the sea behind me into white
rage; and so I go round the world for ever, and from the North
Pole to the South Pole, riding on waves that burn like fire,
diving to the terrible cold deeps for centuries and centuries, for
ever and ever.   I am the Emperor of all the green waters.   I
am the Whale.

JONAH.   Dear me.

WHALE.   I understand that you are running away from God,
Jonah!   That, to me, is a highly diverting circumstance.   Ha,
ha, ha, ha, ha!   Most charming of little prophets, it is dull work
wallowing round the world.   I praise and magnify the good
God, who has given me this pleasant little joke to break the
monotony of my Cetacean existence.   Ho, ho, ho!

JONAH (testily).   I am glad you are pleased.   I do not know
who you are, but I am heartily glad that you are pleased.

WHALE.   I have told you who I am.   And presently you will
have an opportunity to make my better, or worse, acquaintance.
In the meantime, I implore you to remember this: that it is a
useless, undignified, irrational and utterly preposterous action for
the leading citizen of Gittah-Hepher to run away from God.

[The WHALE's voice is silent.   The wind increases.   Storm music is
heard.   Lightning flashes.   Thunder.   The MATE runs swiftly
across the stage and disappears.   JONAH wakes up.]

JONAH.   Hi, there!

[Enter BILSHAN.   There is an ominous slate-blue silence now, but
every now and again a distant babble of voices is heard.]

What's the matter?   What has happened?

BILSHAN.   That's what I am trying to find out.   The ship
shook like a fat man with the ague.   Hi, Captain!

[The CAPTAIN and the MATE come running down from the poop.
They take no notice of BILSHAN and trot sharply across the scene
and exeunt.]

BILSHAN.   Looks pretty serious.   I wonder if . . .

[Wails and shouts are heard.]

Listen to that.

JONAH.   I'm listening.

BILSHAN.   I think we must have hit something.

JONAH.   I think something must have hit us.

BILSHAN.   Funny the Captain not noticing me just now. We're old friends.   I make this trip often.   I wonder if I ought to go up to the poop and ask . . . No.   I'll wait till he comes back.   I don't expect it's anything much.   He's a most competent fellow, the Captain.   I've great confidence in him. . . . How still it is!   It's gone all quiet.

JONAH.   It's as if Jahveh were going to speak.

BILSHAN.   No doubt, no doubt.   A very poetical conception. . . . But we'll learn all about it now.   They're coming back. . . . Well, Skipper, anything serious?

[*The* CAPTAIN *and the* MATE *come back.*]

BILSHAN.   Anything serious, Captain?

CAPTAIN.   Mr Pumiyathon.

MATE.   Aye, aye, Sir.

CAPTAIN.   Pipe all the passengers amidships, Mr Pumiyathon.

MATE.   Aye, aye, Sir.   Bosun!   Pipe all hands amidships.

[BOSUN'S *pipe heard.*]

BILSHAN.   Captain, what's the matter?   Is it anything serious?

CAPTAIN.   Oh, it's you, Mr Bilshan?   You'll hear soon enough

[*A crowd of agitated passengers troop in.*]

CAPTAIN.   Give me a little silence, please, Mr Pumiyathon. That's better.   Ladies and gentlemen, it looks a bit like we are all going to get wet.   We've run into the tail of a tornado, the ship has been struck by lightning, the bow timbers are sprung, she's leaking like a sieve, the starboard bank of oars is smashed, the lateen foresail is torn to ruddy ribbons, and we're labouring like a bullock-cart down by the head.   We could pump her out, and undergird her if we'd time, but there ain't no time.   There's a black scud of wind coming up from the nor'-east at eighty knots an hour, and we'll have our bellies full of green water in a very few minutes. . . . Now you stop howling and listen to me, if you want to get your flat feet on dry land again.   There's something darn funny about this voyage.   I never saw a better horoscope, and I took all the omens before we cast off.   It's my opinion there's some off-shore god got a hand in this.   We're

hoodooed, that's what we are. Now the embarkation office
assured me I've got a cargo of all the religions from Iberia to the
Indies. It may be there's one or two of you here can put in a
word with his private hoodoo and save us from foundering in a
roaring ramstammy of a sea. I want every man-jack and
woman-jane of you to get down to it and try to square your
particular deity. Pray till you split, for it's the only way we can
ride it out, so far as I can see

PASSENGERS. Oh, willah, willah. Alas! O Zagmuk!
O Adonay! O Ishtar! O Osiris! O Baal-Phegor! O
Anaitis! O Mithra! O Poseidon! O Ma of Comana! O
Ma! O Ma!

BILSHAN. Captain.

CAPTAIN. What do *you* want?

BILSHAN. What about us? I mean my lot. I haven't got
a god.

CAPTAIN. Then you'd better look lively and get one.

[*He disappears.*]
[*A* WOMAN *screams.*]

MATE. Stow that, missis. Pipe down, do you hear? Get
on with the praying. What's the name of your god?

WOMAN. Ma of Comana.

MATE. Well, go ahead and talk to your Ma. Suffering
sailor, we're in for the father and mother of a storm.

PASSENGERS. O Mistress of the turquois, pray for us! O
Hellaogabalus! O Artemis!

JONAH. Mr Mate!

MATE. Strike me with scurvy! It's our leisurely friend!
Why aren't you praying?

JONAH. Take me to the Captain.

MATE. Do you think the Captain's got nothing else to do
than blether to the likes of you? Get down on your hunkers
or I'll help you with the toe of my boot.

JONAH. Take me to the Captain.

BILSHAN. Don't be a fool, Jonah. Get down on your
knees and do your bit.

JONAH (*shouting*). Take me to the Captain. Take me at
once, do you hear?

MATE. I'll take you by the neck and twist it round three
times.

JONAH.   Keep your hands off me, you fool.   Take me to the Captain.

[*The* MATE *falls back.*]

BILSHAN.   Look at that cloud.   It's like a great roaring black ram.   It's coming at us.

JONAH.   Captain!!!

[*Re-enter the* CAPTAIN.]

CAPTAIN.   What's this, Mister.   What's this?   Who's this man?

MATE.   I don't know.   He won't pray, and he won't let anyone else pray, and it looks like he's going to shout us all into Fiddler's Green.

CAPTAIN.   Give order there, can't you?   You're interrupting all these religious ceremonies.   Who are you, anyway?

JONAH.   I am a fugitive from the Lord of Heaven and Earth. He has come for me to take me.   Throw me into the sea, that he may take me alone and leave the rest.

CAPTAIN.   What's your religion?

JONAH.   I am a Hebrew.

CAPTAIN.   You are, are you?   Then get out of my way.

JONAH.   I can stop the hurricane.

CAPTAIN.   No, you can't.   Nobody can't.

JONAH.   This tempest is my doing.   You must take me up and throw me into the sea.

CAPTAIN.   My owners have placed the souls of every dog of you under my charge.   No one goes overboard from my ship. If your prayers are no good, get forrard and bear a hand with the pumps.

[*The sound of wind grows ominous.*]

Hold her a point to starboard.   Stand by to brail up the mainsail.   Give way below there.   Heave and break your hearts. It will be on us any minute now.

JONAH.   You can't fight Jahveh!

CAPTAIN.   Can't I?   I'll show him.

[*Exit* CAPTAIN.]

JONAH.   Men, the Captain is mad.   Throw me into the sea.

PASSENGERS.   We are lost, we are lost.

JONAH (*shouting above the storm*).   I have no courage.   I dare not leap myself.   Take me and throw me into the sea.

MATE.   Didn't you hear what the Captain said?   Stand away from that rail.

JONAH. Look! Jahveh's black cloud is coming nearer.

WOMAN. It's racing at us. It's charging at us. Throw him overboard.

PASSENGERS. Yes, yes, over with him, it's our only chance.

MATE. Stand back, you rats. You heard the Captain's orders.

BILSHAN. It's worth trying, Mr Mate. It's worth trying.

MATE. You shut your trap. I have my orders.

PASSENGER. It's a case for a sacrifice.

MATE. Sacrifice my foot!

BILSHAN. Listen, Mr Pumiyathon. We can do it all in order. We can draw lots. You've seen that done before?

MATE (*doubtfully*). Yes, I've seen that done.

BILSHAN. If he's bringing us bad luck, he'll lose in the draw. That's fair and sensible, isn't it?

PASSENGERS. Yes. That's fair. Draw lots. Where is the lottery bag?

BILSHAN. I have it here. Draw everybody and be quick about it.

> [*They draw lots. The tempest rises. An advancing roar is heard.*]

BILSHAN. Quick, quick. Who has drawn the black?

JONAH (*holding up the black bean*). Here it is, do you believe me now?

PASSENGERS. Over with him!

JONAH. Throw me over the side.

MATE. Look's like we're all for Davy Jones anyway. Who happens to be the first doesn't matter. Bear a hand there.

JONAH. Throw me far out.

PASSENGER. The Lord forgive us, friend, and wash our hands from innocent blood.

JONAH. Throw me far.

MATE. One, two, three, heave!

> [*They heave* JONAH *into the sea. The storm ceases suddenly. The sun shines out.*]

BILSHAN. He has gone. Not a sign of him. He sank like a stone.

WOMAN. The wind has dropped. There's the blessed sun. We're saved.

MATE. It couldn't be helped. Lord send it brings us no ill-luck.

WOMAN.   He was a great Prophet.

MATE.   The gods send his death isn't on our heads.   He was a holy man.

CURTAIN.

SCENE IV

The Belly of the WHALE.   JONAH, *solus.*

WHALE.   It is three days and three nights since you became my passenger.

JONAH.   Yes, Whale.

WHALE.   During that time I have been attempting to improve your mind.   It is not a very broad mind, but it contains plenty of room for improvement.   Perhaps I have been a little prolix, but I get so few chances for agreeable conversation.   And I have been very much impressed by your habit of laying down the law and expressing opinions and forming judgments on the Universe without, perhaps, sufficient knowledge of the data involved.   So you will forgive me for having gone into detail rather fully.   Will you forgive me?

JONAH.   Yes.   Oh, yes.

WHALE.   That is very kind of you.   Perhaps I might now summarise a few of the main points of my discourse.   You would wish me to do so, I have no doubt.

JONAH.   It is all one to me.   I am dead.   I thought I might not be dead, because I caught a bad cold and began to sneeze. And dead men don't sneeze.   But I *am* dead.   I am suffering eternal punishment.   Your voice is punishment enough, and it certainly seems to me to be eternal.

WHALE.   Did you speak?   I was aware of a muffled sound that might well have been your voice.

JONAH.   No, no.   It's nothing.   It's nothing.

WHALE.   If you would like to ask me any questions, I shall be happy to do what I can to answer them.

JONAH.   No, no.

WHALE.   I have tried to outline to you the various steps that led up to that remarkable experiment called Mankind.   I have tried to give you a certain grounding in morphology and taxonomy.   I have drawn your attention to the unspeculative and absorptive Amoeba, to the gentle Chlamydomonas, to the humorous Volvox that goes rolling, ever rolling, waving its little pulsellae so cheerily and budding forth its posterity as it rolls. I have pleased you, I hope, with my reflections on the elk, the horned screamer, the liver fluke, the duck-billed platypus, the armadillo, the giraffe, and the charming penguin that stands the winter through balancing its eggs on its toes lest they freeze in the bitter ice. I have entertained you with those pleasing images partly in the hope of relieving your somewhat tedious circumstances. I now ask you to direct your thoughts to the constitution of Matter; and to believe that you and I and the Atlas Mountains and the date-palms and the fleas on a jackal and a dromedary's whiskers are all composed of quadrillions of dancing things, not infinitely little, each like a star behaving like a lunatic in its own orbit . . . things . . .

JONAH. It's a lie. You are lying to me, you liar. You LIAR.

WHALE. Things which are like and yet not like pebbles on a beach; things which are like and yet not like the sounds of harps and of timbrels, the bellowing of bulls and the lowing of sheep; things which are like and yet not like summer lightning; things which are like and yet not like the waves of the sea or the shifting sands of the shore. . . . Jonah?

JONAH. Oh, what? Oh, what?

WHALE (*a little more quietly*). For three days and three nights out of consideration for you, I have abstained from drinking. Would it trouble you very much if I shipped a few gallons? Can you swim?

JONAH. I can swim out of here. You are a sophisticated rhetorician intoxicated with the exuberance of your own verbosity. Drink as much as you like. Only let me out of here. I *must* get out of this!

WHALE. What did you say? Is it all right? Look out, then, Jonah!

[*Darkness and a confused roaring sound. When the lights go up,* JONAH *is standing on a sunny beach.*]

WHALE (*distant*). Dear me! What has happened? Are you all right, Jonah? Are you safe?

JONAH. Yes, O great Fish, I am safe! You have given back to me the sun and the light breezes on my bruised, soaked body; and the kind, dry sand below my feet. O great Fish, wallowing in the lagoon, take back my thanks and blessings with you in your strange journeyings through the cold ocean. All happiness of the sort most pleasing to whales attend you in the green seas.

WHALE. Not at all, not at all. To tell you the truth, I am glad to be quit of you. Thank you for your blessings and take this in return: You and I, in our several ways, are proud monsters. Let us cultivate Humility. You, Jonah, are tempted from time to time to believe that you are a party to the good God's secrets. Into one of them you have penetrated somewhat deeply. It was a dark secret, Jonah. It was the secret of my vast and rumbling belly. I fear that your sojourn has left you little the wiser, but I hope that you know this: To suppose that Almighty God keeps you regularly informed of His Purpose is a foolish assumption. It is almost as foolish as to run away from Him—in which irrational exercise I found you. Good-bye and farewell to you, damp little Prophet. Mark me now! Here I blow!

JONAH.

I called out in my affliction to the Lord,
And He answered me.
Out of the Belly of Hell I cried,
And He heard my voice.

For He cast me into the deep,
Into the heart of the seas;
And the flood was about me
And the waves and the billows passed over me.

And I said: He has cast me out from before His eyes,
Yet will I look again towards the holy Temple.
The waters compassed me about
Even to the soul.

The deep was all about me;
The weeds were wrapped about my head;
I went down to the bottoms of the mountains;
The earth with her bars closed on me forever.

Yet thou hast brought up my life from the pit, O Lord my God.
When my soul fainted I remembered Thee;
And my prayer found Thee, Lord,
In Thy holy Temple.

I am poor and naked.
I have no sacrifice to offer but to pay the debt I have vowed.
I will sacrifice with my soul and my voice and my works.
I will pay the debt which I have vowed and follow no more
    lying vanities.
Salvation is of the Lord!

CURTAIN.

SCENE V

A gallery in the King's palace overlooking Nineveh. The King, ASSUR-
NIRARI, *is sitting on a chaise-longue with his feet up. He is a handsome man of about thirty, with a long, elaborate beard.* SHIPHRA,
*seated on a cushion on the floor, is reading to him from an engraved
tablet.*

SHIPHRA (*reading*). "Etanna looked down through the
eagle's wings and saw the swirl of stars round the first gate of
Heaven far below. It was then that she noticed that the wings
of the eagle no longer moved in a steady sweep, but struck the
air in little, swift, irregular beats. It was then that the thought
came to her that she might not reach the gate of Ishtar. The
gate was gleaming above her like the setting sun shining on a
distant window. She longed for the gate of Ishtar with a great
longing; but the eagle turned his head to her and she could see
that his beak was wide open and his eyes were glazing. In a
voice full of despair, she urged the eagle on and upwards, but his
strength was gone."

KING. And they fell for a million leagues, and Etanna was
dashed in pieces. It is an excellent story, but not very well told.
We should hear what Etanna said to the eagle, and what the
eagle said to Etanna. Why have we no poets nowadays,
Shiphra? Life is very tedious without poets; and it is more
tedious still when the poets we have take a pride in being common-
place and vulgar. I have not met a single interesting man for
the last six months, and only very few interesting women.

SHIPHRA. It is very difficult for ordinary people to sustain
your level of conversation, O Son of the Morning.

KING. I have no level of conversation. Conversation should
be all hills and valleys, and cliffs and ravines and secret caverns.
A level of conversation is the abomination of desolation. Fetch

me the Governor of Nineveh, my darling; I want to speak to
him.

SHIPHRA.   I hear and obey.

[SHIPHRA *goes out. The* KING *rises wearily and looks out over
Nineveh.*   SHIPHRA *returns.*]

I have sent for him.   You will break his heart.   He is such
a solemn person, and he can't understand your jokes.   He and I
have a sign between us.

KING.   A sign?   What sign?

SHIPHRA.   When you are talking to him he stands with his
head respectfully bowed.

KING.   Yes, confound him.   Why can't he look me in the
eyes like a man?

SHIPHRA.   He is looking at my toes.   When I wiggle my
toes he knows that he ought to laugh.

KING.   Dear me.   I never noticed that.   You made him
laugh once at the wrong time and I nearly had him impaled.

SHIPHRA.   I know.   A spider crawled over my foot.

[*Enter the* GOVERNOR OF NINEVEH, *whose name is* NINID-MUKIM-
AHI.   *He kisses the ground between the* KING's *feet and then rises
and stands in a respectful attitude.*]

KING.   Well, my dear Ninid-Mukim-Ahi—and, by the way,
how fortunate you are to have such a divine name—Ninid-
Mukim-Ahi!

[SHIPHRA *wiggles her toes and the* GOVERNOR *laughs politely.*]

GOVERNOR.   I am a child of good fortune, O Son of the
Morning.   I count it my greatest fortune to be your humble
slave.

KING.   Ninid-Mukim-Ahi, I am heavily oppressed by the
tedium of life.

[GOVERNOR *looks anxiously at* SHIPHRA's *toes, but they do not move.*]

GOVERNOR.   I am desolated to hear it.   Is there anything I
can do?

KING.   You can tell me of some of the famous people who
are in Town tonight.

GOVERNOR.   There is a boxer from Ararat called Shim; he
can lift a chariot and the charioteer in his teeth.

KING.   I am not interested in dentistry.   The jawbone of
such an ass delights not me.   Am I a Philistine that you should
kill me in such a manner?

257 K   [39]

[*The* GOVERNOR *catches sight of the wiggle of* SHIPHRA'S *toes just in time as he was about to issue a disclaimer. He laughs heartily.*]

KING.   It may be egotism on my part, but I can see nothing humorous in the thought of such a death. What are you laughing at ?

GOVERNOR (*hastily*).   There is an actress from Tyre who arrived last night. She sings songs most amusingly to the tabor. She is a negress. She practises a new kind of music called swing. Would you like to hear her ?

KING.   I will have no such disgusting songs in Nineveh. She shall swing from the end of a rope. Who else is there ?

GOVERNOR.   I don't know whether you remember Bilshan, the traveller. A rather vulgar fellow, but well-informed and entertaining in his way.

KING.   A traveller, is he ? Has he had adventures ?

GOVERNOR.   It would be very unlike him if he had not.

KING.   Bring him here. He shall tell us of his adventures.

[*The* GOVERNOR *bows, goes to the door and claps his hands.*]

GOVERNOR.   Send up Bilshan the traveller.

[*He turns again to the* KING.]

KING.   Anyone else ?

GOVERNOR.   This morning a Jewish prophet came in by the west gate. I have not had time to examine his credentials, but he seems to be a person of little account.

SHIPHRA.   Do you think so ?

GOVERNOR.   Well, as I say, I've only just learnt of the police report; but the police are quite competent to deal with him if he gives any trouble. I shall go into the matter personally if you wish it.

SHIPHRA.   I have seen this man.

KING.   Have you, sweetheart ? Why didn't you tell me ? You know I like to hear everything you have to tell me.

SHIPHRA.   I should have told you when I got the words arranged properly. My heart was troubled, I did not know what to think.

KING.   This is very extraordinary. What manner of man is he ?

SHIPHRA.   I saw him from my window. He came through the gate with a great crowd of camel-drivers and shepherds. He seemed to be talking all the time, but I could not hear what he

[40]

said for the noise of the camels and the people and the sheep.   He
was a little ragged man, but there was something strange about
him.   Every few yards he stopped and said something to the
crowd, and they were silent and listened to him.   He was only
a little man, but when he spoke to the crowd his body distended
till he looked like a great giant blotting out the street and the
arches of the gateway and the sky above.   Even from where I
sat I could see his eyes burning like live coals.   And then he
turned down the street of Marduk and I lost sight of him.

   KING (*to* GOVERNOR).   Go and bring me this man.

   GOVERNOR (*bending down and touching the ground with his
forehead*).   I hear and obey.

                       [*As he reaches the door the* GOVERNOR *turns.*]

The man Bilshan is here, O Son of the Light.

   KING.   Send him in, and then go fetch me the Jew.

   [GOVERNOR *ushers in* BILSHAN *and then exit.* BILSHAN *enters with a
      confident air in which servility is nicely blended with impudence.*]

   KING.   You are Bilshan, the great traveller ?

   BILSHAN.   I am Bilshan the traveller, O Son of the Light;
but I don't know about great.   That is for you to say.

   KING.   It is, as you say, for me to say.   You may sit down.

                       [KING *and* BILSHAN *sit down.*]

   KING.   Will you have some sherbet, or a little Greek wine ?

   BILSHAN.   No, your Majesty, thanks very much.   I have
just had a little snack at the hotel.

   KING.   Are you comfortable in your hotel ?

   BILSHAN.   Oh, I make myself at home wherever I go.

                       [*He casts a roguish glance at* SHIPHRA.]

   KING.   So I observe. . . . You have travelled far since your
last visit to Nineveh ?

   BILSHAN.   I have been on the road for the best part of a year

   KING.   Have you had any adventures, that could be described
as interesting or astonishing ?

   BILSHAN.   There was one very near thing, on a ship out from
Joppa.   Would you care to hear about that ?

   KING.   Proceed.

   BILSHAN.   We were only a day out when we ran into the tail
of a hurricane.   It blew like an orchestra of devils, and a flash
of forked lightning hit the mast and brought us up all standing.
The Captain told me that he thought we were for it.   You

never saw such a mess as the ship was forrard: the mast down, half the oars gone and steering like a dray. I'm not much of a religious man myself, but I told the Captain that we were in the hands of the gods and we'd better ask them to do something about it. Then a little cocksparrow of a Jew I had met before in Zebulun stood up and gave tongue. He said it was his own private storm and we'd better chuck him overboard if we wanted to see land again. I had a hunch that this was an outside chance, so we chucked him into the ditch. He sank like a stone, and immediately the sky cleared and the sea became as flat as a millpond. The rest of the voyage was what they call uneventful. He was a curious little chap, the Jew. Name of Jonah. He didn't look much, and he was full of conceit, but there must have been something to him. Name of Jonah. It's my opinion he was a magician of sorts.

SHIPHRA.   But he was drowned?

BILSHAN.   Not a shadow of a doubt about that. It's a pity. I'd have liked to have seen more of him. It was no ordinary storm and he stopped it like that.

[BILSHAN *snaps his fingers.*]

SHIPHRA.   I wonder.

KING.   You wonder what, my darling?

SHIPHRA.   It was something I heard a big fellow in the crowd say. He had a voice like a bull. It came floating up to my window.

KING.   What did he say?

SHIPHRA.   It was just a fragment of a phrase. I didn't know what it meant, but the words were, " The man from the sea."

KING.   The man from the sea?

SHIPHRA.   Yes.

KING.   Curious. I have not noticed that you are habitually troubled by an imagination. (*To* BILSHAN.) Your story is not a very good story, but it has had a singular effect on the Lady Shiphra. It has stirred her imagination.

BILSHAN.   Only too delighted to have been of any small service.

KING.   We must see this Jewish prophet.

BILSHAN.   I am afraid you'll have to hunt the beaches from Issicus to the Nile—unless he's fed the fishes by this time. I think that's more likely.

SHIPHRA.   What did you say was the name of your magician?

BILSHAN.   Jonah.
SHIPHRA.   Jonah.

[Enter the GOVERNOR.]

KING.   Well?
GOVERNOR.   I've found the man, O Son of Daylight.
KING.   What man?
GOVERNOR.   The Hebrew Jonah.

[An astonished silence, broken by the KING.]

KING.   Bring him to me.
GOVERNOR.   I hear and obey.

[Exit GOVERNOR.]

KING.   This is very strange.
SHIPHRA.   It is a miracle.
BILSHAN.   Oh, come now! It's only a coincidence. I have
known at least twenty-five Jonahs in my short life. It's quite a
common name. I remember one fat old fellow in Tyre. He
was a pawnbroker. I wasn't so well off as I am now, and I had
dealings with him strictly in the line of business, I don't mind
telling you. It was rather comic. I went into his shop . . .
KING.   You dog, and son of a dog, you are in the presence of
Assur-Nirari, High King of Assyria. When he is in need of
your scabrous anecdotes, he will instruct you accordingly. Till
then remember that you are not in a pot-house.
BILSHAN.   I am sure I had no intention . . .
KING.   If I remember you in half an hour's time I shall lift
my little finger, and from that moment you will have no intention, or sight, or hearing, or anything at all. You have interrupted my conversation in a most impertinent manner.

[Enter the GOVERNOR, *ushering in* JONAH.]

GOVERNOR.   The Prophet Jonah.

[Aside to JONAH.]

Get down on your stomach, man. You are in the presence
of the King.
JONAH.   Sir, I intend no discourtesy; but I reserve that
attitude for the presence of the King of kings. I cannot help it.
I hope you will forgive me.
GOVERNOR.   What insolence!
KING.   We are becoming accustomed to insolence this
morning. Let it pass. They tell me that your name is Jonah
and that you are a Hebrew.
JONAH.   Yes, Lord.

KING. The Hebrews are very interesting people.

JONAH. I have found them so.

KING. You are a stranger in Nineveh?

JONAH. Yes.

KING. From where did you come?

JONAH. I came from the depths of the sea and from the belly of hell.

GOVERNOR. Tut, tut, dear, dear!

KING (*to* BILSHAN). Is this the man of whom you spoke?

BILSHAN (*awestruck*). My Lord, he is very like the man.

KING. This man says that you were thrown into the sea in the midst of a hurricane.

JONAH. He speaks the truth.

KING. Where did this happen?

JONAH. A day's journey out of Joppa.

KING. And yet you are here?

JONAH. And yet I am here.

SHIPHRA. Are you a man or a spirit?

JONAH. A man is a spirit, and a spirit is a man. But I am what you mean by a man.

KING. This is a matter of great interest to me. I cannot think that a man who has been thrown into the sea a day's journey from the shore can have been preserved by the gods unless they had some signal purpose in view.

JONAH. In a manner of speaking, you are right.

GOVERNOR. Fellow, the Son of Daylight is always right.

KING. Be quiet. Tell me, how does it come that you are still alive?

JONAH. The Lord had prepared a great fish.

KING. And the fish swallowed you? Come, come. You can't expect us to believe that.

JONAH. Your capacity for belief is not under my control. Nevertheless it is true.

KING. But that is a solar myth. The Ocean is said to have swallowed my distinguished ancestor the Sun-God . . . and no doubt he did. But you are only a mortal—and rather a shabby-looking one at that.

JONAH. For three days and three nights, I lived in the belly of the fish.

GOVERNOR. Sire, he is an untutored person. He means the interior—the interior.

[44]

KING.   One cannot be a King without becoming something of an expert in liars.   But you have not, to me, the appearance of a liar.

JONAH.   No, my Lord.

KING.   You are not mad, by any chance?

JONAH.   No, my Lord.

KING.   Since I took the right hand of the God Marduk and ascended the Throne of Assyria, I have never heard anything so extraordinary.   How did it feel to be in what my friend Ninid-Mukim-Ahi describes as the interior?

JONAH.   It was dark, narrow, slimy, slippery and noisome. I thought at first that I was dead.   I did not know what it was like to be dead.   And then I knew that Jahveh had spared my life and for what purpose He had spared it.

KING.   You think that there was a purpose behind all this?

JONAH.   I know that there was a purpose.

GOVERNOR.   O Son of the Morning . . .

KING.   Well?   What is it?

GOVERNOR.   I can see that your celestial highness is about to enter upon a sublime train of thought and I interrupt at my peril. But you charged me to remind you.

KING.   Remind me of what?

GOVERNOR.   To-day is the anniversary of the wedding of Ishtar and Marduk.   In a few moments the people will come to the Palace to pay their respects to you as the representative on earth of that divine Bride and Bridegroom.

KING.   If they are silly enough to believe all that nonsense, why shouldn't they?

GOVERNOR.   No reason at all, O Son of the Blessed.   But you wished particularly to inspect the Company of Guards before they formed up before the Palace.

KING.   I remember.   Yes.   Last parade they looked like a congregation of flea-bitten monkeys.   Are they ready?

GOVERNOR.   They have been standing at attention in the sun for the last three hours.

KING.   Good.   Then I shall go.   Wait here, Prophet.   I want to talk to you. . . . And, oh, there is another thing I almost forgot.   Call two sturdy fellows to throw this commercial gentleman out on the back of his neck.

GOVERNOR.   Do you wish him to be bastinadoed as well?

KING.   No.   He is a stranger.   That would be inhospitable.

GOVERNOR.   Go out, fellow, and wait in the antechamber.

BILSHAN.   May I express my appreciation for the honour of this interview?

GOVERNOR.   You may not.   Get out.

BILSHAN.   Oh, all right.

[*Exit* BILSHAN.]

GOVERNOR.   And now, O my Lord . . .

KING (*to* JONAH).   Wait for me.

[*Exeunt* KING *and* GOVERNOR.]

SHIPHRA.   Be seated, Prophet.

JONAH.   I thank you.

[*He sits on the floor.*   SHIPHRA *brings him an amphora and a cup.*]

JONAH.   No.   Please.   I'm sorry.   Thank you.   But I am a teetotaller.

SHIPHRA.   I thought you were.   This is snow water from the mountains.

JONAH.   Oh?   In that case . . . thank you very much.

[*He drinks.*   SHIPHRA *sits down opposite him.*]

SHIPHRA.   It is brought down by convoys of fast mules.   It is carried in little tanks with big umbrellas fixed above them to keep the sun away.   Have you seen one of these convoys?

JONAH.   No.

SHIPHRA.   It is a pretty sight.   You have not been in Nineveh before?

JONAH.   No.

SHIPHRA.   I think you will like Nineveh.   Didn't you think the Great Western Gate was a fine piece of architecture? I saw you coming in.

JONAH.   Did you?

SHIPHRA.   Yes.   There are five hundred different colours in the walls and arch.   The gate itself is covered with gold-leaf. It is made of copper.   It looks like fire in the setting sun. People who haven't seen it before think that the city is burning.

JONAH.   Do they?   Do they indeed?

SHIPHRA.   Have you seen the great fountain in the Market Square?   It runs wine of all sorts on holidays . . . through a hundred spouts.   But I forgot.   You don't like wine.   But there are hundreds of other things to interest you.   Did you see the big avenue of olive trees to your right as you came in?   That leads to the Zoological Gardens.   We have the finest lion park in Asia. The band plays there among the poplars every evening when it gets cool. . . . But you must have seen some of the city. What do you think of it?

JONAH.   It makes me sick to the soul.

SHIPHRA.   Oh, you mustn't say that! Do you know that we have a million people here? The kindest and jolliest in the world. They work hard and they play hard. We have concerts and horse-races and camel-races and the King's Hunt. We've got the finest singers and musicians and the best soldiers and hunters and boxers and wrestlers and some of the prettiest girls. They smell like gardens and tinkle as they walk. You *must* like Nineveh.

JONAH.   Whether I like Nineveh or not is neither here nor there.

SHIPHRA.   But we *like* to be liked. . . . Oh, forgive me for chattering like this; but I must talk on and on or I shall ask you your secret and the King would never forgive me. You have a secret, haven't you?

JONAH.   Yes.

SHIPHRA.   Have you told anybody?

JONAH.   Not here. Not yet.

SHIPHRA.   Will you tell us?

JONAH.   The secret is for you.

SHIPHRA.   Who gave you the secret?

JONAH.   I am the Messenger of the Lord of Hosts.

SHIPHRA.   Who is the Lord of Hosts?

JONAH.   The Creator of Heaven and Earth. The Father of all Mankind.

SHIPHRA.   The God of the Jews?

JONAH.   The God of the Jews. Jahveh-Elohim. Hallowed be His Name.

SHIPHRA.   Is He a very terrible God?

JONAH.   He is very terrible.

SHIPHRA.   You will tell his secret to the King?

JONAH.   Yes.

SHIPHRA.   I wish he would come back. He may have forgotten all about us. He is a good King, but very absent-minded.

[*She goes to the balcony.*]

The Palace Yard is full of people. He will come back here. He usually makes them a little speech from the balcony. They never know what he is talking about, but they cheer like anything. There's always something ironical in his speeches. I know him as well as anybody can, but his jokes are above my head, and the people don't know that they are jokes at all. That pleases him very much. . . . Oh, yes. The Guard has lined up now. He will be here presently. You will tell him your secret, won't you?

JONAH.   I will tell him.

SHIPHRA.   May I be here too?

JONAH.   Everybody may be here. It is for all Nineveh and for all the world.

[*The* KING *and the* GOVERNOR *enter, with rather hurried dignity.*]

KING.   Well . . . now.

GOVERNOR.   My Lord, your speech to the people.

KING.   All right, all right. Jonah, you will dine with me tonight. You have impressed me very deeply. I walked past the ranks of the Guard as if I were in a dream. A fellow dropped his pike and I didn't order him a flogging. I don't know when I have been so interested. . . . You see . . .

[*The* KING *walks up and down while* JONAH *stands firmly but respectfully enough.*]

I believe in a purposive Universe. Myths—any kind of mythology is all very well, but it takes one's mind off the point. By the way, my Court buffoon the other day told me that a myth was a moth's sister.

JONAH.   A moth's sister?

[SHIPHRA *wiggles her toes and the* GOVERNOR *laughs heartily.*]

KING.   There was a truth in that. Myths and Moths are destructive and destructible. A candle is lit. They meddle with the light. And out they go. You agree with me, don't you?

JONAH.   I have nothing to do with myths.

KING.   You are quite right. I suggested earlier that you were yourself a solar myth, but that was discourteous and incorrect. What was I saying? Oh, yes. It is obvious that there is a purpose in natural happenings, and even more obvious that there is one in unnatural happenings. We learn astronomy from meteors and eclipses and psychology from the ravings of madmen. We must study the meaning of your strange adventure. We must seek out its purpose.

ANGEL. Did you feel like a fool when you spoke to the people of Nineveh ?

JONAH. No.   That is true.   If ever a man was inspired, I was that man.   I do wrong to doubt.

> [*The* ANGEL *vanishes.* JONAH *shakes his head and rubs his eyes as if to rid himself of a thought.   He gets up and begins to busy himself with a row of small stones.   Enter* SHIPHRA, *in rather agreeable-looking rags, carrying a basket and pitcher.   She watches him for a moment.*]

SHIPHRA.   What are you doing, Jonah ?

JONAH.   When the hour comes, I shall stand at this stone here and my shadow will fall just short of the little stones there

SHIPHRA.   And that is how you will know ?

JONAH.   That is how I shall know. . . . Who are you ?

SHIPHRA.   Don't you know me, Jonah ?

JONAH.   No.

SHIPHRA.   My name is Shiphra   Don't you remember ? You talked to me kindly in the King's Palace.   But what has happened to your Gourd ?

JONAH.   Never mind about my Gourd.   Why have you come here ?

SHIPHRA.   I had to come.

JONAH.   Are you a devil come to tempt me ?

SHIPHRA.   Do I look like a Devil ?

JONAH.   You have not answered my question.

SHIPHRA.   I am not a Devil.   An Angel sent me to bring you food and drink.

JONAH.   An Angel, eh ?

SHIPHRA.   You look dreadfully tired and hungry.

JONAH.   Put the things down there.

SHIPHRA.   But . . .

JONAH.   Do as I tell you.

SHIPHRA.   Don't send me away, Jonah.   I shall die if you send me away.

JONAH.   Why should I send you away ?   You are nothing to me . . . and you will die anyhow.   I cannot protect you.

SHIPHRA (*sitting down*).   Oh, thank you, Jonah.   If I am to die I shall die with you.

JONAH.   It is not revealed whether I shall die or not.

> [*He sits down at some distance from* SHIPHRA.]

SHIPHRA.   The King and all his people are walking in sack-cloth with ashes on their heads.   They have fasted for nearly forty days.   Whatever they have done, they are sorry for it. Why don't you spare them, Jonah?

JONAH.   Who am I that I should spare them?   I am like the donkey that rebuked Balaam—a poor dumb beast till the Word opened his mouth.

SHIPHRA.   But you can call on your God to save them.

JONAH.   Do you think I have not called?   I cannot bear to think of what I shall see.

SHIPHRA.   But it will be interesting.

JONAH.   It will *not* be interesting.

SHIPHRA.   Then call again on your God.

JONAH.   He will not answer.

SHIPHRA.   Then He will kill all these poor stupid people and all the babies.   How can He kill babies for worshipping idols?

JONAH.   He knows what He is doing.

SHIPHRA.   I wonder.

JONAH.   Don't be blasphemous, woman.

SHIPHRA.   I'm sorry, Jonah.

JONAH.   A lot of difference that will make to Jahveh.

SHIPHRA.   Master . . .

JONAH.   You must not call me Master.   I am only a voice. And be quiet.   If you are to stay here you must not talk.

SHIPHRA.   Very well, Master.

JONAH.   We must sit and wait.

SHIPHRA.   You were grand and beautiful when you spoke to the people.

JONAH.   Are the hot wind and the sun not enough, that I have to listen to the endless tongue of a woman?   Be silent.

SHIPHRA.   I walked seven miles to come here.   See.   My feet are bleeding.

JONAH.   If you will not be quiet you shall walk seven miles back.   Sit quiet for a very few hours and look at Nineveh.   Yet a very little while and no one will ever see it again.

> [*They sit and watch Nineveh in the blazing, growing heat.   Music to denote the passage of time.*]

SHIPHRA (*intoning softly*).

Nineveh was like a pool; Nineveh was like a flower,
So excellent was Nineveh,

Like a flashing jewel with lightnings in its heart
By the wayside was Nineveh.

Sweet at the dawn when the light smoke rose
From the hearths of Nineveh.
Sweet in the dusk with the children at the fountains;
Sweet below the velvet night that curtained our loves;
Sweet in the sunshine with the scarlet coated charioteers
Trotting by the stalls in the coloured bazaar.

[*While she is intoning she moves gradually closer to* JONAH. *He does not repulse her, but gives no sign that he is aware of her.*]

SHIPHRA.

Voices of the cattle; voices of the people;
Voices of harpers, singing songs of Nineveh;
Stilling as the stars rose, smiling at Nineveh.

[*She touches his hand.* JONAH *withdraws his hand sharply.*]

JONAH. Don't touch me. I told you to be quiet. Wait and watch.

[*They sit together in profile, looking towards Nineveh. Solemn music and play of lights returning at last to full daylight and silence.*]

SHIPHRA (*moaning*). It is hot, Jonah. Have we long to wait?

JONAH. No.

SHIPHRA. Did your Lord tell you that the Gourd would wither?

JONAH. No.

SHIPHRA. The Destruction will come soon, now. The sun is crawling down the arch of the great bow. The shadows are growing longer.

JONAH. When my shadow is as long as a man, the Lord Jehovah will fall upon Nineveh. For He has told me.

[*He stands up. His shadow is almost as long as a man.*]

SHIPHRA. It will be time when your shadow reaches the stones.

JONAH. When it reaches the stones. It is almost there.

SHIPHRA. Sit down, Jonah. I don't want your shadow to reach them.

JONAH. Do you hear the stirring of a wind?

SHIPHRA. No. Not yet.

JONAH. Listen then. Listen. Your ears are better than mine. The Trumpet in Zion is about to sound.

SHIPHRA. The shadow has reached the stones!

JONAH. Listen.

SHIPHRA. O Jonah! The people! The poor people! Kneeling there with no sound but the thudding of their poor frightened hearts.

JONAH. Listen. There will be a silence and then the Trumpet. Listen.

[*He raises his arms. Suddenly a chatter of birds and the crowing of a cock are heard. His shadow is past the stones. He drops his hands to his side.*]

SHIPHRA. The shadow has passed the stones.

JONAH. Nothing has happened. Nothing.

[*The* ANGEL *strolls onto the Scene as* JONAH *casts himself on the ground.*]

JONAH. O curse and blast the day that ever I saw the light. Curse my father and my mother and the snivelling brats my brothers. Oh, why did not Jahveh drown me like a gentleman instead of making me a mock and a hissing to those uncircumcised dogs of Chaldeans? O Fool, Fool, Fool!

SHIPHRA. Jonah, look up! Don't go on like that, Jonah.

JONAH (*beating his brow on the ground*). O darkness, come down and hide me. O sands of the desert, cover me. O winds of the desert, blow the foolish, lying words I have spoken into nothing and less than nothing. All living things despise me, for I am utterly ashamed.

ANGEL. Jonah!

[SHIPHRA *cannot see the* ANGEL. *She is wringing her hands in despair over* JONAH.]

JONAH. The Lord has mocked me for his sport.

ANGEL. Jonah, why are you grovelling there with your face begrutten with dust and tears?

JONAH. Go away from me. You are an evil spirit.

ANGEL. Why are you grovelling there like a bad-tempered child? I am anxious to know.

JONAH. It is the INJUSTICE of it. The Lord drove me and scourged me and nearly drowned me and forced me against the revolt of my whole soul to speak the truth to Nineveh. And

[56]

now He has turned the truth into a foolish lie.   He has mocked me and forgotten me.

ANGEL.   Even the Lord, who can do everything, cannot mock you and forget you at the same time.

JONAH.   He has withered me as he withered my companion the Gourd.   The poor little Gourd did nobody any harm.

ANGEL.   You are sorry for the Gourd?

JONAH.   It was a living thing and gave me shelter.

ANGEL.   Yet it was not your child.   You neither planted it nor caused it to grow.   You have pity on a plant that came up in a night and perished in a night.   Will you not allow the Lord to pity Nineveh, that great city, with its hundred and twenty thousand poor souls who don't know their right hands from their left?   And the sheep and the cattle too, Jonah.   Sometimes I think you are a little unreasonable.

[*The* ANGEL *vanishes.*]

JONAH.   Lord. . . .

SHIPHRA.   What's the matter, Jonah?   What are you looking at?   There is nobody.   Nobody but me.

JONAH.   Is that you, Shiphra?   Take hold of me.   Hold on to me.   Oh, Shiphra, I shall die and not live.

SHIPHRA.   Oh, not for years yet, Jonah.   You'll make hundreds of wonderful prophecies before that.   Don't cry, Jonah.

JONAH.   I shall never prophesy again.

SHIPHRA.   O yes, yes, yes!

JONAH.   No.   I have learned today a bitter truth.   I am not in God's confidence.

SHIPHRA.   Yes, you are.   He has changed His mind, that's all.   Surely He can change His mind.

JONAH.   No.   I have never been in His confidence.   I thought he was speaking to me—to me alone.   And all the time He was sending me ridiculous messengers who were more in His confidence than I.   That vulgar blackguard Bilshan.   Little Euodias.

SHIPHRA.   Who is little Euodias?

JONAH.   He spoke to me through jackals and kites.   He spoke to me through that noisy, boring, smelly Whale—and I didn't understand a word of it.   And he talked to me through my skin when he bruised and ducked and burned me.   What

275   [57]

must he think of me ? It is horrible to think that the Almighty
may have a sense of humour.

SHIPHRA. If He hasn't, that is rather a dangerous thing to
say, Jonah.

JONAH. I can't help it. What am I to say ? What am I
to do ? My whole life has given way beneath me. I thought
I was a great Prophet. Everything I did or said was on that
understanding. And now I find that I am nobody. I am only
an Ordinary Man.

SHIPHRA. Oh, no, Jonah ! No, no, no, no, NO, NO, NO,
NO!!

CURTAIN.

THE END OF THE PLAY.

THE SIGN OF THE PROPHET JONAH

A PLAY FOR BROADCASTING

The Author is indebted to the British Broadcasting Corporation for permission to publish this Play

THE SIGN OF THE PROPHET JONAH

WOMAN NARRATOR.   In the deep-sea-caves below the waters about the South Pole there lives a distressed and ancient Whale. His great cruising days are over, and he is so close to disintegration that Time and the sanctions of life and death have become for him misty and confused.   To such as he the waves of seas long evaporated, the forms of sea-creatures long washed to atoms, the voices of men long dead are as real as if the seas still beat, the fishes still swam and the men still spoke.   To that huge, dreaming beast comes the voice of the Prophet Jonah.   It is nearly thirty centuries since the Whale last heard that voice, piping out in an agony of terror from its uneasy interior.   It is a calm and confident voice now.

JONAH.   Ah, my dear Whale, I have found you at last.   Do you remember me?

WHALE (*as if reciting a lesson*).   I do not remember anything at all.   I am a Whale, that most deadly immortal monster. . . . I sail the oceans for ever and ever, lashing the sea in my wake till one would have thought the deep to be hoary.   Or so they say.   I do not remember anything at all.

JONAH.   And yet, Leviathan, you were once the instrument of Providence.

WHALE.   Was I?   In what respect?

JONAH.   Once upon a time you saved ME.

WHALE.   And who are you?

JONAH.   I am a spirit hovering over the waters.   They are of interest to me, those great waters in which I nearly died frustrated and unfulfilled.   For even on them the doom I foretold for Nineveh has fallen.   It is a pleasure to me to revisit them.   It is a pleasure to me to see you, dear and majestic instrument, still held by a thread of life and brooding away time.

WHALE.   I am glad that a spirit can yet feel pleasure.   But you have not yet told me who you are.

JONAH.   I was Jonah, the son of Amittai.   My childhood was spent in Zebulun in the little village of Gittah-Hepher.   As if it were yesterday evening I can see myself with two boys and a girl lying lazily in a field beyond the city gate.   We were watching the sun sink through the yellow and olive haze to the dusty horizon. . . .

[*Fade in of Children's voices.*]

JONAH. Did you ever notice that when the sun gets down just almost to the horizon it bounces like a ball?

JONADAB. Huh! I bet it doesn't!

JONAH. Yes. And it flattens out a bit too. Just as it touches. You watch.

KISH. I bet it doesn't.

JONAH. I bet it does.

KISH. If you can bounce and flatten the sun, why don't you make it stand still—like how Joshua did?

GIRL. Joshua made the sun stand still.

KISH. I know he did. I've just said he did, haven't I?

GIRL. Yes. You said so.

KISH. Then shut up. Nobody asked you to speak.

GIRL. Who asked Jonah to speak?

JONAH. I can speak if I like.

GIRL. Nobody would pay any attention to you unless you said silly things—like that you can bounce the sun.

JONAH. I didn't say I could bounce the sun.

JONADAB. Yes, you did. You're always saying things like that.

KISH. People will think you are cracked. And so you are.

JONADAB. When I grow up, I'm going to be a soldier like Joshua.

JONAH. I'm going to be a Prophet, like Elijah.

KISH. I wish you'd shut up. You are a cocky little beast. This kid is quite right. You're always thinking of silly, mad things to say to make people listen to you.

JONAH. They're not mad things.

JONADAB. Yes, they are. It's a mad thing to say you are going to be Elijah.

GIRL. Somebody's got to be Elijah.

KISH. Not a little, fat, tubby kid like Jonah, anyhow. And I thought I told you to shut up.

GIRL. I'll shut up if I like. And, anyhow, why should I sit and listen to you? Jonah may say silly things, but at least they are interesting things. You talk about nothing but how high you can climb or how high you can jump or how fast you can run. As if a monkey couldn't climb better or a dog run faster or a flea jump higher.

KISH. Look here. If you think I'm going to let a fat-faced girl like you . . .

[4]

JONAH. Look!

KISH. Look where?

JONAH. Look at the sun. It's just setting. Look at the sun.

[*Short silence.*]

GIRL (*in an awed tone*). It bounced!

JONADAB. So it did!

KISH. Only a little bit, though.

GIRL. And it's flattening out now. Look. Just where it's touching the ridge.

KISH. Gosh!

GIRL. Jonah, don't let it! Don't let it flatten any more.

JONAH (*modestly*). All right.

JONADAB. It's all right now. The bit we can see, anyhow.

JONAH. Yes. It's all right now.

KISH. Jonah, I'll race you to the town gate.

JONAH. All right.

KISH. You start us, Jonadab.

JONADAB. No. I'm running too. I can beat Jonah, at any rate.

GIRL. I'll start you, Kish.

KISH. All right. I'm ready.

GIRL. One, two, three. Go!

[*Sound of boys running.*]

KISH. Owch!

JONADAB. What's the matter?

GIRL. Stop, Jonah. He's hurt himself!

JONAH (*distant and still running*). I know.

KISH. Owch! My ankle turned over.

JONADAB. Jonah! Come back!

JONAH (*more distant*). I'm at the gate. I've beaten you both.

JONADAB. No, you haven't. The race is off.

KISH. Ow! Don't touch it!

JONADAB. He is a cocky little beast.

GIRL. All the same . . . It's awfully funny. He said he would win.

JONADAB. No. He hadn't the cheek to say that.

GIRL. He *looked* as if he knew he would win.

KISH. How could he know? He didn't trip me. He was yards behind.

281

GIRL. It was the way he looked. It's getting dark. I'm frightened.

JONADAB. Could you walk if you put your arm round my neck, Kish?

KISH. Yes. I think I could . . . Owch! . . . Yes. I can manage.

JONADAB. Come along, then. What a cad Jonah is!

GIRL. I'm frightened . . .

[*Fading.*]

JONAH'S MOTHER. Jonah, Jonah, where have you been? It's after sunset.

JONAH. I know, Mother. But it's only just after.

MOTHER. You've been running. You're all out of breath.

JONAH. Yes, Mother. . . . Mother, I won a race.

MOTHER. Did you, sonny? That was very nice. Now, wash your hands and face and sit down to supper. I thought the wolves must have eaten you.

JONAH. But I won a race, Mother.

MOTHER. That was very clever of you. Wash yourself. Be quick.

JONAH (*splashing*). I've never won a race before. I beat Jonadab and Kish. Kish is the fastest boy in the village. I beat him.

MOTHER. You mustn't be conceited, Jonah.

JONAH. It isn't conceited to tell the truth. I beat Kish. And Jonadab too. Rachel saw us. She saw me win. I won easily.

MOTHER. Yes, sonny! Now, eat your supper.

JONAH. Of course, I didn't win by running faster than Kish and Jonadab. They're really very good and I can't run very fast.

MOTHER. Don't speak with your mouth full.

JONAH. All right. My mouth's empty now. You see, this is what happened. . . .

MOTHER. And don't bolt your food. . . . Who's that? Oh, Rachel! What do you want? Isn't it time you were home?

GIRL. I wanted to see Jonah.

MOTHER. What about?

GIRL. Nothing. I just wanted to see him. Good night.

MOTHER. What an extraordinary girl!

[6]

JONAH I know why she wanted to see me.

MOTHER. Do you? Why did she want to see you?

JONAH. Because I did a miracle today.

MOTHER. Jonah! Are you feeling quite well?

JONAH. Yes, Mother, I'm all right. But I won the race by a miracle. I wished that Kish would fall, and he fell. It was the only way I could beat him. He's the fastest boy in the village.

MOTHER. But that was very unkind. And not very fair, was it?

JONAH. I thought of that. But if it had been unfair, would the Lord have twisted the boy's ankle just at the very moment I wanted him to? And he laughed at me for telling the truth. And people are punished for that, aren't they, Mother? And it isn't ordinary truth, Mother, like confessing when I stole the peaches from the priest's garden. It's special kind of truth I know inside myself, and I've got to tell it or—or—or bust.

MOTHER. Jonah, I know what you need. You need some senna pods. You'll go straight to bed and I'll boil up some senna pods for you right away. . . .

[Fade. Music.]

JONAH. The years went on and I grew from a peculiar little boy to a strange little man. I was rather fat, and I had thick, curly ginger hair and a small, curly ginger beard. When I looked at people straight in the eye they were afraid of me. At that time the world was as it is now. Men were hating each other and killing each other and nobody knew what was going to happen next. People were very anxious to know what was going to happen, whether it was good or bad, and soon it became known that I could tell them. They came for miles to my little village and I told them the truth in a strong voice. Some things I told them were easy, such as that if they were wicked they would be miserable. Other things were more difficult. I could tell them when the copper-smith's donkey would fall down a well and when they might expect the soldiers to come ravening over their fields and when it was going to thunder. How I knew these things I did not know, but I was fairly certain that God told them to me, and the people were quite sure.

One night I went to bed very pleased with myself. I had spoken very eloquently to over two hundred people at the town gate, and they had crept away in the dark very quietly when I had finished.   Most of them had been weeping.   I could make them cheer or weep exactly as I wished.

I was tired and happy, and I went to sleep quickly.   But in my sleep I began to talk as I had talked to the people at the gate.

[*Music.*]

. . . If thieves came to you, if robbers came to you by night, O you helpless and forlorn, would they not spoil your grape-vines and eat till they were full?   Awake, then, and watch; for the . . . for the . . . Where am I?

I have been asleep.   This is my sleeping-mat and this is my room.   There is the crack in the mud wall with the hole at the foot of it where the little green lizard came through.   And yet it isn't my room.   There is something wrong.   There is a white light in the room, though it isn't daylight.   It should be dark.   And yet the light grows and grows.   It will soon be so bright that I cannot look at it.   Someone is there.   Who is that?   It is a young man.   He is very tall and beautiful. Who are you?

ANGEL.   Are you Jonah?

JONAH.   Yes, Lord.   But who are you?

ANGEL.   Why are you sleeping here on your sleeping-mat?

JONAH.   Yes.   I think I am asleep.   But I was very tired. I had been preaching at the town gate.

ANGEL.   You are to get up and go to Nineveh.

JONAH.   To Nineveh, Lord?   But Nineveh is a great huge rich city.   I should be lost in Nineveh.   I am only a simple village prophet.   And, besides, I am doing good work here.   I don't know what they would do without me.   And Nineveh is very far away.   I shouldn't know how to get there.   I think you must be making some mistake.

ANGEL.   Have you finished?

JONAH.   Yes, Lord.

ANGEL.   Very well, then.   You are to go to Nineveh and cry against it.   The wickedness of Nineveh has come up before the Lord.

JONAH.   But, Lord, a man from Edom went to Nineveh last spring.   They broke his bones and threw him into the river. It is useless to cry against Nineveh. . . . The light is fading. He has gone. . . . I am awake. . . . Oh dear, oh dear, oh dear!   What am I to do? . . . Stand up, Jonah.   Take a deep

[8]

breath. . . . That's better. The word of the Lord has come to you, Jonah, son of Amittai. And Nineveh is as nothing in the Lord's great eye. You are God's prophet, Jonah, son of Amittai. You are God's prophet at last. . . . Jonadab! Wake up and come in here. Jonadab!!

JONADAB (*sleepily*). Here I am, Master.

JONAH. Call the people.

JONADAB. The people? What people?

JONAH. Call all the people of Gittah-Hepher.

JONADAB. But it's after midnight, Master. They have all gone to bed.

JONAH. Do as I tell you.

> [*Hurrying music. Confused voices fading to silence as* JONAH *speaks.*]

People of Gittah-Hepher. . . . In this town where I was born, I have taught you what it has been given to me to teach. I have called you from your beds to tell you that I am about to leave you.

> [*Moans of protest.*]

Tonight I start on a dark and dangerous journey, far from my home and my friends. At the end of that journey lies the mighty and wicked city of Nineveh. I have been charged with the duty of putting the fear of the Lord over Nineveh. I should feel proud and honoured above all mankind. But pity me and pray for me. . . . Farewell.

> [*A pause. Then a babble of voices.*]

WOMAN. He has gone. Shall we ever see him again, Jonadab?

JONADAB. I don't know. He woke me suddenly. He looked like one possessed. I thought I saw a light round his head.

MAN. Nineveh is a terrible place. They have singing and dancing and bear-baiting and cockfights in Nineveh.

ANOTHER MAN. And soldiers and thieves and painted ladies clattering with gold ornaments.

ANOTHER MAN. And chariot-racing and great gilt buildings full of flowers and fountains running wine—or so they say.

MAN. It is strange that Jonah is not afraid.

WOMAN. He *is* afraid.

JONADAB. You must not say things like that.

WOMAN. All the same, it's true. He's afraid. He looked from side to side like a cornered rat.

JONADAB.   Be silent, woman!

WOMAN.   He'll never go to Nineveh! He's a great man here. This is only a little village. He can shout and strut and bawl as much as he pleases and we all think he is a great man. But he won't be a great man in Nineveh. And he knows it.

[*A pause.*]

MAN.   I wouldn't go so far as to say that, but I am rather glad he's gone. He always seemed to me to be a bit narrow-minded.

ANOTHER MAN.   He was always admonishing and threatening and keeping people in order. After all, we were meant to get a little fun out of life.

WOMAN.   I've got a drum hidden in the rafters of my house. Kish has got a fife. Let's have a dance.

JONADAB.   No!

WOMAN.   Who do you think you are? You're not a prophet! Play up, Kish!

[*Music growing wilder and wilder till it becomes blended with the far-away eerie howling of a jackal. It stops suddenly and only the long-drawn wail of the jackal is heard.*]

JONAH.   What's that? What's that? It sounds sometimes like a child crying and sometimes like a lost soul. . . . It's only a jackal. You've heard jackals crying in the night before. But it's dark and lonely and I'm weary.

JACKAL.   Jo-o-o-owowow-onah!

JONAH.   It sounded like my name.

JACKAL (*clearly enough*).   Jonah.

JONAH.   It's still the jackal, but I'm sure I heard my name. What is it? . . . Pull yourself together, Jonah. It's the night and—and being so tired. Three days and three nights. I hardly stopped to rest.

JACKAL.   The sun set on your right, Jonah.

JONAH.   What if it did?

JACKAL.   If you had been going to the North-East it would have set on your left. Nineveh is to the North-East. Where are you going, Jonah?

JONAH.   It's all imagination. Jackals can't talk. My imagination is playing me tricks.

JACKAL.   You're going to Joppa, aren't you, Jonah? Here, boys, Jonah's going to Joppa. Jonah's running away!

[10]

286

JACKAL PACK. Away-ay-ay-ay.

JACKAL. O great bustard, flying up aloft! O starlings, chattering in your nests! O whistling kites! O bears, shambling among the rocks! Jonah is running away from God.

JACKAL PACK. Birds and Beasts: Away-ay-ay-ay. Jonah is running away!

JACKAL. O laughing hyena who roams by himself, do you hear that? Jonah is running away from God.

HYENA. Ha! Ha! Ha! Hahahahahahahahahaha!

JONAH. O peace, rest! Will I never have peace? Will I never have rest? I cannot go to Nineveh. I dare not go.

JACKAL PACK. Away-ay-ay.

STARLINGS. Coward, coward, chattering, bragging coward!

JONAH. They are devils. I must make for the sea. I must put the blue water between me and the devils. I must go on I must go on and on. The sea!

[*Noise of beasts and birds, music, seagulls crying and the sound of waves. Then the sound of wind in cordage, the lapping of water against ships and scattered cries of a busy harbour in the early morning. Sailors are heard singing a Chanty.*]

SAILORS.
Good-bye and farewell to you, ladies of Joppa.
Good-bye, fare you well, Good-bye, fare you well.
Farewell and adieu to you, young Joppa ladies.
Hurrah, my boys, we're Tarshish bound.

NARRATOR. The sun is rising on the seaport town of Joppa and the galley, Semiramis, must cast off from the quay if she is to catch the tide.

[*Weary, ragged, hungry and covered with dust,* JONAH *comes staggering up the Jetty. The* CAPTAIN *is talking to the* MATE *and does not see him at first.*]

CAPTAIN. A fair wind from the landward, Mr Mate.

MATE. Aye, aye, Sir.

CAPTAIN. Time we was casting off. I think we can cast off now, Mr Mate, hey? What do you think?

MATE. Aye, aye, Sir. Stand by to cast off! Look alive there, you palsy-stricken dock rats!

PURSER (*a very polite man*). Oh-er, Captain?

CAPTAIN. Ah, good morning, Purser. Well, what is it?

PURSER. I think there's a passenger coming down the jetty.

CAPTAIN. Wait. I'll get my spectacles. Haven't we got enough passengers?

PURSER. We've still got an empty berth.

MATE. Hold hard, there! . . . Suffering Sailor, what a passenger!

JONAH. Hi!!

PURSER. Are you coming aboard, Sir?

JONAH. May I? Yes, I can pay the fare. Are you bound for Tarshish?

MATE. Tarshish it is. Take your time. There's no hurry. We're only here for your convenience. It doesn't matter if we miss the suffering tide.

CAPTAIN. Mr Mate! Steady as you go, Mr Mate. The poor gentleman is tired.

MATE. This ship's full to the funnel of tired gentleman. This way, you. Look lively. Stow your dunny-bag aft the binnacle.

PURSER. Let me see. Single or return?

JONAH. Single—to Tarshish.

PURSER. That will be half a talent. Thank you!

MATE. Stand by to cast off. Give way, the starboard bank. Easy as you go!

SAILORS.

> A girl asleep with a blue dress on
> (Shake her, Johnny shake her);
> An unsafe couch she's resting on
> (Shake her, lads, and wake her).
> Oh, shake her and wake her,
> For we're bound away to Tarshish,
> Poor old man!

[Sea music.]

JONAH (*drowsily*). He followed me through the wilderness of Tob. I lay like Jacob with a stone for my pillow but I could not sleep. I thought I should never sleep again. I am no prophet. I am a frightened little man. Why should I be hunted through the wilderness? I ran and ran and staggered and fell down and got up again, but the beasts and the birds and the snakes in the socks mocked me. But now I am safe. Now I can sleep. For seventy-two long hours I have had no rest and no sleep. Now I can sleep—sleep—sleep. . . .

[Soft music growing slowly loud and sinister.]

CAPTAIN. I don't like it, Mr Mate.

MATE. No more do I, Sir.

CAPTAIN. The South-Easter's dropped and the sky's like lead. Call all hands to take in sail.

MATE. Aye, aye, Sir.

CHILD. Mummy.

WOMAN. What is it, love?

CHILD. Look at that funny little cloud far over there where the sky meets the sea.

WOMAN. Yes, dear, isn't it funny? It's like a little fat black sheep.

CHILD. It's coming this way.

WOMAN. So it is. Arshak! Wake up! Do you see that cloud?

MAN. What cloud! Oh, yes. My golly, it isn't half moving.

WOMAN. It's coming towards us. It's RACING at us. Oh, Arshak!

MAN. It's bound to be all right. She's a well-found ship and . . . My golly, what an ugly sky!

WOMAN. There's going to be a storm. Put my cloak over your head, dearie.

CHILD. I want to see the black sheep.

MAN. It's a great raging black ram, now. There's the rain.

[*Storm music.*]

[*Shouts, trampling of feet, storm sounds, confusion.* CAPTAIN's *voice tops the tumult.*]

CAPTAIN. Mr Mate!

MATE. Aye, aye, Sir.

CAPTAIN. Call all hands on deck and muster the passengers aft.

MATE. Aye, aye, Sir.

[*Noise. Shouts die down till storm only is heard.*]

CAPTAIN. Ladies and gentlemen, it looks a bit like we are all going to get wet. We've run into the tail of a tornado, and I'm hopeful, all the same, that we may ride it out. If you want to get your flat feet on dry land again, there's two things you've got to do. In the first place we've got to lighten ship. So you'll kindly turn to and dump all your heavy baggage overboard. I wouldn't tell you to do this if it wasn't the only thing to do. In

[13]

the second place, this ship has been struck by lightning, to say nothing of a roaring ramstammy of a sea. It's a hundred to one she'll founder. Now, the passenger list shows that we've got members of forty-two different religions aboard. I want you to get down to it and pray to your gods, whoever they are. Every man jack and woman jane of you. Pray till you split, for it's the only way we can ride it out as far as I can see.

[Tumult.]

PASSENGERS. O Isis! O Osiris! O Poseidon, save us. O Artemis! Come to our aid. O Astarte! O Ma of Comana! O Ma! O Ma!

[Sounds fade and grow as scene changes to another part of the ship.]

MATE. Hi! What's this?

PURSER. It looks like one of the passengers asleep.

MATE. Holy Sailor! Asleep! Wake up, you. Show a leg!

JONAH. Eh! Er! Oh! Ah! I've been asleep, I think.

MATE. I give you first prize for that.

JONAH. I was very tired. I—I lay down. Is it a storm?

MATE. It's the father and the mother of a storm.

[Clap of thunder.]

Listen to that. Why aren't you praying with the rest?

JONAH. Take me to the Captain.

MATE. Do you think the Captain's got nothing else to do than to listen to you? Get down on your hunkers. . . .

JONAH. Take me to the Captain!

[Loud storm music.]

CAPTAIN. What's this, Mister? What's this? Who's this man?

MATE. I don't know. Sir, the steering gear's gone to glory and the larboard bank of oars is burst to matchwood. We're for Fiddler's Green and no mistake.

JONAH. Are you the Captain?

CAPTAIN. What's all this? Who are you?

JONAH. I am a fugitive from the Lord of Heaven and Earth. He has come for me to take me. Throw me into the sea that He may take me alone and leave the rest.

CAPTAIN. I can't do that. I'm responsible to the owners for every man jack and woman jane on my ship. Nobody leaves the ship without my orders.

[14]

JONAH. Throw me into the sea.

A MAN. Captain, we have drawn lots to find who has brought bad luck on the ship. That's the man, Jonah, the Jew. Throw him overboard.

CAPTAIN. Get forrard, you, and bear a hand with the pumps. No man is to be thrown off this ship.

VOICES. We're lost. We are lost.

JONAH (*shouting above the storm*). I have no courage. I dare not leap myself. Take me and throw me into the sea. You cannot fight God.

CAPTAIN. Can't I? I'll show him.

[*More storm noises.*]

MATE. She's shipping it heavily, Sir. Another sea like that last and we go under for good.

JONAH. Throw me over the side.

MATE. Looks like we're all for Davy Jones anyway. Who happens to be first doesn't matter. Bear a hand, two of you, and cast him overboard.

JONAH. Throw me far out.

[*A splash and the storm suddenly stops. A silence.*]

PURSER. He's gone.

WOMAN. The wind has dropped. We're saved.

CAPTAIN. It couldn't be helped. Lord send it brings us no ill luck.

WOMAN. He was a great prophet.

CAPTAIN. Lord send his death isn't on our heads. There's not a sign of him. He sank like a stone.

[*Two or three bars of solemn music followed by curious gurgling sounds.*]

JONAH. In the green dark, at the bottom of the sea, the Lord had prepared a great fish to swallow me. . . .

WHALE. Yes. That was me. . . . It comes back to me. Yes, yes, yes, yes, yes. It comes back to me. I remember the storm. The father and mother of a storm, as you very truly observe. I got a crack from a wave as big as a mountain. I opened my mouth to gasp, and in popped a most indigestible little gobbet. Well, well, well. I remember it all now. It had a singular air of the miraculous about it, now I come to think of it, but at the time I thought mainly of the plaguy dyspepsia you caused

291

JONAH.   You were an instrument of Providence.

WHALE.   It is agreeable to hear you say so, and in some sense consoles me for that prodigious belly-ache.

JONAH.   For three days and three nights I was your unwilling passenger. . . .

[*Fade to muffled voices of* JONAH *and internal rumblings of the* WHALE.]

JONAH.   Where am I ?   I can . . . it's difficult, but I can breathe now.   I can feel my arms and legs.   My legs are over my head.   It is hot and stifling.   All round me is wet and slipperiness and slime.   The stench is dreadful.   Am I dead ?   I did not think it would be like this.

[JONAH *sneezes.*]

I can sneeze.   Dead men don't sneeze.   I am alive.

[*Back to natural conversation between* JONAH *and the* WHALE.]

WHALE.   . . . And kicking, my dear friend.   And kicking! Karwoosh!

JONAH.   At long and last the Lord spoke to you and you vomited out Jonah on the dry land.

WHALE.   With, I hope, the maximum of consideration and the minimum of inconvenience to that excellent man.

JONAH.   Yes.   I found myself on a long, sandy beach, and the blessed sun was shining on my bruised, soaked body.   I saw you wallowing in the lagoon and blessed you and thanked you. . . .

[*Fade.*]

O great fish, O mighty immortal monster!   You have given back to me the sun and the light breezes and the kind, dry sand below my feet.   Take back my thanks and blessings with you in your strange journeys through the cold oceans.   All happiness of the sort most pleasing to whales attend you in the green seas.

WHALE.   Not at all.   Don't mention it.   To tell the truth I am glad to be quit of you.   Thank you for your blessings, and take this in return.   Important little person from Gittah-Hepher, Palestine, it is the Whale who speaks.   There is nothing in the deep waters or the silly dry land to compare with him, to compare with the majesty of his great driving snout, to compare with the fury of his dreadful tail.   I beat the sea before me into a foam and lash the sea behind me into white rage, and traverse

[16]

the world for ever and ever, from Pole to Pole for ever and ever. And the thing that I, the Whale, enjoin upon you, Jonah, is Humility. You are tempted from time to time to believe that you are a party to the good God's secrets. Into at least one of them you have penetrated somewhat deeply. It was a dark secret, Jonah. It was the secret of my vast and rumbling belly. I fear that your visit has left you little the wiser, except in this, that to suppose that Almighty God keeps *you* regularly informed of his Purpose is a foolish assumption. It is almost as foolish as to run away from God—in which undignified and irrational exercise I found you, my Prophet. Go to Nineveh and be good. Good-bye and farewell to you, damp little Jonah. Watch me. Mark me. Here I blow!

JONAH.

I called out my affliction to the Lord
And he answered me.
Out of the belly of Hell I cried
And he heard my voice.
For he cast me into the deep,
Into the heart of the seas;
And the flood was about me
And the waves and the billows passed over me.

And I said: He has cast me out from before His eyes,
Yet will I look again towards the holy Temple.
The waters compassed me about
Even to the soul.

The deep was all about me;
The weeds were wrapped about my head;
I went down to the bottom of the mountains;
The earth with her bars closed on me forever.

Yet thou hast brought up my life from the pit, O Lord
my God.
When my soul fainted I remembered thee.
And my prayer found thee, Lord,
In thy holy Temple.

I am poor and naked,
I have no sacrifice to pay but to pay the debt I have vowed.
I will sacrifice with my soul and my voice and my works.

I will pay the debt that I have vowed and follow no more
  lying vanities.
Salvation is of the Lord.

[Fade and Music.]

JONAH.   So I, Jonah, went to Nineveh to pay my debt.   I
saw it through the desert haze nearly a day's journey away.   By
the roadside were shepherds, watching their sheep, and on the
road were camel-drivers taking great bales of wool and other
merchandise to Nineveh. . . .

[Caravan noises.   Sheep.   Travellers' Song.]

JONAH.   Camel-drivers, I will walk with you.   Shepherds,
bring your sheep and join us.   Walk with me to Nineveh.
SHEPHERD.   Who are you, ragged man, who walks so fast?
JONAH.   I am a man from the depths of the sea.   Come with
me to Nineveh, for I have a message to Nineveh from the
Omnipotent Lord of Hosts. . . .

*[The music is now a rather monotonous March Tune; reinforced
by growing noises as JONAH is presumed to be approaching
Nineveh.   The sound of walking, marching, trotting and padding
feet is heard.   The grunts and bubbling of camels.   The bleating
of sheep and the lowing of cattle.   The creak and clatter of cart
and chariot wheels.   A bagpipe played by a beggar.   A continual sound of human chatter, growing more eager and excited as
the noises and music grow louder.]*

JONAH.   Is this Nineveh?
VOICES.   Yes.   This is the Great Western Gate.   Isn't it
fine?   There are five hundred different colours in the walls and
arch.   Yes, and the gate itself is covered with gold-leaf.   It
looks like fire in the setting sun.   People who haven't seen it
before think that the city is burning.   That huge great building
on the bank of the river is the King's Palace.   It is covered with
gold-leaf too, and there is a big fountain in the middle that runs
wine of all sorts through a hundred spouts.   Isn't it a fine city?
What do you think of it?   You don't find cities like this at the
bottom of the sea!   What do you think of our city, ragged man?
JONAH.   It makes me sick at heart.
VOICES.   Oh, you mustn't say that!   There are the kindest
people here.   You can have great fun.   Singing and dancing
and listening to bands.   And horse-races and camel-races and
the King's Hunt.   We've the finest poets and the finest singers

[18]

and the best soldiers and hunters and boxers in the world and the prettiest ladies.   They smell like gardens and tinkle when they walk.   You *must* like Nineveh.

JONAH.   Whether I like Nineveh or not is neither here nor there.   In forty days there will be no more Nineveh.

[*A silence.*   JONAH *raises his voice to oratorical pitch.*]

I stand here at the Gate as I stood at the gate of my town far away and speak what the Lord has given me to speak.   The Lord has taken hold of the strings of my heart with His hands, and the song He plays on the strings of my heart rings in my head and body with agony and fear.   It is terrible to me to tell you His truth, but there is no other way.   After forty days and forty nights, when the morning sun casts a shadow as long as a man, the birds will be suddenly silent and the beasts of the field will stand still like statues.   Then suddenly there will arise a great wind, and the Wrath of the Lord will fall on Nineveh.   The proud buildings will bend and break and fall down, and doom and destruction will take everything that lives in the city.   It will be useless to fly to the desert or to the hills.   I, Jonah, Son of Amittai, thought once that I could escape that anger.   I know now that it cannot be.   The thunder of the rage of the Lord of Hosts will come upon you, and there will be no escape.   In a little while there will be silence again, and in the waste of the sands no traveller will know where Nineveh has been.

[*Fade.   Music.   The tinkle of fountains in the Palace.*]

JONAH.   They brought word to the King of Nineveh where he sat upon his throne. . . .

KING.   . . . And it is thought that what he said was true ?

MESSENGER.   O King.   It was true.   He was a little ragged man, but he is a great magician.   Lightning came from his eyes, and his body distended till he was like a mighty giant blotting out the skies.   And his voice was the voice of a god, and his words were true.   The people, as many as the eye could see, fell on their knees in the street and tore their garments.   It is true that Nineveh will be destroyed.

KING.   Let it be published through Nineveh by my decree. Let neither man nor beast, herd nor flock, taste anything; let them not feed nor drink water.   But let man and beast be covered with sackcloth and cry mightily to God.   Let every man turn from his evil way and from the violence of his hands.

. . . It may be . . . who can tell ? . . . that God will turn and repent, and turn away from his fierce anger, and we shall not perish.

NOBLES.   We hear and obey.

[Solemn music.]

NINEVEH WOMAN.   We in Nineveh knelt in the street with dust on our heads and watched Jonah go out of the city and climb the foothills till he came to a flat place at the top of the rock. From that he could see the city.   And he placed two lines of little stones.   The distance between them was from his toes to his head.   For he knew that when the day of the destruction of Nineveh would come, if he stood with his feet at one row of stones his shadow would fall so that the shadow of his head touched the second row of stones, and that at that moment there would be a stillness, and everything would happen as he had said.   He sat there day after day in the burning sun, waiting for his prophecy to come true.

Up on his hill, day after day, he could almost hear the beating of the frightened hearts of the people of Nineveh . . . but he could hear nothing else.   God had ceased to speak to him, and he was alone and ill upon his rock.

JONAH.   O Lord, surely I begin to see that I have been made a fool.   So terrible was the message thou gavest me that I could not bear it.   I fled to Tarshish, and thou followedst me to bid me go on.   But now I begin to perceive that my message was lies, and that the destruction of Nineveh was an evil dream. Kill me now, Lord, for it is better for me to die than to live.   I am a shamed and miserable man.

NINEVEH WOMAN.   When Jonah had said this a curious voice came to him—the only voice that came in all these forty days and nights.   All it said was, " Are you very angry, Jonah ? "   And then it was silent again. . . .   But on the thirty-ninth day, when the sky was like brass and the heat was so terrible that Jonah thought he would indeed die, suddenly a fresh, green gourd plant with broad flat leaves grew up between him and the sun and sheltered him from the heat, so that he slept and was refreshed and comforted.

[A few bars of soft music.]

Then the fortieth morning dawned on the day when Jonah said that Nineveh would be destroyed.   And Jonah looked at the gourd and saw that it had withered away.

[20]

JONAH. O gourd, you are withered away, my kind, green gourd, my only companion, the only living thing that came to comfort me in my loneliness and desolation.   Poor gourd; now I am alone indeed.

NINEVEH WOMAN.   He looked towards Nineveh and it was very still.   No smoke rose from the morning fires.   He looked east, and the sun was mounting in the Heavens.   He looked at his little row of stones, and stood up with his feet on the first row. His shadow almost reached the second row.   The time was very near. . . .

JONAH.   My shadow has almost reached the stones.   In a moment there will be a stillness of birds and beasts and then . . . and then . . . It will be terrible, but it will show that I have spoken the truth and not lies . . . that the word of the Lord is true and unshakeable . . . that . . . my shadow has reached the stones . . . a hot wind is beating on the back of my neck . . . and now for the Silence. . . .

[*A cock crows.   There is a clamour of birds and beasts.   A child is heard laughing.*]

JONAH.   Nothing has happened.   Oh, let the earth cover my shame, for I am deceived and a false prophet and a liar and a fool. I am withered like the gourd.   The Lord could not leave me even the good little gourd that has done nobody any harm. . . . O darkness, come down and hide me.   O sands of the desert, cover me.   O winds of the desert, blow the foolish lying words I have spoken into nothing, and less than nothing.   O perish, black day on which I was born.   All living things despise me, for I am utterly shamed.   The Lord has mocked me for His sport.

ANGEL.   Jonah!   Why are you grovelling there with your face all begrutten with dust and tears ?

JONAH.   Go away from me.   You are an evil spirit.

ANGEL.   You have not told me why you are grovelling there like a bad-tempered child.

JONAH.   It is the INJUSTICE of it!   The Lord drove me and scourged me and nearly drowned me and forced me against the revolt of my whole soul to speak the truth to Nineveh.   And now he has turned the truth to a foolish lie.   He has mocked me and forgotten me.   He has withered me as he withered my companion the gourd.

ANGEL.   Even the Lord, who can do everything, cannot forget you and mock you at the same time.   You are sorry for the gourd?

JONAH.   It was a living thing and gave me shelter.

ANGEL.   Yet is was not your child.   You neither planted it nor caused it to grow.   You have pity on a plant that came up in a night and perished in a night.   Will you not allow the Lord to pity Nineveh, that great city, with its hundred and twenty thousand poor souls who don't know their right hands from their left?   And there are the sheep and the cattle too, Jonah. . . .

[*Fade.*]

VOICE OF THE WHALE.   And that is how it happened?

JONAH.   That is how it happened.

VOICE OF THE WHALE.   I am obliged to you for telling me such an interesting story.   And it has all the symptoms of being true. . . . Good-bye, Jonah.

JONAH.   Good-bye, Whale.   Sleep well.

THE END

(40 minutes.)

NOTE.—This play must be taken QUIETLY.   The rhetorical passages should be spoken with intensity, and not shouted.   I have heard several good "religious" broadcast plays spoiled recently because the actor seemed to associate prophecy with ham acting.   I only mention this to re-inforce what I am sure will be the Producer's instructions.

THE DRAGON AND THE DOVE
or
HOW THE HERMIT ABRAHAM FOUGHT THE DEVIL FOR HIS NIECE

A PLAY IN TWO ACTS

The Author stole the Story and the best of the Dialogue from his friend, HELEN WADDELL. *To her and to her splendid book,* THE DESERT FATHERS, *he offers his respectful acknowledgements.*

ACT I

In front of the Curtain, at either corner of the Proscenium, there are two rough stools. You are to imagine that the stools are the sole furniture of the antechamber of the Bishop of Edessa, in Mesopotamia, and that the year is A.D. 400. A WOMAN *in the garments of a* DEACONESS *enters shyly and sits on one of the stools. Shortly after, a brisk young* ABBOT *enters from the other side and takes the other stool. After a seemly pause, he begins to shoot glances at the* DEACONESS *and presently speaks.*

ABBOT. It is cool and pleasant in here in the shade. One is very glad to get out of the heat of the hillside.

DEACONESS. Yes.

ABBOT. You have come to see Bishop Nonnus?

DEACONESS. Yes.

ABBOT. A worthy old man. I have been sent to him by my Bishop—Rufinus of Samosate. Do you know him?

DEACONESS. No.

ABBOT. A good fellow. A funny old fellow. The young monks call him old Grunts, because he does. Like an old boar-pig having his dinner. He screws up his face and beams and cracks his fingers and grunts and hiccups—and he waddles like an old tortoise when he walks. We all love him. A very learned old boy, too. And a good holy man.

DEACONESS. So I have heard.

ABBOT. Have you come far?

DEACONESS. From Hierapolis.

ABBOT. That's a pretty good step. I hope you don't have to wait long for an audience, but I suppose you'll have to. The Bishop here is a good soul, but he doesn't put much value on time. Eternity will be nothing to him, if he gets talking. He's like my Bishop in that. Living in the Desert, that does it. When the Euphrates runs past your cell you don't think anything of it, but after a year or two in Libya you want to live up to your neck in it. . . . In Libya your skin dries and crackles like old leather. I was a Hermit myself for a bit, but Old Grunts took me away from it. He said there was more than one way of serving God. . . . I say, I hope you don't mind me talking to you. Are you very strict in Hierapolis?

301

DEACONESS.   No, not very.   But they enjoin on us a certain degree of austerity.   And they are careful to give us the usual warnings.

ABBOT.   What warnings?

DEACONESS.   Oh, that the Devil may awake in us wicked thoughts by—oh, well—taking the disguise of a monk, for instance.

[*She laughs.*]

ABBOT (*laughing*).   You look very attractive when you laugh. Perhaps you, too, are another favourite disguise of the Devil.

DEACONESS (*suddenly serious*).   Oh, no.   You must not say that.

ABBOT.   We monks are properly warned too, you know. We know that women are the most dangerous of all living creatures.

DEACONESS (*crossing herself*).   It was said by Sara, the Abbess, " I am a woman in sex, but not in spirit ".

ABBOT.   Very well, then.   I shall not think you a Devil if you will pay me the like compliment.

DEACONESS.   I do not think you are a Devil.

ABBOT.   Splendid!   And now, what shall we talk about, for we may have many hours to wait?

DEACONESS.   Do you think we might talk about the Devil?

ABBOT.   Why not?

DEACONESS.   I have often wanted to talk about him, but the other Deaconesses are shocked when his name is mentioned.   I think that is a little foolish of them, don't you?

ABBOT.   Yes.   It is a good thing to know something about the ways and the character of one's enemy.   The holy old men in Libya were often on quite intimate conversational terms with him.

DEACONESS.   So I have heard.   And how can one fight a battle if one doesn't know what sort of a person the enemy's general is?

ABBOT.   How indeed!   And some of the Fathers go further than that.   They say that it is sometimes necessary to fight the Devil with the Devil's weapons.

DEACONESS.   Oh! . . . Oh, do they?

ABBOT.   Yes, indeed.   Did you ever hear the true story of the Holy Old Anchorite, Abraham, and his little Niece who was stolen from him by the Devil?

[4]

DEACONESS.   No.   I haven't heard that story.

ABBOT.   It has been written down by St. Ephraem, the good old man who died in this very city.   I shall tell it to you, if you like.

DEACONESS.   Please do.

ABBOT.   It will help to pass the time.

DEACONESS.   Yes.   It will.   Does the Devil come into the story?

ABBOT.   Not in his own person.   But he is very lively in the background—behind the scenes, as they say in the wicked theatres where actors and even actresses exhibit themselves on the stage for money.

DEACONESS (*crossing herself*).   They have told me of such places.

ABBOT.   It is not of them we speak.   But in the sanctified theatre of your mind you must make yourself see this old man, Abraham the Hermit, sitting in his cell in the Desert, steeping palm-leaves in water and interlacing them into mats; and most of all meditating on the greatest—on the only great things . . .

[*The Curtain parts and shows* ABRAHAM'S *Cell.   It is divided into two by a rough partition, in which there is a little trapdoor about five feet from the ground.   In each half there is a stool and a matting bed.   In each there is a book on a stand.   But on the* ABBOT'S *side there are flowers in a bowl—the only visible sign that* ABRAHAM'S NIECE *lives there.   There is a stone pitcher on* ABRAHAM'S *side, but none on the other.* ABRAHAM, *an old man with a white bushy beard, is weaving a mat of palm-leaves and reading his book.*]

ABBOT.   The story says that the blessed Abraham had a brother; and when his brother died, he left behind him a daughter, a child of seven.   Her father's friends brought her to her uncle.   The old man saw her and had her housed in the outer room of his cell.   There was a small window between the two rooms, and through this he taught her the psalter and other passages of Holy Writ, and she kept vigil with him in praising God, and would sing the Psalms along with him, and tried to copy her uncle in all abstinence.   She was a charming little creature with fair hair and a slight stammer which she never completely lost.   Her uncle had joy to see her so swift and unhesitant in all good, in humbleness, in modesty, in quiet. Twenty years she lived with him in abstinence, even as an

innocent lamb and an untarnished dove.   But the time came
when the Evil One webbed a net for her to the grief and anxiety
of the holy man. . . .

> [MARIA, *a handsome, enthusiastic-looking young woman in a plain
> white garment, comes into her half of the Scene carrying an
> earthenware vessel full of water. She puts it down and goes to the
> trapdoor, opening it from her side.*]

MARIA.   Uncle!

ABRAHAM.   Are you there, my child?

> [*He does not look up.*]

MARIA.   I've been fetching water.

ABRAHAM.   Water is a most instructive element.

MARIA.   Is it, Uncle?

ABRAHAM.   When there is a great deal of it, it is turbulent
and treacherous, and even murderous.   Yet when it separates
itself apart, we see a very good thing.   For in the peace of its
solitude the muddiness settles and the water becomes clear and
honest and reflects very gaily and humbly the lights of Heaven.

MARIA.   I wish I knew how you think of such things.   I
think and think and I see that what you tell me is true, but I can't
think of truths for myself.

ABRAHAM.   We don't think of truths.   They are given to
us if we wait.   And if we cleanse ourselves from our passions.

MARIA.   But I have no passions.

ABRAHAM.   No?   Tell me, if you were walking along the
road and saw a lot of stones and broken pots lying about, and
there, among them, a piece of gold, what would you do?

MARIA.   Well . . . I should know that it wasn't mine.   I
should let it be.

ABRAHAM.   No, but how would it appear to you?   Could
you think of it as if it were one of those stones or broken bits of
pottery?

MARIA.   No.   I should know what it was and that some
people might think it important, but I could easily stop myself
from picking it up.

ABRAHAM.   Then passion is alive in you, but it is bound. . . .
If you were to hear of two people that one loved you and spoke
well of you and that the other hated you and told everybody that
you were a stupid, priggish, spoiled little brat; and then suppose
you saw them coming along the track to see you in your cell;
would you be glad to see them both?

[6]

MARIA.   Well, I should try to make no difference between them.

ABRAHAM.   You would try very hard?

MARIA.   Yes, very hard.   I should *make* myself kind to both of them alike.

ABRAHAM.   Then the passion of hatred is still alive.   You do not wrestle with anything that is dead.   But by the practise of holiness we may keep our passions bound so that they need not trouble us.   They need not trouble us at all.

MARIA.   Yes. . . . I saw the Brother at the well.

ABRAHAM.   The Brother?   What Brother?

MARIA.   The Brother who came to you yesterday and talked and talked.   Or rather you talked, but I heard his voice from time to time and I recognised it when he spoke to me at the well.

ABRAHAM.   I thought he had gone away.

MARIA.   He meant to go this morning, but he said he had still some troubles in his mind and that he might come to you again.

ABRAHAM.   Did he?

MARIA.   He wasn't very sure.   He thought he might settle his difficulties by himself.   I asked him what his difficulties were, and we had quite a long talk.

ABRAHAM.   Did you help him?

MARIA.   I think I did, perhaps.   He said I had.

ABRAHAM.   Hm! . . . What were his difficulties?

MARIA.   He said that when he practised humility he always felt a kind of satisfaction in it.   And he couldn't be sure whether that satisfaction came from God or from the Devil.

ABRAHAM.   You told him, of course, that true humility can never be satisfied, but cries continually like the daughter of the horse-leech?

MARIA.   I didn't tell him that exactly in so many words.

ABRAHAM.   But you told him that his satisfaction was sinful pride in his humility and that it came from the Devil?

MARIA.   No, not exactly that either.   I can't put things as well as you can.   But it was more or less that.

ABRAHAM.   What did you tell him?

MARIA.   I told him I thought he undervalued himself and that he should go on practising humility and not bother.

ABRAHAM.   But that isn't more or less what I said at all.

MARIA.   Oh, isn't it?   I'm sorry.

ABRAHAM.   I hope you may not have nourished the Devil of spiritual pride in that young man's heart.

MARIA.   Oh, no.   I haven't done that.

ABRAHAM.   How do you know ?

MARIA.   He's not that sort of man at all.   He's so gentle and humble and kind.   He helped me to draw the water and he *did* want to know.   Don't be cruel to him if he comes back.

ABRAHAM.   Cruel ?

MARIA.   No, of course you're never cruel.   You're my dear, kind old Uncle, and you couldn't be cruel to a raging lion if it came ramping and roaring into the cell.

ABRAHAM.   Talking of lions, did I ever tell you the story the Abbot Alexander told me of old Paul Helladicus ?

MARIA.   No.   Tell me it.

ABRAHAM.   Alexander went one day to see the old fellow in his cave, and they were sitting talking when there was a knock at the door.   The old fellow went and opened the door and then took a platter of bread and peas and took it out to whoever it was that knocked.   The Abbot thought it must be some pilgrim, so he had a look out of the window—and it was a lion !

MARIA.   Oh, dear !

ABRAHAM.   The Abbot asked the old man about it and he said, " I admonished the great beast, saying, ' If you do no hurt to any living thing, you may come here every day and I will give you food.'   And this is now the seventh month since he has come twice a day for his meals."   After a few days, my friend the Abbot went to buy a wine-jar from the old Solitary and asked how the lion did.   And the old fellow said, " Badly.   The other day he came here for breakfast with blood on his chin, and I said, ' What's this ?   What's this ?   You have been disobedient to me.   You have eaten flesh.   Blessed be God, I will give you no more—devourer of flesh, eating the bread of the fathers !   Go away.   Get out ! '   He didn't want to go away, so I took a rope and folded it in three and hit him with it three times.   And he went away."

MARIA (*laughing*).   Poor lion !   But what a brave old man ! I should have been afraid of the lion.

ABRAHAM.   I don't think so.   There is nothing in this world to be afraid of—except sin.   The old Abbot Nisteron was walking in the desert with a Brother and they met a huge Dragon.   The Brother ran like a hare and the Abbot ran too, and very fast indeed for such an old man.   When they stopped for breath the Brother said, " Were you afraid of the Dragon too ? "   And the Abbot said, " I am not afraid, my son; but it was expedient that I should flee at the sight of the Dragon, that I might not have to flee the spirit of vainglory."

MARIA.   I should think he *was* a little bit frightened.

ABRAHAM.   Maria !   You must not compel me to admonish you.   If the Abbot was frightened, it was a matter between himself and God.   It is none of our affair. . . . It's getting too dark to work.   We shall say our evening prayer and go to bye-byes.

MARIA.   I would like to read a Gospel before I go to sleep. May I light the lamp, if I draw the shutter ?

ABRAHAM.   Yes, yes.   You won't disturb me.   I am weary tonight.   I'm not so young as I once was. . . . Are you ready ?

[*He has put away his work.   Both kneel.*]

ABRAHAM and MARIA.   Blessed Lord, stretch forth Thy great hand between us and the Powers of Darkness on this night. Blessed Son of Mary, watch over us tenderly as thy Mother watched over thee in the cattle stall.   Amen.

[MARIA *lights her rush-light.*   ABRAHAM *continues in prayer for a little and then stretches himself on his mat.*]

MARIA.   Good night, Uncle.   God bless you.

ABRAHAM.   Good night, my child.   God bless you.

[ABRAHAM *turns his face to the wall and is immediately asleep.* MARIA *turns the pages of her missal and begins to read ; but not for long.   She looks into vacancy, thinking.   Then listening.   A knock, very gentle, at the door startles her.   She sits frozen till the knock is repeated.   Then she goes to the door.*]

MARIA.   Who is there ?

MONK (*outside*).   It is I, Brother Absolom.

MARIA.   My Uncle has gone to bed.   You must come to-morrow.

MONK.   Is he asleep ?

MARIA.   Yes.   You must come tomorrow.

MONK.   Open the door a little.   I have something to ask you.

MARIA (*opening the door a chink*).   You must ask it very quietly.   You will wake my Uncle.

MONK.   It is most unfortunate that he should have gone

307

to bed. I could not sleep. I'm disturbed. I'm ill. I'm parched with thirst. Will you give me a drink of water?

MARIA.   But . . .

MONK.   Your Uncle did not teach you to refuse water to a thirsty wayfarer.

MARIA.   No. I'll give you some. But you must go away at once when you have drunk it.

> [MARIA *goes to the water-jug and pours some water into a cup. Her back is to the door and the* MONK *comes into the room. As she turns, she lets the cup fall.*]

MONK.   Don't be afraid. Are you afraid of me? Why are you afraid?

MARIA.   I don't know. . . . Perhaps . . . I'm like the Abbot Nisteron. . . . Perhaps I'm fleeing from the spirit of vainglory.

MONK.   You're trembling.

> [*He takes her hands and forces her gently to her seat.*]

MARIA.   I have spilt your drink.

MONK.   Never mind that. It's very strange that you should be afraid. Today I was in terrible fear. You cannot know what such fear may be, living like a quiet rock flower in your life of piety and virtue. And then you came to me at the well and cast the fear out of me. Then. Out there. In the darkness. Beneath the stars. It came back. The fear. I could not go away till I had seen you.

MARIA.   Poor Brother Absolom. I didn't understand. I'll wake my Uncle and he'll pray for you.

MONK.   No. He can't help me. You alone can give me peace. . . . You're still trembling. Have you taken my fear upon yourself?

MARIA.   I don't know. I can't help trembling.

MONK.   When I am with you I am happy and content. As if I were safe in the Courts of Heaven and you a bright angel. You are bright and beautiful like an angel. You must not be afraid.

MARIA.   I'm foolish. I don't know what it is. I can't help it.

MONK.   Shall I read you a verse or two to quieten you? I shall read in a very low voice, and your Uncle will not waken.

MARIA.   Yes.

[10]

MONK.   I'll read where the book opens: . . . " So Esther was taken unto King Ahasuerus into his house royal in the tenth month in the seventh year of his reign.   And the king loved Esther above all women, and she obtained grace and favour in his sight more than all the virgins; so that he set the royal crown upon her head and made her queen instead of Vashti.   Then the king . . ."

MARIA.   No.   Don't read that.

MONK.   As you wish.—(*He turns some pages.*)—I shall read to you of the love of the Church.   " A garden enclosed is my sister, my bride.   A spring shut up, a fountain sealed.   Thy shoots are an orchard of pomegranates with precious fruits. Henna and spikenard, saffron and cinnamon.   Thou art a fountain of gardens, a well of living waters. . . .   I was asleep (she said) but my heart waked.   It is the voice of my beloved that knocketh saying: Open to me, my sister, my love, my undefiled.   For my head is wet with dew, my curls are full of the drops of the night. . . .   Who is she that looketh forth as the morning, fair as the moon, pure as the sun, terrible as an army with banners ? . . .

" I am my beloved's and my beloved is mine. . . .   Set me then as a seal upon thy heart as a seal upon thine arm: for love is stronger than death."

[*A short silence broken by a groan from the sleeping* ABRAHAM.]

ABRAHAM (*in his sleep*).   Avoid thee, avoid thee, Satan ! Withdraw thy teeth from God's pure Church, the sanctified, the undefiled.

MONK.   Hush !   Has he awakened ?

MARIA.   No.   He is still asleep.   He cries out, sometimes, in his sleep.

MONK.   Come with me.

MARIA.   No.

MONK.   Come with me.

[*He takes her by the hand and leads her to the door.   With the other hand he puts out the light.* ABRAHAM *groans miserably in his sleep.*]

ABRAHAM.   The dove.   The dragon and the dove.   It is gone.   It is all gone.

THE CURTAIN CLOSES.

DEACONESS.   Oh, alas !   Alas !   That the Fiend should dress himself in the garments of a holy man and use the sacred words themselves to fulfil his devilish purpose!

ABBOT.   It is the way of the Fiend.   You shall hear soon how the tables were turned on him and how he was caught in his own trap.   But have patience.   We shall hear what the girl has to say.

[MARIA *comes out from the Curtain and sinks, woebegone, to the ground.*]

MARIA.

Upon the deep tides of my sorrowing,
As a poor sailor by the seas half-drowned,
At their unwitting will I shift and fling.
Nowhere is place of resting to be found,
Nowhere a haven to heal my bitter wound;
For I am dead, and for the dead there no help is.
I by myself have slain myself in this.
Though I can weep and in my heart feel pain
I wot me well I shall not live again.
Sorrow upon me, with deep springs of tears,
What have I done to him who loves me best?
How drenched in bitterness his later years?
How steeped in shame my soul?   I am the foul fiend's jest.

Where shall I go?   What pit is there to hide
All my rank sorrows that so cling and abide?
For I am she forgot that high betrothing
Wherein I was betrothed to Bridegroom pure,
And now, a vessel of contempt and loathing,
Am dead to God and man.   A thing most sure.
Sorrow upon me, I can never more
Sing holy psalms to the old man in his cell.
If God would grant that I might die at his door
And he might lift me up and all be well. . . .
But I am fallen a thousand fathoms in Hell.
I cannot to his window lift mine eyes
Darkened with evil.   My tongue is parched with lies
And can no more change kind and sacred words with him
Whose company is of the spotless cherubim.
I am lost.   I will go wandering to lands unknown
To live a living death.   For hope is gone.

[*She rises and disappears through the Curtain.*]

DEACONESS. Poor thing! And the poor old man, too. How did he take it when he found she had gone?

ABBOT. On the night she went he had a terrible dream. He dreamed that he saw a huge and monstrous dragon, most foul in its aspect and strongly hissing. He saw it come up out of the ground and come to his cell. And there it found a dove and gulped it down and returned again to its den. Abraham thought that this dream signified a new persecution against the Church, for it was a long time before he found that his niece had gone. He thought that she was in meditation, or asleep. He prayed to God for the Church, saying, " Thou that art God, foreseeing all things, Lover of men, thou knowest what this vision may mean." He spent the day in prayer, and the next night the dragon came again, and this time it laid its head under its paws and burst asunder. And the dove was still alive in its belly.

DEACONESS. But . . . I mean to say . . . You tell me, Father, that he spent the day in prayer—and that I can well understand. I have had frightful nightmares myself, once in a way. But didn't he miss his niece?

ABBOT. No. Not then.

DEACONESS. But didn't he say good morning to her? Didn't they sing the daybreak hymn? Didn't he hear the silence when she wasn't moving about in her cell?

ABBOT. No. None of these things. You see, it was a curious thing for a woman to live in a hermit's cell, even if she was his own niece. And when he was in any perturbation of spirit, it was understood between them that she wasn't there at all. If he didn't say, " Good morning, God bless you," she listened till she heard his groanings and his muttered prayers and sat still or walked about like a little mouse until he spoke to her again. Sometimes it lasted for days.

DEACONESS. But if he had taken ill?

ABBOT. He never took ill. He was a hardy old man. He lived on parched grain and dried peas and water from the spring. There was nothing to make him ill.

DEACONESS. I see. I should have been anxious.

ABBOT. Listen. He has wakened from his second dream.

[*The Curtain parts.* ABRAHAM *is on his mat between sleeping and waking.*]

ABRAHAM. Oh! . . . Oh! . . . Oho! Ah, my poor burst

monster, did you think to hold the dove of the Holy Ghost forever in your beastly maw ?

> *[He wakes and sits up.]*

Thank God! It was a dreadful dream, but a happy dream.
Thank God the dove is safe. I feared too much. I should
have had faith. . . . Maria! We shall say our prayers
together. The Lord has sent me a vision that has broken the
bonds of terror. We must thank him for it. . . . Maria!
Are you asleep? Good morning and God bless you. I want
to talk to you! You have been very good and quiet for a long
time. . . . Bless my soul, I don't know how long. . . .
Maria!!

> *[He goes to the trapdoor and listens. As there is no sound, he
> hesitates for a moment and opens the trapdoor.]*

The flowers are dead. The drinking-cup is broken. She
has not slept on her bed.

> *[He leaves the trapdoor and stands, stunned.]*

Now I know what the vision meant! . . . Sorrow upon me,
for a cruel wolf has stolen my lamb, my daughter is made captive. . . .

Lord Christ, Saviour of the World, send Maria my lamb back
to me and restore her to the fold of life, that my old age go not in
sorrow from the world. Despise not my beseeching, Lord, but
be swift to send thy grace to bring her forth unharmed from the
dragon's mouth.

> *[*ABRAHAM *continues silent in prayer. An approaching voice is
> heard singing a hymn. It is a slightly cracked voice, but the
> hymn is a very jovial hymn and is sung with great joviality.]*

EPHRAEM *(without).*

> Hymnum dicat turba fratrum
> Hymnum cantus personet. . . .

> *[*EPHRAEM, *a cheerful, rather diffident old man enters. He has a
> rough crozier in his hand.]*

EPHRAEM. Ab-raham! . . . Oh, I'm sorry, old friend,
you're busy. I'll come another time.

ABRAHAM. Who is it? Ephraem! What a pleasure to see
you! Come in. Come in. Sit down. I'll take off your
sandals. We'll have breakfast and you shall give me all your
news.

EPHRAEM. I spent last night at the monastery at Nitria. I

shall be there for a few days.   They get up very early.   I said early matins and trotted off to see you.   How are you, my dear old friend?

ABRAHAM.   I?   Oh, there's nothing the matter with me. But you must be starving.   Let me see, now, I had some lentils somewhere.

EPHRAEM.   You don't look after yourself enough.   You must remember you aren't so young as you once were.

[ABRAHAM *fetches a platter and a cup of water*.]

EPHRAEM.   These look very good.   But aren't you having any?

ABRAHAM.   No.   Not at present.

EPHRAEM.   Are you fasting again?

ABRAHAM.   No.   Yes.   I don't know.   I'm glad to see you.   How are the good brothers at Nitria?

EPHRAEM.   Never mind the good brothers at Nitria.   You aren't looking yourself.   What's the matter?

ABRAHAM.   I'm all right.

EPHRAEM.   Where is Maria?

ABRAHAM.   She . . . I don't know.

EPHRAEM.   You don't know?   The poor child, I pity her. Your wits go woolgathering up in the sky among the holy angels and you haven't a thought to spare for your own flesh and blood. Go and find her and tell her I'm here.

ABRAHAM.   Ephraem.

EPHRAEM.   Yes?

ABRAHAM.   Do you know the Monk Absolom?

EPHRAEM.   Yes.   Poor fellow.   A very clever fellow and a very eloquent fellow, but I sometimes wonder whether he should have ever gone into the Church.   I forgot.   I sent him to you. What did you make of him?

ABRAHAM.   He seemed penitent.

EPHRAEM.   He may well be.   He got a poor, decent girl into trouble in Alexandria.   The Bishop gave him hard penance for that, poor soul.   I tried to help him, but, as you know, I'm not much of a man of the world.   It's a great defect in a priest. I've got neither your holiness nor the Bishop's humanity.   I'm afraid I'm just a silly old buffer.   Don't let's talk about Absolom. The thought of him makes me miserable, and I don't want to spoil my happiness in seeing you.

ABRAHAM.   God help me.

EPHRAEM.   What's the matter?

ABRAHAM.   Twenty years ago you brought to me my brother's child and gave her into my keeping.   Three days ago you sent me this wretched young man that I might care for him and bring him back to piety and right living.   I have been false to both my charges.

EPHRAEM.   What do you mean?

ABRAHAM.   Two nights ago as I lay on my lazy bed I heard voices.   I often hear voices when I am rapt and dreamy; but I know now that these were the voices of Absolom and my niece.

EPHRAEM.   Oh, dear me.   You don't mean? . . .

ABRAHAM.   Late in the night I had a vision that would have explained all things to me if I had not been besotted and blind. I am a worthless shepherd.   A treacherous watchman.   O Maria, my child, my child!

EPHRAEM.   Where is she?

ABRAHAM.   She has gone.   She has gone away.

EPHRAEM.   Um!   Not with Absolom?

ABRAHAM.   I fear it.

EPHRAEM.   A bad business.

ABRAHAM.   We must find her.

EPHRAEM.   Yes.

ABRAHAM.   And bring her back.

EPHRAEM.   Indeed, indeed. . . .   We must trust in the Lord.

ABRAHAM.   We must also help ourselves.

EPHRAEM.   Indeed.   But Africa is a big place.

ABRAHAM.   It is not too big for me.

EPHRAEM.   What are you going to do?

ABRAHAM.   I shall set out at once.   If I am to search all Africa, the sooner I begin the better.

EPHRAEM.   It is very splendid and, if I may say so, very like you, my dear old friend, to go out into Africa to find one grain among its multitudinous sands; but could we not take thought for a little?

ABRAHAM.   I cannot think.   I must act.

EPHRAEM.   Yes, but consider.   If the girl came back?   If she found the cell empty while you were a thousand miles away questing like an old hound on a lost scent?

ABRAHAM.   You think she will come back?

EPHRAEM.   I think so.

ABRAHAM. And you think that I should wait for her—here?

EPHRAEM. I put it to you for your consideration.

ABRAHAM. And in the meantime she is running, lost and frightened through the dark caves of the Accuser of the Brethren, and I hold back my hand from guiding her. A shepherd goes to the hills for his lost sheep.

EPHRAEM. You employ a figure of speech, Abraham, that is very sacred and beautiful, but perhaps a little misleading in the present instance. Maria is not a sheep. She is a very good and sensible young woman. She will come back.

ABRAHAM. Good and sensible young women go mad. Her goodness and her sense did not save her from the Devil.

EPHRAEM. I have a great deal of confidence in her goodness and sense—in anybody's goodness and sense. The Devil may leap on the good from behind and bear them to the ground, but their goodness lifts them up again. Goodness, my dear Abraham, is a very resilient quality, as I think I have heard you observe in days gone by.

ABRAHAM. Very justly spoken. But, in the meantime, what is happening to my poor child? Are we to sit here and talk like two old poll-parrots while the Fiend works his will?

EPHRAEM. No. I think you should stay here and ask help from the Lord . . . and *will* her to come back. You have a very strong will, Abraham. And, if you do not think that by itself sufficiently practical, there is much that I can do. I am not, as you know, very clever, but can you be calm and listen to me for a moment?

ABRAHAM. Yes, if you don't intend another homily on goodness.

EPHRAEM. No, no. Of course not. As you know, the Bishops have decided that a useless old man like me can be best employed by trotting round the monasteries and churches and keeping everybody in a good humour. Nobody can be angry with a simpleton like me, and they find that the angriest rebukes I am charged with trip out quite pleasantly on my prattling tongue. So the Brethren are not offended and take the matter of the rebuke to themselves while they hardly notice the manner. I think that's true, isn't it?

ABRAHAM. Yes. That's true.

EPHRAEM. Well, then, let me do the searching. I shall

315

have the whole Church helping me, and rumour travels more quickly over Africa than an old hermit with his staff.

ABRAHAM.   You are a very wise man, Ephraem, and you may well be right.

EPHRAEM.   In whatever great circle Maria may wander, it will always have a centre.   This is the centre, here.   She will be drawn to it, and you will be there to receive her.   As for me, the old chatterbox, I shall try continually to hear of her.   If I hear, I'll run to you and tell you.   You may count on that. Then will be the time for you to act.

ABRAHAM.   Then will be the time.   If she is in the Pit of Hell I will go to her, like the man in the heathen story.

EPHRAEM.   I know you will, old friend.

[*He takes* ABRAHAM's *hand and gives it a friendly shake.*]
North, South, East or West.   I'll soon tell you which!

(THE CURTAIN IS DRAWN.)

DEACONESS.   And did he find her?

ABBOT.   Not for two years.

[*A* LAY BROTHER *appears.*]

LAY BROTHER.   My Lord is now at liberty.   Which of you was first?

ABBOT.   The Deaconess was first.

DEACONESS.   Oh, but I can quite easily wait.

LAY BROTHER.   My Lord can only see one of you before refection.

DEACONESS.   Oh, now, that's very awkward.

ABBOT.   Never mind, I shall walk on the terracing, and perhaps the Bishop will invite me to dinner.

DEACONESS.   Are you sure you won't mind?

ABBOT.   That's all right.

DEACONESS.   I do want to hear the rest of the story.

ABBOT.   We shall see.   In the meantime, you mustn't keep the Bishop waiting.

DEACONESS.   Well . . . thank you . . . yes . . . perhaps. . . . It is really very good of you, Father.   I hope you are still here when I come back.

ABBOT.   I shall try to be.   I like a good listener.

[*Exeunt* DEACONESS *and* LAY BROTHER. *The* ABBOT *yawns, stretches himself, and goes out in the opposite direction.*]

END OF ACT I.

ACT II

The ABBOT *enters, takes his seat, and begins to look over a Book of Hours.*
  To him, the LAY BROTHER.

ABBOT.   Well, my son, how goes it ?

LAY BROTHER.   The audience is nearly finished. The voices of the Father Bishop and the holy Deaconess are near the door and have been for the last five minutes.

ABBOT.   She has thought of something else to ask him.

LAY BROTHER.   Women always think of something else at the last moment.

ABBOT.   You are very observant.

LAY BROTHER.   One has to be, in my job.

ABBOT.   You are also very impudent.   You must not categorise holy Deaconesses as women.

LAY BROTHER.   They have some of the characteristics.

ABBOT.   Hold your tongue.

LAY BROTHER.   Curiosity's one.   She asked me to try to keep you till she heard the rest of your story.

ABBOT.   She did, did she ?   Has your reverence any information as to when the Lord Bishop will see me ?

LAY BROTHER.   Not till after refection.   I told you that, Father, didn't I ?

ABBOT.   Perhaps you did.   I must lay your wise words closer to my heart.   Now go away.

LAY BROTHER.   I was going anyhow, Reverend Father.   I must attend my Lord Bishop at his collation.

ABBOT.   When I am a Bishop I shall not have a chatterbox like you breathing down the back of my neck at mealtimes.

LAY BROTHER.   No.   I shall be an Abbot then.

ABBOT.   Not unless you cultivate a little humility.   Get out. Pax vobiscum.

[*Exit the* LAY BROTHER.   *Enter the* DEACONESS.]

DEACONESS.   You haven't gone.   I'm so glad.

ABBOT.   No.   How is the Bishop ?

DEACONESS (*sitting down*).   He is very gracious.   Will you tell me the rest of your story ?

ABBOT.   Yes.   Certainly.   Where was I ?

DEACONESS. The holy Ephraem had promised to seek for the holy Abraham's niece.   What fortune had he in his search ?

ABBOT.   Ah, yes. . . . He had no fortune for a very long time.   He questioned itinerant Friars, he questioned penitents, he questioned everybody.   But no word came of Maria.   Sometimes he had to send out on a false trail.   But Africa had swallowed her as the dragon swallowed the dove in the old man's dream.   He began to think she might be dead.   But Abraham's faith—after the first day—was as steady as a rock.   He believed his second vision and that he would find her.   And at last one day, two years after she had gone, news came to him.

[*The Curtain parts and shows* ABRAHAM, *listlessly setting his cell in order.   He looks very old and weary.   When he speaks, his voice is tired.   To him,* EPHRAEM.   *He is in high, though slightly subdued, spirits.*]

ABRAHAM.   Well ?

EPHRAEM.   I have some news for you.

ABRAHAM.   Praise be the Lord !   What is it ?

EPHRAEM.   May I sit down ?   I am out of breath.

ABRAHAM.   Surely, old friend, surely.

EPHRAEM (*sitting*).   Well. . . . I have found her.

ABRAHAM.   Where is she ?   Is she safe ?   Is she well ?

EPHRAEM.   Yes and no.

ABRAHAM.   Don't answer me like that.   Get your breath and collect your wits and answer me properly.   I will have patience.

EPHRAEM.   She . . . forgive me . . . she is in Memphis. In the suburb called Babylon.

ABRAHAM.   I shall go at once.

EPHRAEM.   Certain things will be required.   They will be here presently.   I pushed on here on my mule while they were still collecting the things.   That is why I'm a little breathless. I am a poor horseman.   Or should it be muleman ?

ABRAHAM.   I don't know.   Go on.   Tell me about Maria.

EPHRAEM.   Yes.   I was right.   The Colonel would be about your build.

ABRAHAM.   What Colonel ?

EPHRAEM.   He isn't exactly a Colonel.   Not now.   In fact he has been converted.   But he used to be a Colonel in the Foreign Legion.   Really a charming man, for one who has been a soldier all his life.   And extremely devout.

ABRAHAM.   But what has this to do with my child?

EPHRAEM.   I was talking to him about her. You see, as I've often told you, I'm not a man of the world. And he had been. And, as I know very little about such things, I naturally asked him. . . .

ABRAHAM.   Asked him what? Where is all this leading?

EPHRAEM.   I knew you of old, you see; and I knew you'd be jumping to start at once, so I wanted to have everything planned and ready. So that there would be no hitch.

ABRAHAM.   Oh, dear, dear! Will you never tell me what has become of my little one? Must I sit listening to this rigmarole of mules and Colonels till my bones crumple up with age and I cannot go to Memphis at all?

EPHRAEM.   Forgive me, my dear old friend. I am so excited that words come charging out of me like the Gadarene swine. A mendicant told me . . . a curious fellow, he was, but I know we can trust him. . . .

ABRAHAM.   Never mind the mendicant. Go on.

EPHRAEM.   Maria is living in an inn in the Babylon quarter of Memphis. He knew her by the mole on her upper lip and the slight hesitation in her speech.

ABRAHAM.   Has she a mole on her upper lip?

EPHRAEM.   Yes. Don't you remember?

ABRAHAM.   I hardly ever saw her. All these twenty years I hardly ever saw her.

EPHRAEM.   But you remember the little stammer in her speech.

ABRAHAM.   Yes. She used to say, " P-pater noster qui es in c-coelis . . . I remember. It was very little. One could hardly notice it. But it was a pretty sound. Like the little broken sounds robins make when they are afraid.

EPHRAEM.   There was no mistaking it.

ABRAHAM.   And she is living . . . in an inn?

EPHRAEM.   Yes. I'm afraid it is a pretty low kind of inn too. Our Lord was born in an inn, but not, I think, in this kind of inn. The Brother said it was always full of soldiers and boxers and actors and musicians and thieves. The Colonel remembered it. He said it had a bad name.

ABRAHAM.   In nomine Patri, Sanctaeque Virginis. . . . Go on.

EPHRAEM.   The mendicant Friar entered it, in his innocence, and asked for bread.   They mocked him and beat him and left him for dead.   He saw Maria.

ABRAHAM.   She brought him help ?

EPHRAEM.   No.   She was with the rest.   The Brother said he thought she laughed with them, but I do not think she did. He cannot be sure.

ABRAHAM.   I must go there.

EPHRAEM.   Wait, wait, wait !   They are heathen.   They are devils.   They would kill you.

ABRAHAM.   Better than I have been mocked and scourged and killed.   Let me be.   Where is my stick ?

EPHRAEM.   What good would it do to Maria if you were killed ?   We must be wise.   Like serpents.

ABRAHAM.   But I must go to her.

EPHRAEM.   You shall go to her.

ABRAHAM.   But I must go at once.

EPHRAEM.   If you go by my way you will travel ten times as quickly.   I have brought you a horse. . . .
And here it comes.

> [*He goes to the doorway.*]

ABRAHAM.   But I have never ridden a horse.

EPHRAEM.   It is a very quiet horse.   It is old like us and patient, like me.   Don't come out.   Sit down.   I have something to show you.

> [ABRAHAM *sits down, bewildered.   Exit* EPHRAEM, *who returns almost immediately dragging a large bundle.*]

(*To someone outside*).   Take the horse down to the spring and give him a drink.   He has a long journey before him, poor old fellow, and we start almost at once. . . . There.

ABRAHAM.   What is that bundle ?

EPHRAEM.   I tried to tell you, but you wouldn't listen.   It is the Colonel's old undress uniform.

ABRAHAM.   But why ?   I don't understand.

EPHRAEM.   We must go cunningly into the country of the enemy.   You must go in disguise.   They will think you are an officer of the Empire.   They will make you welcome.   That is better than a beating.

ABRAHAM.   But I don't look like an officer of the Empire.

EPHRAEM.   You will when you have dressed in the Colonel's clothes.

ABRAHAM.   I see.

[22]

320

EPHRAEM. Make haste, then. I thought you were in a hurry. Take off your gown.

ABRAHAM. I see. You are a clever man, Ephraem. We shall beat the cunning one by cunning. . . . And by the Lord's help.

EPHRAEM. By the Lord's help, certainly. Take off your gown.

THE CURTAIN IS DISCREETLY DRAWN.

ABBOT. Then Abraham made haste to change his appearance —to change almost his whole being, except for the valiant heart beating beneath it all.

DEACONESS. But it will never succeed. Those two old innocents! They haven't the wickedness in them to carry out such a deceit. They will be discovered. All will be lost. The wicked men in the inn will beat him and mock him as they did to the mendicant. He cannot save her that way.

ABBOT. If they have sufficient faith, even the very good can learn deceit very quickly. Be ye wise, said the Apostle, as serpents, and harmless as doves. So it was with this old holy man. Besides, it is always well to remember that the wicked are exceedingly stupid.

DEACONESS. They must be or they wouldn't be wicked. That is certainly true. But I have a sinking in my stomach when I think of that good old man facing fierce danger in that mountebank disguise. . . .

[*The Curtain parts and shows* EPHRAEM *helping* ABRAHAM *to dress.* ABRAHAM *looks absurdly self-conscious in his costume. It is that of a Roman mercenary officer of the fourth century* A.D. *It includes a chainmail hauberk, a tunic ornamented with a quantity of tarnished gilt, blue trousers, a little leather kilt, calf-high black laced boots, gilt spurs, the long, single-edged spatha on the left side and a dagger on the right. Over all there is a short riding-cloak. Yet the most remarkable change in* ABRAHAM'S *appearance is caused by the removal of his beard.* EPHRAEM *holds it in his hand and, in the other hand, a pair of scissors.*]

ABRAHAM. Alas, alas!

EPHRAEM. It had to be, old friend. If thy whiskers offend thee, cut them off and cast them from thee.

ABRAHAM. My beard must have been a source of vanity to me without my knowing. I feel naked without it.

EPHRAEM. You are far from naked. Indeed, you are a most formidable-looking warrior.

ABRAHAM. Am I?

EPHRAEM. You terrify me. Come along. Get your boots on, I have some walnut juice and soot to make you look fierce.

ABRAHAM. Are these boots?

EPHRAEM. Yes.

ABRAHAM. I am told that people die in such things.

EPHRAEM. They die more often in beds.

ABRAHAM. They are very uncomfortable.

EPHRAEM. Nonsense. Have you never worn peas in your sandals?

ABRAHAM. Yes. But that was in a good cause.

EPHRAEM. So is this. Go on. Lace them up. Lace them up.

ABRAHAM. I put peas in my sandals as a remedy against pride. I wonder if soldiers wear these uncomfortable garments for the same purpose? They are very uncomfortable, Ephraem.

EPHRAEM. Well? Well? You should be the last to complain of that. . . . Let me see. The sword to the left and the dagger to the right. Got your boots on? Stand up. The Colonel showed me. Yes. That's it.

ABRAHAM. I suppose soldiers are more subject to sinful pride than even anchorites. It is strange that that never occurred to me before. What have they got to be proud of, I wonder?

EPHRAEM. Wait a bit; the cloak hangs here, I think. Yes. That's the way.

ABRAHAM. They are all hung over with lethal instruments intended to hurt and destroy their unfortunate brothers. They have to do senseless things shouted at them by rude and stupid men. I am very sorry for soldiers?

EPHRAEM. Eh? I'm sorry. I wasn't listening.

ABRAHAM. I said I was very sorry for soldiers.

EPHRAEM. You look as if you were sorry for something. You mustn't look like that. It spoils the whole effect. Now, the helmet. . . .

ABRAHAM. Of course, they practise a certain kind of austerity; and any kind of austerity must have some influence on the character and be pleasing in the sight of the Lord.

EPHRAEM (*trying on the helmet*). Dear, dear. Tut, tut. I thought it wouldn't fit. Never mind. You can carry it.

[24]

ABRAHAM.   Do you think that austerity, practised for its own sake, or even towards some dubious end . . . ?

EPHRAEM.   Walk up and down a little.   You must get used to all that ironmongery.

ABRAHAM.   Yes.   I see that.   (*He walks in an unsoldierly manner.*)   But my mind is troubled on this question.   All that marching and drill in such uncomfortable habiliments would be looked upon by the Fathers as a very severe penance indeed. But soldiers manage to sustain a lively and even jovial appearance with it all.   They . . .

EPHRAEM.   My dear old friend, do you think *you* might manage to sustain a lively and jovial appearance ?   You look to me much liker a sheep going to the slaughter than a gallant son of Mars.

ABRAHAM.   Do I ?

EPHRAEM.   Hold your head up.   Turn your toes in a little. Cultivate a martial stride.   Twist your moustaches fiercely.

ABRAHAM.   Like that ?

EPHRAEM.   No, fiercely.   And step out.   You won't fall. Turn round quickly, stamp your feet.   Hold your sword by the handle.   Now, cough in an offensive manner.

ABRAHAM.   Ahem ?   Is that offensive enough ?

EPHRAEM.   Not quite.   Remember you are fighting the Devil.

ABRAHAM.   Of course.   Yes.   AHEM !

EPHRAEM.   That's better.   You're not afraid of the Devil ! You'll knock his silly head off !   Think of Gideon.   Think of Joshua.   Think of Benaiah the son of Jehoida.   Left.   Right. Left, right.   About turn.   Cough again.   Stop !

ABRAHAM.   What's the matter ?   Was I doing it wrong ?

EPHRAEM.   No, no.   But I nearly forgot.   The Colonel wrote down for me on this piece of paper some soldiers' oaths. Do you think perhaps you could bring yourself to commit some of the milder ones to memory and use them at the inn ?

ABRAHAM.   Are they very . . . soul-destroying ?   Let me see.   Let me see.   " Blood and wounds."   " Stap my vitals." " Split me."   " Heaven punish that crimson Quartermaster."

EPHRAEM.   But you must say them with conviction.   You must think of the Quartermaster as the incarnate spirit of all evil.

ABRAHAM.   Blast the gory Quartermaster !

EPHRAEM.   Now cough !

ABRAHAM. Blast him! Ahem!

EPHRAEM (*crossing himself*).   It is well to be thorough.

ABRAHAM. Yes.   It is well to be thorough.

EPHRAEM. You look every inch a soldier.

ABRAHAM. Do I?

EPHRAEM. Well, almost every inch   And now, here is a bag of money

ABRAHAM. What?

EPHRAEM. A bag of money.   It is from the Brethren.

ABRAHAM. I can't take money.

EPHRAEM. It is the Devil's artillery.   You must take it.

ABRAHAM. No.

EPHRAEM. Yes, yes, yes.   You will spoil everything.   You must act like a soldier—and feel like a soldier—and *be* a soldier. It is only for a little, and the Lord will forgive you.

ABRAHAM. I hope he may.

EPHRAEM. Well. . . The horse has had his drink. . . . What is it they say? Boot and Saddle? Eh? Boot and Saddle.   Come along, I'll help you to climb up.

[*Both go out laughing as the fun of it begins to appeal to them.*]

THE CURTAIN IS DRAWN.

DEACONESS. I told you.   He won't look a bit like a Colonel.

ABBOT.   My dear Sister, how many Colonels have you seen? The old gentleman who looked after the forage for the Second Legion at Alexandria didn't look any smarter than that.

DEACONESS. Perhaps you know best, Father, but, at the same time . . .

ABBOT. I am telling you exactly what happened.   The whole story was written down by Ephraem himself.

DEACONESS. I'm sorry.   Please tell me more.

ABBOT. The old man rode, and he rode on his old white horse, looking and feeling like Death in the Revelation, for he had never bestridden a horse before.   Though the horse went cannily, he fell off once or twice till he learned how to grip firmly the pommel of the saddle and keep his eyes looking between the quadruped's ears.   He went day and night for a hundred and twenty Roman miles, resting only to feed and water his horse and to loosen its girths, for, although he wasn't a horseman, he was a merciful man and merciful to his beast.   In desert places, where he was unlikely to be seen by anyone, he walked beside the horse, leading it.   He felt happier so.   As he walked he recited the less soul-destroying of the oaths the Colonel had written down for him; but he was careful to ask forgiveness in the silence of his soul as each dreadful word sullied the air.   And, in time, he came to Babylon-on-the-Nile.   Night was falling over the ruined tombs of the wicked kings.   As the dew gathered, the scent of corruption rose on the evening air; for, as the women spread sugar and acacia gum to catch flies, so the Lord had spread this Babylon to collect the children of the Evil One.

Through the foul streets they buzzed like caught flies. There was a sound of screaming and foolish laughter, and the sound of bagpipes and flutes and fifes, but never the sound of a psalm.   The old man was weary and sick to the soul.

The name of the Inn to which he had been directed was THE THREE KITTENS OF BUBASTIS.   It merited its evil name.   It was kept by a harridan who might have been the heathen goddess Bubastis herself, so compact of evil was she, so full of the calculating wickedness of the Cat.   You are to picture this murderess lying in wait in the very nest of the Evil One—like a spider on guard.

Then boldly up to the Gates of Hell on his white horse came Abraham.   The first Abraham went forth to do battle with the kings and smote them and brought back his nephew Lot.   The second Abraham, says Ephraem, went forth to do battle with the Devil himself.   So much greater the triumph if he vanquish him and bring home again his niece in safety.

DEACONESS.   Amen to that.

ABBOT.   You are to see a room lit by the filtering dusk from a square, barred window.   It is a low, vaulted room, painted and gilt like a rich woman; but the plaster is broken and the paint is peeling off.   Near the floor, though we cannot see them, are bloodstains.   Round the wall, though we cannot read them, there are hieroglyphs encouraging guests to the commission of the Seven Deadly Sins.   One of them says of Gluttony: "When the belly is full, the heart sits in comfort."   Another says of Pride: "Yourself is the only man you really know. Think well of yourself."   A third says, of Sloth: "Show me tomorrow and I shall bestir myself on its behalf."   Below these hieroglyphs are pictures, done in the Greek fashion, that I can only liken to the dreams of a tortured anchorite.   But mould and flies and the busy rats have answered contempt with con-

325   [27]

tempt, blotting and tearing the wicked artist's work.   On the floor and on the divan are rich and dusty fabrics.   If you could look at them closely you would see the fleas leaping.

> [*The Curtain parts and shows a room in the* THREE KITTENS OF BUBASTIS. *It is nearly dark. The room contains a divan at the back and a low table with cushioned stools. On one of them a* WOMAN *is sleeping with her head on the table. She is dressed in shabby finery, rather like an ancient Egyptian's. We cannot see her face for her head-dress, but when it becomes visible it is scarred and battered like an old barnacled rock. The candle-stick on the table has fallen over. The eerie sound of a bagpipe is heard from somewhere in the house and there is a sudden burst of mirthless laughter—as suddenly silent. An evil-looking* KNAVE, *also in a rather elaborate Egyptian costume comes in carrying a taper. As he lifts and lights the table candles, he disturbs the sleeping* LANDLADY, *and we get the full impact of her terrible face as she raises it and the light falls on it simultaneously.*]

LANDLADY.   Well, rat!   Why did you disturb me?

KNAVE.   It is getting dark, Ma.   Time to light up.

LANDLADY.   What's the good of lighting up?   We can blaze like Hell Fire and nobody will come near us.   It's your fault too.   You lose your temper too quickly.   And then you're too handy with the knife.   Nothing but riff-raff comes here now.

KNAVE.   You know it's not my fault, Ma.   I'm paid to keep order and I keep it.   It's the Priests.

LANDLADY.   The Priests!   O Priests, priests, priests, priests, priests.   In the whole of Africa every second man is a priest. A decent woman can't go out to take the air but she can't move for psalm-singing Praying Jacks.   A poor decent woman can't set up a happy house in jovial, randy little town, but down they come like a flock of hoodie crows and peck up all her substance. Even the good, dirty old magistrates are afraid of them with their, " Yes, Father," and " O Father," and " You don't say so, Father!   How shocking that a naughty dive like the THREE KITTENS should flourish in your pure parish! "   Dirty old men, who used to rollick here with the worst of them.   And here am I with every dinar of my hard-earned capital sunk in this dump and not an obolus of return on my money and a murdering lout like you to keep in idleness and ten lazy sluts of girls eating me out of house and home.   Don't speak to me about priests.   If I had my nails in their skinny throats.

[28]   326

KNAVE (*going to the window*).   They want us to have no fun in this world.   It'd be a poor world without any fun.

LANDLADY.   Giving a decent house a bad name.

KNAVE.   Let them come here, that's all.   Let them come here.

LANDLADY.   Lights.   Lights.   They call me a witch, but I can't make lights, and I can't make venison and I can't make wine, not if they scare away my guests.   If I had all their necks in one skinny neck.

KNAVE.   Ma!   The luck's changed!

LANDLADY.   What's the matter?

KNAVE.   There's an Officer riding down the street.

LANDLADY.   Tyach!!   An Officer.   When did we see an Officer last?   He's only passing through.

KNAVE.   No.   All the beggars are round him, and he's throwing them money.   They're pointing this way.

LANDLADY.   Holy Bubastis, we're going to be raided!

KNAVE.   No.   I think he's drunk.   He can hardly sit on his horse.   He's holding on by its mane.   He's very well put on. He seems to be dripping with baksheesh.   And he's coming here!

LANDLADY.   Run, rat, run.   I'll look after the candles. Go and meet him.   Tell the cook on your way down.   Tell her to get ready everything she's got.   My Liver and Lights, when did I last see an Officer?

[*Exit* KNAVE.   LANDLADY *bustles about, lighting all the candles there are and moving the furniture about in high excitement. Presently the* KNAVE *ushers in* ABRAHAM.   *He is walking stiffly, partly because he is saddle-sore and partly because he is embarrassed.*]

ABRAHAM.   And you'll see that my horse is fed and watered and has some good clean straw to lie on.

KNAVE.   Keep your mind easy about the horse, General. We've good hospitality here for man and beast.

LANDLADY.   Come in, my Lord General, come in.   Sit down.   Make yourself at home.

[ABRAHAM *sits, with some discomfort, on one of the stools.*]

You must be tired.   Have you had a long journey?

ABRAHAM.   Yes.   Oh, yes.   Oh, yes indeed.   I *am* tired. . . . Blast me.

LANDLADY.   Do you think a little tiny drop of Greek wine would do you good ?   Just a little wee tiny drop ?

ABRAHAM.   Yes. Yes, by the Dog. Bring me a huge tankard . . . rot my lungs.

LANDLADY.   Josef, get some wine.

KNAVE.   All right, Ma.

[*Exit* KNAVE.]

ABRAHAM (*calling after him*).   And let it be of the best.

LANDLADY.   Keep your mind at rest on that, honey General. You shall have the best there is in Africa.

ABRAHAM.   Good. Good. There is nothing I like better than a good stoup of wine.

LANDLADY.   You've come to the right place. You shall have your blessed skinful. And now what would you like to eat ?

ABRAHAM.   I should like the best your house can offer.

LANDLADY.   A partridge pie, now ?   Or a hunch of venison ? Or a good fat roast quail ?

ABRAHAM.   I shall have a partridge pie and a haunch of venison and a good fat roast quail.

LANDLADY.   I'll try what I can do. We don't have many visitors at this time of the year. General Antoninus comes here sometimes. Do you know him ?

ABRAHAM.   Yes. Stap my vitals. Very well.

LANDLADY.   A very nice gentleman. A very cheerful, agreeable gentleman indeed.

ABRAHAM.   He is. A fine fellow, by Blazes. A most blazing fine fellow.

LANDLADY.   To think of you knowing Lord Antoninus. How is the dear gentleman ?

ABRAHAM.   Very well, I thank you. Confound his eye-sight.

[*At each of these terrible oaths, the* DEACONESS *is seen to flinch. She can hardly contain herself from speaking.*]

LANDLADY.   That is a mercy. And now, honey-dear General and Captain, what do you say to lying down on that nice soft divan and taking forty winks for yourself ? You are so tired you can hardly sit upright. Just forty winks, and the wine will be here and the dinner will be ready.

[*While she is speaking, she shepherds* ABRAHAM *towards the divan. He is dazed with weariness. He sits on the edge of the divan staring in front of him.*]

[30]

ABRAHAM.   No. I do not wish to sleep. I wish to . . . to make a night of it.

LANDLADY.   And the most joyous night of your life you shall have, soldier darling.

ABRAHAM.   Pray God it may be so.

LANDLADY.   Of course it will. But you'll be all the better for it—all the better for a teeny-weeny cat nap. Put his little footleums up on the divan. That's right. Will mumsy take his horrid sword and dagger away?

ABRAHAM.   No. I shall . . . I shall rest only . . . a few minutes. I shall not sleep. I don't need sleep. Sleep is a waste of time.

LANDLADY.   Surely, surely. It won't be sleep. Just a minute or two of shut eyes. Weary heavy eyelids will lift again when you see the wonderful things I shall have prepared for you. But now they're heavy. Sleepy, heavy eyes. Shut eyes. Old Ma will stroke his forehead.

ABRAHAM.   Don't touch me, woman.

LANDLADY.   Well, well. It's only old Ma. Shut eyes and rest. Shut eyes and rest. Rest. Rest.

[KNAVE *enters carrying wine-skin.* LANDLADY *signals him to be quiet and joins him down stage.*]

Hush, rat. He's asleep.

[*The* KNAVE *takes out a long, shining knife.*]

LANDLADY.   No, you fool. We must find out more about him.

KNAVE.   Do you think he's a spy.

LANDLADY.   If he is, he may have a troop within call.

KNAVE.   He's a queer kind of soldier. Looks more like an old Praying Jack to me.

LANDLADY.   If he is a Praying Jack, I've known one or two that liked their bit of fun. I'll go down to the kitchen to see about his dinner. Don't use the knife unless you have to.

KNAVE.   All right, Ma.

LANDLADY.   Remember that, now. I've told you it gets us a bad name. And you might as well drown yourself as get a bad name in this town. And don't wake him till I come back.

329   M 2   [31]

KNAVE. Right, Ma.

[LANDLADY *goes out. The* KNAVE *stands still, watching* ABRAHAM, *his hand on the hilt of his knife.*]

THE CURTAINS ARE DRAWN.

DEACONESS. Jesu protect him, the brave old man.

ABBOT. He did not sleep. With one eye half open, he watched the murderer at his bedside until they brought his supper. Then he fell to and ate and drank, for he judged it wise to do this, that the Devil might be circumvented.

DEACONESS. O wisdom as of God! O wise understanding of the spirit! O memorable discretion in salvation! Throughout fifty years of abstinence he had never tasted so much as bread; and now, without a falter, he eats meat and drinks strong wine to save a lost soul.

ABBOT. The company of holy angels, rejoicing over the discretion of the blessed man, were mazed at what he ate and drank, light-hearted and nothing doubting, to deliver a soul sunken in the mire.

DEACONESS. O wisdom and understanding! O discrimination of the discerning!

ABBOT. Do you not marvel at this madness, this reversal, when an upright and wise and discreet and prudent man is made, for the time, a reckless fool to snatch a soul from the jaws of the lion, and set free a captive bound, and thrust away from it its chains and its dark prison-house?

DEACONESS. O light of the spirit, illuminating the dark and tortuous ways!

THE CURTAIN PARTS.

[ABRAHAM *is sitting at a heaped-up table, doing his best to be convivial. The* LANDLADY *and the* KNAVE *are waiting on him. They are very assiduous. The* LANDLADY *keeps signing to the* KNAVE *to keep the supply of wine flowing.*]

ABRAHAM. Ha! Ho! An excellent supper, stab and split me!

LANDLADY. We do our best, General Honey, we do our best.

ABRAHAM. But there's something missing.

LANDLADY. Is there, my Lord? I thought we had everything you asked for. Would it be pickled onions? Josef, get some pickled onions.

[32]

KNAVE.   Here they are, Madam.   I didn't forget them.

ABRAHAM.   It is not pickled onions.   It is company.

LANDLADY.   Well, I know I'm very poor company for a gentleman like you, but . . .

ABRAHAM.   Don't be offended, good woman.   Don't be offended.   You are excellent company, but you are busied with many things.   Your mind is on hospitality.   I can only have a half of your company.

LANDLADY.   It's a thousand pities that there isn't another gentleman of your rank staying at the Inn.   You could have had a glorious time together, talking over the wars.

ABRAHAM.   That is as may be.   But we who follow the wars sometimes love a respite from talking of them. . . . Tell me, are there any fine wenches in this town who might cheer a soldier's lonely hour?

LANDLADY.   Wenches?   Why, yes.   But I took you to be a staid and serious gentleman who was past the follies and prattle of wenches.

ABRAHAM.   The appetite for folly dies hard, Mistress.

LANDLADY.   And that's a true word, as I ought to know.

ABRAHAM.   Tell me.   Some time ago I heard talk of a wench; and rot me, it was when we were talking of your inn. A youngish wench, she was, they said.   With—let me see—a mole on her upper lip and a slight stammer in her speech.

LANDLADY.   Who told you of her?

KNAVE.   That's Lalage.

LANDLADY.   Be quiet. . . . Who told you, Honey General?

ABRAHAM.   Collop me if I can remember.   Would it be Antoninus, now?

KNAVE.   That's right, Ma.   He took to her a treat.   Don't you remember?

LANDLADY.   Hm . . A middle-sized girl?

ABRAHAM.   Yes.

LANDLADY.   Sort of darkish-fairish, with grey eyes?

ABRAHAM.   I think Antoninus said her eyes were grey.

LANDLADY.   That might well be Lalage.   A dear girl.   I feel as if she were one of my own daughters.

ABRAHAM.   Do you think she'd share a bite of supper with an old soldier?

LANDLADY.   Well.   She's a very cheerful sort of girl.   Very lively and full of high spirits.   Always ready for a bit of fun.

331   [33]

Yes. She might. . . . Josef, go and see if Miss Lalage's about
and ask her if she'd step down here a moment.

KNAVE (*aside to* LANDLADY). You know very well she's
about. She's been tricking herself up for the last hour.

[*Exit* KNAVE.]

LANDLADY. A fine, lively, high-spirited lass. Yes. I wish
I'd thought of her before. But you see how it is, Sir. I
thought you were one of those serious ones.

ABRAHAM. Then my looks belied me.—Rot me.—You
should never judge by appearances.

LANDLADY (*looking at him doubtfully*). I don't often do.

ABRAHAM. Why do you stare at me? I come, by thunder,
to take my ease at my inn. I am just beginning to be gay and
light of heart and you glower and stare at me as if you had seen a
ghost. Fetch the jade, by Mars and Bacchus, and take yourself
out of here.

LANDLADY. Oh, General Honey, you mustn't speak like
that to poor old Ma.

ABRAHAM. I don't like people to stare at me. You can tell
your wench that too. If she stares at me, I'll throw her down-
stairs.

LANDLADY. Honey Captain, take some more wine. I am
sorry you are out of temper. Miss Lalage won't like it.

ABRAHAM. I am not out of temper. But you must beware
of me if I get so. I am a hard man to my enemies, rot my ribs.

[MARIA *enters. She is heavily painted and tinkles as she walks.*]

LANDLADY. Ah, there you are, duckie. The Captain very
kindly asked if you would dine with him. Isn't he a nice
gentleman? (*Aside.*) Come on. Talk pretty, or I'll have
the skin off your back.

MARIA. Yes. He is a beautiful gentleman.

[*She stares at* ABRAHAM *with an impudent smile on her face. The
smile gradually fades and she looks troubled; but she does not
recognise him. He looks at her steadfastly.*]

LANDLADY. But you mustn't stare at him, love. He doesn't
like that.

ABRAHAM. Well, young lady. Here you come with rings
on your fingers and bells on your toes. Do you feel like a merry
evening?

MARIA. No.

LANDLADY (*in a voice like a file*). What? What do you say?

MARIA. I wish to God I had died three years ago. I should have been merry then.

LANDLADY. What sort of talk is that? Captain, General, I never heard her talk like that before. Nothing but laughing and joking since she came to my house. . . . Have you lost your senses, you fool?

ABRAHAM. Dear me! Dear goodness gracious me! Tears? Do you think I'm your father confessor, come to hear the tale of your sins? Scatter me, what care I for your sins? Sit down, my dear, and cry into a tankard. Slidderkins, that's a poor start to an ambrosial evening!

LANDLADY. Now, isn't that kind of the sweet gentleman? Sit down, honey love, and be yourself.

ABRAHAM. And get you out, Mistress. I'll find means to comfort the wench.

LANDLADY (*sotto voce*). Cheer yourself, you crazy cat, you'll reckon with me if you don't. ' (*Aloud.*) A pleasant evening to you, sweetheart; and to you too, honey Captain, you old rascal!

[*Exit the* LANDLADY. MARIA *sits down opposite* ABRAHAM. *He pours her some wine.*]

ABRAHAM. What ails you, now?

MARIA. I am better. There was something. You reminded me. . . . Oh, it doesn't matter. That's all finished. Are you a stranger in these parts?

ABRAHAM. Yes, by Jupiter, and glad I am of it.

MARIA. Why? Isn't it a beautiful town?

ABRAHAM. I have seen better.

MARIA. You are a great traveller?

ABRAHAM. I have been here and there, stap and rend me. Here and there.

MARIA. I love soldiers. They are so interesting. I mean, they talk in such an interesting way.

ABRAHAM. Do they, hey?

MARIA. Yes. And they're so gentle and kind. Not like merchants. I hate merchants.

ABRAHAM. Why?

MARIA. Oh, I don't know. When I laugh to them or sing

333   [35]

to them or kiss them or dance to them, they are always reckoning up and reckoning up. " How many drachmas is that song worth—or that dance step—or that kiss ? " They can't enjoy themselves like men. They are like those counting machines in the bazaar.

ABRAHAM. Do you like this life ?

MARIA. What does it matter whether I like it or not ? We don't choose when we are going to be born and very few of us choose how we are going to live after that—or how we are going to die.

ABRAHAM. Come, come. You will be crying into the gravy, my lachrymose Lalage. Have a bit of chicken, or whatever it is, and cheer up.

MARIA. I like you. You are—different.

ABRAHAM. Different from what ? Rot me, I wish I were.

MARIA. No. But I mean it. You look all rakish and tanned and bloodthirsty like a soldier, but you. . . .

[She thinks for a moment.]

I remember reading in a book about the " fragrance of austerity ". You've got that, somehow. A lean sort of clean sort of smell, like wind off a moorland. Forgive me for talking like this. But I have become accustomed to garbage, and a whiff of freshness makes me happy. Shall I sing to you ?

ABRAHAM. Yes, if you like.

MARIA. May I sit on your knee while I sing ?

ABRAHAM. Why not ?

[She takes over her winecup and sits on ABRAHAM's knee.]

SONG (*Maria*).

(Note.—*She can sing any antique, playful song she likes. This is a rough version of Horace's 8th Ode in Book ii*).

" *Strike me* ", said Barina, " *dead if I lie to you.*" *Knowing full well that she said it to deceive. Not a hair blew out of place as thunderbolts fell round her. How can I believe ?*

> *She swears like a trooper and looks like a seraph,*
> *Thriving on the wrath of the gods called down ;*
> *Lovelier than ever ; smooth as an amethyst ;*
> *The toast of the Town.*

She makes mothers lock their boys in cellars.
She makes father lock his money up ; and she
Scares young brides with her lee wind blowing
Husbands out to sea—to sea,
Husbands out to sea.

ABRAHAM.   She was a bit of a villain, that Barina, hey ?
(*Sings.*) " Husbands out to sea, to sea. Blows them out to
sea ! "

MARIA.   Wasn't she a villain, old darling ?   And how nicely
you sing.

[*She embraces him.*]

MARIA.   Scrubby old cheeks you have. Never mind.   I
like it.

ABRAHAM (*loudly and heartily*).   And I like it too, by the
Hammer of Hephaestus !

MARIA.   Do you like me ?

ABRAHAM.   Yes.

MARIA.   And I like you.   I am glad you came.

ABRAHAM.   I too am glad I came. . . . But wait one
moment.

[*He puts* MARIA *gently off his knee ; rises ; draws his sword ; goes
to the door ; listens for a moment ; then throws the door open.
The* KNAVE *and the* LANDLADY *tumble into the room on their
hands and knees.*]

ABRAHAM.   A hundred thousand harpies !   Is this the kind
of house you keep ? Spies, hey ? Eavesdroppers, hey ? Cats
and Monkeys ! Begone before I carve you into gobbets, you
sneaking dog and bitch !

[*The* KNAVE *shows his teeth and feels for his knife, but the* LANDLADY
restrains him.]

LANDLADY.   Oh, high Lord, your pardon. We had just
come to find whether you had everything you wanted.

ABRAHAM.   There are two things I don't want, and they are
you. Get out of here. Go back to your kennel. Blast and
blister it, can a gentleman not take his ease without being set
about with snuffling spies ?

LANDLADY.   We are going. I swear you shall not be disturbed again.

ABRAHAM.   See you keep to that ; or it shall be the worse for
you.

335   [37]

LANDLADY.   Good night, honey Lord.
KNAVE.   Good night, Sir.   No offence.

> [*Exeunt* KNAVE *and* LANDLADY. *During this scene,* MARIA *has been frightened at first and then amused. She is now sitting on the divan, laughing.* ABRAHAM *locks the door and throws the big key on the table ; then goes slowly to her.*]

MARIA.   Aren't you the gallant old fire-eater ?   And what a fright you gave them !   I was terrified myself.   Now take off your boots and make yourself at home.

> [ABRAHAM *takes her by the hands and looks at her. Her smile fades.*]

ABRAHAM.   Do you not know me, Maria ?   My heart, was it not I who brought you up ?   What has come to thee, my child ?   Who was it destroyed thee ?   Where is that angel's garb thou didst wear, my daughter ?   Where is thy continence, thy tears, thy vigils, thy holy psalms, thy bed on the ground ? How didst thou fall from heaven's height into this pit, my daughter ?   Why, when thou didst sin, didst thou not tell me ? Why didst thou not come to me there and then ?   I would have done thy penance for thee gladly, and my dear Ephraem too. Why didst thou do this ?   Why didst thou desert me and bring me into this intolerable sorrow ?   How could I be unkind to thee ?   For we are all sinners, save God himself.

> [MARIA *sits motionless like a stone.*]

Maria, child, speak to me.   Wilt thou not speak to me, half of my heart ?   Was it not because of thee, child, that I came here ?   Upon me thy sin, my daughter.   It is I that shall answer for thee to God on the day of Judgment.   It is I that shall give satisfaction to God for this sin.

MARIA.   I cannot look on your face for shame.   And how can I pour out a prayer to God, so foul as I am with the mud of this uncleanness ?

ABRAHAM.   Upon me be the guilt, my daughter; at my hand shall God requite this sin.   Only listen to me . . . and, come, let us go home.   For, look you, there is our dear Ephraem grieving sore for thee.   Don't be afraid.   Don't distrust the mercy of God.   Let our sins be as mountains, His mercy towers above His every creature.   The foolish woman washed the Lord's feet with her tears and dried them with her hair.   What

[38]

care did He take of what she was or of what she had done ? If a spark can set the sea on fire, then can thy sins stain his whiteness. There's nothing new about falling into the mire. The evil thing is to lie there, fallen. So bravely now return again to your place. The Enemy mocked thee falling, but he shall know thee strong in thy rising.

MARIA.   I cannot.   I cannot.

ABRAHAM.   Remember my old age and have pity on it. Have pity on the travail of my poor, white, silly head. Rise up, I implore thee, and come home. Fear not. Mortal man is apt to slip; but if he be swift to fall, he is swift to rise again with the succour of God, who desireth not the death of a sinner, but rather that he be healed and live.

MARIA.   If you are sure that I can do penance and that God will accept my atonement, I shall come as you bid me. And every step of the way I shall kiss the track of your feet, you that so grieved for me and took me out of this cesspit. . . . O what shall I render to Thee for all this, O Lord, my God ?

ABRAHAM.   Rise up, daughter, and let us go home to our cell.

MARIA.   I have some money put by here and some clothes. What do you want me to do with them ?

ABRAHAM.   Leave them. Throw back in the face of the Evil One his wicked wages.

MARIA.   They may try to stop us.

ABRAHAM.   They had better not.

MARIA.   What will you do ?

ABRAHAM.   I have earned many penances this day, my child I shall earn another by striking them dead.

[ABRAHAM *puts his cloak around her and takes up the key and his sword.*]

MARIA.   With your sword ?

ABRAHAM.   With my sword.

MARIA.   But you have never used a sword.

ABRAHAM.   No. But it is easy. One seizes the instrument by the handle, shut's one's eyes and strikes home.

MARIA.   Oh, no, no! Sword play is very difficult.

ABRAHAM.   Nothing is difficult if one has faith.

MARIA.   But have you faith in the sword ?

ABRAHAM.   I shall pray for faith.

337   [39]

MARIA. In that dreadful dream from which I am awake, I have seen the sword used. It is difficult and dangerous.

ABRAHAM. The Lord will strengthen the arm of his swordsman as He did to Gideon and to the Mighty Men of Valour.

MARIA. But they were accustomed to the art. Josef is as swift as a panther. I have seen him avoid a blade that flickered like lightning and lean forward to the fifth rib with his knife. . . . Oh!

> [*She covers her face with her hands.*]

ABRAHAM. Be of good cheer. This is no spirit in which to enter a battle. . . . Besides, we may not meet them.

MARIA. We shall meet them. They watch us as a cat watches a mouse. They will kill you.

ABRAHAM. Then I shall die the joyful death of a Christian martyr.

MARIA. And I shall die the death of a poor, murdered baggage in a house of ill-fame—with all my black sins thick upon me.

ABRAHAM. They would kill you too?

MARIA. Yes.

ABRAHAM (*after a pause*). The Lord has given you sorrow, but He has given you wisdom too, my child. I am a sorry old fool.

> [*He draws himself to his full height, beats with his sword upon the table, making a tremendous noise, and then throws the sword into the corner of the room.*]

MARIA. Oh, what are you doing?

ABRAHAM. Ho! Woman! Landlady! Come here to me!

MARIA. We are lost. We are lost.

> [*Enter the* LANDLADY *with a meat-axe in her hand. She is followed by the* KNAVE, *who has drawn his knife and carries a short lariat with a leaden weight at the end of it.*]

LANDLADY. What's the matter? Is she making trouble? I'll tear her to shreds if she is.

KNAVE. His worship is drunk. I told you it was nothing.

ABRAHAM. I have something to say to you.

LANDLADY. Well, I wish you'd say it a little more quietly. It's this sort of thing that gets us into trouble.

[40]

MARIA (*screaming with fear*).   Uncle, the rope, the rope! He'll throw it round your ankles and then fall on you and stab you!

[*The* LANDLADY *flies at* MARIA.   ABRAHAM *interposes himself and she stops a foot or two from him, cowed by his mild and magnificent eye.*]

LANDLADY.   You misbegotten child of an Ifrit and a Harpy! . . . You must not believe her, Sir.   We never harm our guests.   She is mad.   Don't be afraid.

ABRAHAM.   I am not afraid.

LANDLADY.   What did you wish to say to me, Sir . . . ? Stand back, Josef, it's all right.

ABRAHAM.   I wish to take this woman away with me.

LANDLADY.   Why didn't you say so at first?   I'm delighted she has found favour in your sight, my Lord, though I shall be sorry to lose her.   Of course she is a very valuable girl, and I don't know what we shall do without her; but no doubt we can come to some reasonable bargain.

ABRAHAM (*throwing down a handful of coins*).   That is all I have.   You can take that and welcome.

LANDLADY.   Your honour is pleased to be merry.

ABRAHAM.   I should give you the horse too, but it is not mine.   Now let us pass.

LANDLADY.   Let you pass?   You know very well that won't pay for your supper, let alone anything else.   Oh, no, my good Sir.   I have lived too long in this bad world to be bilked by a moth-eaten, louse-bitten old half-pay soldier man in my own town and in my own house.   Pay for your supper and take yourself out of here.

ABRAHAM.   Woman . . .

LANDLADY.   And don't call me a woman.   We have a rough way here with those who don't pay their shot—soldier or no soldier.

[JOSEF *advances to just behind her, grinning warily and almost dancing on his toes.*]

ABRAHAM.   You would show your teeth at me?

MARIA (*whispering*).   Speak her fair, Uncle.   Oh, speak her fair.

ABRAHAM.   Hush, child . . . Would you show your teeth at me?

339   [41]

LANDLADY.   Show my teeth? Aye, and bite.

ABRAHAM.   Did the lions bite the Prophet Daniel in their den? Did the fire bite Shadrach, Meshach and Abednego in the fiery furnace? Poor foolish woman, you cannot lift your feeble hands against the might of the Lord of Hosts.

LANDLADY.   The man is mad.

KNAVE.   I said he was a Praying Jack.

LANDLADY.   Dead man, you are very bold. We are about to take your life, dead man.

ABRAHAM.   My life? You cannot take my life! You can break the muddy dam that keeps it from the shining, eternal sea. It is for you that my soul is troubled.

LANDLADY.   Indeed now, that is very kind of you; but we are vexed to have put your honour to any sort of trouble.

ABRAHAM (*beginning quietly, but with mounting menace*).   It is well that you should know, poor little ugly woman, what will happen to you if you strike at me. And, although the brute has long since swamped the man in him, my words may even reach the remnant of human wits left to your pitiful slave. If you do this thing, the hands that struck, the feet that brought you to do evil, will be smitten with the palsy, and wither and rot. If the Lord leaves you the means to drag your stricken bodies to the steps of the church for a day's begging, it will only be for the reason that His mercy is infinite.

KNAVE.   Take care, Ma. He's a holy man. He'll put a curse on us.

ABRAHAM.   You are the children of curses. Why should you be afraid of them?

LANDLADY (*violently*).   Josef! Kill the old dog. He will have us both mad like himself. Cut his throat, do you hear?

[KNAVE *stands fast. He is terrified.*]

ABRAHAM (*mildly*).   It seems, mistress, that you will have to do your own work.

LANDLADY (*collapsing to a moaning heap at his feet*).   I can't. I can't. What's the matter with me? I can't.

ABRAHAM (*with an air of philosophical detachment*).   It has always been a matter of astonishment to me that the Devil chooses his ministers so idly. With an almost limitless field of choice, he yet yields his insignia to creatures so obviously inferior as these unfortunate blowflies.

340

LANDLADY. Go. Go away from here. Take the slut with you. I cannot bear this talk.

KNAVE. Don't curse us, master.

ABRAHAM. A moment ago there came into my mouth the word " unfortunate "; and it is indeed true that the Devil finds weaklings in the haplessness of their misfortunes and weaves them into the pattern of his evil designs.

LANDLADY. Stop talking. Go from here. O Nile, wash away this mountain of words!

ABRAHAM. If that be so, it is my duty to try to rescue these children of misfortune.

MARIA. Come now. Another time. We must go at once.

ABRAHAM. Ah, you are there, my child ? I had almost forgotten the matter in hand. We shall go now. But I shall speak to Ephraem and he will send missioners to these poor people, that they may not perish in their misery.

LANDLADY. Take your money and go.

ABRAHAM. Money ? Ah, yes. Ephraem will no doubt find a better use for it than you can. (*He gathers up the money*). And now, God bless you and shine on your darkness. Farewell.

CURTAIN DRAWS AS ABRAHAM AND MARIA GO.

ABBOT. So he set her upon his horse and led it, going before, with joy in his heart, like a shepherd who has found his lost sheep. And when he had come home, he set her in the inner cell which had been his own, and himself dwelt in the outer. Maria remained there in humility of soul, disciplining herself with vigils and stern travails of abstinence, in quiet and modesty bewailing her sin, but with sure hope of pardon. And God the compassionate, who will have no man perish but that all should come to repentence, so accepted her atonement that after three full years He restored health to many at her prayer. For crowds flocked to her, and she would pray to God for their healing, and it was granted her. The blessed Abraham saw her penitence, and gave glory to God.

[*The Curtain opens, disclosing* ABRAHAM *and* MARIA *kneeling, in the cells opposite to those which they occupied at the beginning of the play.*]

MARIA. Be mindful of us, Lover of men, and lead us out of

341   [43]

the prison-house of our sins.   Remember us who are without defence and save us, sinners.

ABRAHAM.   And may Thy grace, that was in this world our aid, gather us under its wings in that great and terrible day.

BOTH.   For with Thee is magnificence, adoration and honour. Amen.

> [*The* ABBOT *and* DEACONESS *have stood up at the opening of the Curtain.*]

END OF THE PLAY.

Printed in Great Britain by
RICHARD CLAY AND COMPANY, LTD.
BUNGAY
SUFFOLK